Prentice Hall
LITERATURE
Timeless Voices, Timeless Themes

Selection Support: Skills Development Workbook

TEACHERS EDITION

THE BRITISH TRADITION

Prentice Hall

Upper Saddle River, New Jersey
Glenview, Illinois
Needham, Massachusetts

ACKNOWLEDGEMENTS

Grateful acknowledgment is made to the following for copyrighted material:

Henry Holt and Company, Inc.

"Loveliest of Trees" by A. E. Housman from THE COLLECTED POEMS OF A. E. HOUSEMAN. Copyright © 1965 by Holt, Rinehart and Winston.

Alfred A. Knopf, Inc.

From "A Dill Pickle" by Katherine Mansfield from THE SHORT STORIES OF KATHERINE MANSFIELD. Copyright © 1920, 1922, 1923, 1924, 1926, 1937 by Alfred A. Knopf, Inc.

Oxford University Press

"Sunday Morning" by Louis MacNeice from THE COLLECTED POEMS OF LOUIS MACNEICE, edited by E. R. Dodds. Copyright © 1966 by The Estate of Louis MacNeice. From "Shore Woman" from WINTERING OUT by Seamus Heaney. Copyright © 1072 by Seamus Heaney.

Note: Every effort has been made to locate the copyright owner of material reprinted in this book. Omissions brought to our attention will be corrected in subsequent printings.

ISBN 0-13-058358-8

1 2 3 4 5 6 7 8 9 10   05 04 03 02 01

CONTENTS

UNIT 1: FROM LEGEND TO HISTORY (449–1485)

UNIT 2: CELEBRATING HUMANITY (1485–1625)

UNIT 3: A TURBULENT TIME (1625–1798)

"**The Seafarer,**" translated by Burton Raffel
"**The Wanderer,**" translated by Charles Kennedy
"**The Wife's Lament,**" translated by Ann Stanford

Build Vocabulary

Spelling Strategy Retain the final e when adding a consonant suffix as in *blithe* + *-ly* to create *blithely*.

Using the Suffix –*ness*

A. DIRECTIONS: Answer each of the following questions, changing the underlined word to a word with the suffix –ness.

1. Why did she think the cake was too <u>sweet</u>? _____

2. How did the <u>bright</u> light affect you? _____

3. Did you think Ryan was <u>eager</u> enough to convince Mrs. Malone that he should be in the band? _____

4. What do you think the teacher thought when Alan was so <u>helpful</u> on Thursday? _____

Using the Word Bank

admonish	compassionate	blithe
rancor	redress	winsomeness
rapture	fervent	
sentinel	grievous	

B. DIRECTIONS: On the line, write the letter of the definition for each word in the right column.

____ 1. fervent

____ 2. compassionate

____ 3. sentinel

____ 4. admonish

____ 5. grievous

____ 6. rancor

____ 7. redress

____ 8. blithe

____ 9. rapture

____ 10. winsomeness

a. ill-will

b. advise; caution

c. expression of joy

d. someone who guards

e. cheerful

f. having great feeling

g. sympathizing; pitying

h. causing sorrow; hard to bear

i. compensation, as for a wrong

j. charm; appeal

C. DIRECTIONS: Circle the letter of the word that best completes each sentence.

____ 1. James was kind and caring; he was a _____ person.
   a. flippant   b. apathetic   c. blithe   d. compassionate

____ 2. It was the queen's ____ hope that her subjects respected her just rule.
   a. grievous   b. fervent   c. blithe   d. important

____ 3. The ____ kept watch over the sleeping troops.
   a. elegy   b. sentinel   c. tradition   d. exile

"The Seafarer," translated by Burton Raffel
"The Wanderer," translated by Charles Kennedy
"The Wife's Lament," translated by Ann Stanford

Grammar and Style: Compound Predicates

A **compound predicate** consists of two or more verbs having the same subject. The complete compound predicate includes the verbs; their modifiers, objects, and complements; and conjunctions.

A. Practice: In each passage, underline the compound predicate, and circle the subject.

1 . . . . and my soul/Called me eagerly out, sent me over/The horizon

2. The world's honor ages and shrinks, . . .

3. I grieved each dawn/wondered where my lord my first on earth might be.

4. . . . the sea took me, swept me back/and forth in sorrow and fear and pain,/showed me suffering. . . .

5. . . . and day by day/All this earth ages and droops into death.

B. Writing Application: Rewrite each sentence so that it has a compound predicate.

1. Hardship groaned around my heart.

_____

_____

_____

2. The weakest survives.

_____

_____

_____

3. Lonely and wretched, I wailed my woe.

_____

_____

_____

4. Ever I know the dark of my exile.

_____

_____

_____

5. I must far and near bear the anger of my beloved.

_____

_____

_____

"The Seafarer," translated by Burton Raffel
"The Wanderer," translated by Charles Kennedy
"The Wife's Lament" translated by Ann Stanford

Reading Strategy: Connecting to Historical Context

Recognizing the historical context and the characteristics of the period in which a work was written helps you notice relevant details and ideas. For example, if you know that Anglo-Saxon culture was male-dominated, you may be able to understand the poet's line: "My lord commanded me to move my dwelling here."

DIRECTIONS: Use your understanding of Anglo-Saxon historical context to help you understand the following excerpts. In the right column, record how your comprehension is affected by what you know. In number 4, find an excerpt that reflects the historical context and explain how it does.

Excerpt	How Historical Context Aids Understanding
1. **"The Seafarer":** "This tale is true, and mine. It tells/How the sea took me, swept me back/And forth in sorrow and fear and pain,/Showed me suffering in a thousand ships, . . . "	1.
2. **"The Wanderer":** "'So have I also, often in wretchedness/Fettered my feelings, far from my kin,/Homeless and hapless, since days of old,/When the dark earth covered my dear lord's face,/And I sailed away with sorrowful heart,/Over wintry seas, seeking a gold-lord . . . '"	2.
3. **"The Wife's Lament":** "I must far and near/bear the anger of my beloved./The man sent me out to live in the woods/under an oak tree in this den in the earth./Ancient this earth hall./I am all longing."	3.
4.	4.

Name _____   Date _____

"The Seafarer," translated by Burton Raffel
"The Wanderer," translated by Charles Kennedy
"The Wife's Lament," translated by Ann Stanford

Literary Analysis: Anglo-Saxon Lyric Poetry

Anglo-Saxon poetry was recited or chanted aloud to an audience by wandering poets. In order to make the poems easier to listen to and to be memorized, they were developed with strong rhythms. Each line has a certain number of beats, or accented syllables—almost always four. Many lines have a **caesura**, or pause, in the middle, after the second beat. Anglo-Saxon poetry also contained **kennings**, two-word metaphorical names for familiar things. Note these examples of rhythm, caesura, and kennings in these lines:

Rhythm: No hárps ríng in his héart, nó rewárds

Caesura: No pássion for wómen, [pause] no wórldly pléasures

Kenning: Nóthing, only the oceán's heáve

1. Mark the syllables that have a strong accented beat (´) in these lines from "The Seafarer."

   But there isn't a man on earth so proud,
   So born to greatness, so bold with his youth,
   Grown so brave, or so graced by God
   That he feels no fear as the sails unfurl.

2. In the lines in passage 1, how many caesuras are there? Write the word that appears before each caesura.

   _____

3. Mark each syllable that has a strong accented beat (´) in these lines from "The Seafarer."

   Those powers have vanished, those pleasures are dead.
   The weakest survives and the world continues,
   Kept spinning by toil. All glory is tarnished.

4. Underline the kenning in these lines from "The Wife's Lament."

   First my lord went out away from his people
   over the wave-tumult. I grieved each dawn
   wondered where my lord my first on earth might be.

from *Tristia* by Ovid
"Far Corners of Earth" by Tu Fu

Build Vocabulary: Words of Exile

The authors of both poems use specific words to evoke the theme of exile. How does each word in the box below help bring across the experience described in each poem? What words might a modern poet use to describe the experience of exile?

A. Directions: For each item, write the word from the box that matches the definition or description. Then write a sentence of your own, using the word in the context of the theme of exile.

besieged	menace	dread	barbarous	impassable

1. under stress, worried

   word: _____ sentence: _____
   _____
   _____

2. incapable of being surmounted

   word: _____ sentence: _____
   _____
   _____

3. intense fear

   word: _____ sentence: _____
   _____
   _____

4. threaten

   word: _____ sentence: _____
   _____
   _____

5. without mercy, harsh or cruel

   word: _____ sentence: _____
   _____
   _____

B. Directions: On the lines, write a word you might use to describe a contemporary experience of exile. Write a sentence using your word.

word: _____ sentence: _____
_____
_____

from *Tristia* by Ovid
"Far Corners of Earth" by Tu Fu

Thematic Connection: Exile

The experiences described in the two poems each take place at a specific time and in a specific place. However, important aspects of the experience of exile are universal: they might be applied to an experience of exile occurring anywhere in the world, whether in ancient times or today.

DIRECTIONS: Complete the chart to trace the connections between the excerpt from *Tristia*, "Far Corners of Earth," and other situations with which you are familiar from literature or real life.

	Tristia	"Far Corners of Earth"	Other Exiles
Reason for exile			
Place of Exile			
Circumstances in Place of Exile			
Mood or Attitude of Person Exiled			

Name _____ Date _____

from *Beowulf,* translated by Burton Raffel

Build Vocabulary

Spelling Strategy The final *e* is dropped when you are adding *-ing* to a word ending in *e*. For example, the *e* in *writhe* is dropped when you are changing it to *writhing*.

Using the Root *-sol-*

The root *-sol-* comes from the Latin *solari*, meaning "to comfort."

A. DIRECTIONS: Explain how the root *-sol-* influences the meaning of the underlined word in each sentence.

1. Before Beowulf arrived, Hrothgar and his Danes were <u>disconsolate</u> over the deeds of Grendel.

_____

2. He <u>consoled</u> his little daughter for the loss of her goldfish by promising to buy her a new one.

_____

3. The Geats grieved <u>inconsolably</u> when the dragon killed their once mighty king, Beowulf.

_____

4. Although she won the <u>consolation</u> tournament, Allison was disappointed in her performance.

_____

Using the Word Bank

reparation	solace	purge
writhing	massive	loathsome

B. DIRECTIONS: For each underlined word, substitute a word or phrase with the same meaning. Write it in the blank following the sentence.

1. Only a hero of Beowulf's strength could hope to lift the <u>massive</u> sword in Grendel's battle hall.

_____

2. The third monster, most <u>loathsome</u> of all, had eight eyes on stalks and was covered with slime.

_____

3. Most epic heroes strive to <u>purge</u> the world of wicked beings.

_____

4. Snakes can move rapidly with their <u>writhing</u> form of locomotion.

_____

5. The badly defeated warrior found <u>solace</u> in the affection of his family.

_____

6. The captured bandits were ordered to give gold to their victims as <u>reparation</u>.

_____

from *Beowulf*, translated by Burton Raffel

Grammar and Style: Appositives and Appositive Phrases

Appositives are words that are placed next to nouns or pronouns to explain the nouns or pronouns more fully. When an appositive is accompanied by modifiers, it is called an **appositive phrase**. Look at these appositive phrases from *Beowulf*:

"Hrothgar, *their lord*, sat joyless / in Herot."

". . . he came riding down, / *Hrothgar's lieutenant*, spurring his horse. . ."

In the first example, the appositive phrase immediately follows the noun *Hrothgar* and provides more information: *Hrothgar* was their lord. The appositive phrase in the second example is separated from the pronoun to which it refers, but it also provides more information: *he* was Hrothgar's lieutenant. These phrases do not change the meaning of the noun or pronoun they refer to; they merely add more information.

A. Practice: In these lines from *Beowulf*, underline each appositive phrase and circle the noun or pronoun to which it refers.

1. He was spawned in that slime,
   Conceived by a pair of those monsters born
   of Cain, murderous creatures banished
   By God, punished forever for the crime
   Of Abel's death.

2. . . . so Herot
   Stood empty, and stayed deserted for years,
   Twelve winters of grief for Hrothgar. . .

3. In his far-off home Beowulf, Higlac's
   Follower and the strongest of the Geats—

4. Soon, fourteen Geats arrived
   At the hall, bold and warlike, and with Beowulf,
   Their lord and leader, they walked on the meadhall . . .

5. Grendel's mother
   Is hidden in her terrible home, in a place
   You've not seen.

B. Writing Application: Combine each pair of sentences by turning one into an appositive or an appositive phrase. Set off the appositives with commas.

1. Fourteen men went with Beowulf. Beowulf was their fearless leader.

_____

2. They sailed in a mighty vessel. Their ship was the master of the sea.

_____

3. Hrothgar welcomed Beowulf and his men to Herot. Herot was the strongest hall ever built.

_____

from **Beowulf**, translated by Burton Raffel

Reading Strategy: Paraphrasing

Long sentences and difficult language can make a piece of writing hard to follow. Don't be discouraged when you come across passages that give you trouble. Instead, use paraphrasing to make sure that you're getting the point of these passages. When you **paraphrase**, you identify the key ideas in a written passage and restate them in your own words. Look at this example from *Beowulf*:

Passage from *Beowulf*	Paraphrased
"I've never known fear, as a youth I fought In endless battles. I am old, now, But I will fight again, seek fame still, If the dragon hiding in his tower dares To face me."	I have been fearless throughout life and will continue to fight if the dragon dares to face me.

DIRECTIONS: Use this graphic organizer to help you paraphrase difficult passages in *Beowulf*. Each time you come across a difficult passage, write it in the column labeled "Passage from *Beowulf*." Then write any difficult words from that passage in the appropriate column. Define each difficult word, either by using the words surrounding it to piece together its meaning or by looking it up in the dictionary. Next, determine the key ideas in the passage, and jot these down in the appropriate column. Finally, use the key ideas, along with your understanding of the difficult words, to paraphrase the passage. One passage has already been paraphrased for you.

Passage from *Beowulf*	Difficult Words	Key Ideas	Paraphrase
No one waited for reparation from his plundering claws: That shadow of death hunted in the darkness, . . .	reparation (making up for wrong or injury) plundering (taking by force, theft, or fraud)	No one expected to be repaid for what Grendel took in his claws. Grendel was a shadow hunting in the darkness.	No one expected to be repaid for what Grendel took. He hunted in the darkness.

from *Beowulf,* translated by Burton Raffel

Literary Analysis: The Epic

The **epic** *Beowulf* is a long narrative poem that recounts the exploits of the legendary warrior Beowulf. Like other epic heros, Beowulf represents good and earns glory by struggling against the forces of evil represented by several monstrous creatures. He represents the values of his nation, culture, and religion. *Beowulf* is a typical epic poem in its serious tone and elevated language, which portrays characters, action, and setting in terms larger and grander than life. The use of **kennings**, two-word metaphorical names for familiar things, is also a particular characteristic of Anglo-Saxon poetry.

DIRECTIONS: Read each passage from *Beowulf.* Then list the characteristics of epic poetry represented in it.

1. So mankind's enemy continued his crimes, / Killing as often as he could, coming / Alone, bloodthirsty and horrible. Though he lived / In Herot, when the night hid him, he never / Dared to touch king Hrothgar's glorious / Throne, protected by God—God, / Whose love Grendel could not know. . . .

_____

_____

_____

_____

_____

2. "Hail Hrothgar! / Higlac is my cousin and my king; the days / Of my youth have been filled with glory. Now Grendel's / Name has echoed in our land: sailors / Have brought us stories of Herot, the best / Of all mead-halls, deserted and useless when the moon / Hangs in skies the sun had lit, / Light and life fleeing together. / My people have said, the wisest, most knowing / And best of them, that my duty was to go to the Danes' / Great king. They have seen my strength for themselves, / Have watched me rise from the darkness of war. . . ."

_____

_____

_____

_____

_____

3. "Grant me, then, / Lord and protector of this noble place, / A single request! I have come so far, / O shelterer of warriors and your people's loved friend, / That this one favor you should not refuse me— / That I, alone and with the help of my men, / May purge all evil from this hall."

_____

_____

_____

_____

_____

Name _____ Date _____

Build Vocabulary: Words of Heroic Values and Beliefs

To describe an epic hero, a writer uses language that evokes actions, values, and beliefs that are associated with the best of a culture or nation. Such words lend grandeur and gravity to the epic saga as it unfolds.

DIRECTIONS: Create in your mind a heroic character of your own, then sketch out an epic narrative involving your hero. Then, using each word listed below, write a sentence that either helps to describe your hero or provides information about his or her adventure.

vanguard: _____

_____

_____

_____

valor: _____

_____

_____

_____

avenger: _____

_____

_____

_____

helm: _____

_____

_____

_____

rite: _____

_____

_____

_____

destiny: _____

_____

_____

_____

"The Prologue" from *Gilgamesh*, translated by David Ferry
from the *Iliad* by Homer

Thematic Connection: The Epic

The long narrative poems called epics not only provide the joy of a thrilling adventure but also, through the actions of the legendary heroes who inhabit the epics, provide a model for the values and behaviors a society admires. The ancient Greeks had the epics of Homer; the Sumerians and Babylonians had their tales of *Gilgamesh*. What epics do we have today? How do they compare with the epics of the ancient world?

DIRECTIONS: Use the chart to compare and contrast *Gilgamesh* and the *Iliad* with contemporary narratives that might qualify as epic. Then write a paragraph in which you compare and contrast today's epic to those of the past.

	Gilgamesh	the Iliad	An Epic of Today: _____
Hero(es)			
Actions			
Themes			
Values and Behaviors			

Comparison and Contrast: _____

_____

_____

_____

_____

_____

_____

_____

_____

_____

from *A History of the English Church and People* by Bede
from *The Anglo-Saxon Chronicle,* translated by Anne Savage

Build Vocabulary

Spelling Strategy To create a plural of a word ending in *y* preceded by a consonant, change the *y* to *i* and add *-es*. For example, the word *promontory* becomes *promontories*.

Using the Suffix *-ade*

A. DIRECTIONS: Match each word in the list to a definition and use the word in a sentence.

ambuscade   1. To block the way _____

barricade   2. A disguise, as a mask _____

masquerade   3. An ambush, or trap _____

promenade   4. From the Latin *prominare*, meaning "to drive forward" _____

_____

Using the Word Bank

promontories	innumerable	stranded	barricaded	ravaged

B. DIRECTIONS: Write the word from the Word Bank that best completes each sentence.

1. _____ people lined up to shake the king's hand.

2. The ship was _____ just off the coast.

3. Lookouts were posted at all the _____.

4. They tried to enter, but the door had been _____.

5. The enemy burned and _____ the town.

C. DIRECTIONS: Put a check mark in the blank next to the synonym for the underlined word or phrase in the sentence.

1. According to Bede there were <u>a vast number of</u> wonderful things in Ireland.
     ____ a. hallowed   ____ b. ravaged   ____ c. innumerable   ____ d. stranded

2. The king wanted to help the townspeople who had been <u>left helpless</u> at the crossroads.
     ____ a. barricaded   ____ b. innumerable   ____ c. hallowed   ____ d. stranded

3. The lighthouses were perched along the <u>cliffs above the ocean.</u>
     ____ a. promontories   ____ b. furlongs   ____ c. cockles   ____ d. barricades

4. The enemy had <u>blocked</u> all the exits and set fire to the building.
     ____ a. stranded   ____ b. barricaded   ____ c. confounded   ____ d. achieved

5. The artist looked at the <u>ruined</u> portrait and shook her head sadly.
     ____ a. hallowed   ____ b. stranded   ____ c. barricaded   ____ d. ravaged

from *A History of the English Church and People* by Bede
from *The Anglo-Saxon Chronicle*, translated by Anne Savage

Grammar and Style: Compound Sentences

A **compound sentence** contains two or more independent clauses (groups of words, with subjects and predicates, that can stand alone as sentences). In a compound sentence, the clauses can be joined by *and, or, but,* or a semicolon.

The following sentence from Bede's *A History of the English Church and People* is broken into two parts; its independent clauses are underlined.

Consequently both summer days and winter nights are long

and

when the sun withdraws southwards, the winter nights last eighteen hours.

A. Practice: The following sentences are from *The Anglo-Saxon Chronicle*. Decide whether each is a compound sentence. Underline the independent clauses within each compound sentence.

1. Then King Alfred commanded longships to be built against the ash-ships.

2. They were nearly twice as long as the others; some had sixty oars, some more.

3. The Danes went out with three ships against them, and three stood higher up the river's mouth, beached on dry land; the men from them had gone inland.

4. Then he stole himself away under the cover of night, and sought the force in Northumbria.

5. Alfred died, who was town reeve at Bath; and in the same year the peace was fastened at Tiddingford, just as king Edward advised, both with the East Anglians and the Northumbrians.

B. Writing Application: Rewrite each group of simple sentences as a compound sentence. Remember that each compound sentence must have at least two independent clauses joined by a conjunction or a semicolon. Use pronouns as necessary.

1. Ireland is broader than Britain. Ireland's climate is superior.

   _____

2. There are no reptiles there. No snake can exist there.

   _____

3. The island abounds with milk and honey. There is no lack of vines, fish, and birds. Deer and goats are widely hunted.

   _____

4. In these latitudes the sun does not remain long below the horizon. Consequently both summer days and winter nights are long.

   _____

5. Britain is rich in grain and timber. It has good pasturage. Vines are cultivated.

   _____

from *A History of the English Church and People* by Bede
from *The Anglo-Saxon Chronicle,* translated by Anne Savage

Reading Strategy: Breaking Down Sentences

Long sentences and complex language can make a piece of writing very difficult to follow. One strategy for reading this type of material is to break down complicated sentences by finding their key parts and their clarifying details. When you have identified the key parts, you will find it much easier to understand the complete sentence. The best way to break down sentences is to ask yourself questions.

Look at this example from Bede's *A History of the English Church and People.*

> Having no women with them, these Picts asked wives of the Scots, who consented on condition that, when any dispute arose, they should choose a king from the female royal line rather than the male.

A. DIRECTIONS: Answer each of the following questions, using the sentence above.

1. What is the main action of the sentence?

   _____

2. Why?

   _____

3. What happened next?

   _____

4. Why?

   _____

   _____

B. DIRECTIONS: Use a graphic organizer like the one here to help you break down difficult sentences in *A History of the English Church and People* and *The Anglo-Saxon Chronicle.* When you come across a long, complicated sentence, write it in the column labeled "Difficult Sentence." Then look for the most important ideas in the sentence or its main action. Write these in the column labeled "Key Ideas." Then look for key details or information that explains the main action. Write those details in the column labeled "Why? What else?" One sentence from *The Anglo-Saxon Chronicle* has been broken down for you as an example.

Difficult Sentence	Key Ideas	Why? What else?
He was king over all the English, except for that part which was under Danish rule; and he held that kingdom for one and a half years less than thirty.	He was king over all the English. He held that kingdom for one and a half years less than thirty (or twenty-eight and one-half years).	except for that part which was under Danish rule

from *A History of the English Church and People* by Bede
from *The Anglo-Saxon Chronicle,* translated by Anne Savage

Literary Analysis: Historical Writing

A historical writing is a factual narrative or record of past events, gathered through observation and outside, or secondary, sources. In the excerpts from *The History of the English Church and People* and *The Anglo-Saxon Chronicle*, the authors do not reveal their sources, but most probably they used their own observations, documents in court or monastic libraries, and stories they heard from others (many probably handed down orally for generations).

DIRECTIONS: On the lines following each quotation, write what source or sources the authors might have used to gather information. Comment on the probable accuracy of the quotation.

1. "The original inhabitants of the island were the Britons, from whom it takes its name, and who, according to tradition, crossed into Britain from Armorica. . . ."

   _____

   _____

   _____

2. ". . . it is said that some Picts from Scythia put to sea in a few long ships and were driven by storms around the coasts of Britain, arriving at length on the north coast of Ireland. Here they found the nation of the Scots, from whom they asked permission to settle, but their request was refused."

   _____

   _____

   _____

3. In agreeing to allow the Picts to take Scottish wives, the Scots said that ". . . they (Picts) should choose a king from the female (Scottish) royal line rather than the male."

   _____

   _____

   _____

4. "They got away because the other ships ran aground. They were very awkwardly aground: three were stranded on the same side of the deep water as the Danish ships, and the others all on the other side."

   _____

   _____

   _____

5. "In the same year, Aethelred passed away, who was an ealdorman in Devon, four weeks before king Alfred."

   _____

   _____

   _____

The Prologue from *The Canterbury Tales* by Geoffrey Chaucer

Build Vocabulary

Spelling Strategy The *shun* sound at the end of a word can be spelled *-tion*, *-sion*, or *-ion*. When adding the suffix *-ion* to a word ending in a silent letter *e*, the *e* is usually dropped. For example, when adding *-ion* to the word *prevaricate*, the silent *e* is dropped to form *prevarication*.

Using the Suffix *-tion*

A. DIRECTIONS: Change each verb into a noun with the suffix *-tion*. Then fill in each blank in the sentences with the appropriate noun.

contribute _____   navigate _____

recreate _____   decorate _____

1. The Knight has in his possession fine horses but wears clothes lacking _____.

2. The Monk prefers hunting for _____ to poring over books and tilling the soil.

3. The Friar gives absolution and an easy penance to those who accompany their confessions with a large financial _____.

4. When it comes to getting a boat from one destination to another, apparently none can compare with the Skipper at _____.

Using the Word Bank

solicitous	garnished	absolution	commission
sanguine	avouches	prevarication	

B. DIRECTIONS: Write the word from the Word Bank that best completes each of the following sentences.

1. The Franklin is probably most _____ when he is dining, since eating well gives him tremendous pleasure.

2. The Friar believes that _____ should come at a price so that people experience painful consequences for their sinful actions.

3. The Miller _____ that just by feeling grain with his thumb he can tell how much it is worth, which is a fairly bold assertion.

4. The Knight's son's garments are _____ with embroidery.

5. The innkeeper is a _____ host, doing all he can to make sure his guests are comfortable and happy.

6. A Pardoner given to _____ ought to be afraid of excommunication.

7. The Friar claims to have a _____ from the Pope to hear confessions.

The Prologue from *The Canterbury Tales* by Geoffrey Chaucer

Grammar and Style: Past and Past Perfect Tenses

Tenses of verbs indicate when events happen. Writers use the **past tense** to show that an action or a condition began and ended at a particular time in the past. They use the **past perfect tense** to clarify that an action or a condition ended before another past action began. The past tense is formed by adding *-ed* or *-d* to the base form of the verb. The past perfect tense uses the helping verb *had* before the past participle of the main verb. This passage from "The Prologue" contains both the past tense and past perfect tense.

> He had his son with him, a fine young Squire,
>
> A lover and cadet, a lad of fire
>
> With locks as curly as if they <u>had been pressed</u>. **past perfect tense**
>
> He was some twenty years of age, <u>I guessed.</u> **past tense**

A. Practice: Read the following sentences. On the line that follows each sentence, list each verb and identify its tense as *past* or *past perfect*.

1. The Knight had followed the chivalric code and had achieved success in many battles.

   _____

2. The Yeoman had burnished his hunting horn clean before he dangled it from a baldric of bright green.

   _____

3. According to the narrator, the Nun had learned fine table manners and so never dipped her fingers in the sauce too deep.

   _____

4. The Oxford Cleric had found no preferment in the church or more worldly employment but, instead, just lived off loans from his friends.

   _____

5. The Franklin had stocked his house with fine wine and all sorts of rich foods and then arrayed his hall table with places for guests.

   _____

B. Writing Application: Read each sentence. On the line that follows it, rewrite it, using the correct form of the verb that appears in brackets.

1. Chaucer [intend] to write 124 tales, but [complete] only 24 by the time he died.

   _____

2. The narrator [decide] to go to Canterbury before he met the other pilgrims but [agree] to travel with them once he made their acquaintance.

   _____

3. The narrator [want] to write down what he [observe] of each pilgrim while he still had the time and space to do so.

   _____

The Prologue from *The Canterbury Tales* by Geoffrey Chaucer

Reading Strategy: Analyzing Difficult Sentences

When you encounter long or involved sentences that seem too difficult to understand, asking yourself *who, what, when, where, why,* and *how* questions can help you figure out their meaning.

DIRECTIONS: Read the following sentences from "The Prologue." Then answer the *who, what, when, where, why,* and/or *how* questions following them to decode their meaning.

He knew the taverns well in every town / And every innkeeper and barmaid too / Better than lepers, beggars and that crew, / For in so eminent a man as he / It was not fitting with the dignity / Of his position, dealing with a scum / of wretched lepers; nothing good can come / Of dealings with the slum-and-gutter dwellers, / But only with the rich and victual-sellers.

1. What and whom did he know well? _____

2. Whom didn't he know as well? Why? _____

    If, when he fought, the enemy vessel sank, / He sent his prisoners home; they walked the plank.

3. What did he do? _____

4. How did he do this? _____

    They had a Cook with them who stood alone / For boiling chicken with a marrow-bone, / Sharp flavoring-powder and a spice for savor.

5. Who "stood alone"? _____

6. For what did he stand alone? _____

    A Doctor too emerged as we proceeded; No one alive could talk as well as he did / On points of medicine and of surgery, / For, being grounded in astronomy, / He watched his patient's favorable star / And, by his Natural Magic, knew what are / The lucky hours and planetary degrees / For making charms and magic effigies.

7. Whom is this about? _____

8. What can he do? _____

9. How does he treat his patients? _____

    But best of all he sang an Offertory, / For well he knew that when that song was sung / He'd have to preach and tune his honey-tongue / And (well he could) win silver from the crowd, / That's why he sang so merrily and loud.

10. What does he do best? _____

11. What does he know he'll have to do when he's done singing? _____

12. Why does he sing so merrily and loud? _____

Name _____ Date _____

The Prologue from *The Canterbury Tales* by Geoffrey Chaucer

Literary Analysis: Characterization

Characterization is the writer's act of creating and developing the personality traits of a character. Chaucer uses both **direct characterization**—that is, stating facts about a personality directly—and **indirect characterization**—that is, revealing personality through details of appearance, thoughts, speech, and/or actions—to develop the vivid personalities of the pilgrims in *The Canterbury Tales*.

DIRECTIONS: Read the following passages from "The Prologue." In each passage, circle any direct statements about the character's personality. Underline statements about the character's appearance, speech, and/or behavior that reveal his or her personality indirectly. Then, on the lines that follow, summarize what the passage conveys about the character's personality.

1. There was also a Nun, a Prioress, / Her way of smiling very simple and coy. / Her greatest oath was only "By St. Loy!" / And she was known as Madam Eglantyne. / And well she sang a service, with a fine / Intoning through her nose, as was most seemly, / And she spoke daintily in French, extremely, / After the school of Stratford-atte-Bowe; / French in the Paris style she did not know. / At meat her manners were well taught withal / No morsel from her lips did she let fall, / Nor dipped her fingers in the sauce too deep; / But she could carry a morsel up and keep / The smallest drop from falling on her breast.

   _____

   _____

2. A Sergeant at the Law who paid his calls, / Wary and wise, for clients at St. Paul's / There also was, of noted excellence. / Discreet he was, a man to reverence, / Or so he seemed, his sayings were so wise.

   _____

   _____

3. A worthy woman from beside Bath city / Was with us, somewhat deaf, which was a pity. / In making cloth she showed so great a bent / She bettered those of Ypres and of Ghent. / In all the parish not a dame dared stir / Towards the altar steps in front of her. / And if indeed they did, so wrath was she / As to be quite put out of charity. / Her kerchiefs were of finely woven ground; / I dared have sworn they weighed a good ten pound, / The ones she wore on Sunday on her head. / Her hose were of the finest scarlet red / And gartered tight; her shoes were soft and new.

   _____

   _____

4. The Miller was a chap of sixteen stone. / A great stout fellow big in brawn and bone. / He did well out of them, for he could go / And win the ram at any wrestling show. / Broad, knotty and short-shouldered, he would boast / He could heave any door off hinge and post, / Or take a run and break it with his head.

   _____

   _____

Name _____ Date _____

Build Vocabulary

Spelling Strategy The *zh* sound is spelled -*si*- as in *derision*.

Using the Root -*cap*- and the Prefix apo-

A. DIRECTIONS: In each sentence, underline the word that contains the root -*cap*- or the prefix *apo*. Then, use your knowledge of the root or prefix to define the word you underlined.

1. The captain turned off the "Fasten Your Seatbelts" sign.

   _____

2. As the waves grew higher, we all grew concerned that the boat might capsize.

   _____

3. The audience had filled the auditorium to capacity.

   _____

4. After insulting the group of businessmen, the engineer returned to the conference room and apologized.

   _____

5. The apothegm the gambler used when he lost was: "You win some, you lose some."

   _____

Using the Word Bank

capital	timorous	derision
maxim	stringent	apothecary
pallor	hoary	prating

B. Directions: Read each series of words. Write the word from the word bank that best fits with the other words in the series.

1. cowardly, fearful, shy _____

2. strict, severe, unkind _____

3. money, property, funds _____

4. saying, truth, principle _____

5. pharmacist, medical person _____

6. ridicule, contempt, mockery _____

7. chattering, talking foolishly _____

8. paleness, white skin, deathly hue _____

9. ancient, gray, white _____

"The Nun's Priest's Tale" and **"The Pardoner's Tale"** from *The Canterbury Tales*
by Geoffrey Chaucer

Grammar and Style: Pronouns

Pronoun Case

Pronoun case refers to the form a pronoun takes to indicate its function in a sentence. Writers use the **subjective case** when the pronoun performs the action—acts as the subject of the sentence—or when it renames the subject. Writers use the **objective case** when the pronoun receives the action of the verb—as a direct or an indirect object—or is the object of a preposition.

> **Subjective case pronouns:** I, we, you, he, she, it, they
> **Objective case pronouns:** me, us, you, him, her, it, them

A. Practice: Underline the pronouns in the following sentences. Then identify the case of each pronoun by writing an *S* for *subjective* or an *O* for *objective* above it.

1. "Little she had in capital or rent, ..."

2. ". . . And Pertelote who heard him roar and scream / Was quite aghast. . . ."

3. "It was a dream, he thought, a fantasy."

B. Application: Complete each sentence by inserting the correct pronoun. Then identify its case by writing an *S* for *subjective* or an *O* for *objective* on the line beside the sentence.

____ 1. If you had to characterize Chanticleer, would you call _____ "vain, proud, and crafty"?

____ 2. The storyteller points out that since _____ was seven days old Pertelote held the heart of Chanticleer controlled.

____ 3. Pertelote is distressed not by Chanticleer's dream but by the fact _____ appears to be so afraid of it.

____ 4. _____ recommends that Chanticleer take herbs to purge from his body the red choler in his blood that caused his disturbing dreams.

Relative Pronouns *Who* and *Whom*

Relative pronouns connect one idea in a sentence to another part of the sentence. The **relative pronouns *who*** and ***whom*** introduce clauses that modify a particular word in the sentence. *Who* acts as the subject of a clause; *whom* may act as a direct object, and indirect object, or the object of a preposition within a clause.

S

The apothecary is the one **who** gave the younger rioter the poison.

OP

The old man was the one to **whom** the three rioters spoke on the road.

C. Practice: Circle the relative pronoun in each sentence, underline the clause it introduces, and draw an arrow from the clause to the word it modifies.

1. It's of three rioters I have to tell / Who long before the morning service bell / Were sitting in a tavern for a drink.
2. There came a privy thief, they call him Death, / Who kills us all round here . . .
3. A certain traitor who singles out / And kills the fine young fellows hereabout.
4. The one who draws the longest, lucky man, / Shall run to town as quickly as he can . . .
5. . . . away he ran / Into a neighboring street, and found a man / Who lent him three large bottles.

"The Nun's Priest's Tale" and **"The Pardoner's Tale"** from *The Canterbury Tales*
by Geoffrey Chaucer

Reading Strategy: Using Context Clues and Rereading for Clarification

Using Context Clues

You can often determine the meaning of an unfamiliar word from its **context**—that is, from the words, phrases, and sentences that surround it. You often have to look for clues to discover a word's meaning. For example, look at the word *sauntered* in the following passage:

> "Grim as a lion's was his manly frown
> As on his toes he sauntered up and down;
> He scarcely deigned to set his foot to ground
> And every time a seed of corn was found
> He gave a chuck, and up his wives ran all."

From the surrounding details about what Chanticleer is doing, you can infer that *saunter* means "to stroll"— maybe even "to stroll with an attitude of pride or self-assurance."

A. DIRECTIONS: Read these sentences from "The Nun's Priest's Tale." Use context clues to determine the meaning of the italicized word. Underline the clues you use. Then write your definition on the line. Finally, check your definition in a dictionary.

1. This Chanticleer began to groan and *lurch* / Like someone sorely troubled by a dream, / And Pertelote who heard him roar and scream / Was quite aghast and said, "O dearest heart, / What's ailing you? Why do you groan and start?"

   _____

2. "For shame," she said, "you timorous *poltroon!* / Alas, what cowardice!"

   _____

3. "The first of them found *refuge* in a stall / Down in a yard with oxen and a plow. / His friend found lodging for himself somehow / Elsewhere, by accident or destiny, / Which governs all of us and equally."

   _____

Rereading for Clarification

You can go back and **reread** a passage in order to **clarify** what it means. Sometimes you might be surprised at how much more you understand the second or third time.

B. DIRECTIONS: Reread the following sentences from "The Pardoner's Tale." Write down what becomes clearer to you.

1. Be on your guard to meet such an adversary, / Be primed to meet him everywhere you go.

   _____

2. "Away with him as he has made away / With all our friends. God's dignity. To-night!"

   _____

3. ". . . if it be your design / To find out Death, turn up this crooked way / Towards that grove. I left him there [Death] today / Under a tree, and there you'll find him waiting."

   _____

"The Nun's Priest's Tale" and **"The Pardoner's Tale"** from *The Canterbury Tales*
by Geoffrey Chaucer

Literary Analysis: Parody and *Exemplum* (Anecdote)

Mock-Heroic Style

By using a **parody,** writers use inflated language more suitable to describe heroes and their epic battles to show the ridiculousness of some trivial matter that is taken too seriously. Chaucer tells about a common barnyard occurrence in the example from "The Nun's Priest's Tale"—the attack of a fox on a chicken coop—as though he were narrating a grand scene within some epic poem. Chaucer also displays his rooster and hen as if they were courtly lovers, a tradition he uses to enrich his mock-heroic satire.

> O woeful hens, louder your shrieks and higher
> Than those of Roman matrons when the fire
> Consumed their husbands, senators of Rome,
> When Nero burnt their city and their home.

A. DIRECTIONS: Write *yes* on the line next to each passage if it is an example of parody, and *no* if it is not.

1. _____ Jerry courageously decided he could postpone the fateful moment no longer. Slowly and gravely, he donned the proper uniform until he was clad in sneakers, shorts, and a T-shirt. He found his gracious mother on the porch and bade her farwell. "I will return," he promised her as he marched fearlessly to do battle with the overgrown lawn, using as his loyal steed the new power mower his father had entrusted to his care the week before.

2. _____ He walked into the diner and sat down on one of the stools. He had only forty cents left in his coin purse. That was all the money he had in the world. "Excuse me, miss," he asked the waitress. "How much coffee will forty cents get me?"
   "Maybe half a cup," she answered.
   "O.K.," he said.
   She brought the pot over and poured coffee into his cup until it was full.

Exemplum **(Anecdote)**

An *exemplum* is an anecdote that serves as an example to illustrate a truth or moral. "The Pardoner's Tale" is an *exemplum* used to teach that greediness is a disastrous way of life.

B. DIRECTIONS: In the lines that follow, record four lines from "The Pardoner's Tale" that help to illustrate the moral the Pardoner is trying to teach.

1. _____

2. _____

3. _____

4. _____

"Elizabeth II: A New Queen," *The London Times*

Build Vocabulary: Words of Royalty

The affairs of kings and queens and royal families are complicated. Protocols and traditions dating back hundreds of years guide and dictate every occasion. These traditions accordingly have their own vocabulary. A number of such words can be found in the newspaper account of Queen Elizabeth II's accession to the crown.

DIRECTIONS: For each "royal" word below, write a sentence that uses the word correctly in the context of a new monarch taking a throne.

accession: _____

_____

proclamation: _____

_____

sittings: _____

_____

allegiance: _____

_____

succession: _____

_____

abdication: _____

_____

ceremonial: _____

_____

commissioning: _____

_____

dominions: _____

_____

pageantry: _____

_____

"Elizabeth II: A New Queen," The London Times

Thematic Connection: A National Spirit

Although she exercises no sovereign power, Queen Elizabeth II remains the foremost symbol of the British nation. While some Britons argue against the need for the monarchy, others contend that the British royal family's role as national symbol helps to bind together a diverse people, serving to strengthen the national spirit. Who serves the same purpose in democratic nations with no tradition of a monarchy?

DIRECTIONS: Think about how a national spirit is symbolized by supplying information below. Use the articles on Queen Elizabeth II and what you know about the British royal family to fill in the ovals of the chart. Then, on the lines beneath the chart, list your ideas about a national symbol for the United States.

Who

When

Political or Constitutional Role

Symbolic Role

The British Monarch: A National Symbol

Problems

The United States: A Proposal for a National Symbol:

_____

_____

_____

_____

_____

from *Sir Gawain and the Green Knight*, translated by Marie Borroff
from *Morte d'Arthur* by Sir Thomas Mallory

Build Vocabulary

Spelling Strategy When two vowels occur together, the vowel sound in the syllable is usually the long sound of the first vowel, and the second vowel is silent; as in *entreated*.

Using the Root *-droit-*

A. DIRECTIONS: The word root *-droit-* means "right." In the following sentences, decide whether the italicized word is used properly. If it is, write "correct." If it is not, rewrite the sentence using the correct form of a word with the root *-droit-*.

1. Because of his *adroitness* with a football, Charley was unable to make the football team.

   _____

2. Amber was very *adroit* at gymnastics, so she knew she would never go to the Olympics.

   _____

3. Marla is no longer *maladroit* in her movements now that she takes ballet lessons.

   _____

4. Tad prides himself on his *maladroitness*, having never broken a leg in all his years as a skier.

   _____

Using the Word Bank

assay	adjure	feigned
adroitly	largesse	righteous
entreated	peril	interred

B. DIRECTIONS: Each excerpt below is from one of the poems. Choose the word from the Word Bank that best matches the meaning of the italicized word or phrase.

1. If there be one so willful my words to *prove*, Let him leap hither lightly. . . . _____

2. He proffered, with good grace, His bare neck to the blade, And *pretended* a cheerful face. . . .

   _____

3. . . . those that I did battle for in *just* quarrels, _____

4. First I ask and *appeal* to you, how you are called

   That you tell me true. . . . _____

5. Sir Mordred did his devoir that day and put himself in great *danger*. _____

6. . . . Withdrew the ax *skillfully* before it did damage. _____

7. . . . and there they *pleaded with* Sir Mordred . . . _____

8. . . . contrary both to *noble spirit* and loyalty belonging to the knights . . . _____

9. "What man is there here *buried* that you pray so fast for?" _____

from *Sir Gawain and the Green Knight,* translated by Marie Borroff

from *Morte d'Arthur* by Sir Thomas Mallory

Grammar and Style: Comparative and Superlative Forms

The **comparative form** of an adjective or adverb compares two things. The **superlative form** of an adjective or adverb compares more than two things to the highest degree.

Comparative: . . . Grow green as the grass and *greener*, it seemed . . .

Superlative: . . . *Worthiest* of their works the wide world over . . .

A. Practice: Identify which form of adjective is used in each sentence.

1. Aparna sold a larger amount of her jewelry at the art fair this year than she did last year.

   _____

2. The early recording was finer than the new one. _____

3. Jordan holds the record for the largest number of cans collected during a food drive.

   _____

4. This painting is even more beautiful than the last one. _____

5. Monday was the coldest day of the month. _____

B. Writing Application: Rewrite the following sentences, using the appropriate comparative or superlative form of the adjective or adverb in parentheses.

1. Marcie is the (compassionate) person I know.

   _____

   _____

2. Katrusha will be (happy) working outdoors than in an office this summer.

   _____

   _____

3. Fresh fruit and a bagel makes a (nutritious) breakfast than coffee and a donut.

   _____

   _____

4. Angelo explained to his grandfather that writing a letter is (easy) with a computer than with a pen and paper. _____

   _____

5. Up in the hills, it's always (chilly) in the morning before the sun comes up.

   _____

   _____

from *Sir Gawain and the Green Knight,* translated by Marie Borroff
from *Morte d'Arthur* by Sir Thomas Mallory

Reading Strategy: Summarize

Summarizing is one way to check your understanding of what you have read. A summary briefly states the main point and key details in your own words. A summary is always much shorter than the original, but it must reflect the original accurately. Look at this example from *Morte d'Arthur.*

Passage	Key Ideas and Events	Summary
King Arthur smote Sir Mordred under the shield, with a thrust of his spear, throughout the body more than a fathom. And when Sir Mordred felt that he had his death's wound, he thrust himself with the might that he had up to the burr of King Arthur's spear, and right so he smote his father King Arthur with his sword holden in both his hands, upon the side of the head, that the sword pierced the helmet and the casing of the brain.	King Arthur speared Sir Mordred. Sir Mordred felt that he was dying from the wound, but he forced himself to hit King Arthur in the head.	Sir Mordred and King Arthur fought a terrible battle. Sir Mordred was killed and King Arthur was wounded in the head.

DIRECTIONS: Use this graphic organizer to summarize this excerpt.

Passage	Key Ideas and Events	Summary
. . . Sir Lucan departed, for he was grievously wounded in many places. And so as he walked he saw and harkened by the moonlight how that pillagers and robbers were come into the field to pill and to rob many a full noble knight of brooches and bracelets and of many a good ring and many a rich jewel. And who that were not dead all out there they slew them for their harness and their riches. When Sir Lucan understood this work, he came to the King as soon as he might and told him all what he had heard and seen.		

from *Sir Gawain and the Green Knight,* translated by Marie Borroff
from *Morte d'Arthur* by Sir Thomas Mallory

Literary Analysis: Medieval Romance

Medieval romances were the popular adventure stories of the Middle Ages. Originally cast in verse, they were later sometimes told in prose. In England, the best known of the medieval romances involve King Arthur and his knights.

DIRECTIONS: Following is a series of characteristics of medieval romances. On the lines below each characteristic, cite at least two details from *Sir Gawain and the Green Knight* and *Morte d' Arthur* that illustrate the characteristic.

1. Medieval romances convey a sense of the supernatural.

   Sir Gawain and the Green Knight: _____

   _____

   Morte d' Arthur: _____

   _____

   _____

2. Medieval romances give a glamorous portrayal of castle life.

   Sir Gawain and the Green Knight: _____

   _____

   Morte d' Arthur: _____

   _____

   _____

3. Chivalric ideals—bravery, honor, courtesy, fairness to enemies, respect for women—guide the characters.

   Sir Gawain and the Green Knight: _____

   _____

   Morte d' Arthur: _____

   _____

   _____

4. Medieval romances are imbued with adventure.

   Sir Gawain and the Green Knight: _____

   _____

   Morte d' Arthur: _____

   _____

   _____

Letters of Margaret Paston
"Lord Randall," "The Twa Corbies," "Get Up and Bar the Door,"
and **"Barbara Allan,"** Anonymous

Build Vocabulary

Spelling Strategy The ô sound may be spelled *au*, as in *assault*.

Using the Root *-cert-*

A. Directions: Use context and the meaning of the word root *-cert-* to write a definition of the italicized word in each sentence below.

1. Margaret Paston was *certain* her son would defend Caister.

   _____

2. The ringing of the church bells was like a death *certificate* for Sir John Graeme.

   _____

3. With *certitude*, the man and his wife determined neither would bar the door.

   _____

Using the Word Bank

alderman	enquiry	succor	certify
remnant	ransacked	asunder	assault

B. Directions: On each line, write the word from the Word Bank that has the same meaning as the italicized word or phrase in the sentence.

1. Two thieves broke into a house and *pillaged* every room in search of valuables. _____

2. The *official* voted against a proposal to raise parking meter rates in her district. _____

3. The only *remainder* of the delicious meal was a spoonful of mashed potatoes. _____

4. After I knocked on the door, I heard the *question* "Who's there?" from behind it._____

5. The pirates planned to *violently attack* the trade ship and steal any cargo on board. _____

6. Nurse Florence Nightingale offered *aid* to wounded soldiers during the Crimean War.

   _____

7. The explosives expert recommended using dynamite to blow the boulder *into pieces*.

   _____

8. Only an anthropologist will be able to *verify* whether the artifact is authentic._____

Letters of Margaret Paston
"Lord Randall," "The Twa Corbies," "Get Up and Bar the Door,"
and **"Barbara Allan,"** Anonymous

Grammar and Style: Direct Address

Direct address refers to the way a character in a story or poem speaks to someone or something. A character who uses direct address is speaking directly to a person or a thing, and not simply speaking about it. The person or thing being addressed is referred to by a name, a title, or a descriptive phrase, which is always set off by commas in writing.

The italicized words in these lines from "Get Up and Bar the Door" and "Lord Randall" are examples of direct address.

" 'My hand is in my hussyfskap, *Goodman*, as ye may see;' "

" 'O yes, I am poison'd; *mother*, make my bed soon,' "

A. Practice: This stanza is from "Lord Randall." Circle the examples of direct address.

"Where gat ye your dinner, Lord Randall, my son?

Where gat ye your dinner, my handsome young man?"

"I dined wi' my true-love; mother, make my bed soon,

For I'm weary wi' hunting, and fain wald lie down."

B. Writing Application: In this ballad, underline any line that contains an example of direct address and add the correct punctuation to it.

"Are you hungry Lord Randall for there's plenty to eat,

and I'll spread it all out on the table.

Eat hearty my love of the bread and the broth.

Fill up as much as you are able."

"Now surely my darling there's room in you still.

Won't you try some more delicate eel?

'Twas a pleasure dear man to cook you this food.

It's as good as the love I feel."

"Be off stupid hounds there's no scraps for you!

They are all for my love to keep strong.

Now go home gentle knight you've eaten quite well,

and your sleep will be deep and long."

Letters of Margaret Paston
"Lord Randall," "The Twa Corbies," "Get Up and Bar the Door,"
and **"Barbara Allan,"** Anonymous

Reading Strategy: Understanding Dialect

Dialect is the form of a language spoken by people in a particular region or group. Poetry and prose written in dialect can be difficult to understand because the vocabulary and the pronunciation of certain words are unfamiliar. You can make sure you understand what you are reading by translating the dialect to modern English. Following are some strategies you can use to do this.

1. Use footnotes to find the meaning of words no longer used in modern English.

2. Use the context of the sentence to figure out what a word or phrase means.

3. Read the word aloud to figure out if it sounds like a word in modern English.

In this line from "The Twa Corbies," the two instances of Scottish-English dialect are italicized: "'And I'll *pike* out his bonny blue *e'en*;'" **1. e'en:** Eyes.

The footnote explains the meaning of *e'en*. You can use context and the sound of the word *pike* to figure out that it means "poke." Now the sense of the line is clear: "And I'll poke out his bonny blue eyes."

DIRECTIONS: Read the stanzas from "The Twa Corbies" and underline all instances of dialect in them. Then rewrite the stanzas, using modern English in place of the dialect.

As I was walking all alane,

I heard twa corbies[1] making a mane.[2]   **1. twa corbies:** Two ravens.

The tane unto the tither did say,   **2. mane:** Moan.

"Whar sall we gang and dine the day?"

"In behint yon auld fail dyke,[3]   **3. fail dyke:** Bank of earth.

I wot[4] there lies a new-slain knight;   **4. wot:** Know.

And naebody kens[5] that he lies there   **5. kens:** Knows.

But his hawk, his hound, and his lady fair."

_____

_____

_____

_____

_____

_____

_____

_____

_____

Letters of Margaret Paston
"Lord Randall," "The Twa Corbies," "Get Up and Bar the Door,"
and **"Barbara Allan,"** Anonymous

Literary Analysis: Letter and Folk Ballad

A **letter** can range from a short note to a detailed narrative. It usually begins with the date and a greeting followed by the body and a closing. A **folk ballad** is a narrative poem by an unknown author that was originally meant to be sung. Most ballads are made up of four-line stanzas in which the second and fourth lines rhyme. Other typical characteristics include a refrain, or a regularly repeated line or group of lines, dialogue, and repetition. The letters and the folk ballads in this selection contain details that reveal some of the challenges of medieval life.

A. DIRECTIONS: Use this graphic organizer to record the details of some challenges of medieval life about which you have read. First, write the title of the selection and details from it in the first column. Then describe the challenge in the second column. Use details from a ballad and from a letter. Examples are provided for you.

Title and Details	Challenge
Title: "Get Up and Bar the Door" **Details:** The wind sae cauld blew . . .; ". . . there's nae water in the house,"	Houses did not have indoor plumbing. Going outside to get water in winter was probably an unpleasant and difficult chore.
Title: "The Letters of Margaret Paston" **Details:** . . . I would that you should send home your brothers . . . to take control and to bring in such men as are necessary for the safeguard of the place . . .	In the Middle Ages, landowners had to use force of their own to protect their land from political officials who also used force to try to take it away.
Title: **Details:**	
Title: **Details:**	

"How Siegfried Was Slain" from *The Nibelungenlied,*
translated by A. T. Hatto

Build Vocabulary: Language of Perils and Adventures

To tell a story of adventure, a writer needs to use vivid vocabulary that effectively describes the perils the hero must face.

DIRECTIONS: Choose the word from the box that when used to replace a word or phrase in the sentence will retain the sentence's meaning. Then write a sentence of your own for the word.

daring	ill-omened	sinister	noble
quarry	thwarted	dispatched	treacherous

1. In an incredible act of boldness, Sir Hans rode alone against the dragon.

   word: _____ sentence: _____

   _____

2. The dream involving the winter storm turned out to be a cruel portent.

   word: _____ sentence: _____

   _____

3. The prince was defeated in his plan to enslave the kingdom.

   word: _____ sentence: _____

   _____

4. With a thrust of his lance, the prince killed the dragon.

   word: _____ sentence: _____

   _____

5. The prince and his hunting party found themselves not the hunters but the hunted.

   word: _____ sentence: _____

   _____

6. The dignified queen did not flinch in the face of danger.

   word: _____ sentence: _____

   _____

7. With an evil laugh, the dark prince signaled his intentions.

   word: _____ sentence: _____

   _____

8. The twisting path down the mountainside was incredibly dangerous.

   word: _____ sentence: _____

   _____

"How Siegfried Was Slain" from *The Nibelungenlied*,
translated by A. T. Hatto

Thematic Connection: Perils and Adventures

Many aspects of an adventure story are universal: a brave protagonist, a plot full of twists and turns, the overcoming of a variety of dangers, an evil enemy. An adventure story is made special, however, when the specific context of time and place is presented in rich detail. In what historical context does *The Nibelungenlied* take place? What facets of daily life or social structure affect the action?

DIRECTIONS: Use the chart below to list facts about the historical context of the era in which Siegfried's story takes place. One entry has been included in each column. Then, create a companion list of facts and details that would provide the context for an adventure tale that is set in the contemporary United States. List any facts or details you think might be of interest to a reader or might in some way affect the action of an adventure tale.

Medieval Europe	Contemporary United States
high mortality rate	longer life expectancy

Sonnets 1, 35, and 75 by Edmund Spenser
Sonnets 31 and 39 by Sir Philip Sidney

Build Vocabulary

Spelling Strategy The long sound of the vowel a can be spelled in several different ways. Two examples are *ei* as in *deign* and *ay* as in *assay*.

Using Forms of *Languished*

A. DIRECTIONS: Fill in the blanks in the following sentences with the appropriate form of the word *languished*: *languish* (verb), *languid* (adjective), or *languor* (noun).

1. Maria's _____ caused her mother to worry.

2. The _____ breeze offered little relief from the sweltering heat.

3. Jamie's severe depression causes him to grow more _____ daily.

4. Keats continued to _____ from the effects of tuberculosis.

5. As I watched the dreamy _____ of the slow-moving river, I could feel my eyelids grow heavy.

Using the Word Bank

deign	assay	devise
wan	languished	balm

B. DIRECTIONS: Match each word in the left column with its definition in the right column. Write the letter of the definition on the line next to the word it defines.

____ 1. balm   a. try or attempt

____ 2. wan   b. weak

____ 3. assay   c. lower oneself

____ 4. deign   d. grew weak

____ 5. devise   e. something that heals

____ 6. languished   f. plan

C. DIRECTIONS: On the lines that follow, write a paragraph describing the thoughts of a lover who is longing for his beloved. Use each word in the Word Bank at least once in your paragraph.

_____

_____

_____

_____

_____

_____

Unit 2: Celebrating Humanity (1485–1625)

Sonnets 1, 35, and 75 by Edmund Spenser
Sonnets 31 and 39 by Sir Philip Sidney

Grammar and Style: Capitalization of Proper Nouns

A noun that names a specific person or thing is a **proper noun** and should be **capitalized**. Some writers, especially poets, give the names of some things a human quality by treating them as if they are proper nouns. Sir Philip Sidney addresses the moon as if it were a person, for example, and emphasizes his intention by capitalizing *Moon*.

A. Practice: Capitalize any proper noun or other word requiring capitalization in the sentences below.

1. When my mother was in the hospital, kate Chapman sent her a beautiful plant.

2. Oh, dawn, why must you arrive so soon?

3. My brother tom will start at southridge high school next year.

B. Writing Application: Write two sentences for each of the following words. The first sentence should use the word as a noun in a way that should be capitalized. In the second sentence, use the word as a noun in a way that should NOT be capitalized. Sentences using the first word have been done as an example.

nightingale carpenter	wind cook	bill street

1. Florence Nightingale was the founder of modern nursing.

   The nightingale sang throughout the night.

2. _____

   _____

3. _____

   _____

4. _____

   _____

5. _____

   _____

6. _____

   _____

Sonnets 1, 35, and 75 by Edmund Spenser
Sonnets 31 and 39 by Sir Philip Sidney

Reading Strategy: Paraphrasing

Poetic language often uses condensed imagery to convey the poet's ideas. **Paraphrasing,** or restating passages in your own words, can help you understand and explore a poem's meaning. When paraphrasing poetry, look for the main ideas within the imagery. Think about what the images might be representing and how those images convey a bigger theme.

Spenser, Sonnet 1, lines 1-3: "Happy ye leaves when as those lily hands,/which hold my life in their dead doing might,/Shall handle you and hold in love's soft bands, . . . "

Paraphrase: The pages of a book are happy when held in the beautiful, soft hands of my beloved, hands that also hold me in their power.

DIRECTIONS: In the chart below, paraphrase One of Spenser's sonnets and one of Sidney's sonnets.

Try these tips as you paraphrase a sonnet:

• Break down the sonnet into parts (octaves, quatrains, sestets, or couplets).

• Paraphrase parts, not every line.

• Focus on complete thoughts.

Sonnet	Paraphrase

© Prentice-Hall, Inc.

Sonnets 1, 35, and 75 by Edmund Spenser
Sonnets 31 and 39 by Sir Philip Sidney

Literary Analysis: The Sonnet and Sonnet Sequence

A **sonnet**, a lyric poem of fourteen lines, originated in Italy. The Italian, or Petrarchan, sonnet is divided into two parts. The first eight lines form the *octave* and the next six lines the *sestet*. While the Italian sonnet had a fairly strict rhyme scheme, English poets took many liberties with the sonnet form. Sir Philip Sidney used an *abab abab* rhyme scheme in addition to the Italian *abba abba* rhyme scheme for the octave. In the sestet, Sidney's rhyme schemes were *cdcdee, cddcee,* or *ccdeed.* The Spenserian sonnet, named for Edmund Spenser, uses the *abab, bcbc, cdcd, ee* rhyme scheme. Usually there is no break in a Spenserian sonnet between the octave and the sestet.

Recognizing the Sonnet Form

A. DIRECTIONS: In the following sonnet by Edmund Spenser, bracket and label the stanzas with their rhyme schemes.

> Lyke as a ship that through the ocean wyde,
> By conduct of some star doth make her way,
> Whenas a storme hath dimd her trusty guyde,
> Out of her course doth wander far astray.
> [5] So I whose star, that wont with her bright ray,
> Me to direct, with cloudes is overcast,
> Doe wander now in darknesse and dismay,
> Through hidden perils round about me plast.
> Yet hope I well, that when this storme is past
> [10] My Helice the lodestar of my lyfe
> Will shine again, and looke on me at last,
> With lovely light to cleare my cloudy grief.
> Till then I wander carefull comfortlesse,
> In secret sorrow and sad pensivenesse.

Sonnet Sequence

B. DIRECTIONS: A **sonnet sequence** is a group of sonnets linked by subject matter or theme, and following certain conventions. Compare two of the sonnets from the sonnet sequence *Astrophel and Stella* by Sir Philip Sidney by answering the following questions about Sonnets 31 and 39.

1. To what inanimate object is each sonnet addressed?
   a. Sonnet 31 is addressed to the _____.
   b. Sonnet 39 is addressed to _____.

2. The speaker in each sonnet desires something from the one addressed.
   a. In Sonnet 31, he wants _____.
   b. In Sonnet 39, he wants _____.

3. Both poems are lyric and reflect the speaker's feelings.
   a. In Sonnet 31, he feels _____ about the way women treat men.
   b. In Sonnet 39, he feels a _____ for peace.

Sonnets 29, 106, 116, and 130 by William Shakespeare

Build Vocabulary

Spelling Strategy When adding a suffix that begins with a vowel to a word that ends in a silent letter *e*, the *e* is usually dropped. For example, when adding the suffix *-ing* to the word *prefigure*, the silent *e* is dropped to form *prefiguring*.

Using the Root *-chron-*

A. DIRECTIONS: The root *-chron-* comes from the Greek word *khronos*, meaning "time." Complete the following paragraph using the *-chron-* based words provided.

synchronize	chronic	chronologer
synchronicity	chronicle	chronology

Mr. Khronos has suffered from anxiety all his life. Some say he's a _____

worrier. His problem is that he's always watching the clock. He has to—it's his job. As a

_____ of geological history, he measures time in terms of fixed periods

and events. When not at work, Mr. Khronos collects clocks and keeps a _____

of his purchases. Once, a friend bought him a Felix the Cat clock at the very same moment he

was picking one out for himself at another store. Talk about _____! Not

surprisingly, he has managed to _____ all the timepieces in his house to

Greenwich Mean Time. At some time in the future, someone will probably write the

_____ of the life and times of Mr. Khronos.

Using the Word Bank

scope	sullen	chronicle
prefiguring	impediments	alters

B. DIRECTIONS: Write the word from the Word Bank that best matches each situation that follows.

1. She was imagining her future life as his wife. _____

2. The father of the bride did all he could to stop the wedding. _____

3. The groom oversaw the extent of the crisis. _____

4. He kept a careful account of the key events in their relationship. _____

5. Her mother's wedding dress fit the bride nearly perfectly, but some pieces of old lace needed replacing. _____

6. After her father put a stop to the wedding, she fell silent for weeks. _____

Name _____ Date _____

Sonnets 29, 106, 116, and 130 by William Shakespeare

Grammar and Style: Participles as Adjectives

Participles are verb forms that often end in *-ing* or *-ed*. They can sometimes be used as adjectives to modify nouns or pronouns. When a participle functions as an adjective, it must appear near the noun or pronoun it modifies. Shakespeare's descriptive writing is enhanced by the skillful use of participles as adjectives:

O, no! It is an *ever-fixed* mark / That looks on tempests and is never shaken. (Sonnet 116)

Yet well I know / That music hath a far more *pleasing* sound. (Sonnet 130)

A. Practice: Shakespeare's Sonnet 128, which is not in your text, appears below. Underline participles used as adjectives. Circle the noun or pronoun each participle modifies.

How oft, when thou, my music, music play'st

Upon that blesséd wood whose motion sounds

With thy sweet fingers when thou gently sway'st

The wiry concord that mine ear confounds,

Do I envy those jacks that nimble leap

To kiss the tender inward of thy hand,

Whilst my poor lips, which should that harvest reap,

At the wood's boldness by thee blushing stand.

To be so tickled they would change their state

And situation with those dancing chips

O'er whom thy fingers walk with gentle gait,

Making dead wood more blest than living lips.

Since saucy jacks so happy are in this,

Give them thy fingers, me thy lips to kiss.

B. Writing Application: Make each of these sentences more descriptive by adding a participle used as an adjective to modify the noun or pronoun shown in italics.

1. During his time, Shakespeare had a public reputation as a *playwright*.

   _____

2. Shakespeare's plays were performed at the *Globe Theater*. _____

3. In 1593, a *plague* broke out in London, forcing the city's theaters to close.

   _____

4. Shakespeare's sonnets have a *variety* of themes. _____

5. The later sonnets focus on a "dark lady," and the grief she causes the *speaker*.

   _____

Name _____ Date _____

Sonnets 29, 106, 116, and 130 by William Shakespeare

Reading Strategy: Relating Structure to Theme

Readers **relate structure to theme** in literature by looking at how the form of a work influences what is being said. The form of the sonnet—its three quatrains and ending couplet—molds its contents. An idea, situation, or problem is usually presented in the first eight or twelve lines. This means that thoughts must be shaped to fit three quatrains, while the final couplet provides a succinct conclusion in a burst of rhyme. For example, Sonnet 130 examines the features of the speaker's beloved one by one, each time making a case against overstating her worth. The descriptions are beautifully suited to the concise format of the quatrain as each line builds on the last, leading to the surprising conclusion in the couplet.

DIRECTIONS: Use this graphic organizer to help you understand the relationship of structure and theme in Shakespeare's sonnets. As you read each sonnet, use the middle column to summarize in a sentence or two what the initial idea, situation, or problem is. Then, in the last column, briefly describe what you think the concluding couplet is saying.

Unit 2: Celebrating Humani (1485–1625)

Sonnet	Idea, Situation, or Problem	Conclusion
Sonnet 29		
Sonnet 106		
Sonnet 116		
Sonnet 130		

Name _____   Date _____

Sonnets 29, 106, 116, and 130 by William Shakespeare

Literary Analysis: Shakespearean Sonnet

Read the following sonnet by Michael Drayton (1563–1631). First indicate the rhyme scheme by writing the appropriate letters on the lines at the right. Then answer the questions that follow the poem.

Calling to mind since first my love began _____

Th'incertain times oft varying in their course. _____

How things still unexpectedly have run, _____

As please the Fates, by their resistless force, _____

[5] Lastly, mine eyes amazedly have seen _____

Essex great fall, Tyrone his peace to gain. _____

The quiet end of that long-living Queen, _____

This King's fair entrance, and our peace with Spain, _____

We and the Dutch at length ourselves to sever. _____

[10] Thus the world doth, and evermore shall reel, _____

Yet to my goddess am I constant ever, _____

Howe'er blind Fortune turn her giddy wheel. _____

Though heaven and earth prove both to me untrue, _____

Yet am I still inviolate to you. _____

Lines 7–10 refer to the failure of the Earl of Essex (Robert Devereux) to conquer the Earl of Tyrone (Hugh O'Neill), to the death of Elizabeth I, who was succeeded by James I, and to other historical events.

1. According to the rhyme scheme, is Drayton's sonnet an example of Shakespearean form or of Petrarchan form? _____

2. What is the premise stated in the poem? _____

   _____

3. What is the conclusion stated in the poem? _____

   _____

4. In what way is Drayton's philosophy similar to Shakespeare's? _____

   _____

Sonnets 18 and 28 by Petrarch
Sonnets 69 and 89 by Pablo Neruda

Build Vocabulary: Language of Love Poetry

A number of words found in the sonnets of Petrarch and Neruda may seem rather ordinary by themselves, but in the context of a love sonnet they take on a special aura. Recognizing how words take on special meanings depending on their context will help you better appreciate works of literature and will add depth to your own writing.

DIRECTIONS: Write the word from the box that best fits each clue that follows. Then, on the lines, write a sentence of your own using the word. Your sentence should relate to the theme of love, and read as if it were a line from a love poem.

Unit 2: Celebrating Humanity (1485–1625)

beauties	sublime	muse	vanquished
woe	prospects	light	destiny

1. hopes or chances _____

_____

_____

2. inspiration _____

_____

_____

3. of the moon, in that it is a fine place to woo _____

_____

_____

4. it was meant to be _____

_____

_____

5. what I felt when my lover left _____

_____

_____

6. overcome by feeling _____

_____

_____

7. these can be internal or external _____

_____

_____

8. a special feeling _____

_____

_____

Sonnets 18 and 28 by Petrarch
Sonnets 69 and 89 by Pablo Neruda

Cultural Connection: Love Poetry

The quotation "Love makes the world go 'round" is found in the works of writers as diverse as Lewis Carroll and W. S. Gilbert, as well as in anonymous lyrics of a French song. The subject of love is all around us, in the music that pipes over the airwaves and the plots of stories in film and television. How do contemporary images of love compare with the ideas and themes in the works of Petrarch and Neruda?

DIRECTIONS: Use the graphic organizer to arrange your thoughts on the subject of love and to describe how romantic love is portrayed in the poetry you read and in contemporary culture. In each box, include such topics as how the object of love is portrayed, how the outcome of the love affair is presented, what metaphors are used to describe the emotion, whether love is portrayed as an ideal or more realistically, and so on.

Petrarch

Neruda

Love

Contemporary Song

Contemporary Film

from *Utopia* by Sir Thomas More
Elizabeth's Speech Before Her Troops by Queen Elizabeth I

pages 264- 270 (handwritten)

Build Vocabulary

Spelling Strategy You may think of the prefix *sub-* as meaning "under" or "below." However, sometimes it has the meaning "close to" or "after," as it does in the word *subsequently*.

Using the Root *-sequent-*

A. DIRECTIONS: The word root *-sequent-* means "following in time or order." On a separate sheet of paper, rewrite each sentence by replacing the underlined word or phrase with one of the following words.

consequence	sequentially	non sequitur	sequel	inconsequential

1. His outrageous behavior appeared to be a <u>result</u> of the tragedy.

2. Following the death of the queen, his everyday troubles seemed <u>trivial.</u>

3. These crucial events, from earliest to latest, do indeed flow <u>in order by time.</u>

4. I saw "Young Emperor," the original episode, but missed "Old Emperor," which is the <u>following episode.</u>

5. After making her first point, she delivered a <u>remark that had no bearing on what she had just said.</u>

Using the Word Bank

confiscation	sloth	subsequently	abrogated
forfeited	fraudulent	treachery	stead

B. DIRECTIONS: Complete each sentence with an appropriate word from the Word Bank.

1. The monarch's _____ of property was like death to his people.

2. He was a detestable man, displaying his _____ as a soldier displays a medal.

3. The king requested the lieutenant general escort the queen in his _____, for he trusted him like a brother.

4. The ruler's _____ promises were revealed by his heir to the throne.

5. When she _____ the death penalty, the once-doomed prisoners cheered like exhilarated school boys.

6. Noble monarchs, who live to serve their people, know nothing of _____.

7. Because the jester was as entertaining as a stone, he _____ his turn to cheer up the queen.

8. The king unwittingly consumed a vial of poison; _____ he died.

from *Utopia* by Sir Thomas More
Elizabeth's Speech Before Her Troops by Queen Elizabeth I

Grammar and Style: Complex Sentences

Complex sentences contain a main clause and one or more subordinate clauses relating to that clause. The main clause, which can appear anywhere in the sentence, can stand by itself. However, the subordinate clauses are dependent on the main clause. Complex sentences are useful for showing relationships between ideas, such as time, logic, or cause and effect. In the following complex sentence from *Utopia*, note the position of the main clause, which is italicized.

He ought to shake off either his sloth or his pride, for the people's hatred and scorn arise from these faults in him.

A. Practice: In the space provided, combine each pair of simple sentences to make a complex sentence. Use connecting words (subordinate conjunctions) like *but, because, when, although,* and *who.*

1. The royals loved their jester. He never failed to make them laugh.

_____

2. The general worshipped his queen. He was still forced to fight against her.

_____

3. The king called for an end to taxes. His subjects cried for joy.

_____

B. Writing Application: Revise the following paragraph by making some of the simple sentences into complex sentences. Use connecting words such as *because, although, when, after, before, until,* and *if.*

The queen enjoyed her morning ritual. She drank her tea. She read the paper. Then, she watered the plants in her room. She didn't trust her staff with such delicate specimens. Her Majesty ate a delicious royal breakfast. She strolled the grounds of the main house. The groundskeeper spoke with her about landscaping matters. The resident rabbit was scared off by their voices. The queen extended her stroll. It was a sure sign that her mood had soured. She continued on a long walk. The dignitaries from France arrived. It seemed she might be cross. The queen still looked cheerful.

_____

_____

_____

_____

_____

_____

_____

_____

from *Utopia* by Sir Thomas More

Elizabeth's Speech Before Her Troops by Queen Elizabeth I

Reading Strategy: Summarizing

Unit 2: Celebrating Humanity (1485–1625)

Long, complex passages can make a piece of writing difficult to follow. **Summarizing** these passages by briefly restating the main idea can help you in your reading. Look at this example from Queen Elizabeth's "Speech Before Defeating the Spanish Armada."

> Let tyrants fear; I have always so behaved myself that, under God, I have placed my chiefest strength and safeguard in the loyal hearts and good will of my subjects.

Summary: The Queen has every faith in her subjects' loyalty.

DIRECTIONS: Use the graphic organizer below to help you summarize the difficult passages in the speeches of Sir Thomas More and Queen Elizabeth I. As you read, write any difficult passages in the first column of the chart. In the next column, jot down the main idea of the passage. Note the supporting ideas, and record these in the third column. Finally, summarize the main idea of the passage in your own words. One example has already been done for you.

Passage	Main Idea	Supporting Ideas	Summary
And that therefore a prince ought to take more care of his people's happiness than of his own, as a shepherd ought to take more care of his flock than of himself.	A prince should put his people's happiness before his own.	A shepherd must look after his sheep before he cares for himself.	A prince should be more concerned with his subjects' welfare than with his own.

from *Utopia* by Sir Thomas More
Elizabeth's Speech Before Her Troops by Queen Elizabeth I

Literary Analysis: The Monarch as Hero

Both the fiction and nonfiction of the English Renaissance portray monarchs as heroes. These men and women are often drawn as superhuman archetypes: they forfeit their lives for the sake of their kingdoms; their power and generosity know no bounds; they are perfect, larger-than-life human beings. Some of these characterizations are realistic, while others are the exaggerations of an adoring public or high-minded leader. Notice Queen Elizabeth's personal sense of heroism in this excerpt from "Speech Before Defeating the Spanish Armada":

> And therefore I am come amongst you at this time, not as for my creation or sport, but being resolved, in the midst and heat of the battle, to live or die amongst you all. . . .

The people under the monarchies during the English Renaissance had great expectations of their rulers, as the rulers often did of themselves. Generosity, courage, and intelligence are among the qualities monarchs were expected to possess.

DIRECTIONS: Answer the following questions on the lines provided.

1. Look back over the selections by Sir Thomas More and Queen Elizabeth I to find individual words or phrases that you think characterize the monarch as hero. Use some of these words in a brief description of a heroic Elizabethan monarch.

_____

_____

_____

_____

2. How do heroic characteristics help monarchs rule? Use examples from More's speech to support your answer.

_____

_____

_____

_____

3. Do you think heroism, as opposed to simple trustworthiness and solid character, was a necessary quality in the monarchs of the time? Why or why not?

_____

_____

_____

_____

Build Vocabulary

Spelling Strategy Most suffixes change the part of speech of the base word. Sometimes more than one suffix is added to a word. The noun *righteousness* was formed from the adjective *righteous*, which was formed from another adjective, *right*.

Using the Root -*stat*-

A. DIRECTIONS: Combine the word root -*stat*-, which means "to stand," with each prefix or suffix listed below to make a word. Then use that word in a sentence.

1. Suffix -*ic* Word: _____

   Sentence: _____

2. Prefix *thermo*- Word: _____

   Sentence: _____

3. Suffix -*ion* Word: _____

   Sentence: _____

4. Suffix -*us* Word: _____

   Sentence: _____

Using the Word Bank

righteousness	stature	prodigal
entreated	transgressed	

B. DIRECTIONS: The questions below consist of a related pair of words in CAPITAL LETTERS followed by four lettered pairs of words. Choose the pair that best expresses a relationship similar to that in the pair in capital letters.

____ 1. RIGHTEOUSNESS : INJUSTICE ::
    a. pleasure : pain   c. anger : emotion
    b. accurate : correct   d. rule : control

____ 2. TRANSGRESS : DISOBEY ::
    a. break : rule   c. argue : quarrel
    b. shade : tree   d. hope : future

____ 3. ENTREAT : FORGIVENESS ::
    a. ask : favor   c. work : achieve
    b. answer : deny   d. deny : admit

____ 4. PRODIGAL : FORTUNE ::
    a. careful : careless   c. height : mountain
    b. glass : windows   d. wasteful : possessions

____ 5. STATURE : MAN ::
    a. archer : skill   c. agility : dancer
    b. inches : feet   d. speaker : listener

from The King James Bible

Grammar and Style: Infinitive Phrases

Infinitive phrases are made up of the word *to* followed by the base form of a verb (*to run, to sing*) plus its complements (*to run swiftly, to sing loudly*) and/or its objects (*to run swiftly home*) and its modifiers (*to sing loudly in the shower*). An infinitive phrase can function as a noun, an adjective, or an adverb.

Noun: *To praise God* was David's intention. (subject)

All his life he had loved *to sing psalms of praise*. (direct object)

Adjective: He believed that God had the power *to supply all his needs*. (modifies *power*)

Adverb: He was a devout man, quick *to turn to God for help*. (modifies *quick*)

A. Practice: Underline the infinitive phrases in the sentences. Then indicate whether each phrase functions as a noun, an adjective, or an adverb by writing *N, ADJ,* or *ADV* on the line following the sentence, and tell how the phrase functions in the sentence.

1. Reginald is afraid to raise his hand in class. _____

2. Mary Ann refused to answer the question. _____

3. The store is looking for someone to work evenings. _____

B. Writing Application: Fill in the blank in each sentence with an infinitive phrase. Then write *N, ADV,* or *ADJ* to indicate whether the infinitive functions as a noun, an adverb, or an adjective.

1. _____ is a doctor's most important responsibility. _____

2. We'll be ready when you give the signal _____. _____

3. The whole class stopped _____. _____

4. Andrew is working _____. _____

5. People do not have the right _____. _____

6. Michael always loved _____. _____

from The King James Bible

Reading Strategy: Inferring Meaning

Some passages from the Bible include difficult language and images that require you to make inferences, or draw conclusions, about the meaning of the passage. You can **infer meaning** by using the following strategy. First, ask yourself what you already know about the words or images in the passage. Second, look for context clues that help you understand the meaning. Look at this example from Psalm 23 showing how you can infer meaning.

Biblical Passage	What I Know	Context Clues
Thou preparest a table before me in the presence of mine enemies; thou anointest my head with oil; my cup runneth over.	I know that he's speaking to God and that he is using metaphors.	The psalm begins with the phrase "The shepherd," which means God is taking care of him; anointing with oil is probably a sign of honor; a cup that runs over must refer to having more than enough.

From these clues, the reader can infer that God is protecting the poet from his enemies, honoring him, and providing him with all that he needs.

DIRECTIONS: Use this chart to help you infer the meaning of difficult passages in *The King James Bible*. Each time you come across a difficult passage, write it in the column labeled Biblical Passage. In the next column, write what you know about the words or ideas in the passage. Then write clues to the meaning that you find in the context. Finally, combining what you know together with the context clues, write what you think the passage means.

Biblical Passage	What I Know	Context Clues	Meaning

© Prentice-Hall, Inc.

from The King James Bible

Literary Analysis: Psalms, Sermons, and Parables

Psalms, sermons, and parables are literary forms found in the Bible. A **psalm** is a lyric poem or a sacred song praising God. A psalm usually contains figurative language. Many psalms were originally written to be sung. A **sermon** is a speech with a moral or religious message, usually spoken by one person to a group. A **parable** is a short story that conveys a moral or religious lesson. Parables have simple plots and often contain dialogue.

DIRECTIONS: Read each passage and answer the questions that follow.

1. And he arose, and came to his father. But when he was yet a great way off, his father saw him, and had compassion, and ran, and fell on his neck, and kissed him. And the son said unto him. Father, I have sinned against heaven, and in thy sight, and am no more worthy to be called thy son.

   But the father said to his servants, Bring forth the best robe, and put it on him; and put a ring on his hand, and shoes on his feet.

   What elements in this passage are characteristic of parables?

   _____

   _____

2. Behold the fowls of the air: for they sow not, neither do they reap, nor gather into barns; yet your heavenly Father feedeth them. Are ye not much better than they?

   a. What is the religious message in the passage?

   _____

   b. Is this a psalm, sermon, or parable?

   _____

3. He maketh me to lie down in green pastures; he leadeth me beside the still waters.

   He restoreth my soul: he leadeth me in the paths of righteousness for his name's sake.

   a. What figures of speech are used in this passage?

   _____

   b. To whom does *He* refer?

   _____

   c. What elements in this passage are characteristic of psalms?

   _____

from _A Man for All Seasons_ by Robert Bolt

Build Vocabulary: Language of Power

In _A Man for All Seasons_, Robert Bolt examines the tensions in a struggle for power. His success in exploring this topic stems largely from his careful choice of words, as well as from his focus on relationships among characters.

DIRECTIONS: Use each listed word in a sentence of your own on the theme of power.

1. licentious: _____

_____

2. trust: _____

_____

3. pride: _____

_____

4. Majesty: _____

_____

5. honest: _____

_____

6. crown: _____

_____

7. respect: _____

_____

8. truth: _____

_____

9. opposition: _____

_____

10. unjust: _____

_____

from *A Man for All Seasons* by Robert Bolt

Thematic Connection: Power of Contemporary Rulers

King Henry VIII and Sir Thomas More were historical figures—real men who actually came into conflict in the early 1500's. One of the men died a martyr's death as a result of the conflict. While Henry VIII and Sir Thomas More are worthy of study in and of themselves, it is also useful to consider them as archetypes in the examination of the exercise of power. Consider the following questions:

- What were the sources of each man's power?

- How did each man choose to exercise his power?

- Whose power was the stronger and why?

- What costs did each man suffer as a result of the power he wielded or the power which he faced?

DIRECTIONS: Use the entries to examine the way two or three contemporary leaders exercise power, in the context of what you learned about power in *A Man for All Seasons*. In the two upper portions, write a brief sketch about both Henry VIII and Sir Thomas More, answering the questions posed in the paragraph above. Then, choose two leaders from recent history or today's headlines. Using the given phrase as a beginning, draw parallels between the figures you've chosen and the two men depicted by Robert Bolt in the play.

King Henry VIII

_____
_____
_____
_____
_____
_____
_____
_____

Like Henry VIII, _____
_____
_____
_____
_____
_____
_____

Sir Thomas More

_____
_____
_____
_____
_____
_____
_____
_____

Like Sir Thomas More, _____
_____
_____
_____
_____
_____
_____

The Tragedy of Macbeth, Act I, by William Shakespeare

Build Vocabulary

Spelling Strategy The long sound of the vowel *e*, as in the word *be*, is usually spelled by the digraph *ie*, as in *liege*. However, there are exceptions, such as *either*, *caffeine*, and *leisure*.

Using Words About Power

A. DIRECTIONS: *The Tragedy of Macbeth* is a play about the misuse of political and personal power. There are many words in the English language that have political associations. Here are a few such words you will find in Shakespeare's play: *thane, earl, lord, king, traitor.* Think of other words that might apply to political situations and relationships in the United States. For example, in the United States there are no lords or kings but there is a president. On the lines below, write as many words having to do with American political relationships as you can think of.

_____   _____   _____

_____   _____   _____

Using the Word Bank

valor	treasons	imperial	liege	sovereign

B. DIRECTIONS: Fill in each blank with the word from the Word Bank that best completes the sentence.

1. Macbeth's _____ in battle was unsurpassed.

2. "Acts of betrayal against the king are _____!" cried the general.

3. "I bring news of the battle, my _____," the messenger whispered to the king.

4. King Duncan is the _____ ruler of Scotland.

5. Macbeth's _____ virtues have impressed the king.

C. DIRECTIONS: In each sentence that follows there is a word in italics. Choose the lettered word or phrase that is closest in meaning to the word in italics, and write the letter of your choice in the blank.

____ 1. The military leader wanted to preserve his *sovereign* power.
    a. economic   b. meager   c. supreme   d. brave

____ 2. *Valor* is a trait that is associated with heroism in battle.
    a. lightning   b. courage   c. beauty   d. ferocity

____ 3. The rebels attempted to strip the queen of her *imperial power.*
    a. supreme authority   b. religious beliefs   c. army   d. court

____ 4. The subject bowed before his *liege.*
    a. royal personage   b. high-ranking general   c. witch   d. doctor

____ 5. He was arrested and jailed for *treason.*
    a. losing a great battle   b. joining forces with a soldier   c. attaining imperial wisdom   d. committing a crime against his country

Name _____ Date _____

The Tragedy of Macbeth, **Act I,** by William Shakespeare

Grammar and Style: Action Verbs and Linking Verbs

Action verbs express physical or mental action. **Linking verbs** connect the subject of a sentence with a complement that either renames or modifies the subject. Linking verbs include forms of *be, seem, taste, sound, look, become, appear, feel,* and *smell.*

> **Action verbs:** "Who was the thane *lives* yet,
>
> But under heavy judgment *bears* that life
>
> Which he *deserves* to lose."
>
> **Linking verbs:** "The rest *is* labor, which is not used for you.
>
> I'*ll be* myself the harbinger, . . ."

A. Practice: Each of the quotations below is from *The Tragedy of Macbeth.* Underline the action verbs and circle the linking verbs.

1. But in a sieve I'll thither sail,
   And like a rat without a tail
   I'll do, I'll do, I'll do.

2. Hover through the fog and filthy air.

3. Live you, or are you aught
   That man may question?

4. Speak if you can: what are you?

5. . . . He bade me, from him, call thee Thane of Cawdor;
   In which addition, hail, most worthy Thane!
   For it is thine.

6. The sin of my ingratitude even now
   Was heavy on me: thou art so far before,
   That swiftest wing of recompense is slow
   To overtake thee.

7. The King comes here tonight.

B. Writing Application: If the underlined verb in each sentence is an action verb, rewrite the sentence using a linking verb. If the underlined verb is a linking verb, rewrite the sentence using an action verb.

Example: Macbeth <u>speaks</u> of his unhappiness. (action verb)

Rewritten: Macbeth seems unhappy *or* Macbeth is unhappy.

1. Lady Macbeth <u>sees</u> a way to make her husband king.

_____

2. The witches <u>are</u> evil.

_____

3. King Duncan <u>trusts</u> Macbeth completely.

_____

4. Duncan's sons <u>look</u> guilty.

_____

5. Macbeth <u>wants</u> the crown for himself.

_____

The Tragedy of Macbeth, Act I, by William Shakespeare

Reading Strategy: Using Text Aids

Playwrights use stage directions to help readers, actors, and directors understand how a play should look when it is staged. Stage directions can give play readers hints about mood, setting, movement, and characters' intentions. For example, look at the opening stage directions of *The Tragedy of Macbeth*:

> *An open place.*
> [*Thunder and lightning. Enter* THREE WITCHES.]

With very few words William Shakespeare has told you a great deal about the play you are about to read.

1. Where does the scene take place?

   In "An open place," a place where there are no trees, hills, or houses.

2. What is going on at this place?

   "Thunder and lightning." The weather is bad, and the mood is a little frightening.

3. Who is in the scene?

   "Three witches enter." Right away, the reader can tell that something strange is about to happen.

DIRECTIONS: Stage directions can guide the reader to a better understanding of a play's action. Use a graphic organizer like this one to help you pick up hints from the stage directions.

Act/Scene	Characters	Setting	Specific Action
Act I, Scene i	Three witches	An open place	Thunder and lightning. Three witches enter.

Notes in the margin of *The Tragedy of Macbeth* and other plays provide another useful tool to aid you in your reading. To get more from what you read, it's a good idea to see if you can figure out an annotated term or expression before you look at the margin note. Usually the context of the play provides clues to the meaning. Look at the following lines from *The Tragedy of Macbeth*:

> **MALCOLM.** . . . He died
>
> As one that had been studied[3] in his death,
>
> To throw away the dearest thing he owed[4]
>
> As 'twere a careless[5] trifle.

The lines may seem confusing at first. But if you look at the context, you will find hints about the meaning. The context makes it clear that Malcolm is praising the Thane of Cawdor for the noble way in which he died. According to Malcolm, the Thane's death turned out to be his greatest achievement. Knowing this, when you read "He died / As one that had been studied in his death," you might be able to guess that *studied* means "prepared for" or "rehearsed." Then, to check your interpretation, look at the margin note.

Name _____ Date _____

Literary Analysis: Elizabethan Drama

In the years before Elizabeth I came to power in England, troupes of actors traveled the English countryside performing religious plays. They performed wherever they could: in the courtyards of inns, in town squares, and in open areas on the outskirts of villages. Many of the plays they presented were based on biblical stories.

During the Elizabethan period, the style of English drama changed radically. Permanent theaters were built, giving actors not only an artistic home, but also the luxury of perfecting certain aspects of presentation. Plays began to veer away from religious themes. Instead, audiences found themselves watching plays about familiar problems and events. Playwrights used poetic language and rich imagery to tell a wide variety of stories—from dramas about tragic figures to comedies about hapless lovers. This kind of theater, with its nonreligious entertainment value, became very popular. Audiences loved watching plays about characters with motivations and feelings they could understand. They came to the theater to laugh and cry and to see their own lives mirrored in the stories of others.

DIRECTIONS: Answer the following questions about Act I of *The Tragedy of Macbeth.*

1. What might the three witches represent to an audience used to watching plays with religious themes?

   _____

   _____

   _____

2. In what ways might the content of the following speech be said to echo the religious sentiments of Shakespeare's audience?

   > . . . But I have spoke
   > With one that saw him die, who did report
   > That very frankly he confessed his treasons,
   > Implored your Highness' pardon and set forth
   > A deep repentance . . .

   _____

   _____

   _____

3. In the following speech, what is Lady Macbeth saying about her husband's character? How might such sentiments about Macbeth win an audience's sympathy?

   > Glamis thou art, and Cawdor, and shalt be
   > What thou art promised. Yet do I fear thy nature;
   > It is too full o' the milk of human kindness
   > To catch the nearest way. Thou wouldst be great,
   > Art not without ambition, but without
   > The illness should attend it. . . .

   _____

   _____

   _____

The Tragedy of Macbeth, **Act II,** by William Shakespeare

Build Vocabulary

Spelling Strategy Many words end in an unstressed syllable spelled with a consonant +
-*le*, as does *palpable*. To add -*ly*, drop the -*le*: *palpably*. To add other endings, drop the final
-*e* except when it spells a separate syllable: *wrestling, trickled, puzzlement.*

Using the Root -*voc*-

A. Directions: The word root -*voc*- means "voice" or "calling." Read each definition and then
choose the word that best completes each sentence.

evocative (adj.), calling forth an emotional response
provocative (adj.), serving to provoke or stimulate
vocation (n.), a summons or strong inclination to a particular state or course of action; the
   work at which a person is regularly employed
vociferously (adv.), marked by or given to insistent outcry
vocalize (adj.), to give voice to

1. The witches speak to Macbeth _____; they will not be quieted.

2. Macbeth finds the witches' predictions very _____.

3. The setting of the first scene in *Macbeth* is _____ of loneliness.

4. Macbeth's _____ at the beginning of the play might be said to be that of a warrior.

5. Lady Macbeth is able to _____ a horrifying idea that her husband has
   only thought about.

Using the Word Bank

augment	palpable	stealthy
multitudinous	equivocate	predominance

B. Directions: Each question below consists of a pair of words in CAPITAL LETTERS followed
by four lettered pairs of words. Choose the pair that best expresses a relationship similar to
that expressed in the pair in capital letters.

____ 1. MULTITUDINOUS : MANY ::
    a. gigantic : large
    b. some : few
    c. up : down
    d. survive : prosper

____ 2. AUGMENT : PREVENT ::
    a. terrify : frighten
    b. beg : plead
    c. hollow : empty
    d. help : hinder

____ 3. STEALTHY : OBVIOUS ::
    a. quiet : healthful
    b. adventuresome : timid
    c. fat : heavy
    d. polluted : filthy

____ 4. PALPABLE : TANGIBLE ::
    a. stealthy : furtive
    b. shy : outgoing
    c. few : multitudinous
    d. ambitious : lazy

____ 5. EQUIVOCATE : DECEPTION ::
    a. whine : exhibit
    b. beautiful : attractive
    c. death : die
    d. sing : song

____ 6. PREDOMINANCE : WEAKNESS ::
    a. valor : courage
    b. success : failure
    c. happiness : gladness
    d. selfishness : miserliness

Unit 2: Celebrating Humanity (1485–1625)

The Tragedy of Macbeth, Act II, by William Shakespeare

Grammar and Style: Commonly Confused Words: *Lie* and *Lay*

Many people find it difficult to distinguish between the words *lie* and *lay*. A few simple rules can help you use these words correctly every time.

Lie means "to lie down or recline."

Example: I'm going to *lie* down before dinner.

Lay means "to place."

Example: *Lay* the king's robe over the chair.

The past tense of *lie* is *lay*; the past participle is *lain*.

Example: Macbeth devised his plot while the king *lay* sleeping; the king had *lain* in his bed scarcely two hours when he was murdered.

The past tense of *lay* is *laid*; the past participle is *laid*.

Example: Lady Macbeth *laid* the king's robe aside; the robe had been *laid* in the king's blood after the murder.

A. Practice: If the underlined verb form in each sentence is correct, write *OK* in the blank. If it is incorrect, write the correct verb form on the blank.

_____ 1. Morning came but still the revelers <u>lay</u> in their beds.

_____ 2. Lady Macbeth <u>laid</u> the daggers down by the sleeping guards.

_____ 3. Foul deeds <u>lie</u> heavily upon the conscience.

_____ 4. The porter had already gone to <u>lay</u> down when Macduff arrived.

_____ 5. The servants will <u>lie</u> the table for a great feast.

B. Writing Application: Follow the directions to write sentences using *lie* and *lay* correctly.

1. Use *lie* to tell about taking a nap.

_____

2. Use *laid* in reference to putting away some clothes.

_____

3. Use *lain* to describe the dust on an old piece of furniture.

_____

4. Use *lay* to describe a sleeping cat.

_____

5. Use *lying* to describe someone who is sleeping in the next room at the moment.

_____

6. Use *laying* to describe a hen producing an egg.

_____

Name _____ Date _____

The Tragedy of Macbeth, Act II, by William Shakespeare

Reading Strategy: Reading Verse for Meaning

Some readers see that a text is written in verse and automatically assume they will have a difficult time understanding it. Verse texts can indeed seem more complicated than prose. However, there are many tools a reader can use to break verse down into manageable and understandable ideas. A good strategy is to read verse passages for the ideas that they present rather than simply as individual lines of poetry. One way to do this is to read the lines aloud in order to better follow complete sentences or thoughts. If you stop at the end of each line, rather than reading all the way to the end of the thought, you will probably become confused. Pay close attention to punctuation to note where a sentence ends. If you reach the end of the thought in a passage and you don't understand what you've read, go back through the passage slowly, paraphrasing as you go. Look at this example from Act II of *The Tragedy of Macbeth.*

> **MALCOLM.** This murderous shaft that's shot
> Hath not yet lighted, and our safest way
> Is to avoid the aim. Therefore to horse;
> And let us not be dainty of leave-taking,
> But shift away. There's warrant in that theft
> Which steals itself when there's no mercy left.

1. How many sentences are there in this passage?

_____

2. Paraphrase the first sentence.

_____

_____

3. Paraphrase the next two sentences.

_____

_____

_____

4. What is the basic thrust of the passage?

_____

_____

As you continue reading *The Tragedy of Macbeth,* break long passages down into individual sentences and restate the sentences in your own words.

© Prentice-Hall, Inc.

The Tragedy of Macbeth, **Act II,** by William Shakespeare

Literary Analysis: Blank Verse

Blank verse consists of lines of poetry written in iambic pentameter. Each line contains five poetic feet of stressed and unstressed syllables. The form is flexible and versatile and can produce the effect of smooth, natural speech in a way that other metrical patterns cannot. For this reason, Shakespeare relied primarily on blank verse throughout his plays. However, Shakespeare occasionally used prose, especially for the speech of characters from lower stations in life. He also employed occasional rhymes when it seemed appropriate to a particular character: The witches in *The Tragedy of MacBeth,* for example, often speak in rhymes. Finally, like most dramatists of the English Renaissance, Shakespeare often used one or more rhymed lines of dialogue to signal that a scene had ended or that new players must make their entrances, in this way alerting offstage players or other members of the company.

Following is a series of passages from *The Tragedy of Macbeth.* On the line below each passage, identify it as "prose," "rhyme," or "blank verse." Then scan the lines that are in blank verse by marking the stressed and unstressed syllables.

1. **SECOND WITCH.** When the hurlyburly's done.

   When the battle's lost and won.

   _____

2. **ROSS.** I'll see it done.

   KING. What he hath lost, noble Macbeth hath won.

   _____

3. **ROSS.** The King hath happily received, Macbeth,

   The news of thy success. And when he reads

   Thy personal venture in the rebel's fight,

   His wonders and his praises do contend

   Which should be thine or his.

   _____

4. **LADY MACBETH (Reads).** They met me in the day of success; and I have learned by the perfect'st report they have more in them than mortal knowledge. When I burned in desire to question them further, they made themselves air, into which they vanished.

   _____

The Tragedy of Macbeth, Act III, by William Shakespeare

Build Vocabulary

Spelling Strategy *Soluble* and *solvable* are two words that mean the same thing: "Capable of being solved." However, *soluble* has the additional meaning of "capable of being dissolved (in liquid)."

Using the Prefix *mal-*

A. DIRECTIONS: The prefix *mal-* means "bad or badly," or "poor or poorly." Rewrite each sentence, replacing the underlined word or words with a word that contains the prefix *mal-*.

1. The airplane engine continued to <u>function poorly</u> during a routine inspection.

   _____

2. Sheri was <u>poorly adjusted</u> to her new school environment.

   _____

3. The doctor said my problem with digesting proteins came from <u>improper absorption</u> of certain nutrients.

   _____

4. Every time Tomas comes for a visit, I remember that he is a <u>person who is not content.</u>

   _____

5. The company was cited for <u>wrongdoing.</u>

   _____

Using the Word Bank

indissoluble	dauntless	jocund
infirmity	malevolence	

B. DIRECTIONS: For each item, choose the lettered word or phrase that is most nearly *opposite* in meaning to the numbered word. Write the letter of your choice in the blank.

_____ 1. infirmity
    a. bad mood   c. sickness
    b. good cheer   d. good health

_____ 2. jocund
    a. grumpy   c. elderly
    b. sickly   d. sleepy

_____ 3. indissoluble
    a. easily undone   c. often repeated
    b. not to go forward   d. not to be heard

_____ 4. dauntless
    a. agreeable   c. hapless
    b. humorless   d. fearful

_____ 5. malevolence
    a. happiness   c. good will
    b. ill feelings   d. desire

Unit 2: Celebrating Humanity (1485–1625)

***The Tragedy of Macbeth,* Act III,** by William Shakespeare

Grammar and Style: Subject-Verb Agreement

The **subject and verb** in a sentence must **agree**, or be the same in number. That means that a singular subject takes a singular verb and a plural subject takes a plural verb.

Singular subject and singular verb:

<u>Macbeth</u> <u>murders</u> Duncan.

Plural subject and plural verb:

The <u>witches</u> <u>predict</u> that Macbeth will become king.

Determining whether to use a singular or plural verb can be difficult when there are other words or phrases between the subject and its verb.

Example: Macbeth, despite his pangs of conscience, (*does, do*) kill King Duncan.

The subject of the sentence is *Macbeth*, not *pangs*, so the verb form is singular: *does*.

A. Practice: Underline the correct form of the verb in each sentence.

1. ". . . Command upon me, to the which my duties / (*Is, Are*) with a most indissoluble tie / For ever knit."

2. "Your spirits (*shines, shine*) through you."

3. The three murderers (*attempts, attempt*) to do away with Banquo and Fleance.

4. Of the two, only Banquo (*is, are*) killed.

5. (*Has, Have*) Macbeth and his wife gotten away with murder?

B. Writing Application: Look at each of the following sentences and decide whether its subject and verb agree. If the sentence is correct, write *OK* on the line. If the sentence is incorrect, rewrite it, replacing each italicized word with one that agrees with its subject or verb.

1. The three murderers who were hired by Macbeth *is* upset when Fleance *escape*.

_____

2. Macbeth is shocked that no one else *see* the ghost of Banquo.

_____

3. The other dinner guests *are* appalled at Macbeth's behavior.

_____

4. Lady Macbeth *become* alarmed when she sees that Macbeth is out of control.

_____

5. She *tell* the dinner guests that Macbeth is prone to this kind of fit.

_____

The Tragedy of Macbeth, **Act III**, by William Shakespeare

Reading Strategy: Reading Between the Lines

Often *what* a character in a play says is not as important as *why* he or she says it. For example, shortly after the beginning of Act III, Banquo speaks to Macbeth:

> **BANQUO.** Let your Highness
> Command upon me, to the which my duties
> Are with a most indissoluble tie
> For ever knit.

If you were to take Banquo's words at face value, you would think that he is a most loyal subject to King Macbeth. However, in a speech just before Macbeth enters the scene, Banquo voices not only his suspicions about what criminal acts Macbeth might have committed in order to achieve the throne, but also his own hopes for the future regarding the throne. Therefore, you must assume that Banquo has a very good reason for not confronting Macbeth. With this thought in mind, you can begin to see how the character of Banquo, like that of Macbeth, serves as more positive embodiment of the play's themes of deception and the quest for power. Such "reading between the lines" can help you understand more than simply what the words say.

DIRECTIONS: Use the following questions to help you analyze and read between the lines of Act III of *The Tragedy of Macbeth*. As you continue through the play, remember to look for the intentions behind each character's words by asking yourself similar questions.

> **MACBETH.** Both of you
> Know Banquo was your enemy.
> **BOTH MURDERERS.** True, my lord.
> **MACBETH.** So is he mine, and in such bloody distance
> That every minute of his being thrusts
> Against my near'st of life. . . .

1. What is Macbeth telling the murderers about his relationship to Banquo?

_____

_____

2. Why does he tell them this?

_____

_____

> **MACBETH.** [to **MURDERER**] Thou art the best o' th' cutthroats.
> Yet he's good that did the like for Fleance;
> If thou didst it, thou art the nonpareil.

3. What is Macbeth saying about the murderer's deeds?

_____

_____

4. Why is he saying this?

_____

_____

© Prentice-Hall, Inc.

The Tragedy of Macbeth, Act III, by William Shakespeare

Literary Analysis: Conflict

In literature, as in life, **conflict** is a struggle between two opposing forces. It is an essential dramatic element; it builds tension and holds the reader's interest. Without conflict there can be no drama. There are many conflicts within Shakespeare's *The Tragedy of Macbeth.* Some of them are external conflicts that take place between characters with opposing goals. Others are internal conflicts that take place within the consciousness of certain characters. Often conflict begins in one scene and escalates throughout a number of scenes that follow. For example, the fact that Banquo is with Macbeth when the witches make their prophesies in Act I leads to conflict between the two men in later scenes.

DIRECTIONS: Answer the following questions, and then find a quotation from Act III of *The Tragedy of Macbeth* that supports your answer.

1. In Scene i, what is the conflict between the murderers and Banquo?

   _____

   _____

   _____

   _____

   Quotation: _____

2. Why is Banquo in conflict with Macbeth?

   _____

   _____

   _____

   _____

   Quotation: _____

3. Why does Macbeth experience an internal conflict at the state dinner?

   _____

   _____

   _____

   _____

   Quotation: _____

4. Why is Lady Macbeth in conflict with Macbeth during the state dinner?

   _____

   _____

   _____

   _____

   Quotation: _____

The Tragedy of Macbeth, **Act IV**, by William Shakespeare

Build Vocabulary

Spelling Strategy The letter *c* combines with the *i* of the suffix *-ious* to spell the *sh* sound, as in *pernicious* and *judicious*.

Using the Root *-cred-*

A. DIRECTIONS: Remember that the word root *-cred-* means "belief." Use the following words to complete the sentences.

credibility	credence	credentials

1. The news reporter had to show his _____, or proof of his profession, to get into the crime scene.

2. The mayor's _____ was ruined when it was discovered that he had stolen funds from his office.

3. Those accusations are completely ridiculous; I give them no _____ whatsoever.

Using the Word Bank

pernicious	judicious	sundry
intemperance	avarice	credulous

B. DIRECTIONS: Match each word in the left column with its definition in the right column. Write the letter of the definition on the blank next to the word it defines.

____ 1. pernicious	a. lack of restraint
____ 2. judicious	b. greed
____ 3. sundry	c. tendency to believe readily
____ 4. intemperance	d. showing good judgment
____ 5. avarice	e. various
____ 6. credulous	f. highly injurious or destructive

C. DIRECTIONS: Use words from the Word Bank to fill in the blanks in these sentences.

1. King Duncan was known as a wise and _____ ruler.

2. When it comes to power and fortune, Macbeth shows great _____.

3. Had Banquo been less _____ about Macbeth's evil intentions, he might have been able to save his own life.

4. Macbeth's control of Scotland had a _____ effect upon the country.

5. The murderers had committed _____ crimes before they killed Banquo.

6. Macbeth's _____ manifested itself when he had Banquo killed.

The Tragedy of Macbeth, **Act IV,** by William Shakespeare

Grammar and Style: Possessive Forms

You can write the **possessive form** of a singular noun by adding *'s: girl's, boy's, king's*. For the possessive of most plural forms, simply add an apostrophe: *creditors', goddesses', countries'*. However, some plural forms that do not already end in *s* do need an *'s: men's, women's, children's*. Remember that you don't add an apostrophe to make a word plural.

A. Practice: Decide which is the correct form of the noun in each sentence: the plural, the singular possessive, or the plural possessive. Circle your choice.

1. The three (*witches/witch's/witches'*) stirred the bubbling cauldron.

2. Each (*glass's/glasses'/glasses*) stem was covered with dust.

3. Macbeth looked into the three weird (*sisters/sister's/sisters'*) cauldron.

4. (*Scotlands/Scotland's/Scotlands'*) future is in jeopardy.

5. These (*ladies'/lady's/ladys'*) opinions are good enough for me.

6. The (*Macbeths/Macbeth's/Macbeths'*) castle stands on a hill.

7. (*Rosses/Ross's/Rosses'*) warning can't save Lady Macduff from her fate.

B. Writing Application: Use the possessive form of each underlined word or phrase to write a sentence based on *The Tragedy of Macbeth*. The first one has been done for you.

1. The lives of the <u>characters</u>

   The characters' lives have been changed forever by the bloody deeds of Macbeth.

2. The eight <u>kings</u>

   _____

3. The escape of <u>Fleance</u>

   _____

4. The prophesies of the three <u>apparitions</u>

   _____

5. The words of the <u>messenger</u>

   _____

6. The deeds of the <u>murderers</u>

   _____

Name _____ Date _____

Reading Strategy: Using Your Senses

In today's commercial theater environment, with its elaborate sets and extravagant special effects, it is difficult to imagine a time when a stage setting consisted of little more than a bare floor. Yet when Shakespeare was writing and producing his plays, theaters used almost nothing in the way of scenic design. Theatergoers depended on the words of the play to transport them to another time and place. Shakespeare was a master of poetic language. His plays contain rich, vivid imagery that allows audiences to experience dramatic moments through the senses of sight, hearing, smell, taste, and touch.

DIRECTIONS: You will get more from what you read if you use your senses to try to see, hear, smell, taste, and feel the things Shakespeare's characters say. In the graphic organizer below, read each quotation from Act IV of *The Tragedy of Macbeth* and decide which of the senses it appeals to. Some quotations may appeal to more than one sense. Use the blank spaces in the graphic organizer to analyze other sensory images throughout the rest of the text.

Quotation	Appeals to Sense(s) of
"This tyrant, whose sole name blisters our tongues / Was once thought honest . . ."	
". . . To offer up a weak, poor, innocent lamb / T' appease an angry god."	
"Each new morn / New widows howl, new orphans cry . . ."	
"Double, double, toil and trouble; / Fire burn and caldron bubble."	
"Thy crown does sear mine eyelids."	

Name _____ Date _____

The Tragedy of Macbeth, **Act IV**, by William Shakespeare

Literary Analysis: Imagery

Imagery can create responses from any of the reader's senses: sight, hearing, touch, smell, or taste. Written images can illuminate for the reader the meaning of both individual moments and patterns of meaning that run throughout the text. Look at this imagery-laden quotation from the First Witch in *The Tragedy of Macbeth*, Act IV.

> "Pour in sow's blood, that hath eaten
> Her nine farrow, grease that's sweaten
> From the murderer's gibbet throw into the flame."

This passage contains visual imagery: "sow's blood"; a mother pig eating her nine young. It also contains imagery of touch: "grease" from the noose that hangs a murderer; grease added to a "flame."

Paying attention to imagery can guide you to a deeper understanding of the text. As you read, be on the lookout for repeated imagery; for example, think about the image of blood that runs throughout the entire text of *The Tragedy of Macbeth*. Blood as an image can mean many different things: loyalty, guilt, revenge, death, brotherhood, parent-child relationship, royalty, and so on. Think about the significance of each of these ideas within the plot of the play.

DIRECTIONS: Read the following passages from *The Tragedy of Macbeth* and identify the imagery in each. Then write the connection, or what the image makes you think of.

1. "When shall we three meet again? / In thunder, lightning, or in rain?"

   Imagery: _____

   Connection: _____

2. "Stars, hide your fires; / Let not light see my black and deep desires . . ."

   _____

   _____

3. "I have no spur / To prick the sides of my intent, but only / Vaulting ambition, which o'er-leaps itself / And falls on th' other . . ."

   Imagery: _____

   Connection: _____

4. "But now I am cabined, cribbed, confined, bound in / To saucy doubts and fears . . ."

   Imagery: _____

   Connection: _____

The Tragedy of Macbeth, Act V, by William Shakespeare

Build Vocabulary

Spelling Strategy The ending -ous makes adjectives out of some nouns, such as clamorous from clamor, famous from fame, and treasonous from treason.

Using the Root -turb-

A. Directions: Knowing that the word root turb- means "to disturb," create a sentence using each of the following italicized words.

perturbed, adj., greatly disturbed in mind

turbine, n., a machine that changes the movement of a fluid into mechanical energy

turbojet, n., an airplane powered by turbines

turbid, adj., cloudy, muddy; mixed up or confused

1. _____

2. _____

3. _____

4. _____

Using the Word Bank

perturbation	pristine	clamorous	harbingers

B. Directions: Match each word in the left column with its definition in the right column. Write the letter of the definition on the line next to the word it defines.

____ 1. perturbation   a. noisy

____ 2. pristine   b. forerunners

____ 3. clamorous   c. pure; untouched; unspoiled

____ 4. harbingers   d. disorder

C. Directions: Use words from the Word Bank to fill in the blanks in the sentences.

1. Macbeth's honor, which was once _____, is now soiled with the blood of a murdered king.

2. The three witches are _____ of Macbeth's wretched fate.

3. The natural order of the heavens has experienced severe _____.

4. The people have become _____; they are insistent that the king should be dethroned.

Unit 2: Celebrating Humanity (1485–1625)

Name _____ Date _____

The Tragedy of Macbeth, **Act V**, by William Shakespeare

Grammar and Style: Pronouns and Antecedents

Pronouns are words that take the place of nouns to avoid awkward repetition. See the following example:

> Macbeth was a great soldier, but Macbeth's ambition got the better of Macbeth. Macbeth's wife, Lady Macbeth, was just as ambitious as Macbeth. Together, Macbeth and Lady Macbeth devised a plot to kill King Duncan.

Notice the monotonous repetition of the names *Macbeth* and *Lady Macbeth*. By using pronouns to avoid such repetition, the paragraph can read as follows:

> Macbeth was a great soldier, but <u>his</u> ambition got the better of <u>him.</u> <u>His</u> wife, Lady Macbeth, was just as ambitious as <u>he.</u> Together, <u>they</u> devised a plot to kill King Duncan.

The second paragraph flows much better than the first because pronouns have been used in place of proper nouns. The word or group of words to which each pronoun refers is its **antecedent**. As you use pronouns in your own writing, make sure they agree with their antecedents in gender, number, and person.

A. Practice: Read the following sentences and write the correct pronoun in each blank.

1. Macbeth becomes king of Scotland after _____ kills King Duncan.

2. Banquo, once Macbeth's good friend, later becomes _____ bitter enemy.

3. Lady Macduff and _____ children are killed.

4. Macbeth might have gotten away with murder but _____ conscience kept playing tricks on _____.

5. Lady Macbeth imagines blood on _____ hands out of guilt.

6. Macduff and Malcolm lead an army against Macbeth, and Macduff later kills _____.

B. Writing Application: Rewrite the following sentences using pronouns in place of the underlined names.

1. When Macduff hears of the death of <u>Macduff's</u> children, <u>Macduff</u> determines to seek justice against Macbeth.

   _____

   _____

2. The three witches give Macbeth information that makes <u>Macbeth</u> feel <u>Macbeth</u> can't lose in battle against <u>Macbeth's</u> enemies.

   _____

   _____

3. Lady Macbeth spends several nights sleepwalking and washing <u>Lady Macbeth's</u> hands over and over again.

   _____

   _____

The Tragedy of Macbeth, **Act V,** by William Shakespeare

Reading Strategy: Inferring Beliefs of the Period

The plays of William Shakespeare include many works of dramatic genius with much to say about the course of human events and history. In many ways these plays are universal; they transcend ethnic and cultural boundaries with their tales of fallen heroes, star-crossed lovers, and misguided nobles. But Shakespeare's plays also tell a reader quite a bit about the time period in which Shakespeare himself lived. The playwright applied many of the philosophies, beliefs, and superstitions of his day to illuminate the historical periods about which he wrote. As you look back over *The Tragedy of Macbeth,* ask yourself which ideas might be specific to the time period when William Shakespeare lived and which ones might be said to cross boundaries of time and place.

DIRECTIONS: You can get more from what you read by analyzing a play or story for its historical perspectives. Use the graphic organizer below to find and keep track of places in the play that reveal something about the time in which the author lived. Two of the boxes are filled in for you. Fill in the rest with other examples from the text.

Quotation	Meaning
THIRD WITCH: "All hail, Macbeth, that shalt be king hereafter!"	Macbeth seems to take this prophesy as the whole truth. People who lived in Shakespeare's time may have believed that certain individuals could read the future.

Name _____ Date _____

The Tragedy of Macbeth, **Act V,** by William Shakespeare

Literary Analysis: Shakespearean Tragedy

Throughout the ages—from ancient times to the present day—people have been fascinated by dramatic tragedy. One of the reasons for this is that tragedy allows readers to see themselves and their own potential for self-destruction. Each tragedy rests upon the premise that the tragic hero brings about his or her own downfall, often because of an inborn weakness in character or personality, a tragic flaw. This flaw can be any one of a number of things: pride, lust, greed, and so on. In a typical Elizabethan or Greek tragedy, the tragic hero begins the play as a respected, usually high-born, member of society. His or her virtues are described at length during the early scenes. In *The Tragedy of Macbeth*, for example, we first meet Macbeth as a hero in battle, a loyal supporter of King Duncan, a good husband, and an excellent friend. With all these wonderful qualities, what could Macbeth want that he does not already possess? What could possibly go wrong? The answer is, of course, human nature. With all the things Macbeth has, he wants most acutely that which he *doesn't* have. His ambition becomes his master, his tragic flaw.

DIRECTIONS: Think about Macbeth's tragic flaw and answer the following questions.

1. If Macbeth had never met the three witches, do you think the events of the play would have turned out the same way? Give reasons for your answer.

_____

_____

_____

_____

_____

_____

2. Is Macbeth aware of how ambitious he is? Find at least one quote from the text that supports your response.

_____

_____

_____

_____

_____

_____

3. Do you think Lady Macbeth is certain of her husband's ambition before Macbeth kills King Duncan? Find at least one quotation from the text that supports your response.

_____

_____

_____

_____

_____

_____

Name _____ Date _____

Build Vocabulary: Language of Tragedy

A tragedy gains it force through the terrible twists of its plot. Its effect, however, can be heightened by the skillful use of vivid vocabulary.

DIRECTIONS: Choose the word from the box that best completes each sentence below.

prophesied	burden	oracles	wreck
pestilence	sorrows	guilt	destroying

1. The seer warned that a _____ would strike the land if the king did not reform his ways.

2. Staring at the car _____, he couldn't fail to ponder how the driver caused his own demise.

3. Farnsworth _____ that the birth of the twins would spell doom for the family's future.

4. Knowing there was no way to escape his fate was a terrible _____ to bear.

5. The _____ that he felt for what he had done to his father caused him many sleepless nights.

6. "You're _____ your family," the old woman shrieked at the prince.

7. The _____ that befell the Stuart family were almost too much for them to bear.

8. The message of the _____ is clear: the children of the family will wreak vengeance upon their parents.

from *Oedipus the King* by Sophocles

Literary Connection: Dramatic Tragedy

Having its roots in the literature of the ancient Greeks, tragedy has been explored again and again in the literature of the world. In contemporary times, authors have continued to revisit the concept of tragedy. Some authors have rewritten older tragedies in modern contexts, as in Jane Smiley's *A Thousand Acres*, which places the tale of King Lear on a modern farm. Other authors have created entirely new conceptions of the tragic. In your recent reading, you met two of the greatest tragic heroes in literature: Macbeth and Oedipus. How are these two characters the same? How are they different? How do they compare with a tragic character you might encounter in a contemporary work of literature or film?

DIRECTIONS: Use the chart below to explore the concept of dramatic tragedy, comparing the characters in your recent reading with a character from a prospective contemporary literary work or film. In the upper diagram, describe Macbeth and Oedipus as tragic heroes, including any similarities you find between them in the intersecting part of the circles. Below, continue your comparison by writing a sketch of a character of your own creation who might appear in a contemporary tragedy.

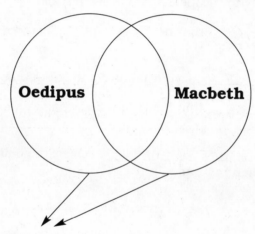

Contemporary Tragic Character:

_____

_____

_____

_____

_____

_____

_____

_____

_____

Works of John Donne

Build Vocabulary

Spelling Strategy The suffix *-ity* is more common than the suffix *-ety*. Examples include *chastity*, *sanctity*, and *laity*. When the word stem ends in *i*, *-ety* is used to avoid two *i*'s in a row, as in *propriety*, *anxiety*, and *piety*.

Using the Prefix *inter-*

A. DIRECTIONS: Each of the following sentences includes an italicized word which contains the prefix *inter-*, meaning "between," "among," or "with each other." Using one of the three meanings, fill in each blank with a phrase that completes the sentence and reveals the meaning of the italicized word.

1. An expert in *international* affairs understands the relations _____.

2. At the town's main *intersection*, two highways _____.

3. When a person *intercedes* between two disputing friends, she is _____.

4. *Intervals* in a series of events mean periods of time _____.

5. When a reporter and politician take part in an *interview*, they talk _____.

Using the Word Bank

contention	piety	intermit	covetousness
profanation	laity	trepidation	breach

B. DIRECTIONS: Write a word or words from the Word Bank to complete each sentence.

1. Strong disagreement over the proper role of the congregation caused a

   _____ between the priests and the _____.

2. The active _____ over the family house did _____

   briefly after the death of the grandfather.

3. The congregation approved of George's obvious _____ when he entered

   the cathedral because they believed it to be evidence of his _____.

4. The guide reminded the tourists to remove their shoes before entering the mosque, explain-

   ing that wearing shoes would be a _____.

5. The child gazed at the toy-shop display with undisguised _____.

© Prentice-Hall, Inc.

Works of John Donne

Grammar and Style: Active and Passive Voice

When the subject of a sentence performs the action of the verb, the verb is in the **active voice**. When the subject receives the action of the verb, the verb is in the **passive voice**. This passage from "Meditation 17" shows how Donne uses both the active voice and the passive voice:

Active voice: And when she *buries* a man. . . .

Passive voice: . . . every chapter must *be* so *translated*.

A. Practice: Rewrite the passive sentences below in the active voice. Write "active" on the line if the sentence is already in the active voice. The first sentence has been done for you.

1. Her eyes were cast up toward the sky.
   She cast her eyes up toward the sky.

2. God forgives us for coveting another's afflictions.
   _____

3. Death is enslaved by fate, chance, kings, and desperate men.
   _____

4. The two lovers are represented by the image of a drawing compass with two legs.
   _____

5. The poet is begging his love not to mourn his departure.
   _____

B. Writing Application: Create a meaningful sentence from the nouns and verbs in each group. Use the voice identified in the parentheses, and add any necessary words. The first sentence has been done for you.

1. boy, train, horse (passive voice)
   The horse was trained by the boy.

2. artist, draw, circle, compass (active voice)
   _____

3. lovers, separate, death (active voice)
   _____

4. earth, erode, sea (passive voice)
   _____

5. Donne, dismiss, employer (passive voice)
   _____

6. poet, weep, sigh, lover (active voice)
   _____

Works of John Donne

Reading Strategy: Recognizing the Speaker's Situation and Motivation

To understand a poem it may be helpful to recognize the situation and motivation for the speaker's words. What does the poem tell you about the speaker's circumstances? Are the words a cry of the heart? A song? A lament? As you read poetry, ask yourself about the speaker's motives for speaking, and identify the situation that gives rise to the speech.

DIRECTIONS: The chart records some of the speaker's words from the poem "Song" in one column and an inference about the speaker's situation and motive for speaking in the second column. Continue adding the speaker's words and his possible motives as you read the poem.

Speaker's Words	Motivation
"Sweetest love, I do not go, For weariness of thee."	He has to leave his beloved. He wants to reassure her that he still loves her and is not tired of her.

Unit 3: A Turbulent Time (1625–1798)

Works of John Donne

Literary Analysis: Metaphysical Poetry

Metaphysical poetry uses conceits and paradoxes as devices to convey the poet's message. A **metaphysical conceit** is an elaborate metaphor comparing very different ideas, images, or objects. The metaphysical poets used conceits that ranged from elaborate images developed over many lines to simple images presented in only a line or two.

DIRECTIONS: On the lines following each excerpt, write what is being compared and explain the meaning of the conceit or metaphor expressed.

1. Death be not proud, though some have called thee
   Mighty and dreadful, for thou art not so;
   For those whom thou think'st thou dost overthrow,
   Die not, poor death, nor yet canst thou kill me.
   From rest and sleep, which but thy pictures be,
   . . .
   One short sleep past, we wake eternally. . .

_____

_____

_____

_____

_____

_____

_____

_____

_____

_____

2. If they be two [souls], they are two so
   As stiff twin compasses are two;
   Thy soul, the fixed foot, makes no show
   To move, but doth, if th' other do.

_____

_____

_____

_____

_____

_____

_____

_____

_____

Build Vocabulary

Spelling Strategy When suffixes are added to words ending in *y*, the *y* is usually changed to *i* when it is preceded by a consonant. So when the archaic word *thy*, meaning "your," is pluralized by adding *-ne*, the *y* changes to *i*: *thine*, or "yours." A modern example is the plural form of *company—companies*. If preceded by a vowel, *y* usually does not change. For example, the plural of *money* is *moneys*.

Using Archaic Words

A. DIRECTIONS: The following poem by Ben Jonson contains archaic words that are no longer used in modern English. Underline each archaic word and write an appropriate modern English word above it.

How, best of kings, dost thou a scepter bear!

How, best of poets, dost thou laurel wear!

For such a poet, while thy days were green,

Thou wert, as chief of them are said t'have been.

("To King James" by Ben Jonson)

B. DIRECTIONS: Use the clues below to fill in the crossword puzzle with the appropriate archaic word.

Across

2. you
3. Past tense form of the verb *to be*

Down

1. Second-person singular form of *do*
2. to have
4. your

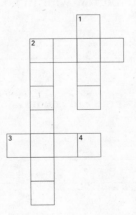

"On My First Son," "Song: To Celia," and **"Still to Be Neat"**
by Ben Jonson

Grammar and Style: The Placement of *Only*

In the first line of Ben Jonson's "Song: To Celia" ("Drink to me only with thine eyes"), the placement of *only* conveys the meaning that the speaker wishes Celia to drink to him using just her eyes, not drinking from a cup. Placing the word *only* in a different position in the line conveys a different or an unclear meaning, as these examples show:

Drink only to me with thine eyes. ("Drink to me and no one else.")

Only drink to me with thine eyes. ("Just drink to me and do nothing else" or "Drink to me and no one else.")

A. Practice: The following sets of sentences contain the modifier *only* placed in two different ways. In the blank, write the letter of the lettered sentence that conveys the meaning of the underlined sentence.

_____ 1. Mary Ann brought nothing but cookies.
    a. Mary Ann brought only cookies.
    b. Only Mary Ann brought cookies.

_____ 2. Jeremy is the one person who can lead.
    a. Jeremy can be only a leader.
    b. Only Jeremy can be a leader.

_____ 3. I have just one sister, whose hobby is taking long walks.
    a. My sister's only hobby is taking long walks.
    b. My only sister's hobby is taking long walks.

B. Writing Application: Rewrite each sentence inserting the modifier *only*; then explain the meaning of the sentence.

1. We saw the dark forest through the window in the cabin.

_____

Meaning: _____

_____

2. I came to you for advice, not to borrow your radio.

_____

Meaning: _____

_____

3. Our day together was spent listening to the music we both loved—jazz.

_____

Meaning: _____

_____

"On My First Son," "Song: To Celia," and "Still to Be Neat"
by Ben Jonson

Reading Strategy: Hypothesizing

Hypothesizing—making informed guesses about what you are reading based on information in the passage —and confirming your hypothesis helps you better understand what the writer is trying to say. You can hypothesize from the first line of a poem, and further reading may confirm or disprove your hypothesis. For example, in the first three lines of the poem "Still to Be Neat," Jonson says

> Still [always] to be neat, still to be dressed,
> As you were going to a feast;
> Still to be powdered, still perfumed;

You might hypothesize that the speaker does not appreciate a perfectly-groomed woman. Line 6 helps confirm that hypothesis: "All is not sweet, all is not sound." And lines 7 and 8, make clear his preference: "Give me a look, give me a face / That makes simplicity a grace."

DIRECTIONS: Use the table below to help you hypothesize about passages in the poems and to confirm or disprove your hypotheses. In the left column, write the lines that lead to a hypothesis. Write your hypothesis in the second column. In the third column, write the phrases or lines that confirm (or disprove) your hypothesis. In the fourth column, confirm your hypothesis, or state a new hypothesis based on the additional information. The first row has been completed for you.

Lines on Which Hypothesis is Based	Hypothesis	Lines Supporting or Disproving Hypothesis	Final Hypothesis
1. "Farewell, thou child of my right hand, and joy;" ("On My First Son," line 1)	Since the poet uses the term *farewell*, this poem is probably about a child who is dying or has died.	Line 3: "Seven years thou wert lent to me" Line 7: "To have so soon scaped world's and flesh's rage" Line 9: "Rest in soft peace"	These lines and phrases verify that the speaker's son has died.
2.			
3.			
4.			

Unit 3: A Turbulent Time (1625-1798)

"On My First Son," "Song: To Celia," and **"Still to Be Neat"**
by Ben Jonson

Literary Analysis: Epigrams

An **epigram** is a short poem in which brevity, clarity, and permanence are emphasized. Short epigrams or lines from epigrams are often used as inscriptions on buildings or statues, or as an epitaph for a gravestone. For example, the lines "Rest in soft peace, and, asked, say here doth lie/Ben Jonson his best piece of poetry" is a good epitaph for Jonson's son. The English poet Samuel Taylor Coleridge wrote the following epigram to define epigrams:

> What is an epigram? A dwarfish whole,
> Its body brevity, and wit its soul.

A. DIRECTIONS: Read each of the excerpts below and circle those that can be considered epigrammatic.

1. Mary had a little lamb,
   Its fleece was white as snow.

2. Give me a look, give me a face,
   That makes simplicity a grace;

3. Drink to me only with thine eyes.

4. To err is human, to forgive divine.
   (Alexander Pope, *Essay on Criticism*)

5. What's in a name? That which we call a rose
   By any other name would smell as sweet.
   (Shakespeare, *Romeo and Juliet*)

B. DIRECTIONS: On the lines below, write two short two- or four-line epigrams: one in praise of friendship and the other as an epitaph.

_____
_____
_____
_____
_____
_____
_____
_____
_____
_____
_____
_____
_____

"To His Coy Mistress" by Andrew Marvell
"To the Virgins, to Make Much of Time" by Robert Herrick
"Song" by Sir John Suckling

Build Vocabulary

Spelling Strategy In most one-syllable words ending in *e*, such as *wane*, *mate*, and *site*, the preceding vowel has a long vowel sound. By removing the *e* from the end of these three examples, one creates three completely different words with a short vowel sound: *wan*, *mat*, and *sit*.

Using Related Forms of *prime*

A. Directions: Each of the following sentences includes an italicized form of the word *prime*, which means "first in importance" or "first in time." Write a second sentence that uses the same word and that demonstrates the word's meaning.

1. The *primary* reason for going to the zoo was to observe the snow leopard.

   _____

2. Those young artists are *primarily* interested in improving their skills.

   _____

3. The *primacy* of the president is unquestioned.

   _____

4. They hoped to have a good voter turnout for the *primary*.

   _____

5. The runner was in her *prime* when she won the Olympic trials.

   _____

coyness	amorous	languish	prime	wan

Using the Word Bank

B. Directions: In each blank, write a word from the Word Bank to complete the sentence.

1. At your age, you are just entering your _____.

2. His flirting showed his _____, since he never made a date.

3. She looked with _____ eyes at her new husband.

4. When she left him, he became _____ and went to bed.

5. When her husband left for the army, she began to _____ in despair.

© Prentice-Hall, Inc.　　　　　　　　　　Coy Mistress/Virgins/Song　**87**

Unit 3: A Turbulent Time (1625–1798)

"To His Coy Mistress" by Andrew Marvell
"To the Virgins, to Make Much of Time" by Robert Herrick
"Song" by Sir John Suckling

Grammar and Style: Irregular Forms of Adjectives

The comparative and superlative forms of most adjectives are created by adding the endings *-er* and *-est* or *more* and *most* to the positive form. For example, the comparative form of the adjective *cold* is *colder;* its superlative form is *coldest*. Irregular forms of comparative and superlative adjectives are not created in this predictable way. This passage from "To His Coy Mistress" contains the irregular adjective *last,* which here is a superlative form of *late*.

> An age at least to every part,
> And the *last* age should show your heart.

The table below contains examples of irregular adjectives in their positive, comparative, and superlative forms.

Positive Form	Comparative	Superlative
late	later	last
many	more	most
little	less or lesser	least

A. Practice: Underline the irregular adjective in each sentence. Then identify its form by writing *comparative* or *superlative* on the line.

1. What is the best poem you have ever read? _____

2. Which do you think is the better poem, "To His Coy Mistress" or "Song"?

   _____

3. More people in that class have read the poems of Andrew Marvell than the poems of Robert Herrick. _____

4. The worst thing you can do when reading poetry is hurry through it. _____

5. Students spend less time studying Sir John Suckling than William Shakespeare.

   _____

B. Writing Application: Rewrite each sentence below, replacing the irregular adjective in parentheses with its correct comparative or superlative form.

1. It is (*good*) to read the poem now while you are not so tired rather than after you have studied hard all day.

   _____

2. Although they also studied Shakespeare and Milton, (*many*) students preferred the metaphysical poets.

   _____

3. The judges decided that the (*good*) poem of all those they had read was written by a high-school student.

   _____

"To His Coy Mistress" by Andrew Marvell
"To the Virgins, to Make Much of Time" by Robert Herrick
"Song" by Sir John Suckling

Reading Strategy: Inferring Speakers' Attitudes

The tone and words in a poem can expresses the attitude of the speaker toward the poem's subject or person he or she is addressing. You can better understand the poem if you **infer**, or figure out, this attitude from what the speaker is saying. You'll find clues to the speaker's attitude in the poem's words, images, and rhythms. For example, look at the words used by the speaker in Robert Herrick's "To the Virgins, to Make Much of Time."

Then be not coy, but use your time,
And, while ye may, go marry;
For, having lost but once your prime,
You may forever tarry.

It can be inferred from the speaker's use of words like *coy, marry,* and *tarry* that the speaker's attitude is one of lighthearted earnestness. The words suggest both joyfulness and an urgent message. The rhythm of the lines is quick and full of energy, which seems to reinforce the speaker's enthusiasm for his subject.

DIRECTIONS: Read the following examples from the poems. Then answer the questions.

Unit 3: A Turbulent Time (1625–1798)

1. What is the image in these lines from "To the Virgins, to Make Much of Time" and what attitude does it express?

   And this same flower that smiles today
   Tomorrow will be dying.

   _____

   _____

2. What do the words "at my back" suggest about the speaker's attitude in "To His Coy Mistress" and what attitude does it imply?

   But at my back I always hear
   Time's wingè d chariot hurrying near:

   _____

   _____

3. What is the speaker's attitude in the first line of "Song," and how has it changed in both the second stanza and the third stanza?

   Why so pale and wan, fond lover?
   . . .
   Why so dull and mute, young sinner?
   . . .
   Quit, quit, for shame; this will not move . . .

   _____

   _____

   _____

"To His Coy Mistress" by Andrew Marvell
"To the Virgins, to Make Much of Time" by Robert Herrick
"Song" by Sir John Suckling

Literary Analysis: *Carpe Diem* Theme

Examples of the **theme** of *carpe diem*, which is Latin for "seize the day," can be found throughout world literature. Robert Herrick's poem "To the Virgins" contains lines that are frequently cited as an example of this theme.

> Gather ye rosebuds while ye may,
> Old time is still a-flying;
> And this same flower that smiles today
> Tomorrow will be dying.

The metaphor of the rosebuds is a particularly appropriate symbol for the *carpe diem* theme. The rose is one of the most beautiful of flowers, yet it lives only a short time.

DIRECTIONS: Answer the following questions.

1. In the opening lines of "To the Virgins, to Make Much of Time," Herrick uses the image of rosebuds as a symbol of the *carpe diem* theme. What other image does he use as a symbol in the poem?

_____

_____

2. How do the following lines from "To the Virgins, to Make Much of Time" reinforce the *carpe diem* theme?

> That age is best which is the first,
> When youth and blood are warmer:
> But being spent, the worse, and worst
> Times still succeed the former.

_____

_____

3. In the opening lines from "To His Coy Mistress," the speaker implies that coyness is a crime. How does the speaker use the *carpe diem* theme to justify this implication?

> Had we but world enough, and time,
> This coyness lady were no crime.

_____

_____

4. What other lines from "To His Coy Mistress" reinforce the *carpe diem* theme? Give one example.

_____

_____

5. In "To His Coy Mistress," what is the speaker's purpose in trying to convince his listener that life is short? Use an example from the poem to support your statement.

_____

_____

"Freeze Tag" by Suzanne Vega
"New Beginning" by Tracy Chapman

Build Vocabulary: Language of Time

Poets Suzanne Vega and Tracy Chapman explore the concept of time in their poetry. The words they and other writers use to describe time relationships have common connections. Even simple words take on important meanings when used in the context of time.

DIRECTIONS: Write a word or phrase from the box to complete each sentence.

beginning	cycle	fragments	past
change	fading	indecision	wake up

1. At the _____ of my reflection, I felt nervous, but later I began to feel more comfortable.

2. My memories of those days long ago are _____ with each passing year.

3. If we want to catch the sunrise, we'll have to _____ before the dawn.

4. We mustn't mourn the _____, but look with hope to the future.

5. When I remember times past, I sometimes recall disconnected _____ of disjointed events.

6. My favorite times of the year are when the seasons _____.

7. Sometimes time seems to stand still, and I am frozen in _____ as to what to do next.

8. Some consider the passing of the years to be a never-ending chain of events; I like to think of time passing as an endless _____ in which events are revisited again and again.

Unit 3: A Turbulent Time (1625–1798)

"Freeze Tag" by Suzanne Vega
"New Beginning" by Tracy Chapman

Cultural Connection: Theme of Time

You have read works by two seventeenth-century poets and two contemporary songwriters writing on the **theme of time**. What images do these four writers use to convey their feelings about time? What similarities can you find between the two sets of writers? Do they use any of the same images? What images would you use to write about the same theme?

DIRECTIONS: Use the chart below to record the images used by the different poets in their works. Decide which images of Marvell and Herrick still have resonance or meaning today. Use these images to start a list of your own that you believe you might use in a poem or song that explores the theme of time.

Images of Time

Marvell
Herrick
Vega
Chapman
My Images

Build Vocabulary

Spelling Strategy If an adjective ends in *-ant*, its parallel noun forms end in *-ance* or *-ancy*. For example, a noun form of the adjective *suppliant* is *suppliance*. If an adjective ends in *-ent*, its parallel forms end in *-ence* or *-ency*. For example, two noun forms of the adjective *transcendent* are *transcendence* and *transcendency*.

Using the Root *-lum-*

A. DIRECTIONS: Each of the following sentences includes an italicized word that contains the word root *-lum-*, which comes from the Latin word meaning "light" or "lamp." Fill in each blank with a word or phrase that completes the sentence and reveals the meaning of the italicized word.

1. When you flip the switch to *illuminate* the room, you _____.

2. When the physicist described the star's *luminance*, she was talking about its

   _____.

3. Because the face of the watch is *luminescent*, the hands and numbers are

   _____ enough to be read in the dark.

Using the Word Bank

semblance	illumine	transgress
guile	obdurate	tempestuous
transcendent	suppliant	ignominy

B. DIRECTIONS: Write the word from the Word Bank that best completes each analogy.

1. Trickery is to _____ as judgment is to wisdom.

2. _____ is to yielding as agitated is to peaceful.

3. Happiness is to joy as appearance is to _____.

4. _____ is to dishonor as pride is to conceit.

5. Ignorant is to educated as _____ is to calm.

6. _____ is to darken as love is to hate.

7. Obey is to comply as violate is to _____.

8. Imploring is to _____ as observant is to watchful.

9. Curious is to inquisitive as _____ is to exceeding.

Unit 3: A Turbulent Time (1625–1798)

Poetry of John Milton

Grammar and Style: Correct Use of *Who* and *Whom*

Who and **Whom** are relative pronouns that refer to or relate to another word or idea in the sentence. *Who* is the subject of a verb; *whom* is the object of a verb or preposition. Milton uses *who* and *whom* correctly in these lines from *Paradise Lost*.

> . . . Be it so, since he
> *Who* now is sovereign can dispose and bid
> What shall be right: farthest from him is best,
> *Whom* reason hath equaled, force hath made supreme

In the second line, *who* is the subject of the verb "is." In the last line, *whom* is the object of the verb "hath equaled."

A. Practice: Read each sentence and decide whether *who* or *whom* has been used correctly. Circle those words that have been used incorrectly.

1. John Milton, whom was born in 1608, was an English poet who attended Cambridge University.

2. Milton, who most people know as a poet, was also active in politics.

3. When King Charles I, who was Catholic, was overthrown, Oliver Cromwell, whom was Protestant, took over the reigns of government.

4. Milton, who was very well educated in the classics, was given a government position by Cromwell, to who he gave his loyalty.

5. After Charles II gained the throne, Milton, whom had opposed Charles I, was imprisoned.

6. Andrew Marvell, with who Milton had long been friends, helped Milton regain his freedom.

B. Writing Application: Rewrite each sentence, using *who* or *whom* correctly.

1. (*Who, Whom*) has not read Milton's greatest work, *Paradise Lost?*

_____

2. Milton, (*who, whom*) was totally blind by age forty-four, was a man for (*who, whom*) the loss of sight must have been especially tragic.

_____

3. Milton, (*who, whom*) said he wanted to write something so important that later generations would not let it die, kept writing despite his blindness.

_____

4. Many of those people (*who, whom*) know Milton's work best claim he is one of the greatest poets (*who, whom*) ever lived.

_____

5. About (*who, whom*) do you think he wrote the poem, "When I Consider How My Light Is Spent"?

_____

Poetry of John Milton

Reading Strategy: Breaking Down Sentences

Milton's poetry is sometimes difficult to read and understand because of its long and complex sentence structure. Milton frequently shifts the order of the clauses to add emphasis to certain ideas. The main clause may appear in the middle or at the end of the sentence. One way to un-ravel the meaning of sentences that confuse you is to break them down into the main clause and supporting details.

DIRECTIONS: Use the table below to help break down confusing sentences and decipher their meaning. The following passage has been used as a model.

> There the companions of his fall, o'erwhelmed
> With floods and whirlwinds of tempestuous fire,
> He soon discerns, and welt'ring by his side
> One next himself in power, and next in crime,
> Long after known in Palestine, and named
> Beelzebub. . . .

Main Clause	Supporting Ideas
1. "He soon discerns"	His companions are overwhelmed with floods and whirlwinds of fire. One of them is weltering by his side. Beelzebub is next to Satan in power and crime.
2.	
3.	
4.	

© Prentice-Hall, Inc.

Unit 3: A Turbulent Time (1625-1798)

Poetry of John Milton

Literary Analysis: Epic Poetry

Milton chose to write *Paradise Lost* in blank verse. The poet rejected the idea of rhymed verse, claiming, "The measure is English Heroic Verse without (rhyme), as that of Homer in Greek and of Virgil in Latin; (rhyme) no longer being necessary." Milton thought rhymed verse was "trivial and of no true musical delight" and that the true musical delight in poetry came from the fit of the syllables and the meter of the sentences from one verse to another.

DIRECTIONS: Scan the following lines of blank verse from *Paradise Lost* to show the basic iambic pentameter of the verse.

Of man's first disobedience, and the fruit

Of that forbidden tree, whose mortal taste

Brought death into the world, and all our woe,

With loss of Eden, till one greater Man

Restore us, and regain the blissful seat,

Sing Heav'nly Muse, that on the secret top

Of *Oreb* , or of *Sinai*, didst inspire

That shepherd, who first taught the chosen seed. . . .

from "Eve's Apology in Defense of Women" by Amelia Lanier
"To Lucasta, on Going to the Wars" and **"To Althea, from Prison"**
by Richard Lovelace

Build Vocabulary

Spelling Strategy Two common word endings which sound very similar are -ent and-ant, as in the words *insistent* and *inconstant*. Parallel forms of these words, such as *insistence* and *inconstancy*, retain the same vowel patterns in their endings.

Using Terms with *Breach*

Amelia Lanier uses the word *breach* in "Eve's Apology in Defense of Women." *Breach* means "breaking" and is often used in phrases related to the law, such as "breach of contract" or "breach of the peace."

A. DIRECTIONS: Rewrite each of the following sentences to include the word *breach*.

1. Richard said, "The owner of that car should be cited for disturbing the peace."

   _____

   _____

2. The subcontractor who failed to build the foundation on time was cited for breaking the contract.

   _____

   _____

3. The knights finally broke through the town's defenses.

   _____

   _____

Using the Word Bank

breach	discretion	inconstancy

B. DIRECTIONS: The questions below consist of a related pair of words in CAPITAL LETTERS followed by four lettered pairs of words. Choose the pair that best expresses a relationship *similar* to that in the pair in capital letters.

_____ 1. BREACH : CONTRACT ::
    a. break : broken
    b. running : legs
    c. excavation : archaeological site
    d. engine : train

_____ 2. INDISCRETION : DISCRETION ::
    a. indecisive : unsure
    b. fidelity : faithful
    c. love : loveless
    d. cowardice : courage

_____ 3. INCONSTANCY : FICKLENESS ::
    a. true : faithful
    b. insolvency : solvent
    c. lightning : quickly
    d. hard : soft

from "Eve's Apology in Defense of Women" by Amelia Lanier
"To Lucasta, on Going to the Wars" and **"To Althea, from Prison"**
by Richard Lovelace

Grammar and Style: Correlative Conjunctions

Correlative conjunctions are pairs of conjunctions that connect two words or groups of words. Stylistically, correlative conjunctions allow writers to link words clearly and elegantly. Examples of correlative conjunctions are *both . . . and, either . . . or, not so . . . as, neither . . . nor,* and *not only . . . but also.*

The following lines from "Eve's Apology in Defense of Women" shows two different uses of correlative conjunctions.

Before poor Eve had *either* life *or* breath . . .

Yea, having power to rule *both* Sea *and* Land . . .

A. Practice: Underline the correlative conjunctions in each of the following sentences.

1. Lanier's poetry is both sincere and insightful.

2. The reader is forced to wonder whether Eve was justly punished or if Adam should have shared the blame.

3. Richard Lovelace was neither a Catholic nor a Puritan.

4. Lovelace was both arrested and imprisoned by anti-Royalists.

5. The poetry that Lovelace wrote while in prison was not only beautiful but also some of his finest.

B. Writing Application: Use correlative conjunctions to combine the following pairs of sentences into one sentence.

1. In "Eve's Apology in Defense of Women" Lanier says that Adam is guilty of sin. She also says that Eve is guilty of sin.

_____

_____

2. Lovelace's tone is coy in his poem about going to war. His tone is also quite serious.

_____

_____

3. The poem addressed to Althea is playful in its imagery. The poem addressed to Lucasta is less playful.

_____

_____

4. "To Althea, from Prison" is a poem about love. It is also a profound statement on the nature of freedom.

_____

_____

from "Eve's Apology in Defense of Women" by Amelia Lanier
"To Lucasta, on Going to the Wars" and **"To Althea, from Prison"**
by Richard Lovelace

Reading Strategy: Using Historical Context

The poems by Lanier and Lovelace were inspired by specific social and historical circumstances. Think about the **historical context** when you read these works by asking yourself whether the ideas, assumptions, and beliefs expressed are typical of the era in which the work was written. Ask also if these ideas are a response to events of the period.

Evidence of loyalty and ideas of honor can be found in both of Lovelace's poems. In "To Lucasta, on Going to the Wars," Lovelace says "I could not love thee, Dear, so much,/Loved I not honor more" (lines 11–12). In "To Althea, from Prison," the poet celebrates "The sweetness, mercy, majesty,/And glories of my King" (lines 19–20). By understanding the historical context, you can reach a deeper understanding of the poems and the poets.

DIRECTIONS: Place the poems of Lanier and Lovelace into historical context using the chart below. Use the biographies and background on page 444 of the textbook to learn more about the poets and the events to which they were responding. As you read the poems, look for evidence of the events and circumstances of the era.

Poem	Historical Event, Assumption, or Belief	Evidence of Historical Context Within Poem
"Eve's Apology in Defense of Women"		
"To Lucasta, on Going to the Wars"		
"To Althea, from Prison"		

Unit 3: A Turbulent Time (1625–1798)

Name _____ Date _____

from "Eve's Apology in Defense of Women" by Amelia Lanier
"To Lucasta, on Going to the Wars" and **"To Althea, from Prison"**
by Richard Lovelace

Literary Analysis: Tradition and Reform

Tradition and **reform** go hand in hand. Political and social reformers usually propose ideas that are based on new readings of traditional stories familiar to most everyone in the culture. Bible episodes are often used to inspire reform. For example, Lanier reinterprets the story of Adam and Eve in support of her proposals to reform the treatment of women. Traditional stories, parables, fables, and books have always influenced reform because these stories help to form the basic beliefs of a culture.

DIRECTIONS: Use the following excerpts from "Eve's Apology in Defense of Women" to answer each of the following questions. Give examples from the selection quoted as evidence to support your interpretation.

1. In the following excerpt, when Lanier writes "Her fault though great, yet he was most to blame," what "fault" does she refer to? What does she say about the fault?

   But surely Adam can not be excused,
   Her fault though great, yet he was most to blame;
   What weakness offered, strength might have refused,
   Being lord of all, the greater was his shame. . . .

   _____

   _____

   _____

   _____

2. According to Lanier, what is the difference between Adam's guilt and Eve's guilt in the following excerpt? Whose is the greater?

   If Eve did err, it was for knowledge sake;
   The fruit being fair persuaded him to fall. . . .

   _____

   _____

   _____

   _____

3. According to Lanier, what knowledge or privilege do men claim in the following excerpt? Are men correct in claiming this knowledge for themselves?

   Yet men will boast of knowledge, which he took
   From Eve's fair hand, as from a learned book.

   _____

   _____

   _____

   _____

from *The Diary* by Samuel Pepys
from *A Journal of the Plague Year* by Daniel Defoe

Build Vocabulary

Spelling Strategy The suffixes *-ible* and *-able*, as in the words *combustible* and *lamenta-ble*, both mean "capable of" or worthy of." If you're not sure which ending to use, keep in mind that new words, such as *machine-washable* and *skiable*, always use the suffix *-able*.

Using the Prefix *dis-*

A. DIRECTIONS: The prefix *dis-* can mean "apart," "not," "opposite of," or "absence of." The words below all contain the prefix *dis-*. The parentheses contain information about the word root for each word. Fill in each blank with a form of the word from the list.

dispel (*pellere* = "to drive")   distribute (*tribuere* = "to allot")

disgrace (*grazia* = "grace")   disheveling (*chevel* = "hair")

disinfect (*infecter* = "to infect")   disgust (*gustus* = "a taste")

1. The wind blew fiercely, _____ Rob's neatly combed hair.

2. Anita groaned as her teacher began to _____ the test.

3. The first thing Albert did after moving into his new apartment was to clean and _____ the bathroom.

4. Gazing at his sister's messy room, Leroy could feel nothing but _____.

5. Because he had broken the law, the president resigned in _____.

6. Nancy posted a sign to _____ the rumors that school would be closed Friday.

Using the Word Bank

apprehensions	abated	lamentable
combustible	malicious	discoursing
distemper	importuning	prodigious

B. DIRECTIONS: Match each word in the left column with its definition in the right column. Write the letter of the definition on the line next to the word it defines.

____ 1. apprehensions   a. huge

____ 2. abated   b. begging

____ 3. combustible   c. flammable

____ 4. lamentable   d. distressing

____ 5. malicious   e. disease

____ 6. discoursing   f. talking about

____ 7. distemper   g. fears

____ 8. importuning   h. deliberately harmful

____ 9. prodigious   i. lessened

from _The Diary_ by Samuel Pepys
from _A Journal of the Plague Year_ by Daniel Defoe

Grammar and Style: Gerunds

Gerunds are verb forms that end in -_ing_ and function as nouns. Like nouns, gerunds can be preceded by articles. For example, in Defoe's phrase "nobody put on black or made a formal dress of mourning for their nearest friends," the word _mourning_ is a gerund. Gerunds are often mistaken for present participles, which are also verbs ending with -_ing_. Present participles, however, function as verbs or as adjectives modifying nouns and pronouns.

A. Practice: For each phrase, write _gerund_ if the word is a gerund. Write _not a gerund_ if it is not.

____ 1. Some of our maids _sitting_ up late last night . . .

____ 2. and the _cracking_ of houses at their ruin . . .

____ 3. the voice of _mourning_ was truly heard. . . .

____ 4. the plague _raging_ in a dreadful manner . . .

____ 5. the buriers . . . gathered about him, _supposing_ he was one of those poor . . . creatures

B. Writing Application: Write a sentence using each of the following words as a gerund.

1. summarizing

_____

_____

_____

2. bicycling

_____

_____

_____

3. farming

_____

_____

_____

4. chewing

_____

_____

_____

5. performing

_____

_____

_____

from *The Diary* by Samuel Pepys
from *A Journal of the Plague Year* by Daniel Defoe

Reading Strategy: Drawing Conclusions

When reading a text, you can discover more than the writer is explicitly stating by using evidence to **draw conclusions**. In *The Diary*, for example, Pepys does not say he is afraid that he or his wife and family may get sick and die of the plague. However, you might draw that conclusion when he lists all the people he knows who have recently died and mentions how closely he interacted with them. Drawing conclusions is like solving a mystery. First, you look for clues the writer has left in the text, and then you use those clues to figure out what the writer is saying "between the lines."

DIRECTIONS: Read the following excerpts from *The Diary* and *A Journal of the Plague Year*. Below each excerpt, write one conclusion that you can draw from it.

From *The Diary* by Samuel Pepys

1. . . . Jane called us up . . . to tell us of a great fire they saw in the city. So I rose . . . but, being unused to such fires as followed, I thought it far enough off; and so went to bed again and to sleep. About seven rose again . . . and saw the fire not so much as it was and farther off. So to my closet to set things to rights after yesterday's cleaning.

   Conclusions: _____

   _____

   _____

   _____

From *A Journal of the Plague Year* by Daniel Defoe

2. I went all the first part of the time freely about the streets, though not so freely as to run myself into apparent danger. . . .

   Conclusions: _____

   _____

   _____

   _____

3. . . . people that were infected and near their end, and delirious also, would run to those pits, wrapped in blankets or rugs, and throw themselves in, and, as they said, bury themselves.

   Conclusions: _____

   _____

   _____

   _____

Unit 3: A Turbulent Time (1625–1798)

from *The Diary* by Samuel Pepys

from *A Journal of the Plague Year* by Daniel Defoe

Literary Analysis: Diary or Journal

A **diary** or **journal** is a day-to-day description of the writer's experiences. Some diaries offer important insights into historical events or periods, and historians use diaries to research these events and eras. Reading historical diaries can also help a reader imagine what it would have been like to live through a particular event, because the diarist can give a first-person account usually not found in history texts.

A. DIRECTIONS: As you read the following excerpt from *The Diary*, think like a historian—look for clues that might explain why the Great Fire of London caused so much damage. In the space below the excerpt, list at least five factors that might explain why the fire spread so far.

Having stayed, and in an hour's time seen the fire rage every way . . . and the wind mighty high and driving it into the city; and everything, after so long a drought, proving combustible, even the very stones of churches. . . . So I was called for, and did tell the King and Duke of York what I saw, and that unless his Majesty did command houses to be pulled down nothing could stop the fire. They seemed much troubled, and the King commanded me to go to my Lord Mayor from him, and command him to spare no houses, but to pull down before the fire every way. . . . To the King's message he cried, like a fainting woman, "Lord! what can I do? I am spent: people will not obey me. I have been pulling down houses; but the fire overtakes us faster than we can do it." . . . So he left me, and I him, and walked home, seeing people all almost distracted, and no manner of means used to quench the fire. The houses, too, so very thick thereabouts, and full of matter for burning, as pitch and tar, in Thames Street, and warehouses of oil. . . .

1. _____

2. _____

3. _____

4. _____

5. _____

B. DIRECTIONS: Answer the following questions on the lines provided.

1. Diaries and journals offer historians a unique view of the past. If you were to keep a detailed journal of daily activities, what type of information might a historian of the future learn from reading it?

_____

_____

2. Defoe's *Journal of the Plague Year* is actually a novel written in journal form. How would the effect of the novel on the reader be different if it were written as a regular narrative story?

_____

_____

_____

from *Gulliver's Travels*
by Jonathan Swift

Build Vocabulary

Spelling Strategy Most words that start with the prefix *ex-*, such as *expostulate* and *expedient*, are spelled without a hyphen. However, compound words in which *ex-* means "former" require a hyphen: *ex-president*, *ex-wife*, and *ex-mayor*.

Using the Root *-jec-*

A. DIRECTIONS: Each of the following sentences includes an italicized word that contains the word root *-jec-* meaning "throw." Fill in the blank with a word or phrase that completes the sentence and reveals the meaning of the italicized word.

1. The criminal hung his head in *abject* misery; he looked completely _____.

2. The last time my grandmother had an *injection* was when she got _____.

3. My uncle liked to *interject* things into the conversation; he always had something to

_____.

Using the Word Bank

conjecture	expostulate	schism
expedient	habituate	odious

B. DIRECTIONS: The questions below consist of a related pair of words in CAPITAL LETTERS followed by four lettered pairs of words. Choose the pair that best expresses a relationship *similar* to that in the pair in capital letters.

____ 1. SCHISM : GROUPS ::
    a. whole : pieces
    b. storm : clouds
    c. division : parts
    d. separation : separate

____ 2. ODIOUS : HATEFUL ::
    a. broken : fixed
    b. peaceful : calmer
    c. odium : vileness
    d. lovely : beautiful

____ 3. CONJECTURE : INFERENCE ::
    a. confer : talk
    b. speak : statement
    c. relate : relative
    d. go : leave

____ 4. EXPOSTULATE : EARNESTLY ::
    a. reason : incorrect
    b. apologize : sincerely
    c. vilify : villain
    d. swim : gladly

Unit 3: A Turbulent Time (1625–1798)

Name _____ Date _____

Grammar and Style: Correct Use of *Between* and *Among*

When you write, knowing how to use the prepositions *between* and *among* correctly can help you avoid making needless mistakes. Here are some rules to keep in mind:

Use *between* to refer to two items or two groups of items:

There is a special bond *between* the king of Brobdingnag and Gulliver.

Use *among* to refer to more than two items:

Many *among* us feel the same way Gulliver felt.

A. Practice: Fill in the blank using either *between* or *among*.

1. The Lilliputians and the Blefuscudians had many disputes _____ them.

2. Of course, many Lilliputians probably bickered _____ themselves as well.

3. There were vast differences _____ Brobdingnag and England.

4. _____ the nobility of Brobdingnag, intelligence was rated very highly.

5. Gunpowder was the subject of a debate _____ Gulliver and the king.

B. Writing Application: Write two sentences that use each of the following words, one sentence using *among* and one using *between*.

argument

1. _____

2. _____

gossip

3. _____

4. _____

dispute

5. _____

6. _____

communication

7. _____

8. _____

Name _____ Date _____

Reading Strategy: Interpreting

Good satire is packed with social and political references, but writers of satire are also concerned with telling a good story. They wrap their satirical observations inside the story to comment in a humorous way. To **interpret** satire, the reader needs to know the historical context of the time it was written.

Satirical works that survive their own historical time period, such as _Gulliver's Travels_, do so because they address questions of universal human interest. For example, Gulliver describes the effects of gunpowder to the king of Brobdingnag. To ingratiate himself with the king, Gulliver proudly tells him about the enormous destruction that can be perpetrated by mixing a few simple ingredients and discharging the mixture with the help of a small spark. To Gulliver's surprise, the king is horrified by this notion. In fact, the king becomes so upset by the "evil genius, enemy to mankind" who must have first conceived of gunpowder, that he tells Gulliver never to mention the subject again. Swift uses this discussion to point up the problem of unbridled violence and the need for pacifism in the world. Since violence continues to be a societal and political problem to this day, Swift's satirical commentary retains its relevance.

DIRECTIONS: To interpret satirical works, you must look for the author's intended meaning. Use this graphic organizer to analyze and interpret material from _Gulliver's Travels_. One example has been completed for you.

Quotation	Meaning	Relevance Today
1. "He observed, that among the diversions of our nobility and gentry I had mentioned gaming."	It is clear by the questions the king asks that Swift thinks of gambling as a disease and an addiction that ruins lives.	The problem of gambling addiction still exists today.
2.		
3.		
4.		

from *Gulliver's Travels*
by Jonathan Swift

Literary Analysis: Satire

Satire uses wit and humor to ridicule vices, follies, and abuses. The intent, however, is rooted in a hope for reform: Satirists hope their work will open people's eyes to the real state of affairs in a society and do something about it. Irony and sarcasm are important tools of satirists, whose tone may be gentle and amused, or bitter and vicious. Jonathan Swift is one of the most famous and widely read satirists in English and *Gulliver's Travels* one of his most enduring works.

A. DIRECTIONS: Plan a satire of your own by writing out the following steps:

1. Name an institution or custom you believe merits criticism. It may be an organization or custom within your community, your state, the nation, or the world.

   _____

   _____

2. What aspect of this institution or custom deserves criticism? What vice or folly do you want to reveal?

   _____

   _____

3. Describe a setting that could be used in a satire about your subject. The setting can be the actual one, humorously disguised or, like Jonathan Swift's in *Gulliver's Travels*, it can be highly fanciful.

   _____

   _____

4. Name and briefly describe a character or two who will represent ordinary people who must deal with the institution or custom.

   _____

   _____

5. Describe an event—something the characters do or something that happens to them—that will highlight the aspect you wish to criticize.

   _____

   _____

6. Practice using verbal irony. Describe the institution or custom you are satirizing, or have a character comment on it, making sure the comment says the opposite of what is really meant. Make a statement that seems to defend the institution or custom but actually reveals the institution's shortcomings.

   _____

   _____

   _____

   _____

from *An Essay on Man* and from *The Rape of the Lock*
by Alexander Pope

Build Vocabulary

Spelling Strategy When adding suffixes to words such as *haughty* and *merry*, in which the final *y* is preceded by a consonant, the *y* usually changes to an *i*. For example, *haughty* becomes *haughtier*, *haughtiest*, and *haughtily*; *merry* becomes *merrier*, *merriest*, and *merrily*.

Using Related Words: Words About Society

A. DIRECTIONS: Read each of the lines from *The Rape of the Lock*. Describe the significance of the underlined word in upper-class British society during Alexander Pope's time. Use a dictionary if needed.

1. To taste awhile the pleasures of a <u>court</u> . . .

   _____

2. Who gave the <u>ball</u>, or paid the visit last . . .

   _____

3. A third interprets motions, looks, and eyes;/At every word a <u>reputation</u> dies.

   _____

4. <u>Snuff</u>, or the <u>fan</u>, supply each pause of Chat. . . .

   _____

   _____

5. Now to the <u>baron</u> fate inclines the field.

   _____

Using the Word Bank

| obliquely | plebeian | destitute |
| assignations | stoic | disabused |

B. DIRECTIONS: Write the word from the Word Bank that best completes each sentence.

1. If Sir Plume thought he could get away with a lock of Belinda's hair, she certainly

   _____ him of that notion.

2. In Pope's time beggars lived on the street and were completely _____.

3. Sometimes ladies and gentlemen made secret _____ with one another.

4. If a person gives you a sidewise glance, he or she is looking at you _____.

5. The nobleman was considered by many to be haughty because he rarely spoke to those

   whom he considered _____, or lower class.

6. The _____ remained calm and collected while others reacted to the

   news emotionally.

Name _____ Date _____

from *An Essay on Man* and from *The Rape of the Lock*
by Alexander Pope

Grammar and Style: Inverted Word Order

In his mock epic poem *The Rape of the Lock*, Alexander Pope often uses **inverted word order**. When poets invert word order, or change the normal word order of subject-verb-complement, they often do so to maintain a regular rhythm or to emphasize certain important words. Inverting words also frees the poet to use interesting words as end rhymes. Here is an example of inverted word order from *The Rape of the Lock*:

> The rebel knave, <u>who dares his prince engage,</u>
>
> Proves the just victim of his royal rage.

Here is the same excerpt written in normal English word order:

> The rebel knave, <u>who dares engage his prince,</u>
>
> Proves the just victim of his royal rage.

Inverting the word order in this case facilitates the end rhyme, *engage* and *rage*.

A. Practice: These lines from *The Rape of the Lock* contain inverted word order. On the lines, rewrite each line using normal English word order.

1. His giant limbs in state unwieldy spread . . .

   _____

2. Clubs, diamonds, hearts in wild disorder seen . . .

   _____

3. The nymph exulting fills with shouts the sky. . . .

   _____

4. "Let wreaths of triumph now my temples twine. . . ."

   _____

5. While nymphs take treats, or assignations give . . .

   _____

B. Writing Application: Write endings for each couplet below using inverted word order. Try to maintain the rhythm of the first line and use end rhymes. The first one has been done for you.

1. But while my brother lies asleep in bed,

   <u>His wife cold water pours upon his head.</u>_____

2. When winter weather goes from bad to worse,

   _____

3. In springtime when the heart may turn to love

   _____

4. How happy are the children in the park

   _____

from *An Essay on Man* and from *The Rape of the Lock*
by Alexander Pope

Reading Strategy: Recognizing Author's Purpose

In *The Rape of the Lock*, Pope satirizes high society by focusing his wit and poetic talents on a petty incident that takes place among members of the wigged and powdered London upper-crust set. With elevated language and allusions to mythology, Pope deflates London society, exposing its silliness and shallowness. In the following passage, Pope appears to compliment the depth and grandeur of upper-class London society, but is really ridiculing such people by exposing their pettiness and the shallowness of their conversations.

> Hither the heroes and the nymphs resort,
> To taste awhile the pleasures of a court;
> In various talk th' instructive hours they passed,
> Who gave the ball, or paid the visit last;
> One speaks the glory of the British Queen,
> And one describes a charming Indian screen;
> A third interprets motions, looks, and eyes;
> At every word a reputation dies.

DIRECTIONS: Use the chart below to interpret the author's purpose in examples from the *The Rape of the Lock*. The left column contains a quote from the poem. In the right column, interpret the meaning underlying the author's words. The first one has been done for you.

Quotation	Author's Purpose
"To arms, to arms!" the fierce virago cries, / And swift as lightning to the combat flies. / All side in parties, and begin th' attack; / Fans clap, silks rustle, and tough whalebones crack . . .	1. Pope mocks the high-society ladies and gentlemen whose "arms" are fans, silk dresses and suits, and the whalebone stays of corsets.
Meanwhile, declining from the noon of day, / The sun obliquely shoots his burning ray; / The hungry judges soon the sentence sign, / And wretches hang that jurymen may dine; / The merchant from th' Exchange returns in peace, / And the long labors of the toilet cease.	2.
The skilful nymph reviews her force with care: / Let spades be trumps! she said, and trumps they were.	3.
The meeting points the sacred hair dissever / From the fair head, forever, and forever!	4.
When, after millions slain, yourself shall die; / When those fair suns shall set, as set they must, / And all those tresses shall be laid in dust, / This lock, the Muse shall consecrate to fame, / And midst the stars inscribe Belinda's name.	5.

from *An Essay on Man* and from *The Rape of the Lock*
by Alexander Pope

Literary Analysis: Mock Epic

A **mock epic** uses the epic form for humorous effect. The key feature of a mock epic is its treatment of a trivial subject in an elevated style, thus showing how ridiculous it is. A mock epic tells a story of "heroes" doing "great deeds," but the heroes and deeds are actually petty. A mock epic, like a true epic, may use gods and other supernatural elements. *The Rape of the Lock* is a masterpiece of mock epic.

DIRECTIONS: Explore the characteristics of the mock epic by answering these questions.

1. What is the subject of *The Rape of the Lock*?

_____

_____

_____

2. What makes these lines humorous?

Here, thou, great Anna! whom three realms obey,
Dost sometimes counsel take—and sometimes tea.

_____

_____

_____

3. As in a true epic, mighty forces "draw forth to combat on the velvet plain." What war is then described in detail?

_____

_____

_____

4. Figures from mythology take an interest in the events described. Quote a line that shows their involvement.

_____

_____

_____

5. An epic celebrates the immortal fame of its heroes. Cite lines in which Pope makes a similar claim for his.

_____

_____

_____

**from *The Preface to A Dictionary of the English Language* and from *A Dictionary of the English Language* by Samuel Johnson
from *The Life of Samuel Johnson* by James Boswell**

Build Vocabulary

Spelling Strategy The basic pattern in English is to use *-ity* as a noun ending, as in the words *credulity* and *malignity*. The noun ending *-ety* is used for some words, such as *anxiety*, *piety*, and *variety*, to avoid having two *i*'s in a row.

Using the Root *-dict-*

A. Directions: The words that follow each contain the word root *-dict-*, from the Latin for "to say." Information about the prefix or suffix of each word is contained in parentheses. On the line, write the word that best completes each sentence.

> dictate (*-ate* = "act on")
>
> dictator (*-or* = "one that does something")
>
> diction (*-ion* = "action or process")
>
> predict (*pre-* = "before")

1. When the _____ seized power, he immediately censored the newspapers.

2. Because their scientific instruments were precise, the meteorologists were able to _____ accurately the arrival of the storm.

3. The executive began to _____ her speech into the tape recorder.

4. The actor's good _____ enhanced his reading of the short story.

Using the Word Bank

recompense	caprices	adulterations	propagators	risible
abasement	credulity	malignity	pernicious	inculcated

B. Directions: Match each word in the left column with its definition in the right column. Write the letter of the definition on the line next to the word it defines.

____ 1. adulterations   a. condition of being put down or humbled

____ 2. risible   b. tendency to believe too readily

____ 3. inculcated   c. strong desire to harm others

____ 4. caprices   d. causing serious injury; deadly

____ 5. abasement   e. impressed upon the mind by repetition

____ 6. propagators   f. prompting laughter

____ 7. malignity   g. those who cause something to happen or to spread

____ 8. credulity   h. reward, payment

____ 9. pernicious   i. whims

____ 10. recompense   j. impurities

Unit 3: A Turbulent Time (1625–1798)

from *The Preface to A Dictionary of the English Language* and from *A Dictionary of the English Language* by Samuel Johnson
from *The Life of Samuel Johnson* by James Boswell

Grammar and Style: Commas with Parenthetical Expressions

Parenthetical expressions are words, phrases, or clauses which interrupt the main part of a sentence to comment on it or to give additional information. Listed below are several common parenthetical expressions.

I am sure	after all	incidentally	naturally	on the other hand
I believe	by the way	indeed	nevertheless	
I think	for example	in fact	of course	to tell the truth
I hope	however	in my opinion	on the contrary	

Wherever parenthetical expressions occur in a sentence—at the beginning, the middle, or the end—they need to be set off from the main part of the sentence by commas. The following examples are from *The Life of Samuel Johnson.*

But however that might be, this speech was somewhat unlucky. . . .

That, Sir, I find, is what a very great many of your countrymen cannot help.

A. Practice: For each of the following sentences, identify the parenthetical expression by underlining it. Then insert commas to set off the expression from the rest of the sentence.

1. The character of Samuel Johnson has I trust been so developed in the course of this work. . . .

2. Man is in general made up of contradictory qualities. . . .

3. Ridicule has gone down before him, and I doubt Derrick is his enemy.

4. . . . so that the unavoidable consciousness of his superiority was in that respect a cause of disquiet.

5. . . . his poetical pieces in general have not much of that splendor. . . .

B. Writing Application: Use each parenthetical expression below in a sentence.

1. on the contrary

_____

2. incidentally

_____

3. to tell the truth

_____

4. on the other hand

_____

5. indeed

_____

from *The Preface to A Dictionary of the English Language* and from *A Dictionary of the English Language* by Samuel Johnson

from *The Life of Samuel Johnson* by James Boswell

Reading Strategy: Establishing a Purpose

When you **establish a purpose** before reading, you are able to

- focus on the information you wish to find.

- add the knowledge you have gained to your framework of prior knowledge on the subject.

- increase your concentration and ability to retain what you have read.

- increase your pleasure in reading because you are taking an active rather than a passive part in the process.

DIRECTIONS: Establish a specific purpose for reading the excerpts from *A Dictionary of the English Language* and *The Life of Samuel Johnson*. After you have set a purpose, use the following KWL chart to record what you Know about the subject, what you Want to find out, and what you Learned from your reading.

Selection	What I Know	What I Want to Find Out (Purpose for Reading)	What I Learned
from The Preface to *A Dictionary of the English Language*			
from *A Dictionary of the English Language*			
from *The Life of Samuel Johnson*			

from *The Preface to A Dictionary of the English Language* and **from *A Dictionary of the English Language*** by Samuel Johnson

from *The Life of Samuel Johnson* by James Boswell

Literary Analysis: Dictionary

Samuel Johnson's *Dictionary* was not the first to attempt to include all the English words in one volume. However, it was the first dictionary to set a standard for how all English words should be used. Today's English dictionaries list and define words and provide information about their pronunciation, meanings, history, and usage. A modern dictionary entry may also contain a word's spelling, syllabication, pronunciation in phonetic symbols, part(s) of speech and the definitions for the word in each part of speech, illustrative sentences, synonyms, how to use the word correctly, and when to use it. Some entries contain a history of the word, correct grammatical usage of the word, illustrations, antonyms, idioms, and foreign words and phrases. Modern dictionaries may also contain roots and other combining forms, abbreviations, and bibliographic and geographic entries. Electronic dictionaries on computers have expanded the capabilities of dictionaries. If you are unsure of a spelling, you can enter an approximation of the word and be given choices of possible entries. When looking for a word that fits a particular meaning, you can search the dictionary by entering one or more of the key words that might be found in its definition.

A. Directions: Read the entry for *gang* in Johnson's dictionary and list the different pieces of information he supplies about the word; then look up the word *gang* in a modern dictionary and note the similarities and differences in the kinds of information supplied. Fill in the Venn diagram to show the similarities and differences between Johnson's dictionary and a modern dictionary.

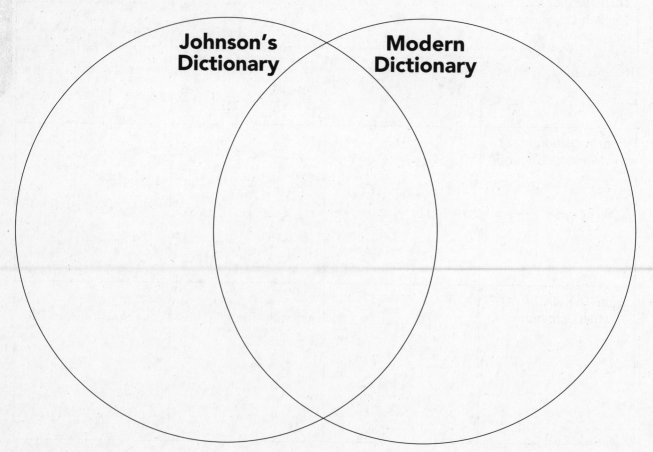

Johnson's Dictionary

Modern Dictionary

"Elegy Written in a Country Churchyard" by Thomas Gray
"A Nocturnal Reverie" by Anne Finch, Countess of Winchilsea

Build Vocabulary

Spelling Strategy When *y* is added to a word ending in *e*, such as *venerable* and *ignoble*, the *e* is usually dropped: *venerably* and *ignobly*.

Using the Prefix *circum-*

A. DIRECTIONS: Each of the following sentences includes an italicized word that contains the prefix *circum-* (or *circ-*), meaning "around." Fill in the blank with a word or phrase that completes the sentence and reveals the meaning of the italicized word.

1. When a path is *circuitous*, it _____.

2. When a person *circulates* at a party, he or she _____

   _____.

3. A *circus* takes place in _____.

4. If a patient is *circumambulating* the grounds, he or she is_____

   _____.

Using the Word Bank

penury	circumscribed	ingenuous	ignoble
nocturnal	temperate	venerable	forage

B. DIRECTIONS: Write a word or words from the Word Bank to complete each sentence.

1. It is so cold here that I'm tempted to move someplace where the weather is

   _____.

2. The pasture is full of rich _____ for the cattle to graze on.

3. Finch's poem describes _____ phenomena such as moonlight.

4. Gray describes the churchyard occupants as _____ regardless of

   their _____, or poverty.

5. The judge described the ex-senator as lowly and _____ for taking

   advantage of his _____, unsuspecting constituents.

6. The teacher _____ the topics for the final essay by requiring that they

   focus on plot.

Unit 3: A Turbulent Time (1625–1798)

"Elegy Written in a Country Churchyard" by Thomas Gray
"A Nocturnal Reverie" by Anne Finch, Countess of Winchilsea

Grammar and Style: Pronoun-Antecedent Agreement

You will find it easier to understand densely constructed poetry if you learn to recognize **pronoun-antecedent agreement**. Look, for example, at this excerpt from "A Nocturnal Reverie":

> In such a night, when every louder wind
> Is to *its* distant cavern safe confined;
> And only gentle Zephyr fans *his* wings,
> And lonely Philomel, still waking, sings;
> Or from some tree, famed for the owl's delight,
> *She*, hollowing clear, directs the wanderer right. . . .

Reading carefully, you will note that *its* in line 2 refers to line 1 and its antecedent *wind*. The pronoun *his* in line 3 refers to its antecedent, the proper noun *Zephyr*. The pronoun *She* in line 6 refers to its antecedent, the proper noun *Philomel* in line 4.

When using pronouns, make sure that the pronoun you choose agrees with its antecedent.

A. Practice: Circle the word in parentheses that correctly completes each sentence.

1. The children patiently await (*his, their*) father's return.

2. Which one of the sons was (*his, their*) father's favorite?

3. The cows and the sheep are going to (*its, their*) pen for the night.

4. Thomas Gray enjoyed the churchyard for (*his, its*) mournful reminders about the past.

5. Gray's lonely musings reveal (*his, their*) serious frame of mind.

B. Writing Application: For each of the antecedents below, write a sentence that uses a correct pronoun. Underline the pronoun in your completed sentence.

1. My sister and I _____

    _____.

2. The mothers and the children _____

    _____.

3. The cemetery _____

    _____.

4. Thomas Gray _____

    _____.

5. Anne Finch, Countress of Winchilsea, _____

    _____.

"Elegy Written in a Country Churchyard" by Thomas Gray
"A Nocturnal Reverie" by Anne Finch, Countess of Winchilsea

Reading Strategy: Paraphrasing

Poetry presents readers with challenges different from those presented by prose. Poetry often uses dense language and imagery, which some readers find difficult to follow. **Paraphrasing** is a useful tool to help guide you through complex poetic passages. Look at the following example from Gray's "Elegy."

Original:

Full many a gem of purest ray serene
The dark unfathomed caves of ocean bear:
Full many a flower is born to blush unseen,
And waste its sweetness on the desert air.

Paraphrase:

Many precious gems are never seen by human eyes because they exist deep in the ocean. Many flowers bloom without ever being seen; their sweet smells dissipate in the desert.

DIRECTIONS: Use the chart below to help you break down difficult passages in Thomas Gray's "Elegy Written in a Country Churchyard." When you encounter complex material, read it over twice; then try to paraphrase the meaning of the words. Continue reading to make sure that your paraphrase makes sense with regard to the rest of the poem. An example has been completed for you.

Original	Paraphrase
1. "The boast of heraldry, the pomp of power,/And all that beauty, all that wealth e'er gave,/Awaits alike the inevitable hour./The paths of glory lead but to the grave." ("Elegy," lines 33–36)	Having a noble birthright, power, wealth, and beauty doesn't matter; in the end, everyone dies.
2.	
3.	
4.	
5.	

Elegy/Nocturnal Reverie **119**

"Elegy Written in a Country Churchyard" by Thomas Gray
"A Nocturnal Reverie" by Anne Finch, Countess of Winchilsea

Literary Analysis: Preromantic Poetry

The poems of Thomas Gray and Anne Finch celebrate the formal style of eighteenth-century poetry while at the same time ushering in the emotional expressiveness of the coming Romantic movement. Unlike many other poets of the time, Gray and Finch managed to create poems that stirred not only readers' minds but their emotions. In poems such as Gray's "Elegy Written in a Country Churchyard," for example, readers found themselves compelled and emotionally drawn to insights about the lives and deaths of common rural people, those whose existence supposedly held little meaning for the rest of the world. By concentrating on life's mysteries, the unanswerable questions that mark human experience, Gray and Finch were able to create poems of universal appeal and lasting literary significance.

DIRECTIONS: Read the lines from "Elegy Written in a Country Churchyard" and "A Nocturnal Reverie" and answer the questions that follow.

> Some village Hampden, that, with dauntless breast,
>   The little tyrant of his fields withstood,
> Some mute inglorious Milton here may rest,
>   Some Cromwell guiltless of his country's blood.

1. What is Gray saying about the lives of the common people laid to rest in the churchyard?

   _____

   _____

> Yet even these bones from insult to protect
>   Some frail memorial still erected nigh,
> With uncouth rhymes and shapeless sculpture decked,
>   Implores the passing tribute of a sigh.
>
> Their name, their years, spelt by the unlettered Muse,
>   The place of fame and elegy supply:
> And many a holy text around she strews,
>   That teach the rustic moralist to die.

2. What statement does Gray make about the importance of honoring the dead?

   _____

   _____

> In such a night, let me abroad remain,
>   Till morning breaks, and all's confused again;
> Our cares, our toils, our clamors are renewed,
>   Or pleasures, seldom reached, again pursued.

3. How does being outside at night affect the speaker? How does this feeling exemplify pre-romantic poetry?

   _____

   _____

from *The Analects* by Confucius
from The Declaration of Independence by Thomas Jefferson

Build Vocabulary: Language of Governing

These two works spell out the common beliefs that bind people together. They both use language that describes the proper relationship between the governors and the governed.

DIRECTIONS: Fill in the crossword puzzle below with words related to governing that fit the clues provided.

authority	consent	equal	homage	moral
order	political	powers	principles	respect
right	rules	separate	superior	trusts

Across

1. special kind of party
6. basic beliefs
8. freedom of the press, for example
9. the same
11. pay ____; show allegiance or reverence
12. state of peace and observance of the law
13. consideration
14. set apart

Down

1. a government derives them from the people
2. believes in
3. approve
4. ethical
5. higher in rank or value
7. legal ability to act
10. ____ of the game

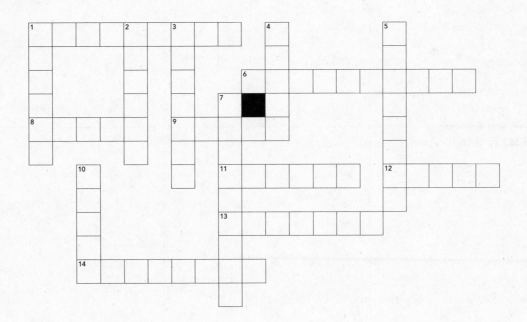

Unit 3: A Turbulent Time (1625–1798)

from *The Analects* by Confucius
from The Declaration of Independence by Thomas Jefferson

Cultural Connection: Governors and the Governed

Though it is many centuries old, *The Analects* of Confucius still represents the philosophical, ethical, and social beliefs of the Chinese people. Similarly, The Declaration of Independence, written to articulate the reasons why Americans separated from Britain, is also considered a key document in defining what it means to be an American. Both documents, in their own way, provide a guide for behavior of both rulers and the ruled.

DIRECTIONS: Use the chart below to develop a profile of the ideal citizen and ideal ruler based on the ideas of Confucius and Jefferson. State the main ideas from each document, and then go on to make inferences beyond the examples provided in the texts.

	Confucius	Thomas Jefferson
The Ideal Citizen		
The Ideal Ruler		

"On Spring" by Samuel Johnson
from "The Aims of the Spectator" by Joseph Addison

Build Vocabulary

Spelling Strategy The *sh* sound at the beginning of the words *ship* and *shell* is commonly spelled *sh*, but there are many other ways to spell this sound. For example, when the *sh* sound is combined with the suffix *ious*, the resulting syllable can be spelled *tious*, as in the word *con-tentious*.

Using the Root *-spec-*

A. Directions: Each of the following sentences includes an italicized word which contains the word root *-spec-* from a Latin word meaning "to look." Fill in the blank with a word or phrase that completes the sentence and reveals the meaning of the italicized word.

1. When the detective *inspected* the room, he _____.

2. If she studied every *aspect* of the problem, she _____.

3. If you behold a *spectacle*, you _____.

Using the Word Bank

procured	divert	speculation	transient
affluence	contentious	trifles	embellishments

B. Directions: Write the word from the box that best completes each sentence.

1. I don't know how he _____ the canoe, but it certainly made the trip more enjoyable.

2. I like her painting because she manages to describe a place or person without

   _____ .

3. He was concerned that too much time was being spent on _____ during the meetings.

4. The houses in Great Neck were large and hinted at the _____ of the neighborhood.

5. Her brother seemed sad, so she tried to _____ him with a game of checkers.

6. Whether or not the candidate would run for office was merely a matter for

   _____ .

7. After the season, the pitcher realized how fleeting and _____ were the joys of playing.

8. Because of their bickering, the partners' relationship could be described as

   _____ .

© Prentice-Hall, Inc.

On Spring/Aims of the Spectator **123**

"On Spring" by Samuel Johnson
from "The Aims of the Spectator" by Joseph Addison

Grammar and Style: Adjective Clauses

Adjective clauses are clauses that qualify or further describe the nouns or pronouns preceding them. These clauses begin with the relative pronouns *who, whom, which, that*, and *whose*. The following lines from "On Spring" and *The Aims of the Spectator* show examples of adjective clauses.

It may be laid down as a position *which will seldom deceive* . . .

There is another set of men that I must likewise lay a claim to, *whom I have lately called the blanks of society* . . .

It was said of Socrates *that he brought philosophy down from heaven, to inhabit among men* . . .

A. Practice: Underline the adjective clause in each of the following lines. In the blanks, write the relative pronoun with which the adjective clause begins.

1. Samuel Johnson's *Dictionary of the English Language*, which was wildly popular in its day, greatly influenced the format of later dictionaries.

   _____

2. Irony and satire were popular tools of writers who hoped to make their mark in eighteenth-century literature.

   _____

3. The art of essay writing, which many writers hold to be among the most difficult, dates to the sixteenth century.

   _____

B. Writing Application: Write an adjective clause that uses the relative pronoun shown in parentheses to qualify or further describe each noun below.

1. the poet (*whose*)

   _____

2. a barking dog (*that*)

   _____

3. the president (*whom*)

   _____

4. ironic essays (*that*)

   _____

5. the dancer (*who*)

   _____

"On Spring" by Samuel Johnson

from "The Aims of the Spectator" by Joseph Addison

Reading Strategy: Drawing Inferences

Both Samuel Johnson and Joseph Addison use subtle irony, complex attitudes, and shades of meaning in their essays. As you read their essays you need to **draw inferences** to reach logical conclusions about what the writers mean. For example, in the third paragraph of "The Aims of the Spectator" Addison writes

> . . . in the next place, I would recommend this paper to the daily perusal of those gentlemen whom I cannot but consider as my good brothers and allies, I mean the fraternity of spectators, who live in the world without having anything to do in it; and either by the affluence of their fortunes or laziness of their dispositions have no other business with the rest of mankind but to look upon them.

Addison is saying that there is a type of person who does not frequently engage or interact with people or the outside world. In the pages of *The Spectator* these people will find a means to engage the outside world that will enable them to make sense of it and understand its workings. Although Addison counts himself among this "fraternity," you can infer from the use of the word "laziness" that he has some ambivalent feelings about these people.

DIRECTIONS: Use this chart to draw inferences about ideas or attitudes that Johnson or Addison leave unstated. Write down passages that seem unclear, and make logical connections between what the writer says and what he might mean. One passage has been chosen and an inference shown to help you.

Passage or Statement	Inference that Can Be Drawn
1. "I hope to increase the number of these by publishing this daily paper, which I shall always endeavor to make an innocent if not an improving entertainment, and by that means at least divert the minds of my female readers from greater trifles."	Addison is mocking the trivialities with which most women are forced to occupy their time.
2.	
3.	
4.	
5.	

Unit 3: A Turbulent Time (1625–1798)

"On Spring" by Samuel Johnson
from "The Aims of the Spectator" by Joseph Addison

Literary Analysis: Essay

An **essay** is a piece of short prose that explores a single topic. The word *essay* comes from a French word meaning an "attempt" or "a test." The word was first applied to the writing of Montaigne (1533–1592), a Frenchman whose essays dealt with the questions of life. Although Montaigne's essays were "attempts" to find answers to these enduring questions, they did not always end with definite answers. Montaigne wrote on a number of subjects, but he said that his aim was always to learn about himself.

In his essay "On Spring" Johnson "attempts" to relate the significance and meaning of springtime to our lives. In *The Aims of the Spectator* Addison is "trying" to express his goals for the periodical by describing its usefulness to different types of people. Both essays cause the reader to reflect on his or her own relationship to the given topic.

DIRECTIONS: Read the following excerpts from the essays and answer the questions on another sheet of paper. Give quotations from the essay to support your interpretation.

from "The Aims of the Spectator"

I shall be ambitious to have it said of me that I have brought philosophy out of closets and libraries, schools and colleges, to dwell in clubs and assemblies, at tea tables and in coffeehouses.

1. What is Addison's ultimate goal for *The Spectator?* Give evidence to support your ideas.

from "The Aims of the Spectator"

As they lie at the mercy of the first man they meet, and are grave or impertinent all the day long, according to the notions which they have imbibed in the morning, I would earnestly entreat them not to stir out of their chambers till they have read this paper, and do promise them that I will daily instill into them such sound and wholesome sentiments as shall have a good effect on their conversation for the ensuing twelve hours.

2. How would you describe the type of person Addison is writing about in this passage? How does Addison believe *The Spectator* will benefit this type of person?

from "On Spring"

A French author has advanced this seeming paradox, that very few men know how to take a walk; and, indeed, it is true, that few know how to take a walk with a prospect of any other pleasure than the same company would have afforded them at home.

3. How does the paradox that Johnson cites relate to the topic of the essay as a whole? What does the ability to "take a walk" have to do with Johnson's topic?

Name _____ Date _____

Build Vocabulary: Language of Social Awareness

Many essays deal with important social issues. To understand such essays completely, you need to master vocabulary that deals explicitly with social awareness.

DIRECTIONS: Write the word from the box that best fits each numbered line within the paragraph.

privacy	certainty	discussion	survival	wrong	problems
pain	stability	predictability	world	participation	

I can't say with (1)_____ how the life of the man on the corner had

spiraled downward, what in his past had gone so terribly (2)_____

that he was left to make his way on the street, alone. His life was full of

(3) _____. The often faceless people one meets on the streets lead des-

perate lives, with every day bringing a new test of (4) _____. Some-

times I think that beyond finding food and shelter, the worst trial of being homeless is the

lack of (5)_____: the rest of us wake up and begin our days knowing

something of what lies ahead of us; we have a (6)_____ in our lives

that we may find boring, but which provides us with a certain mooring that guides us

through the day. This psychological salve is not part of the daily

(7)_____ of the homeless. Shunned by passersby, told to move along

by police, there is no (8)_____ for them in the everyday workings of so-

ciety. The (9)_____ of hunger and the batterings of the cold are condi-

tions most of us can scarcely imagine. We might begin a (10)_____ of

the effects of an enforced (11)_____ as well.

"Homeless" by Anna Quindlen

Literary Connection: The Essay

Samuel Johnson's and Joseph Addison's informal essays "On Spring" and *The Aims of the Spectator* are examples of a writing style that gained popularity in the eighteenth century. These essays had a conversational and familiar tone that included sketches of characters and lively anecdotes. Informal essay writing continues today, as shown by Anna Quindlen's "Homeless." Although more serious in subject matter, Quindlen's essay uses a personal and conversational tone. What topics might you explore in an informal essay?

DIRECTIONS: Use the questions below to help plan an essay of your own on a topic that concerns you. Utilize Anna Quindlen's essay on the homeless, as well as the other essays you read in this section, as a guide for planning your own writing.

1. What is my topic? What issue will I explore?

   _____

   _____

   _____

   _____

2. What will be my point of view on the topic?

   _____

   _____

   _____

   _____

3. What characters might I sketch to personalize my essay?

   _____

   _____

   _____

   _____

4. What lively anecdotes might I include to make the essay more interesting and accessible?

   _____

   _____

   _____

   _____

   _____

   _____

   _____

   _____

"To a Mouse" and **"To a Louse"** by Robert Burns
"Woo'd and Married and A'" by Joanna Baillie

Build Vocabulary

Spelling Strategy The suffix that sounds like *shun* at the end of a word may be spelled in any of the following ways: *-cion*, *-tion*, or *-ssion*. Most words ending in *shun* use the *ti* spelling, like *discretion*. A few words use the *ci* spelling (*suspicion*) or the *ss* spelling (*possession*). In words ending with *-sion*, *si* is usually pronounced *z*, as in *vision*.

Using the Suffix *-some*

A. DIRECTIONS: The following words all contain the suffix—*some*, meaning "having specific qualities." Using the word's context along with what you know about this suffix, write a definition of each *itlaicized* word in the blank.

1. At first the jokes were funny, but they became *tiresome.*

   _____

2. When Jerome went to the zoo, he thought the snakes were *loathsome*, but Janelle enjoyed them.

   _____

3. Bees abuzzing around your head at a picini are so *bothersome*, aren't they?

   _____

Using the Word Bank

dominion	impudence	winsome
discretion	inconstantly	

B. DIRECTIONS: Write a word from the Word Bank to answer each question.

1. Which word means most nearly the opposite of *imprudence*? _____

2. If you observe someone acting rudely toward a stranger, what word might you use to describe such behavior? _____

3. Which word is closest in meaning to *changeably*? _____

4. Which word describes a monarch's authority over his or her subjects? _____

5. What word might you use to describe a person who has a charming manner and appearance? _____

© Prentice-Hall, Inc.

Mouse/Louse/Married **129**

"To a Mouse" and **"To a Louse"** by Robert Burns
"Woo'd and Married and A'" by Joanna Baillie

Grammar and Style: Interjections

An **interjection** is a word or phrase that can stand by itself and that is used to express emotion. Consider these examples from "To a Louse."

My sooth! right bauld ye set your nose out. . . .

O, Jenny, dinna toss your head. . . .

Notice that an exclamation mark often follows an interjection to show the strong emotion being expressed.

A. Practice: Underline the interjection in each sentence.

1. My gosh! There's a bug in that woman's hair.

2. Hey! It's only a louse.

3. Good grief! You say that as if a louse were nothing at all to have in your hair.

4. Aha! It's not a louse—it's a bee!

5. Yikes! I remember when a bee flew into my mother's hair while she was driving.

6. I didn't think she would stop the car in time! Whew! It was close.

B. Writing Application: For each of the following interjections, write a sentence that incorporates it. Punctuate each interjection by using an exclamation mark.

1. well

_____

2. hurrah

_____

3. hey

_____

4. alas

_____

5. whoa

_____

6. oh

_____

7. my goodness

_____

"To a Mouse" and **"To a Louse"** by Robert Burns
"Woo'd and Married and A'" by Joanna Baillie

Reading Strategy: Translate Dialect

A **dialect** is the language and speech habits of the members of a particular group, class, or region. Each dialect has its own unique grammar, pronunciation, and vocabulary. Robert Burns and Joanna Baillie wrote their poems in the Scottish dialect of English. Their use of dialect made their poems more accessible and familiar to their contemporaries in Scotland. Modern readers can use a number of different strategies to **translate dialect**:

- Read footnotes to get definitions.
- Use context to guess meaning.
- Speak words aloud and listen for similarities to standard English words.
- Look for similarities between printed dialect words and English words.
- Note apostrophes, which often signal that a letter has been omitted.

DIRECTIONS: After reading the following lines from "To a Mouse," translate each word in italics, identifying the strategy you used to determine each word's meaning.

1. "I wad be laith to *rin* an' chase thee / Wi' murd'ring pattle."

_____

_____

_____

2. "I doubt na, *whyles*,[8] but thou may thieve;"

_____

_____

_____

3. "Thy wee bit *housie*, too, in ruin!"

_____

_____

_____

4. "An' *lea'e* us nought but grief an' pain,"

_____

_____

_____

5. "An' forward, though I *canna* see,"

_____

_____

_____

[8]whyles: At times.

Mouse/Louse/Married **131**

"To a Mouse" and **"To a Louse"** by Robert Burns
"Woo'd and Married and A'" by Joanna Baillie

Literary Analysis: Dialect

Robert Burns was one of the first poets to write verse that incorporated the Scottish dialect of English. **Dialect** is the language, chiefly the speech habits and patterns, of a particular social class, region, or group. Usually dialect differs from the standard form of the language because it possesses its own unique grammar, pronunciation, and vocabulary.

In "To a Mouse," Burns's use of dialect adds to the poem's appeal and the reader's appreciation. If the poem had been written in standard English, it would lack the sense of immediacy and the color achieved in such lines as:

That wee bit heap o' leaves an' stibble, / Has cost thee mony a weary nibble!

By using Scottish dialect, Burns succeeded in capturing his people's tenderness for and intimacy with nature and their shared acceptance of the prospect of "nought but grief an' pain" in the wake of "promised joy."

DIRECTIONS: The following lines are from "To a Mouse." Rewrite each line in standard English and explain the effect that the use of Scottish dialect alone can achieve.

1. "Wee, sleekit, cow'rin', tim'rous beastie,"

   _____

   _____

   _____

2. "A daimen icker in a thrave / 'S a sma' request:"

   _____

   _____

   _____

3. "An' naething, now, to big a new ane,"

   _____

   _____

   _____

4. "To thole the winter's sleety dribble, / An' cranreuch cauld!"

   _____

   _____

   _____

5. "But, Mousie, thou art no thy lane,"

   _____

   _____

   _____

"The Lamb," "The Tyger," "Infant Sorrow," and **"The Chimney Sweeper"**
by William Blake

Build Vocabulary

Spelling Strategy Both the long and short *i* sounds are usually spelled with either an *i* or a *y*. Some words containing the long *i* sound are *high*, *my*, and *aspire*. Some words containing the short *i* sound are *hit*, *symmetry*, and *sinews*.

Using the Root *-spir-*

A. DIRECTIONS: Each of the following sentences includes an italicized word that contains the word root *-spir-*, which means "breath" or "life." Fill in each blank with a word or phrase to complete the sentence and reveal the meaning of the italicized word.

1. If the young woman is *spirited*, she _____.

2. If he was *dispirited* by the bad news, he _____.

3. If we waited to see what would *transpire*, we _____.

4. If the council member's term *expired*, it _____.

5. If the poem *inspires* the reader, it _____.

Using the Word Bank

vales	symmetry	aspire

B. DIRECTIONS: Match each word in the left column with its definition in the right column. Write the letter of the definition on the line next to the word it defines.

____ 1. vales   a. balance of forms

____ 2. symmetry   b. hollows

____ 3. aspire   c. seek after

C. DIRECTIONS: Complete each sentence by filling in the blank with one of the words from the word bank.

1. The rolling hills and grassy _____ were the landscape of his earliest memories.

2. Early on he learned to appreciate the veins of leaves, the wings of butterflies—in short, all of nature's _____.

3. With all of these influences it was only natural that he would _____ to become a nature photographer.

Unit 4: Rebels and Dreamers (1790–1832)

"The Lamb," "The Tyger," "Infant Sorrow," and **"The Chimney Sweeper"**
by William Blake

Grammar and Style: Commonly Confused Words: *Rise* and *Raise*

The forms of the irregular verb *rise*, which means "to get up," are often confused with those of the regular verb *raise*, which means "to lift or elevate." The forms of the verb *rise* are *rise*, *rose*, *had risen*. The forms of the verb *raise* are *raise*, *raised*, *had raised*. Note the following examples:

Rise

Present: We *rise* early in the morning.

Past: I *rose* before the sun came up.

Past Participle: We *had risen* early in order to catch the first train.

Raise

Present: He *raises* the canoe onto the truck's roof.

Past: I *raised* the bookshelf up a few inches.

Past Participle: She *had raised* both of the ladders onto the platform.

A. Practice: Underline the forms of the verb *rise* or *raise* in each of the following lines. In the blank, identify whether the verb is a form of *rise* or *raise* and identify the form in which it appears. The first one is done for you.

1. The King <u>rose</u> one morning and decided he wanted to conquer the world.

   rise: past tense _____

2. One night the King had a dream that the sun had risen in the west.

   _____

3. He called his ministers into council and raised the issue of conquest.

   _____

4. They raised that was composed of the land's most skilled and courageous knights.

   _____

5. He took this dream as a bad omen and doubts rose in his mind.

   _____

B. Writing Application: Rewrite each sentence using the verb tense of *rise* or *raise* indicated in parentheses.

1. The sun had risen over the far horizon. (present)

   _____

2. We rise and gather up our camp equipment. (past)

   _____

3. Abigail and John raised the kayak onto the roof of the car. (past participle)

   _____

4. I watch as morning mist rises from the nearby river. (past)

   _____

5. I had raised the tent yesterday and now I had to take it down. (past)

   _____

"The Lamb," "The Tyger," "Infant Sorrow," and **"The Chimney Sweeper"**
by William Blake

Reading Strategy: Using Visuals as a Key to Meaning

When you read any form of literature that has accompanying illustrations, you can **use the visuals as a key to meaning** by studying the details of the illustrations and thinking about how they relate to the information provided by the author's words. Look at visuals and consider how they support or add to information about characters or events. Blake's vivid illustrations accompany both "The Lamb" and "The Tyger." A late-nineteenth-century engraving, accompanies the poems "The Chimney Sweeper" and "Infant Sorrow" in your textbook. By looking closely at the details of these illustrations you can gather clues about Blake's meaning and about the characters, ideas, or situations described in the poems.

DIRECTIONS: Use the graphic organizer below to help you use the visuals as a key to Blake's meaning. Study the illustrations as you read each poem. Gather and chart clues that support or add to information in the poems. The first one has been done for you.

Poem	What the Illustrations Add to the Meaning
"The Lamb"	1. One of the lambs in the illustration is eating from the boy's hand, supporting the description of the lamb as meek and docile.
"The Tyger"	2.
"The Chimney Sweeper"	3.
"Infant Sorrow"	4.

"The Lamb," "The Tyger," "Infant Sorrow," and **"The Chimney Sweeper"**
by William Blake

Literary Analysis: Symbols

Poets sometimes create their own **symbols**, but frequently they draw on symbols that should be familiar to everyone. Such symbols come from religious texts such as the Bible, as well as from stories that are common throughout a culture, such as a fairy tale or a beloved book. The more associations the reader can make with a given symbol in a poem, the richer the appreciation of the poem.

DIRECTIONS: Following are some of the symbols in Blake's poetry. For each symbol, give one symbolic meaning and identify the source of the symbolic connection.

1. lamb

    Meaning: _____

    Source: _____

2. fire

    Meaning: _____

    Source: _____

3. swaddling bands

    Meaning: _____

    Source: _____

4. child

    Meaning: _____

    Source: _____

5. anvil

    Meaning: _____

    Source: _____

6. angel

    Meaning: _____

    Source: _____

Introduction to *Frankenstein* by Mary Wollstonecraft Shelley

Build Vocabulary

Spelling Strategy Most words ending in the suffix that sounds like *seed* use the *-cede* spelling. For example, *accede, recede, precede,* and *secede* all end in *-cede.* However, there are four words that use the spelling *-ceed* or *-sede*: *exceed, proceed, succeed,* and *supersede.*

Using Related Words: *Phantasm* and *Fantasy*

A. DIRECTIONS: The word *phantasm* means "supernatural form or shape." It is related to the word *fantasy*, which means "a product of the imagination." Each italicized word in the following sentences is related to *phantasm* or *fantasy*. Replace each one with a synonymous word or phrase. Write the new word or phrase on the line following the sentence.

1. To Dexter, the shadows looked like a parade of *fantastic* creatures. _____

2. When Sono opened her eyes, the *phantasm* was still there. _____

3. Angela liked to *fantasize* about quitting her job and moving to Alaska. _____

4. Scowling, Greg pronounced, "If you think you're entitled to another week of vacation, you're living in a *fantasy* land!" _____

5. The special effects in that movie were *phantasmagorical*! _____

Using the Word Bank

appendage	ungenial	acceded
platitude	phantasm	incitement

B. DIRECTIONS: Fill in each blank with a word from the Word Bank to complete the sentence.

1. Alex _____ to Lori's request not to reveal the plans for the surprise party.

2. Without much imagination, the speaker often used a _____ like "All's well that ends well."

3. The shimmering mist in Margo's office turned out to be steam from her teacup, not a _____.

4. The stock market always seems to crash during the _____ weather of October.

5. Tasha's encouragement was all the _____ Li needed to convince her to apply for the job.

6. Dan's pencil looked like an extra _____ growing above his ear.

Unit 4: Rebels and Dreamers (1790–1832)

Introduction to *Frankenstein* by Mary Wollstonecraft Shelley

Grammar and Style: Past Participial Phrases

A **past participle** is the form of a verb that is used along with a form of the verb "to have." In the following sentences, the past participle is italicized.

Juan wasn't hungry because he had already *eaten*.

I have *had* enough of your teasing!

A **past participial phrase** is a phrase that includes a past participle and acts as an adjective. The past participle and all the other words in the phrase work together to modify a noun or pronoun. In the following sentence, the past participial phrase is italicized.

Percy Bysshe Shelley wrote a ghost story *based on his childhood experiences*.

The past participial phrase "based on his childhood experiences" acts as an adjective for the noun "story."

A. Practice: Underline the past participial phrase in each sentence below, and circle the word it modifies.

1. The illustrious poets also, annoyed by the platitude of prose, speedily relinquished their uncongenial task.

2. . . . he advanced to the couch of the blooming youths, cradled in healthy sleep.

3. Eternal sorrow sat upon his face as he bent down and kissed the foreheads of the boys, who from that hour withered like flowers snapped from the stalk.

4. He would hope that, left to itself, the slight spark of life which he had communicated would fade. . . .

B. Writing Application: Rewrite each of these sentences, adding a past participial phrase that acts as an adjective to modify the italicized word.

1. On Friday, all her best *students* were late to class.

_____

2. The *plants* on Sara's windowsill withered and died.

_____

3. The *house* was more dilapidated than haunted.

_____

4. Several of the *stuffed animals* were in danger of falling to the floor.

_____

5. *Samuel* did not listen to the train conductor's announcements and consequently missed his stop.

_____

_____

Introduction to *Frankenstein* by Mary Wollstonecraft Shelley

Reading Strategy: Predicting

Making predictions about what will happen in a literary work keeps you involved in your reading. Use clues that the writer provides, along with what you learn about the characters and the pattern in which the work is organized. As you read, check your predictions and revise them as necessary.

DIRECTIONS: In the lines following each excerpt, record what predictions you might make about Mary Shelly's novel Frankenstein.

1. "'How I, then a young girl, came to think of, and to dilate upon, so very hideous an idea?'"

_____

_____

_____

2. "I busied myself to think of a story—a story to rival those which had excited us to this task. One which would speak to the mysterious fears of our nature . . . "

_____

_____

_____

3. " . . . various philosophical doctrines were discussed, and among others the nature of the principle of life and whether there was any probability of its ever being discovered and communicated."

_____

_____

_____

4. "When I placed my head on my pillow, I did not sleep, nor could I be said to think. My imagination, unbidden, possessed and guided me, gifting the successive images that arose in my mind with a vividness far beyond the usual bounds of reverie."

_____

_____

_____

Unit 4: Rebels and Dreamers (1790–1832)

Name _____   Date _____

Introduction to *Frankenstein* by Mary Wollstonecraft Shelley

Literary Analysis: The Gothic Tradition

To the Romantics of the early nineteenth century, the **Gothic** elements of mystery, variety, richness, and primitive wildness suggested the natural, free, authentic aspects of life that they valued. The Gothic novel was characterized by mystery, chivalry, and horror. The Gothic tradition emphasized setting and plot more than character; often, an atmosphere of brooding and terror pervaded Gothic novels.

DIRECTIONS: Answer the following questions about how Mary Shelley's Introduction to *Frankenstein* reflects the Gothic tradition.

1. How might the Swiss setting in which Mary Wollstonecraft Shelley found herself in the summer of 1816 have inspired her to write a Gothic novel?

   _____

   _____

   _____

   _____

   _____

   _____

2. How did the stories that the writers read to amuse themselves help produce a frame of mind conducive to Gothic writing?

   _____

   _____

   _____

   _____

   _____

3. How is the waking dream that Mary Wollstonecraft Shelley describes characteristic of the Gothic tradition?

   _____

   _____

   _____

   _____

   _____

"The Oval Portrait" by Edgar Allan Poe

Build Vocabulary: Language of the Supernatural

A supernatural horror story gains its success from a gripping plot and the appropriate use of the conventions of the genre. In addition, a writer must use vocabulary that evokes a mood of supernatural suspense. Sometimes, words that in and of themselves do not evoke such a mood gain their power from the context in which they are used.

DIRECTIONS: Choose the word from the box that best completes each numbered blank within the paragraph. Then, write a sentence of your own using the word in the context of the supernatural.

spirited	delirium	dreamy
fancy	spell	secret

   In my dream, I walked down a hallway lined with paintings so (1) ____ that I felt a sense of (2) ____ . A door opened at the end of the hall, and a young child stood quietly, her eyes in a (3) ____ state. Then, as if a curtain parted to reveal a (4) ____ , the (5) ____ was broken. The child had turned into an old crone, who cackled in a deep voice: "What is your (6) ____ , my sweet?"

1. word: _____ sentence: _____

   _____

   _____

2. word: _____ sentence: _____

   _____

   _____

3. word: _____ sentence: _____

   _____

   _____

4. word: _____ sentence: _____

   _____

   _____

5. word: _____ sentence: _____

   _____

   _____

6. word: _____ sentence: _____

   _____

   _____

"The Oval Portrait" by Edgar Allan Poe

Cultural Connection: Supernatural Horror

Supernatural horror stories have fascinated—and terrified—readers since the genre was developed in the eighteenth century. In recent decades, such tales have made the transition to film, television, and radio. Whatever the form, a tale of supernatural horror makes uses of a number of devices: suspense, psychological terror, dreamlike states, and the semblance of reality.

DIRECTIONS: Use the chart below to identify some of the devices used by Edgar Allan Poe and by the author of a more recent work of supernatural horror. Then, use the third column of the chart to plan a supernatural horror story of your own, using the completed entries as a guide.

Devices	"The Oval Portrait"	Recent Horror Story	Your Horror Story
suspense			
psychological terror			
dreamlike states			
semblance of reality			

Poetry of William Wordsworth

Build Vocabulary

Spelling Strategy In American English, the ending -ize is used in several hundred words, such as *anatomize*, whereas the ending -ise is used in only about thirty common words, such as *exercise*.

Using Related Words: *Anatomize*

A. DIRECTIONS: Answer the following questions about *anatomize* and words related to it.

1. What does *anatomize* mean? _____

2. What type of tool might an anatomist use? _____

3. If someone were making an anatomic study of mole rats, would she be more interested in the rats' feeding habits or in their internal organs? _____

4. In 1958, Robert Travers wrote a book called *Anatomy of a Murder*. How do you think the book treats the crime in question? _____

Using the Word Bank

recompense	roused	presumption	anatomize
confounded	sordid	stagnant	

B. DIRECTIONS: Each item below consists of a related pair of words in CAPITAL LETTERS followed by four lettered pairs of words. Choose the pair that best expresses a relationship similar to that expressed in the pair in capital letters. Circle the letter of your choice.

_____ 1. EGOTIST : PRESUMPTION ::
    a. traitor : treachery
    b. doctor : stethoscope
    c. coward : bravery
    d. lawyer : summation

_____ 2. CONFOUNDED : CLEAR-HEADED ::
    a. enraged : even-tempered
    b. amused : laughing
    c. saddened : regretful
    d. wondrous : awesome

_____ 3. RECOMPENSE : SALARY ::
    a. fairness : injustice
    b. indebtedness : mortgage
    c. heat : perspiration
    d. interest : payment

_____ 4. ROUSED : EXCITED ::
    a. sympathetic : saddened
    b. curious : uninterested
    c. offended : insulted
    d. sleeping : awakened

_____ 5. SORDID : FILTHY ::
    a. frigid : lukewarm
    b. amusing : ridiculous
    c. untimely : early
    d. angry : irate

_____ 6. SWAMP : STAGNANT ::
    a. ocean : salty
    b. river : flowing
    c. pond : tidal
    d. lake : frozen

_____ 7. ANATOMIZE : DISSECT ::
    a. infantilize : mature
    b. categorize : difference
    c. prioritize : equate
    d. analyze : study

Unit 4: Rebels and Dreamers (1790–1832)

Poetry of William Wordsworth

Grammar and Style: Present Participial Phrases

A participle is a verb that is used as an adjective: The *folded* blanket is warmer. A present participle uses the present tense: A *rolling* stone gathers no moss. A **present participial phrase** consists of a present participle plus one or more words that modify it. The entire phrase is used as an adjective.

Example: *Walking down the street,* I ran into my friend Ken.

A. Practice: Read each of the following lines from "Lines Composed a Few Miles Above Tintern Abbey." If the underlined words are a present participial phrase, write "yes." If not, write "no" and explain why not.

1. "And passing even into my purer mind / . . . feelings too/Of unremembered pleasure . . ."

_____

2. "we are laid asleep/In body, and become a living soul. . . ."

_____

3. "Have hung upon the beatings of my heart . . ."

_____

4. "more like a man/Flying from something that he dreads . . ."

_____

5. "The sounding cataract/Haunted me like a passion . . . "

_____

B. Writing Application: Rewrite each of the following sentences, adding a present participial phrase that modifies the subject.

1. I lost my key.

_____

2. That dog looks like my dog.

_____

3. The car is out of control.

_____

4. The man seems familiar.

_____

5. The movie is great!

_____

Poetry of William Wordsworth

Reading Strategy: Using Literary Context

Romantic poets and writers, like Romantic musicians and artists, were revolutionary in their time. They were revolting against an earlier literary movement called the European Enlightenment. The Enlightenment stressed intellect and reason. It said that all people were essentially the same, no matter who they were or where they lived. The Romantics stressed the importance of emotions over reason, and believed in the importance of each individual's expression, based on his or her own feelings and life experiences.

DIRECTIONS: Use this graphic organizer to help you record Romantic elements from Wordsworth's poems. When you find a passage that exemplifies Romantic ideals, think about it. Decide why it exemplifies the Romantic period rather than the European Enlightenment. One passage has already been chosen and analyzed for you.

Passage	Why Passage Characterizes Romantic Period, Not Enlightenment
1. "But oft . . . / . . . I have owed to them / . . . sensations sweet,/ Felt in the blood, and felt along the heart;/ . . . feelings too/Of unremembered pleasure . . ." ("Tintern Abbey," lines 25–30)	It describes the emotional response that memories of the landscape provoked in the narrator rather than describing the landscape rationally and realistically.
2.	
3.	
4.	
5.	

Poetry of William Wordsworth

Literary Analysis: Romanticism

During the European Enlightenment, a period that preceded Romanticism, writers and poets believed that intellect and reason were the most important aspects of humanity. They also felt that life was a universal experience for all people, no matter their background or living situation. Romanticism argued against those beliefs. Romantic poets felt that emotions were at least as important as reason, if not more so. They felt that each individual was unique, and that each person's individual life and experiences were important. They also believed that turning away from intellect and toward emotions would lead one away from society and technology and closer to nature.

DIRECTIONS: Read the lines from the poems, and answer the questions that follow.

> Though changed, no doubt, from what I was when first
> I came among these hills; when like a roe
> I bounded o'er the mountains, by the sides
> Of the deep rivers, and the lonely streams. . . .
> ("Tintern Abbey")

1. How does the narrator describe his younger self? What is he implying with these descriptions?

_____

_____

> Little we see in Nature that is ours;
> We have given our hearts away, a sordid boon! . . .
> . . . —Great God! I'd rather be
> A Pagan suckled in a creed outworn;
> So might I, standing on this pleasant lea,
> Have glimpses that would make me less forlorn;
> Have sight of Proteus rising from the sea;
> Or hear old Triton blow his wreathed horn.
> ("The World Is Too Much with Us")

2. Do you think that Wordsworth really wished he could believe in ancient Greek gods? If you do, explain why. If you don't, explain what he meant instead.

_____

_____

> Milton! thou should'st be living at this hour:
> England hath need of thee. . .
> . . . Thy soul was like a Star, and dwelt apart:
> Thou hadst a voice whose sound was like the sea:
> Pure as the naked heavens, majestic, free. . . .
> ("London, 1802")

3. How does Wordsworth describe Milton? Why do you think he describes him this way?

_____

_____

"The Rime of the Ancient Mariner" and **"Kubla Khan"**
by Samuel Taylor Coleridge

Build Vocabulary

Spelling Strategy In American English, words ending in the sound -ence usually end with the spelling -nce, as in reverence. However, many do end with the -nse spelling, such as tense, suspense, offense, and nonsense.

Using the Root -journ-

A. DIRECTIONS: Each of the following words contains the Latin root -journ-, which comes from the French and Latin words for "day." For each of the following sentences, choose one of the five words or phrases to replace the italicized word or phrase.

adjourn	du jour	journal
journalism	journey	

1. The long day's *trip* had wiped me out completely. _____

2. I'm not so interested in writing fiction; I prefer *reporting*. _____

3. Kevin wrote all of his secret sorrows in his *diary*. _____

4. At midnight, the council finally decided that it was time for the meeting *to end for the day*.

_____

5. Maggie ordered the radish salad and the soup *of the day*. _____

Using the Word Bank

averred	sojourn	expiated
reverence	sinuous	tumult

B. DIRECTIONS: Choose the letter of the description that best fits each word below. Write the letters on the lines provided.

____ 1. tumult
    a. commotion
    b. height
    c. depth
    d. gathering

____ 2. sinuous
    a. weak
    b. strong
    c. straight
    d. curving

____ 3. averred
    a. expressed ignorance
    b. stated to be true
    c. stated to be false
    d. defended weakly

____ 4. expiated
    a. breathed
    b. blamed
    c. explained
    d. atoned

____ 5. sojourn
    a. stay for a while
    b. visit briefly
    c. travel widely
    d. carry to

____ 6. reverence
    a. sadness
    b. veneration
    c. revisitation
    d. abhorrence

"The Rime of the Ancient Mariner" and **"Kubla Khan"**
by Samuel Taylor Coleridge

Grammar and Style: Inverted Word Order

In standard English word order, the subject precedes the verb, the verb precedes the direct object, and a prepositional phrase follows the word it modifies. Sometimes a writer uses **inverted word order** to achieve a certain effect. The following lines from "Kubla Khan" provide an example.

Inverted word order: In Xanadu did Kubla Khan/A stately pleasure dome decree. . . .

Normal word order: Kubla Khan did decree a stately pleasure dome in Xanadu. . . .

A. Practice: For each of the following phrases, identify the sentence parts that have been inverted. Then rewrite the phrase or sentence, using normal word order.

from "The Rime of the Ancient Mariner":

1. "At length did cross an Albatross. . . ."

   _____

   _____

2. "Instead of the cross, the Albatross/About my neck was hung."

   _____

   _____

from "Kubla Khan":

3. "Where was heard the mingled measure/From the fountain and the caves."

   _____

   _____

4. "A damsel with a dulcimer/In a vision once I saw. . . ."

   _____

   _____

B. Writing Application: Rewrite each of these sentences using inverted word order.

1. I saw a sprite in that light.

   _____

2. His fingers wrapped around the pole; I knew that it would snap.

   _____

3. We came to the port to see the boats.

   _____

4. The man and his dog ran up the walk to fetch the injured bird.

   _____

5. Soft music slipped into my ears and sent me right to sleep.

   _____

"The Rime of the Ancient Mariner" and **"Kubla Khan"**
by Samuel Taylor Coleridge

Reading Strategy: Analyzing Poetic Effects

One of the primary characteristics that sets verse apart from prose is the range of poetic and sound devices commonly used in poetry. These devices enhance the musical qualities of the language by pleasing the ear, but they also serve to emphasize meaning and create mood. By paying attention to these devices you can become more sensitive to the nuances and effects of poetic language. The following are several different types of sound devices:

alliteration: repetition of consonant sounds at the beginnings of words

consonance: repetition of consonant sounds at the ends of words

assonance: repetition of vowel sounds in nearby words or syllables

internal rhyme: rhymes occurring within a poetic line

ordinary repetition: repetition of entire words

DIRECTIONS: Use this chart to keep track of poetic effects as you read "The Rime of the Ancient Mariner" and "Kubla Khan." Each time you encounter a poetic sound device, write the example in the left column. Then, in the right column, explain the effect of the device, or how it enhances the text. The first passage has been done for you.

Line or Phrase	Device	Effect
1. "Water, water, every-where,/Nor any drop to drink." ("Rime," lines 121–122)	repetition and alliteration	Repetition of the word *water* and of the *w* sound emphasizes the amount of water. Repetition of the *dr-* sound in *drop* and *drink* also emphasizes the lack of drinking water. The differing alliteration in each line contrasts the amount of water with the lack of drinking water.
2.		
3.		
4.		
5.		

Unit 4: Rebels and Dreamers (1790–1832)

"The Rime of the Ancient Mariner" and **"Kubla Khan"**
by Samuel Taylor Coleridge

Literary Analysis: Poetic Sound Devices

Alliteration is the repetition of a consonant sound at the beginnings of words. **Consonance** is the repetition of consonant sounds in stressed syllables with dissimilar vowel sounds. **Assonance** is repetition of vowel sounds in stressed syllables with dissimilar consonant sounds. **Internal rhyme** is the use of rhyming words within a line.

DIRECTIONS: In each of the following passages from "The Rime of the Ancient Mariner" and "Kubla Kahn," certain letters are italicized. For each passage, write on the line the sound device that is used.

1. "As who pursued with ye*ll* and b*l*ow" _____

2. "The ice did spl*it* with a thunder-f*it*" _____

3. "*H*e *h*olds *h*im with *h*is skinny *h*and" _____

4. "The ship was ch*eered*, the harbor cl*eared*" _____

5. "And we did spea*k* only to brea*k*" _____

6. "*R*ed as a *r*ose is she" _____

7. "All in a h*o*t and c*o*pper sky" _____

8. "The Wedding G*uest* he beat his br*east*" _____

9. "The death f*i*res danced at n*igh*t" _____

10. "The *f*air breeze blew, the white *f*oam *f*lew" _____

11. "His *f*lashing eyes, his *f*loating hair!" _____

12. "A *d*amsel with a *d*ulcimer" _____

13. "For *h*e on *h*oneydew *h*ath fed," _____

14. "And c*l*ose your eyes with h*o*ly dread" _____

15. "And from this chasm, with c*ea*seless turmoil s*ee*thing" _____

"She Walks in Beauty," from *Childe Harold's Pilgrimage,* and **from** *Don Juan*
by George Gordon, Lord Byron

Build Vocabulary

Spelling Strategy When the suffix *-ous* is added to an existing word that ends in a consonant, such as *poison*, you can usually just add on the suffix: *poisonous*. However, when the existing word ends with a vowel, the vowel is either dropped or changed. For example, *beauty* + *-ous* = *beauteous*, *pity* + *-ous* = *piteous*, *adventure* + *-ous* = *adventurous*, and *fame* + *-ous* = *famous*.

Using the Suffix *-ous*

A. Directions: The following words all contain the suffix *-ous*, meaning "full of." In the blanks, complete each sentence with the appropriate word or words from the list.

famous	delicious	miraculous	rebellious
ominous	adventurous	humorous	

1. The mushrooms tasted _____, but they were poisonous.

2. The _____ hero walked forward boldly into the storm, undeterred by
   the _____ lightning flashing all around him.

3. The politician was _____ for always beginning his speeches with a
   _____ anecdote.

4. Maude made a _____ recovery following cardiac surgery.

5. Feeling _____, Theo refused to celebrate the holidays.

Using the Word Bank

arbiter	tempests	torrid
fathomless	retort	insensible
credulous	copious	avarice

B. Directions: Match each word in the left column with its definition in the right column. Write the letter of the definition on the line next to the word it defines.

____ 1. retort   a. willing to believe

____ 2. credulous   b. numb

____ 3. copious   c. plentiful

____ 4. avarice   d. greed

____ 5. insensible   e. storms

____ 6. fathomless   f. reply with a wisecrack

____ 7. arbiter   g. too deep to measure

____ 8. tempests   h. very hot

____ 9. torrid   i. judge

"She Walks in Beauty," from *Childe Harold's Pilgrimage,* and from *Don Juan*
by George Gordon, Lord Byron

Grammar and Style: Subject and Verb Agreement

Every verb form that you write should agree in number with the noun that is its subject. A singular subject must have a singular verb, and a plural subject must have a plural verb.

Singular subject and verb: *Time writes* no wrinkle on thine azure brow. . . .

Where *a thought* serenely sweet *expresses*/How pure, how dear its dwelling place.

Plural subject and verb: *Time and adversity write* no wrinkle on thine azure brow. . . .Where *thoughts* serenely sweet *express*/How pure, how dear their dwelling place.

A. Practice: Check each of the following sentences to see if its subject and verb agree in number. If they agree, write *agree* in the blank next to the sentence. If they do not agree, write the correct form of the verb in the blank next to the sentence. If there are two verbs, be sure to write the correct form of each in the blank.

1. She *walks* in beauty, like the night. . . . _____

2. The smiles that win, the tints that glow, but *tells* of days in goodness spent . . .

    _____

3. There *are* a pleasure in the pathless woods. . . . _____

4. These *is* thy toys, and, as the snowy flake, / They *melts* into thy yeast of waves. . . .

    _____

5. their decay/*Have dried* up realms to deserts. . . . _____

6. *Roll* on, thou deep and dark blue ocean—*roll!* _____

B. Writing Application: Write a sentence using each word or phrase below as the subject. Make sure that the verb agrees with the subject in each case.

1. raindrop

    _____

2. dancer

    _____

3. coffee and tea

    _____

4. olives

    _____

5. strangers

    _____

6. grammar

    _____

"She Walks in Beauty," from *Childe Harold's Pilgrimage*, and from *Don Juan*
by George Gordon, Lord Byron

Reading Strategy: Questioning

Poetry is meant to be read several times. You might read a poem once to get a general sense of its themes. On another reading, you might focus on the language and rhythm of the poem. Next you might pay special attention to its images. At least one of your readings should be devoted to achieving a basic understanding of what the poet is trying to communicate. You can do this by reading actively—asking questions about the poem and answering them. Ask questions that use the words *who, what, where, when,* and *why.* For example, consider the excerpt in your textbook from *Childe Harold's Pilgrimage*:

- **Question:** *What* does the speaker hope to communicate? **Answer:** He expresses admiration for the ocean.

- **Question:** *Why* does the speaker admire the ocean? **Answer:** Humans and human activities are insignificant in comparison to the ocean; the ocean is unchanging; it rules its domain and cannot be tamed by humans.

DIRECTIONS: Read the excerpt in your textbook from *Don Juan.* Write questions about the poem using the words listed below. Then answer your questions.

1. Who _____
   _____?
   _____
   _____

2. What _____
   _____?
   _____
   _____

3. What _____
   _____?
   _____
   _____

4. Why _____
   _____?
   _____
   _____

5. Why _____
   _____?
   _____
   _____

Unit 4: Rebels and Dreamers (1790–1832)

"She Walks in Beauty," from *Childe Harold's Pilgrimage,* and from *Don Juan*
by George Gordon, Lord Byron

Literary Analysis: Figurative Language

To build powerful images, writers use **figurative language**, or figures of speech. Through figurative language, things that might at first seem completely unrelated are linked together.

Similes make comparisons using the word *like* or *as:*
   The empty house was like a tomb.

Metaphors make comparisons without using *like* or *as:*
   The empty house was a tomb.

Personification gives human characteristics to nonhuman subjects:
   The empty house whispered of its past.

A. DIRECTIONS: Following are passages from various poems. On the line at the right, identify the figure of speech that is used in each passage.

1. "The lowered pulses of the river beat. . ." _____

2. "I tell you the past is a bucket of ashes." _____

3. The fields "were patched like one wide crazy quilt . . ." _____

4. ". . . drowsy lights along the paths/Are dim and pearled" _____

5. "The twigs are snapping like brittle bones." _____

B. DIRECTIONS: Following is a series of items beside which are listed various types of figurative language. Describe each item in a sentence using the figure of speech indicated.

1. storm clouds (personification) _____

_____

_____

2. courage (personification) _____

_____

_____

3. spring rain (simile) _____

_____

_____

4. an eagle (personification) _____

_____

_____

5. the motorcycle (metaphor) _____

_____

_____

"Ozymandias," "Ode to the West Wind," and **"To a Skylark"**
by Percy Bysshe Shelley

Build Vocabulary

Spelling Strategy The suffix -*ity* is used more often than the suffix -*ety* to end nouns in English. For example, *calamity* and *atrocity* both end in -*ity*. The suffix -*ety* is used when -*ty* is added to adjectives ending in -*e*, as in *nicety* and *safety*, and when -*ty* is added to word stems ending in -*i*, as in *satiety*, *anxiety*, and *variety*.

Using the Root -*puls*-

A. DIRECTIONS: The word root -*puls*- means "push" or "drive." Using your knowledge of the word root -*puls*- and the information in parentheses, replace each italicized word or phrase with a word that includes the word root -*puls*-. Write the new word on the line that follows the sentence.

compulsive (*com*- = with)	repulse (*re*- = against)
pulsar (-*ar* = of or relating to)	impulsiveness (*im*- = toward)

1. Astronomers began to pick up waves of electromagnetic radiation that were being emitted from a previously unknown *neutron star*. _____

2. Because he is *a/an obsessive* shopper, Isaiah can't save money. _____

3. Maddie regretted her *spontaneity* after she threw her book out the window. _____

4. The army used tanks to *drive back* the attacking forces. _____.

Using the Word Bank

visage	verge	sepulcher	impulse
blithe	profuse	vernal	satiety

B. DIRECTIONS: Fill in each blank with a word from the Word Bank.

1. Mary visited the graveyard to put flowers by her ancestor's _____.

2. It was difficult to stop the flooding because the flow of water was so _____

3. The _____ equinox signals the first day of spring.

4. Don't ever show your sorry _____ around here again!

5. After the pie-eating contest, Harold was beyond _____; he was on the _____ of being sick.

6. José loved his grandmother, but her _____ response to even the most depressing events irritated him.

7. When the rescue ship sailed into the harbor and unloaded the survivors, Sarah obeyed her sudden _____ to kneel and kiss the solid ground.

"Ozymandias," "Ode to the West Wind," and **"To a Skylark"**
by Percy Bysshe Shelley

Grammar and Style: Subjunctive Mood

The **subjunctive mood** is used to refer to possible rather than actual actions. For example, writers use the subjunctive mood to suggest that something might happen, express doubt that something will happen, voice a desire for something to happen, or note that if one action occurs another is likely to follow. The subjunctive can be formed with the plural past tense of the verb *to be (were)* or with helping verbs like *could, would,* or *should.*

Subjunctive:	**Not subjunctive:**
The skylark could fly away.	The skylark will fly away.
The skylark should fly away.	The skylark is flying away.
I insist that the skylark fly away.	The skylark flew away.
The skylark would fall out of the sky, were it not to spread its wings and fly.	The skylark has flown away.

A. Practice: Underline the subjunctive verbs in the following verses from "Ode to the West Wind."

If I were a dead leaf thou mightest bear;
If I were a swift cloud to fly with thee;
A wave to pant beneath thy power, and share
The impulse of thy strength, only less free
Than thou, O uncontrollable! If even
I were as in my boyhood, and could be
The comrade of thy wanderings over Heaven,
As then, when to outstrip thy skyey speed
Scarce seemed a vision; I would ne'er have striven
As thus with thee in prayer in my sore need.

B. Writing Application: Rewrite each of the following sentences, changing the verb form to the subjunctive. Be sure to change the rest of the sentence too, if necessary.

1. That apple cannot fall far from the tree.

   _____

2. Samantha will hurt herself when she loses her balance on those slippery steps.

   _____

3. I am sorry you are not happy about this decision.

   _____

4. Marty refused to resign from the company.

   _____

5. Bruno is not able to talk, even though he may want to—he's only a dog.

   _____

"Ozymandias," "Ode to the West Wind," and "To a Skylark"
by Percy Bysshe Shelley

Reading Strategy: Responding to Imagery

Poets use descriptive language, or **imagery**, to make their writing seem more real and vivid to the reader. They do this by appealing to a reader's physical senses with visual details, sounds, smells, tastes, and textures. In order to respond to a poem's imagery, you must use your imagination and draw on your life experience. For example, you might respond to Shelley's mention of rain by imagining what rain feels like against your skin.

DIRECTIONS: As you read these poems, copy several passages that contain vivid images in the first column of the graphic organizer below. In the second column, describe the image in your own words. Include details that Shelley implies but may not specifically mention. Remember to include sounds, smells, tastes, and textures, as well as sights, if appropriate. In the third column list the senses (sight, hearing, touch, smell, or taste) through which the image can be experienced.

Passage	Description of Image	Senses
1. "Round the decay / Of that colossal wreck, boundless and bare, / The lone and level sands stretch far away." ("Ozymandias," lines 12–14)	The statue is surrounded by a vast empty desert where it is dry and hot and there is no sound but the wind.	sight, touch, sound
2.		
3.		
4.		
5.		

"Ozymandias," "Ode to the West Wind," and **"To a Skylark"**
by Percy Bysshe Shelley

Literary Analysis: Imagery

Poets use vivid **imagery** for many reasons. Appealing to a reader's senses of sight, hearing, taste, smell, and touch can make the poem seem more real to the reader. Certain images may also inspire a reader to respond with feelings of awe, disgust, fear, desire, amusement, or joy, to name just a few. But poets do not use images purely to keep the reader's interest—often, the images in a poem help to develop the poem's theme. For example, in "To a Skylark," Shelley uses imagery to reinforce the theme of creativity. He compares the bird to the moon, a poet, a highborn maiden, a glowworm, and a rose. The subject of each image emits or creates a beautiful thing: The moon and glowworm both emit light, the poet creates poetry, the maiden sings, and the rose emits a pleasant odor.

DIRECTIONS: Answer the following questions on the lines provided.

> . . . Two vast and trunkless legs of stone
> Stand in the desert. Near them, on the sand,
> Half sunk, a shattered visage lies, whose frown,
> And wrinkled lip, and sneer of cold command . . .
> ("Ozymandias," lines 2–5)

1. To what senses does this image appeal?

   _____

2. What emotions might this image provoke in a reader?

   _____

   _____

3. How is this image related to the theme of the poem?

   _____

   _____

   _____

> Nothing beside remains. Round the decay
> Of that colossal wreck, boundless and bare,
> The lone and level sands stretch far away.
> ("Ozymandias," lines 12–14)

4. To what senses does this image appeal?

   _____

5. What emotions might this image provoke in a reader?

   _____

   _____

6. How is this image related to the theme of the poem?

   _____

   _____

Poetry of John Keats

Build Vocabulary

Spelling Strategy When -ing is added to a word ending in a consonant, such as *teem*, simply add the -ing to the original word: *teeming*. However, when the original word ends in an -e, such as *bake*, the -e is dropped: *baking*. Exceptions are *eyeing* and *dyeing*.

Using the Suffix -age

A. DIRECTIONS: Each of the following sentences contains an italicized word ending with the suffix -age, one meaning of which is "state, condition, or quality." Using the word's context along with what you know about this suffix, write a definition of each *italicized* word in the blank.

1. The backyard always floods because of poor *drainage.*

   _____

2. Alfred and Olivia wanted nothing more than to be joined in *marriage.*

   _____

3. The terrorists kept their prisoners in *bondage* for thirty days.

   _____

4. The war led to a great *shortage* of many goods.

   _____

5. The garage and its contents lay in *wreckage* around me.

   _____

Using the Word Bank

ken	surmise	gleaned
teeming	vintage	requiem

B. DIRECTIONS: Fill in the blank in each sentence with the correct word from the word bank.

1. I _____ that the trouble began long before we got here.

2. He _____ as much information as he could from the newspaper article.

3. The cathedral choir sang a _____ at his funeral.

4. Jack just bought a Model T to add to his collection of _____ cars.

5. The bag of rotten apples was _____ with ants.

6. The secrets of the universe are far beyond my _____.

Poetry of John Keats **159**

Poetry of John Keats

Grammar and Style: Direct Address

Direct address is the calling of a person or thing by name. Terms of direct address are generally set off by commas. This device can create a tone of intimacy and provide information about the person or thing being addressed as well as the writer's thoughts or feelings about the subject being addressed. The following lines from "When I Have Fears That I May Cease to Be" show the use of direct address:

> And when I feel, *fair creature of an hour,*
> That I shall never look upon thee more . . .

A. Practice: The following passages from "Ode on a Grecian Urn" contain examples of direct address. Underline the words of direct address within each passage.

1. Thou still unravished bride of quietness

   Thou foster child of silence and slow time,

   Sylvan historian, who canst thus express

   A flowery tale more sweetly than our rhyme . . .

2. Fair youth, beneath the trees, thou canst not leave

   Thy song, nor ever can those trees be bare. . . .

3. Ah, happy, happy boughs! that cannot shed

   Your leaves, nor ever bid the Spring adieu . . .

4. O Attic shape! Fair attitude! with brede

   Of marble men and maidens overwrought . . .

B. Writing Application: Rewrite the following sentences using one form of direct address in each sentence.

1. I wish I could forget you and your wicked birds.

   _____

2. Some day you will all see that I'm no child, that I knew the truth.

   _____

3. If only you would look my way, you'd know my mind.

   _____

4. I wonder what secrets hide behind those bricks of yours.

   _____

5. Did you know that the sight of you knocks me speechless?

   _____

Poetry of John Keats

Reading Strategy: Paraphrasing

Keats's nineteenth-century language and complex figures of speech can be difficult to understand. If you come to the end of a stanza and have no idea what you have just read, go back and read each phrase or sentence one at a time. Once you've identified the spots that are giving you trouble, you can **paraphrase** them, or restate them in your own words. Read the following example from Keats's "On First Looking into Chapman's Homer":

> Oft of one wide expanse had I been told
>
> That deep-browed Homer ruled as his demesne:
>
> Yet did I never breathe its pure serene
>
> Till I heard Chapman speak out loud and bold. . . .

Paraphrase:
I had often been told of a great place, ruled by the thoughtful Homer. However, I never breathed its pure air until I heard Chapman speak of it loudly and boldly.

The paraphrased version uses simple words and phrases in the place of more difficult ones and rearranges the order of the sentence parts. Once you have paraphrased the passage you can more easily see that the "wide expanse," or "great place," refers to Homer's poetry and that Chapman's speaking of this place refers to his translation of Homer's work.

DIRECTIONS: Paraphrase the following difficult passages from Keats's poems. Use the footnotes and a dictionary, if necessary, to define difficult words.

from "When I Have Fears That I May Cease to Be":

1. "When I have fears that I may cease to be

   Before my pen has gleaned my teeming brain . . ."

   _____

   _____

from "Ode to a Nightingale":

2. "Fade far away, dissolve, and quite forget

   What thou among the leaves hast never known,

   The weariness, the fever, and the fret. . . ."

   _____

   _____

   _____

3. "Perhaps the selfsame song that found a path

   Through the sad heart of Ruth, when, sick for home,

   She stood in tears amid the alien corn . . ."

   _____

   _____

Name _____   Date _____

Literary Analysis: Ode

The **ode** is a long lyric poem with a serious subject. Written in an elevated style, the ode usually honors its subject and addresses it directly. There are three types of odes in English. The **Pindaric ode** is written in sets of three stanzas and is modeled after the odes of the Greek poet Pindar. Pindar's odes were chanted by a chorus onstage, in the Greek dramatic tradition. With the first stanza, or strophe, the chorus moved to the right; with the second, or antistrophe, it moved to the left. For the third and final stanza, or epode, the chorus stood still. In the English Pindaric ode, the strophes and antistrophes have one stanza pattern and the epode has another. The **Horatian ode** is modeled after the odes of the Roman poet Horace. It is homostrophic, or contains only one type of stanza, and tends to be more restrained and meditative in tone. Finally, the **irregular ode** contains no set strophic pattern.

DIRECTIONS: Fill in the following table to determine which type of odes Keats has written. When analyzing the stanzas, be sure to count out the number of lines, rhyme scheme, and meter for each stanza.

	"Ode to a Nightingale"	"Ode on a Grecian Urn"
Number of stanzas		
Number of lines per stanza		
Rhyme scheme(s)		
Meter(s)		
Type of ode		

"The Lorelei" by Heinrich Heine

Haikus by Bashō, Yosa Buson, and Kobayashi Issa

Build Vocabulary:
Emotional Language of Romantic Lyric Poetry

Poetry gains an aura of romantic lyricism through the use of vocabulary that is rich in emotion.

DIRECTIONS: Choose the word from the box that best completes each line of poetry below. Write the word you choose on the line.

sadness	vision	anguish	devoured
cry	clouds	veiled	cold
beautiful	reflected		

1. Filled with _____, I began to weep.

2. The _____ overhead framed a majestic sky of possibility.

3. Her face I found _____ in the still waters of the lake.

4. Their hearts remained _____ from each other's charms.

5. The loss of love led to an _____ that knew no bounds.

6. She entered the room, a _____ of loveliness.

7. I was _____ by longing, as a hungry traveler takes his meal.

8. With a _____ of pain, she watched her lover disappear into the mist.

9. _____ does not begin to describe my lover.

10. The _____ of winter, the heat of summer, mark the passing of the year.

"The Lorelei" by Heinrich Heine
Haikus by Bashō, Yosa Buson, and Kobayashi Issa

Literary Connection: Contemporary Lyrical Works

The purpose of romantic lyric poetry is to create a highly emotional response in the reader. The presentation of images of nature, the description of everyday occurrences, and the offering of universal experiences are all utilized by the romantic lyric poet to elicit this response. The subject of a romantic lyric poem could be a classic story, as in "The Lorelei," or stark, simple images of nature, as in the haiku.

DIRECTIONS: Use the chart below to list the attributes of romantic lyric poetry as seen in "The Lorelei" by Heinrich Heine and in the haiku of Bashò, Buson, and Issa. Then list ideas for a contemporary lyrical work of your own in both forms. Consider which form would work best for the presentation of a particular topic. If you wish to offer an observation on nature, for example, you might write a haiku rather than a narrative poem.

"The Lorelei" Elements of Romantic Lyric Poetry	**Haiku** Elements of Romantic Lyric Poetry

My Ideas

My Ideas

"Speech to Parliament: In Defense of the Lower Classes"
by George Gordon, Lord Byron
"A Song: 'Men of England'" by Percy Bysshe Shelley
"On the Passing of the Reform Bill" by Thomas Babington Macaulay

Build Vocabulary

Spelling Strategy When endings that start with a vowel are added to words ending in *e*, the *e* is usually dropped. For example, when *-ing* or *-ion* is added to *decimate*, the resulting words are spelled *decimating* and *decimation*.

Using the Roots *-deci-* or *-deca-*

A. DIRECTIONS: Each of the words in the left column contains the roots *-deci-* or *-deca-*, meaning "ten." Match each word with its definition in the right column. Write the letter of the definition on the line next to the word it defines.

____ 1. decade

____ 2. decimal

____ 3. decahedron

____ 4. decibel

____ 5. decathlon

a. an athletic contest consisting of ten events

b. a solid figure with ten plane surfaces

c. a period of ten years

d. a fraction expressed in base 10

e. a numerical expression of the relative loudness of sounds

Using the Word Bank

impediments	decimation	efficacious
emancipate	balm	inauspicious

B. DIRECTIONS: Choose the letter of the word or phrase that is most nearly the same as each numbered word. Write the letters on the lines provided.

____ 1. inauspicious
    a. unlikeable
    b. unmentionable
    c. unfavorable
    d. uneasy

____ 2. emancipate
    a. trap
    b. free
    c. enliven
    d. elevate

____ 3. balm
    a. something disturbing
    b. something healing
    c. something flat
    d. something powdery

____ 4. efficacious
    a. affluent
    b. effusive
    c. efficient
    d. effective

____ 5. impediments
    a. obstructions
    b. detours
    c. pedestals
    d. openings

____ 6. decimation
    a. harm
    b. destruction
    c. support
    d. addition

Unit 4: Rebels and Dreamers (1790–1832)

"Speech to Parliament: In Defense of the Lower Classes"
by George Gordon, Lord Byron
"A Song: 'Men of England' " by Percy Bysshe Shelley
"On the Passing of the Reform Bill" by Thomas Babington Macaulay

Grammar and Style: Correlative Conjunctions

Correlative conjunctions work in pairs to link two words or groups of words of equal importance. Writers use correlative conjunctions such as *just as . . . so (too)* and *whether . . . or*, to present their ideas in a balanced manner. The following lines from "Speech to Parliament: In Defense of the Lower Classes" show how a pair of correlative conjunctions works in a sentence.

When we were told that these men are leagued together, *not only* for the destruction of their own comfort, *but* of their very means of subsistence, can we forget that it is the bitter policy . . . unto the third and fourth generation!

A. Practice: Underline the correlative conjunctions in each of the following sentences.

1. It is widely believed that both Shelley and Byron are among the most important English poets of the early nineteenth century.

2. Do you know whether Lord Byron is considered a Romantic or a Victorian writer?

3. Neither Byron nor Shelley possessed Thomas Babington Macaulay's qualifications as a statesman.

4. Just as repetition can underscore a poem's musicality, so too can it intensify the persuasiveness of a piece of oration.

5. The anthology contains not only examples of Shelley's verses but also a selection of his personal letters.

B. Writing Application: Rewrite each pair of sentences below as a single sentence. In your sentence, use the pair of correlative conjunctions that appears in brackets.

1. You may write your research report on the life and literary works of Percy Bysshe Shelley. You may write your report on the life and literary works of Mary Shelley. [*either . . . or*]

_____

2. Poets must consider carefully the connotations of the words they choose to express their ideas. Poets must consider with great care the sound of the words they use. [*not only . . . but also*]

_____

3. If you are writing a speech, you must pay close attention to your audience. If you are writing a persuasive essay, you must pay close attention to your audience. [*whether . . . or*]

_____

4. Samuel Taylor Coleridge was not as politically active as Shelley. John Keats was not as politically active as Shelley. [*neither . . . nor*]

_____

"Speech to Parliament: In Defense of the Lower Classes"
by George Gordon, Lord Byron
"A Song: 'Men of England'" by Percy Bysshe Shelley
"On the Passing of the Reform Bill" by Thomas Babington Macaulay

Reading Strategy: Setting a Purpose for Reading

If you **set a purpose for reading**, you can focus your attention on particular aspects of a literary work and enrich your reading experience. For instance, if you decide to read "A Song: 'Men of England'" for pleasure, you might take special note of Shelley's use of language, his sound devices, and his passionate tone. On the other hand, you could choose to read the poem to identify its Romantic characteristics; in this case, you might pay close attention to the poet's use of nature imagery and to his challenging attitude about employers' poor treatment of workers.

DIRECTIONS: This graphic organizer can help you set a purpose for reading, note specific passages in the literature, and reflect on these passages in light of your purpose. Before reading, state your purpose in the center box. Then, as you read, write down at least four passages from the work that relate to or answer your purpose. Beneath each quoted passage, explain how it deepens your understanding and helps fulfill your purpose.

Purpose

Passages

Unit 4: Rebels and Dreamers (1790–1832)

"Speech to Parliament: In Defense of the Lower Classes"
by George Gordon, Lord Byron
"A Song: 'Men of England' " by Percy Bysshe Shelley
"On the Passing of the Reform Bill" by Thomas Babington Macaulay

Literary Analysis: Political Commentary

Political commentary, or opinions on political and social issues, can be delivered in a variety of literary forms, including speeches, essays, poems, letters, and even novels. Effective political commentators identify the ideas they wish to express, choose an appropriate literary form, and tailor their message to a particular audience. For instance, the subject of Lord Byron's commentary is a defense of the actions of workers who destroyed factory equipment to protest losing their jobs. Knowing that his audience would be members of Parliament, Byron wrote his commentary as a speech and addressed his remarks (in respectful but confrontational language) directly to his listeners. Being a member of the House of Lords as well as a poet, Byron understood that oration was the most productive form for communicating ideas to a large group of statesmen. He also believed that his fellow legislators must be challenged openly about their responsibilities toward the unemployed workers.

DIRECTIONS: Choose one of the three literary works in this section. After reading the selection, answer the following questions.

1. How would you describe the author's message in a sentence or two? Identify two or three sentences in which the author addresses this central idea.

   _____

   _____

   _____

2. What goal do you think the author hopes to achieve with this commentary?

   _____

   _____

   _____

3. Why do you think the author chose to write in this literary form?

   _____

   _____

   _____

4. How would you describe the audience for this political commentary?

   _____

   _____

   _____

5. List several examples of language or ideas that reflect the author's awareness of his audience.

   _____

   _____

   _____

"On Making an Agreeable Marriage" by Jane Austen
from *A Vindication of the Rights of Woman* by Mary Wollstonecraft

Build Vocabulary

Spelling Strategy When adding a suffix to a word ending with silent *e*, the *e* is usually dropped. For example, *grave + ity = gravity, scarce + ity = scarcity, complete + tion = completion, vindicate + ion = vindication.*

Using the Root *-fort-*

A. DIRECTIONS: Each of the following sentences includes an italicized word that contains the word root *-fort-*, meaning "strong." Fill in the blank with a word or phrase that completes the sentence and reveals the meaning of the italicized word.

1. A musical analogy Mary Wollstonecraft might have used is that while women were expected to play the piano softly and prettily, men could be counted on to play *fortissimo*,

   _____.

2. The *fortress* stood upon a hill and was _____.

3. Jane Austen wrote to her friend Fanny to provide *fortification* for Fanny to make up her own mind about marriage. Austen wanted to _____ Fanny's resolve.

4. Mary Wollstonecraft put a lot of *effort* into her essay on woman's rights. It was a

   _____ to put her deepest feelings into words.

Using the Word Bank

scruple	amiable	vindication
solicitude	fastidious	specious
fortitude	preponderates	gravity

B. DIRECTIONS: In the following paragraph, fill in the blanks using words from the Word Bank.

Jane Austen wrote to Fanny out of (1) _____ with regard to her friend's

future marriage. Austen's argument was certainly not (2) _____,

or deceptively attractive. To Austen, choosing the right husband was a matter of great

(3) _____. In Austen's mind, there was no need to provide

(4) _____ for *not* marrying someone; one either loved the other person

or one didn't. She had no regard for women who behaved in a false manner by only pretend-

ing to care for someone. Nor did Austen advocate being so (5) _____

as to be pleased by no man. She recommended a clear head, an open heart, and

(6) _____ of spirit. Austen's philosophy seemed to be that if one of

those things (7) _____ over the others, all is lost. Although she had

no (8) _____ about speaking her mind, Austen's tone remained

(9) _____ throughout her letter to Fanny.

Agreeable Marriage/Rights of Woman **169**

"On Making an Agreeable Marriage" by Jane Austen
from *A Vindication of the Rights of Woman* by Mary Wollstonecraft

Grammar and Style: Commas in a Series

It is important to be consistent when using a grammatical device such as **commas in a series**. Although it is usual to use commas in a series to ensure clear writing, modern rules of grammar also allow for omitting the final comma before a conjunction. Look at these examples.

Final comma: Jane Austen recommends that young women be amiable, discerning, and scrupulous when it comes to choosing a mate.

No final comma: She warns against loveless marriage, a fastidious nature and specious behavior.

Each of the sentences above is correct in terms of proper usage. However, if the two example sentences were to appear within the same piece of writing, they would create a consistency problem. Remember that whichever comma style you decide to employ, you must use it consistently throughout a single piece of writing.

A. Practice: Decide whether each of the sentences uses series commas appropriately. If a sentence does not use series commas correctly, rewrite the corrected sentence on the blank line. If the sentence is correct as written, write *correct* on the blank line.

1. Fanny, and her friends, and family addressed the problem of her impending marriage.

   _____

2. Fanny might have spoken to Ellen, Jane or any of Jane's sisters.

   _____

3. You might say that honesty, happiness, and respect are the three main requirements for a happy marriage.

   _____

4. Mary Wollstonecraft felt that young women were taught to behave in a deceptive, conniving, and, ridiculous way.

   _____

B. Writing Application: Follow the directions to create sentences that correctly use commas in a series.

1. Write a sentence that uses three adjectives about women's societal roles according to Mary Wollstonecraft.

   _____

   _____

2. Write a sentence about the possible importance of a large family in Mary Wollstonecraft's day.

   _____

   _____

3. Write a sentence about love and marriage in Jane Austen's day.

   _____

   _____

Name _____ Date _____

"On Making an Agreeable Marriage" by Jane Austen
from *A Vindication of the Rights of Woman* by Mary Wollstonecraft

Reading Strategy: Determining the Writer's Purpose

It is particularly important to **determine the writer's purpose** when you're reading essays, speeches, or works of social commentary. Authors of these works can have a variety of purposes. Some seek to explain an issue or a process; others attempt to persuade a certain group or society in general to think in a particular way. Still others write to incite their audience to take action.

DIRECTIONS: Use this graphic organizer to help you record and analyze Mary Wollstonecraft's purpose for writing "A Vindication of the Rights of Women." For each paragraph write down clues that reflect the author's tone and attitude. Decide what you think the author's purpose was. Then think about how the paragraph affected your own opinion on the topic. The first paragraph has been analyzed for you.

Author's Tone/Attitude	Author's Purpose	Personal Reaction
Paragraph 1: The author takes a tone that reveals her to be saddened and frustrated by the way women of her generation are being educated. She feels strongly that women are sacrificing their intellects in order to gain the attentions of men. Wollstonecraft keeps her tone low-key, but it is clear that the situation she is writing about also makes her angry.	The author is attempting to persuade readers that women have been unfairly treated.	Some of the points about society that Wollstonecraft makes are still relevant today. Many women act nice or pretend they're not overly intelligent so that men won't feel threatened.
Paragraph 2:		
Paragraph 3:		
Paragraph 4:		
Paragraph 5:		

Agreeable Marriage/Rights of Woman **171**

"On Making an Agreeable Marriage" by Jane Austen
from *A Vindication of the Rights of Woman* by Mary Wollstonecraft

Literary Analysis: Social Commentary

Mary Wollstonecraft and Jane Austen were writers who were enormously gifted in the art of **social commentary**. These women looked closely at the world around them, thought deeply about what they saw, and put their views down on paper for the betterment and enjoyment of others. For example, Austen begins her letter to her niece by gently prodding Fanny to remember all her gentleman friend's wonderful qualities. But Austen's letter slowly transforms into an appeal to consider carefully before accepting a marriage proposal, and thereby avoid a marriage of convenience or a marriage for the sake of money. Her point, in the end, is that there is nothing worse than marriage without mutual affection and respect. Austen, who remained unmarried throughout her brief life, was nonetheless able to view the institution of marriage with great perception and evenhandedness.

DIRECTIONS: Read the excerpts from the selections and answer the questions that follow.

> And from the time of our being in London together, I thought you really very much in love.—
> But you certainly are not at all—there is no concealing it.—What strange creatures we are!—It
> seems as if your being made secure of him (as you say yourself) had made you Indifferent.
>
> (from "On Making an Agreeable Marriage")

1. What point does Austen make about the fickle nature of some human relationships?

   _____

   _____

   _____

   _____

> It is acknowledged that they spend many of the first years of their lives in acquiring a smattering of accomplishments; meanwhile strength of body and mind are sacrificed to libertine notions of beauty, to the desire of establishing themselves—the only way women can rise in the world—by marriage. And this desire making mere animals of them, when they marry they act as such children may be expected to act—they dress, they paint, and nickname God's creatures. Can they be expected to govern a family with judgment, or take care of the poor babes whom they bring into the world?
>
> (from *A Vindication of the Rights of Women*)

2. What point is Wollstonecraft making about women's place in society?

   _____

   _____

   _____

   _____

   _____

   _____

from the Screenplay of *Sense and Sensibility* and Diaries
by Emma Thompson

Build Vocabulary: Language of Social Awareness

Many essays deal with important social issues. To understand such essays completely, a reader needs to master vocabulary that deals explicitly with social awareness.

DIRECTIONS: Choose the word from the box that best completes each sentence.

private	fortune	politician	church
army	idle	useless	circumstances
inherited	orator		

1. This organization attempts to improve the _____ of recent immigrants to the country.

2. The activist's advice was never to let yourself be _____: always continue to work toward a particular goal.

3. We must not look to an elected _____ to solve our problems.

4. Those in _____ business must also keep the concerns of the community in mind.

5. A powerful _____ can sway great numbers of people to a point of view through his or her use of the spoken word.

6. The clothing drive will be held in the hall of a local _____.

7. Although I feel it is sometimes _____ to continue, I'll keep on fighting for justice.

8. We planned our voter registration campaign as if we were an _____ heading into battle.

9. She _____ her concern for others from her grandmother, who also had dedicated herself to bettering society.

10. The software developer had pledged to use her _____ in a campaign for adult literacy.

from the Screenplay of *Sense and Sensibility* and Diaries
by Emma Thompson

Thematic Connection: Contemporary Social Reformers

Jane Austen's novel *Sense and Sensibility* describes a society that had certain expectations of men and women and in which social class determined and limited many choices. Other writers of the era, such as Shelley, Byron, and Wollstonecraft, further explored in poetry and prose the injustices of their time. What contemporary injustices have reformers attempted to address in recent years? What parallels can you find between the concerns of today and those addressed in the selections you read in this section?

DIRECTIONS: In the column on the left, list the issues that concerned each writer and the particular work in which the writer explored the issue. In the column on the right, list the area in which each reformer or activist sought, or is seeking, to improve conditions. Then use the chart entries to compare and contrast the concerns and sensibilities of the authors you read in this section with the goals of contemporary social reformers.

Writer	Works/Issues
Austen	
Shelley	
Byron	
Wollstonecraft	

Issues	Reformer/Activist
	Cesar Chavez
	Princess Diana
	Martin Luther King, Jr.
	Willie Nelson

from "In Memoriam, A.H.H.," "The Lady of Shalott," "Ulysses," and from
The Princess: **"Tears, Idle Tears"** by Alfred, Lord Tennyson

Build Vocabulary

Spelling Strategy Words ending in a silent *e* drop the *e* before a suffix that begins with a vowel. Thus *diffuse + ive* becomes *diffusive*, and *wane + ing* becomes *waning*.

Using Medieval Words

The Word Bank word *churls* is an Old English word meaning "farmers or peasants." In his poems, Tennyson uses a number of medieval words to add atmosphere and help create the setting.

A. DIRECTIONS: Using the context of the sentence, write a definition of each underlined Old English or other medieval word.

1. Roland earned 100 gold crowns as the village blacksmith, and so was obligated to tithe 10 crowns to the parish.

   _____

2. The knight, smiling, raised only his buckler to fend off the wooden swords of the children who had gathered around him.

   _____

3. Only the old woman's eyes were visible from within the folds of the wimple wrapped around her head.

   _____

Using the Word Bank

diffusive	churls	waning	furrows

B. DIRECTIONS: Choose the letter of the word or phrase most nearly *similar* in meaning to each numbered word. Write the letter of your choice in the blank.

____ 1. diffusive
   a. polluted
   b. fervent
   c. dispersed
   d. alternate

____ 2. churls
   a. attitudes
   b. coarse persons
   c. emblems
   d. assigned duties

____ 3. waning
   a. bathing
   b. waxing
   c. expanding
   d. declining

____ 4. furrows
   a. grooves
   b. ponders
   c. plants
   d. lairs

from "In Memoriam, A.H.H.," "The Lady of Shalott," "Ulysses," and from
The Princess: **"Tears, Idle Tears"** by Alfred, Lord Tennyson

Grammar and Style: Parallel Structure

Sometimes for effect, writers repeat words and phrases, or place them in grammatically similar clauses or structures. **Parallel structure** adds rhetorical and emotional power through rhythm, repetition, and emphasis. Writers may use single words, infinitive phrases, prepositional phrases, or clauses in parallel structure.

A. Practice: Underline each parallel structure in the following passages and identify its grammatical element.

1. There she sees the highway near

   Winding down to Camelot:

   There the river eddy whirls,

   And there the surly village churls,

   And the red cloaks of market girls,

   Pass onward from Shallot.

2. Let Love clasp Grief lest both be drowned,

   Let darkness keep her raven gloss.

   Ah, sweeter to be drunk with loss,

   To dance with death, to beat the ground. . .

B. Writing Application: Create sentences with parallel structure for each of the following items, using the prompts provided.

1. (Repeat article *the*) Damsels, abbot, shepherd, page, and knight may see Camelot, but not the Lady of Shallot.

   _____

   _____

2. (Make one sentence with compound verbs) In order to bear the fate of the curse, the Lady should not look at Camelot. She should not wonder about it. She should not dream of the town. She must not go to it.

   _____

   _____

3. (Make infinitive phrases of gerunds) Sharing, striving, questioning, and discovering is living, whatever one's age, says Tennyson in "Ulysses."

   _____

   _____

4. (Repeat brief rhetorical questions) What are faith, friendship, memory, and life itself? "In Memoriam, A.H.H." asks these essential questions about relationships in the face of death.

   _____

   _____

from "In Memoriam, A.H.H.," "The Lady of Shalott," "Ulysses," and **from**
Princess: **"Tears, Idle Tears"** by Alfred, Lord Tennyson

Reading Strategy: Judging the Poet's Message

Beneath the surface of most poetry are powerful messages about some of life's big issues—love, death, and war, for example. You can apply your critical judgement and experiences to the work to determine whether you think the poet's views are accurate. As you look at a poem, notice clues about the poet's message. What is the message? Do the ideas follow logically? Is the evidence appropriate and relevant? Are Characters and situations true to life? How does it relate to your own experiences or observations of life? Once you have answered these questions, you can make your own judgment about the validity of the poet's message.

DIRECTIONS: In the following chart, record y9ur own experiences and then make a judgment about each excerpt.

Poet's Message	+ My Experiences/ Observations of Life	= My Judgment of Poet's Message
Far off thou art, but ever nigh/I have thee still, and I rejoice:/1 prosper, circled with thy voice;/I shall not lose thee though I die. ("In Memoriam, A.H.H.")		
I am a part of all that I have met;/Yet all experience is an arch wherethrough/ Gleams that untraveled world, whose margin fades/ Forever and forever when I move. ("Ulysses")		
Tear, idle terars, I know not what they mean,/Tears from the depth of some divine despair/Rise in the heart and gather to the eyes,/In looking on the happy autumn fields,/And thinking of the days that are no more. ("Tears, Idle Tears" from The Princess)		

from "In Memoriam, A.H.H.," "The Lady of Shalott," "Ulysses," and from
The Princess: **"Tears, Idle Tears"** by Alfred, Lord Tennyson

Literary Analysis: The Speaker in Poetry

We can truly understand a poem only when we understand who is speaking and what moti-vated him or her to do so. In Tennyson's "Ulysses," the hero is an adventurer who not only re-veals his longing to roam "with a hungry heart," but also attempts to persuade his aging follow-ers and subjects that he and his band should leave the kingdom and "sail beyond the sunset."

DIRECTIONS: On the lines, describe what Ulysses reveals in each quotation about his own thoughts and feelings or how he hopes to persuade his listeners with his words. Remember that both ordinary subjects and Ulysses's fellow adventurers are listening to him speak.

1. How dull it is to pause, to make an end, / To rust unburnished, not to shine in use!

_____
_____
_____
_____
_____

2. This is my son, mine own Telemachus, / To whom I leave the scepter and the isle / Well-loved of me, discerning to fulfill / This labor, . . .

_____
_____
_____
_____
_____

3. . . . My mariners, / Souls that have toiled and wrought, and thought with me— / That ever with a frolic welcome took / The thunder and the sunshine, . . .

_____
_____
_____
_____
_____

4. 'Tis not too late to seek a newer world. / Push off, and sitting well in order smite / The sounding furrows; . . .

_____
_____
_____
_____
_____

"My Last Duchess," "Life in a Love," and **"Love Among the Ruins"**
by Robert Browning
Sonnet 43 by Elizabeth Barrett Browning

Build Vocabulary

Spelling Strategy Many words, such as the Word Bank word *munificence*, end in *-ence*. Be careful not to confuse their spellings with words that end in *-ance*.

Using the Suffix *-ence*

A. DIRECTIONS: Answer each of the following questions, changing the underlined word to a word with the suffix *-ence*.

1. Why was Alan absent from the meeting?

_____

_____

2. How did the class behave when there was an observer present?

_____

_____

3. Why did the teacher praise the diligent students?

_____

_____

4. How did the suspect prove he was innocent of the charge?

_____

_____

Using the Word Bank

countenance	officious	munificence	dowry
eludes	vestige	sublime	minions

B. DIRECTIONS: Match each word in the left column with its definition in the right column. Write the letter of the definition on the line next to the word it defines.

____ 1. countenance   a. overly eager to please

____ 2. officious   b. state of being generous; lavish

____ 3. munificence   c. avoids or escapes

____ 4. dowry   d. inspiring admiration through greatness or beauty

____ 5. vestige   e. face

____ 6. sublime   f. natural talent, gift, or endowment

____ 7. minions   g. attendants or agents

____ 8. eludes   h. trace; bit

"My Last Duchess," "Life in a Love," and **"Love Among the Ruins"**
by Robert Browning
Sonnet 43 by Elizabeth Barrett Browning

Grammar and Style: The Use of *Like* and As

Like, meaning "similar to," is used to compare nouns or pronouns. It introduces a prepositional phrase, which consists of a preposition and a noun or pronoun. *As* is a subordinating conjunction and is used to compare actions. It introduces a clause with a noun and a verb. Look at the following examples from poems by Robert Browning and Elizabeth Barrett Browning:

Strangers *like* you . . .
I love thee purely, *as* they turn from Praise.

A. Practice: Correctly complete each of the following sentences by writing either *like* or *as* on the line.

1. Robert Browning wrote many dramatic monologues, _____ "My Last Duchess."

2. A dramatic monologue reads _____ lines from a play.

3. The Duke in "My Last Duchess" doesn't act _____ I'd expect an aristocrat to act.

4. Elizabeth Barrett Browning's "Sonnet 43" has fourteen lines _____ all sonnets do.

5. Many of her sonnets, _____ "Sonnet 43," are well-known love poems.

6. The scene described in "Love Among the Ruins" sounds _____ ruins in Italy or Greece.

B. Writing Application: Write a paragraph in which you describe another famous love story like the one between Robert Browning and Elizabeth Barrett. Use *like* and *as* at least once each.

_____

_____

_____

_____

_____

_____

_____

_____

_____

_____

_____

© Prentice-Hall, Inc.

"My Last Duchess," "Life in a Love," and **"Love Among the Ruins"**
by Robert Browning
Sonnet 43 by Elizabeth Barrett Browning

Reading Strategy: Making Inferences About the Speaker

When you read a poem, look for meaning behind the speaker's words and actions. Make inferences about the speaker's thoughts, feelings, and motivations. Be aware, too, that the speaker's words sometimes reveal more than he or she realizes.

DIRECTIONS: Read the following lines from "My Last Duchess" and "Love Among the Ruins." Answer the questions related to each set of lines.

from "My Last Duchess" (lines 24–28)

. . . she liked whate'er
She looked on, and her looks went everywhere.
Sir, 'twas all one! My favor at her breast,
The dropping of the daylight in the West,
The bough of cherries some officious fool
Broke in the orchard for her . . .

1. What can you infer about the Duke's attitude toward his wife?

   _____

   _____

2. What can you infer about the Duke's personality from lines 27–28?

   _____

   _____

from "Love Among the Ruins" (lines 67–72)

When I do come, she will speak not, she will stand,
Either hand
On my shoulder, give her eyes the first embrace
Of my face,
Ere we rush, ere we extinguish sight and speech
Each on each.

3. What can you infer about the speaker's feelings for the woman?

   _____

   _____

4. What can you infer about the speaker's attitude toward love?

   _____

   _____

"My Last Duchess," "Life in a Love," and **"Love Among the Ruins"**
by Robert Browning
Sonnet 43 by Elizabeth Barrett Browning

Literary Analysis: Dramatic Monologue

A **dramatic monologue** is a speech, sometimes to a silent listener, in which a character indicates a setting and a dramatic conflict. In the monologue, this character reveals his or her inmost feelings, sometimes without knowing it.

A. DIRECTIONS: Complete the following chart. Indicate the setting and names or general identities of the speaker and listener, and summarize the conflict in each poem.

Poem	Setting	Speaker	Listener	Conflict
"My Last Duchess"				
"Life in a Love"				
"Love Among the Ruins"				

B. DIRECTIONS: Write your answers to the following questions.

1. How does the presence of the silent listener in "My Last Duchess" build dramatic tension?

_____

_____

_____

2. Do you think the dramatic conflict in "Life in a Love" will be resolved? Explain.

_____

_____

_____

3. How does the title "Love Among the Ruins" express the poem's dramatic conflict?

_____

_____

_____

"You Know the Place: Then" by Sappho
"Invitation to the Voyage" by Charles Baudelaire

Build Vocabulary: The Language of Relationships

Both Sappho and Charles Baudelaire are exploring a particular kind of relationship in the poems offered in this section. To accurately characterize an aspect of a relationship, a writer must use the right noun, verb, or adjective.

DIRECTIONS: Write a word from the box that best matches each clue. Then, use the word in a sentence of your own relating to a relationship. You might wish to use the poems as inspiration for your sentences.

leave	waiting	sacred	deep
love	treacherous	richness	pleasure

1. describing someone who can't be trusted: _____

   sentence: _____

2. describing something quite rewarding: _____

   sentence: _____

3. opposite of *unease* or *pain*: _____

   sentence: _____

4. synonym of *depart*: _____

   sentence: _____

5. quality represented by Aphrodite: _____

   sentence: _____

6. word with a length that belies its meaning: _____

   sentence: _____

7. pertaining to religion: _____

   sentence: _____

8. might be done with impatience: _____

   sentence: _____

"**You Know the Place: Then**" by Sappho
"**Invitation to the Voyage**" by Charles Baudelaire

Cultural Connection: Relationships

Our lives are made up of relationships of all kinds. The relationships that immediately spring to mind are those of an interpersonal nature: romantic relationships, family relationships, relationships with friends. But the relationships human beings have with larger forces in society are also important. What important societal relationships color human existence? How might these relationships be explored in poetry?

DIRECTIONS: Use the chart to explore the different kinds of relationships in which human beings engage and how each kind of relationship might be explored in poetry. Begin by identifying the kind of relationship considered by both Sappho and Baudelaire in their respective poems. Then list the images they use to explore this relationship. Go on to identify other kinds of relationships that might be categorized under the general headings given, listing images you might use in a poem describing the relationship.

Poem	Relationship Explored	Images
"You Know the Place: Then" by Sappho		
"Invitation to the Voyage" by Charles Baudelaire		

Category	Relationship	Images
Political		
Environmental		
Psychological		

from *Hard Times* by Charles Dickens

from *Jane Eyre* by Charlotte Brontë

Build Vocabulary

Spelling Strategy For words ending in silent *e*, drop the *e* before a suffix beginning with a vowel. For example, the suffix *-ed* added to the word *comprise* forms the Word Bank word *comprised*.

Using the Root *-mono-*

In *Hard Times*, Charles Dickens describes the "plain, bare, *monotonous* vault of a schoolroom. . . ." The Greek word root *mono-* means "single" or "alone." Therefore, *monotonous* means "having a single 'tone,'" or "dull and unwavering."

A. DIRECTIONS: Complete each sentence with a word from the box.

monolithic	monophony	monosyllabic	monogram

1. The old library was a _____ stone structure.

2. His initials formed a _____ on his writing paper.

3. The song was a simple _____, without harmonizing parts.

4. The teacher repeated the _____ word *facts*.

Using the Word Bank

monotonous	obstinate	adversary	indignant
approbation	obscure	comprised	sundry

B. DIRECTIONS: For each numbered word, choose the word or phrase that is most *similar* in meaning. Write the letter of your choice on the line provided.

____ 1. monotonous
    a. alone
    b. quiet
    c. exciting
    d. dull

____ 2. obstinate
    a. approving
    b. displeased
    c. stubborn
    d. slow

____ 3. adversary
    a. opponent
    b. partner
    c. student
    d. teacher

____ 4. indignant
    a. thoughtful
    b. displeased
    c. agreeable
    d. strict

____ 5. approbation
    a. punishment
    b. lesson
    c. approval
    d. plan

____ 6. obscure
    a. vague
    b. correct
    c. clear
    d. lonely

____ 7. comprised
    a. organized
    b. taught
    c. argued
    d. contained

____ 8. sundry
    a. few
    b. angry
    c. ridiculous
    d. various

from *Hard Times* by Charles Dickens
from *Jane Eyre* by Charlotte Brontë

Grammar and Style: Punctuation of Dialogue

For the **proper punctuation of dialogue**, observe the following rules:

- Place commas and periods within closing quotation marks. Place a comma introducing a quotation before opening quotation marks.

    "Yes**,**" the young girl explained**,** "my name is Sissy**.**"

- Place question marks and exclamation marks within closing quotation marks when they end quotations, and outside closing quotation marks when they belong to a sentence that includes a quotation.

    Miss Scatcherd cried out, "You disagreeable girl**!**"
    "Why doesn't she wish to leave Lowood**?**" Jane wondered.
    Was it Gradgrind who said, "Stick to Facts, sir!"**?**

A. Practice: Read the following lines of dialogue from *Hard Times* and *Jane Eyre*. Where they are needed, place quotation marks correctly in relation to commas, periods, exclamation points, and question marks.

1. After a pause, one half of the children cried in chorus, Yes, Sir!

2. You must paper it, said Thomas Gradgrind, whether you like it or not.

3. Fact, fact, fact! said the gentleman.

4. Why, thought I, does she not explain that she could neither clean her nails nor wash her face, as the water was frozen?

B. Writing Application: Rewrite the following, placing commas and quotation marks where they are needed.

I thought I heard Mr. Gradgrind shout Just give me facts! Did he really say Facts alone are needed in life?

In response to his statements, the fearful children in the room said Yes, sir!

I don't understand Sissy Jupe said.

What is so difficult to understand? Mr. Gradgrind asked. Just stick to facts. Root out everything else.

_____

_____

_____

_____

_____

_____

_____

_____

from *Hard Times* by Charles Dickens

from *Jane Eyre* by Charlotte Brontë

Reading Strategy: Recognizing the Writer's Purpose

A **writer's purpose** is his or her reason for writing a literary work. An author might write a novel for one or more of the following reasons: to address a social problem, to satirize a particular institution, or to entertain readers with humor or adventure. To understand a writer's purpose, pay close attention to the details he or she uses to describe characters, events and ideas. These details reveal the writer's attitude, or feelings, toward what he or she is describing. The writer's attitude, in turn, suggests his or her purpose.

DIRECTIONS: As you read the selections, try to determine the writer's purpose by answering the following questions.

Hard Times

1. In Chapter 1 of *Hard Times*, what details does Dickens use to describe the schoolroom? What details does he use to describe the physical appearance of "the speaker" in the schoolroom? What might these details say about the author's attitude and purpose?

_____

_____

_____

2. What details does Dickens use to create a contrast between Sissy Jupe and Bitzer? Why does Sissy clash with her teachers? What might the incident surrounding Sissy indicate about the author's attitude and purpose?

_____

_____

_____

Jane Eyre

3. What details does Brontë give about Miss Scatcherd and her treatment of Helen Burns? What might these details reveal about the author's attitude and purpose?

_____

_____

_____

4. What two contrasting outlooks are presented in the discussion between Helen and Jane? What does the conversation reveal about their character and their school? Why might this discussion be important to the author's purpose?

_____

_____

_____

from *Hard Times* by Charles Dickens
from *Jane Eyre* by Charlotte Brontë

Literary Analysis: The Novel and Social Criticism

A **novel** is a long work of fiction, usually featuring a complex plot, major and minor characters, a significant theme, and several settings. Like many novelists in nineteenth-century England, Charles Dickens and Charlotte Brontë created the fictional worlds in their novels to reflect real people and social institutions. Through their novels, they could comment on what they saw as problems and injustices in their society. This type of commentary through fiction is known as **social criticism**.

DIRECTIONS: Examine the social criticism in *Hard Times* and *Jane Eyre* by answering the following questions.

Hard Times

1. Of Thomas Gradgrind, Dickens writes: ". . . he seemed a kind of cannon loaded to the muzzle with facts, and prepared to blow [the students] clean out of the regions of childhood at one discharge." What is Dickens's attitude toward Thomas Gradgrind's teaching style? Why is this passage an example of social criticism?

   _____

   _____

2. When Mr. Gradgrind addresses student Sissy Jupe, he refers to her only as "girl number twenty." Why does he refer to her in this way? What viewpoint is Dickens criticizing by drawing attention to this? What aspect of the school is he criticizing?

   _____

   _____

Jane Eyre

3. Helen explains why she was punished by saying "'I seldom put, and never keep, things in order; I am careless; I forget rules; I read when I should learn my lessons; I have no method; and sometimes I say, like you, I *cannot bear* to be subjected to systematic arrangements. This is all very provoking to Miss Scatcherd, who is naturally neat, punctual, and particular.'" Are Helen's "faults" truly bad? In this passage, what is Brontë criticizing about the world in which the two girls live?

   _____

   _____

4. While Jane feels anger when she is treated unfairly, Helen, who is older, says only: "'degradation never too deeply disgusts me, injustice never crushes me too low: I live in calm, looking to the end.'" How much value does Helen place on her life? In what ways are Helen's statements a criticism of what she has been taught at Lowood?

   _____

   _____

from *War and Peace* by Leo Tolstoy

Build Vocabulary: The Language of Human Experience

Great literature tries to find just the right words for all aspects of human experience. Mastering a wide-ranging vocabulary is necessary to appreciate literary works. Having a well-rounded vocabulary will also be invaluable as you make your own literary attempts.

DIRECTIONS: Choose the word from the box that best completes the sentence in each numbered item below. Write the word in the blank.

blunders	inspired	panic	guilty
dignity	ashamed	pitiful	abandon
intuition	greatness		

1. Aggie was mortified at her own _____ when she first arrived at the party.

2. The two _____ orphans made even the battle-hardened soldiers feel moved.

3. I was so thrilled by the music that it _____ me to take up the violin.

4. Who would _____ those shivering kittens by the side of the road?

5. The general's true _____ was revealed by the outcome of the war.

6. The old gentleman showed _____ and held his head high in spite of the taunts of the young people.

7. My face turned red; I was _____ when I realized to whom I had been speaking.

8. The foot soldiers scattered in a _____ when the enemy cavalry attacked.

9. _____ told her that it might be best if she didn't go into town today.

10. From his expression it was clear that he felt _____ about taking the last piece of pie.

Name _____ Date _____

from *War and Peace* by Leo Tolstoy

Literary Connection: The Novel

The most enduring novels, such as *Hard Times, Jane Eyre,* and *War and Peace,* explore human experiences in a way that sheds light on other situations and circumstances. Such universality gives these novels a depth of meaning that goes beyond the narratives themselves.

DIRECTIONS: Develop a plot outline for a proposed novel of your own. Your work should take as its theme universal situations. First, review such themes from the three novels as summarized in the graphic organizer. Then use the lines that follow to sketch out a plot outline for your proposed novel.

Hard Times	*Jane Eyre*	*War and Peace*
• difficult experiences at school or away from home • conflict among young people or between young people and their elders • allowing one's imagination to be stifled in the pursuit of reason	• dealing with the complications of friendship and loss • the difficulty in finding a home • the tensions of romantic relationships	• the tragedy of war • the problems of leadership and command • the fickleness of public opinion

"Dover Beach" by Matthew Arnold
"Recessional" and **"The Widow at Windsor"** by Rudyard Kipling

Build Vocabulary

Spelling Strategy Whenever you hear a long vowel sound followed by a single consonant in the final syllable of a word, you can be sure that the word is spelled with a final, silent *e*, as in the word *contrite*.

Using the Root *-domi-*

A. DIRECTIONS: From the Latin *dominus*, English acquires several words whose meanings relate to the word's meaning of "lord" or "master." Keep this in mind as you answer questions about some words that include the *-domi-* root. Use a dictionary if you wish.

1. How is someone who *dominates* different from someone who *domineers*?

   _____

2. Portuguese and Brazilian royalty are allowed to add the word *Dom* to their names, as a sign of their status. What, in your opinion, does this signify?

   _____

3. What is an *indomitable* enemy?

   _____

Using the Word Bank

tranquil	cadence	turbid	dominion	contrite

B. DIRECTIONS: Match each word in the left column with its definition in the right column. Write the letter of the definition on the line next to the word it defines.

____ 1. cadence   a. repenting for sin

____ 2. contrite   b. murky

____ 3. dominion   c. free from disturbance

____ 4. tranquil   d. rhythmic sequence

____ 5. turbid   e. power

"Dover Beach" by Matthew Arnold
"Recessional" and **"The Widow at Windsor"** by Rudyard Kipling

Grammar and Style: Present Tense

The **present tense** of a verb expresses an action or a state of being that is occurring now. A present tense verb may also express a general truth. Following are several examples of sentences from "Dover Beach" that contain present tense verbs.

The sea *is* calm tonight.
The tide *is* full, the moon *lies* fair
Upon the straits:

Arnold, in particular, uses many present tense verbs in his poem. This helps readers feel close to the ideas the poet is expressing.

A. Practice: Place a check mark next to each sentence whose main verb is in the present tense.

_____ 1. Arnold's and Kipling's lives overlap by twenty-three years.

_____ 2. Both poets lived during Queen Victoria's reign.

_____ 3. Kipling receives the Nobel Prize for Literature in 1907.

_____ 4. A Nobel Prize carries with it great distinction.

_____ 5. Matthew Arnold was never honored with such an award.

_____ 6. His ideas, however, are admirable.

_____ 7. In a volume on social criticism, Arnold urges people to base their lives on the "best that has been thought and said in the world."

_____ 8. Kipling, on the other hand, is known as an imperialist, though perhaps a cautious one.

_____ 9. After a long absence, he returned to India at the age of seventeen.

_____ 10. Many of Kipling's writings display his affection for Indian life.

B. Writing Application: Write four original sentences according to the following instructions.

Write two sentences in the present tense about a captivating view you have seen, whether of the ocean, a mountain, or a cityscape.

1. _____

_____

2. _____

_____

Write two sentences in the present tense about a parade you have watched or in which you have participated.

3. _____

_____

4. _____

_____

"Dover Beach" by Matthew Arnold

"Recessional" and **"The Widow at Windsor"** by Rudyard Kipling

Reading Strategy: Drawing Conclusions

As we read, sometimes we piece together information in order to **draw conclusions** based on that information. Readers who do this can enhance their understanding of a poem or story. At the beginning of "Dover Beach," for example, readers may think that the poem is simply about a person admiring a view of the ocean. Then, at the end of the second stanza, the cadence of the waves brings the "eternal note of sadness in." This should raise a question in readers' minds. Why is there sadness? As readers continue, they should be able to draw a conclusion as to why the speaker of the poem feels sadness.

DIRECTIONS: As you read each poem, record two sets of details from which you draw conclusions about the speaker's attitude toward events in the poem or toward the larger subject of the poem. An example has been provided for you.

"Dover Beach"

Details	Conclusions
"eternal note of sadness"; Sophocles heard it; "human misery"; "Sea of Faith" once full but now retreating	The speaker feels the world is a lesser place—a sadder place—because people don't have the faith in God they once did.

"Recessional"

Details	Conclusions

"The Widow at Windsor"

Details	Conclusions

Name _____ Date _____

"Dover Beach" by Matthew Arnold
"Recessional" and **"The Widow at Windsor"** by Rudyard Kipling

Literary Analysis: Mood as a Key to Theme

The feelings that a poem creates in the reader make up the **mood** of the poem. How you feel after you read a poem can give you a hint as to the poem's central idea, or **theme**.

If you go away from a poem feeling happy, the poem likely expressed an optimistic outlook or a pleasing image. If, however, a poem's theme has to do with the evils of imperialism, for example, it probably will not contain optimism or pleasing images. A reader might come away from such a poem feeling threatened, sober, or scared. Those feelings can be a clue that the poem's central idea is to be taken seriously.

To create mood, poets use vivid images and words that have emotional appeal. Notice how Matthew Arnold creates a rhythm that imitates the sound of the ocean. Notice, too, the vivid verbs and adjectives he uses, which have more emotional appeal than less colorful language.

> Listen! you hear the grating roar
> Of pebbles which the waves draw back, and fling,
> At their return, up the high strand,
> Begin, and cease, and then again begin,
> With tremulous cadence slow, and bring
> The eternal note of sadness in.

DIRECTIONS: Following each passage, describe the mood of the passage—the feelings the passage creates in you—and indicate the words or phrases that create that mood. Then interpret those feelings in connection with the theme of that poem.

1. lines 9–14 from "Dover Beach" (see above)

_____

_____

2. lines 13–18 from "Recessional":

> Far-called, our navies melt away—
> On dune and headland sinks the fire—
> Lo, all our pomp of yesterday
> Is one with Nineveh and Tyre!
> Judge of the Nations, spare us yet,
> Lest we forget—lest we forget!

_____

_____

3. lines 36–40 from "The Widow at Windsor":

> Take 'old o' the Wings o' the Mornin',
>   An' flop round the earth till you're dead;
> But you won't get away from the tune that they play
>   To the bloomin' old rag over'ead.
>   (Poor beggars!—it's 'ot over'ead!)

_____

_____

"Condition of Ireland," *The Illustrated London News*
"Progress in Personal Comfort" by Sydney Smith

Build Vocabulary

Spelling Strategy To form the plural of many nouns, add *s* or *es*. For example, the plural form of *requisite* is the word *requisites*.

Using the Humors

The Illustrated London News article describes problems faced by the Irish as melancholy, or sad. The word *melancholy* originally meant "black bile," which is one of the four principal humors, or liquids, that people believed controlled health and personality. The other humors were yellow bile, blood, and phlegm. Modern English contains words originating from the theory of humors.

A. DIRECTIONS: Answer the following questions, based on clues given about the humors.

1. Phlegm is a thick, slow-moving fluid, so a *phlegmatic* person probably feels

   _____.

2. A person controlled by the warm, life-giving flow of blood can be described as *sanguine*, or

   _____.

Using the Word Bank

requisites	sanction	exonerate
melancholy	indolence	depredation

B. DIRECTIONS: For each sentence, choose the Word Bank word that best completes its meaning. Write the word on the line.

1. Some landowners were lazy, and everyone suffered from this _____.

2. The writer will _____ people who meant no harm.

3. More food, more cultivation, and more employment were the _____ for maintaining the Irish in existence.

4. When walking at night without streetlights, the writer felt exposed to danger and

   _____.

5. The law gave landowners the _____ and encouragement to evict people.

6. They could not get over the _____ sight of people needing to work for food.

Unit 5: Progress and Decline (1833–1901)

"Condition of Ireland," *The Illustrated London News*
"Progress in Personal Comfort" by Sydney Smith

Grammar and Style: Coordinating Conjunctions

A **coordinating conjunction** links two sentence parts of the same grammatical kind. The seven coordinating conjunctions are *and, but, or, nor, yet, so,* and *for.* Notice the use of coordinating conjunctions in the following passages.

from **"Condition of Ireland"**

> The present condition of the Irish...has been mainly brought on by ignorant *and* vicious legislation. . . .
>
> We shall fully consider that question before we quit the subject, *but* we shall now only say . . .

from **"Progress in Personal Comfort"**

> . . . I now glide without noise *or* fracture, on wooden pavements.

A. Practice: Read the following passages from "Progress in Personal Comfort" and "Condition of Ireland." Underline any coordinating conjunctions that you find.

1. I can walk, by the assistance of the police, from one end of London to the other, without molestation; or, if tired, get into a cheap and active cab . . .

2. Calmly and quietly, but very ignorantly . . . did the decree go forth which has made the temporary but terrible visitation of a potato rot the means of exterminating, through the slow process of disease and houseless starvation, nearly the half of the Irish.

B. Writing Application: Rewrite each of the following pairs of sentences, connecting them with a coordinating conjunction.

1. Most people believe progress is always good. "Condition of Ireland" reveals something different.

_____

_____

2. In the name of economic progress, many people suffered. Many people died.

_____

_____

3. The Poor-Laws were supposed to provide relief for the people in Ireland. The laws instead caused the people's destruction.

_____

_____

4. People lost their land. They lost their livelihoods.

_____

_____

5. "Condition of Ireland" calls for compassion. It calls for change.

_____

_____

"Condition of Ireland," *The Illustrated London News*
"Progress in Personal Comfort" by Sydney Smith

Reading Strategy: Distinguishing Emotive and Informative Language

Emotive language includes words, phrases, and examples that appeal to a reader's feelings. **Informative language** conveys facts. Often emotive language is woven into the informative language of an essay to capture the interest and emotions of readers and to reveal the attitude of a writer toward his or her subject.

DIRECTIONS: As you read the selections, identify examples of emotive and informative language. In each of the following passages from the selections, underline emotive language and circle informative language. Then analyze the emotive words in the passages to determine the writer's attitude toward a particular subject or idea.

"Condition of Ireland"

1. The Poor-Law, said to be for the relief of the people and the means of their salvation, was the instrument of their destruction. In their terrible distress, from that temporary calamity with which they were visited, they were to have no relief unless they gave up their holdings.

   Attitude _____

2. Calmly and quietly, but very ignorantly—though we cheerfully exonerate the parties from any malevolence; they only committed a great mistake, a terrible blunder, which in legislation is worse than a crime—but calmly and quietly from Westminster itself . . . did the decree go forth . . .

   Attitude _____

"Progress in Personal Comfort"

3. It took me nine hours to go from Taunton to Bath, before the invention of the railroads, and I now go in six hours from Taunton to London! In going from Taunton to Bath, I suffered between 10,000 and 12,000 severe contusions, before stone-breaking Macadam was born.

   Attitude: _____

4. There were no banks to receive the savings of the poor. The Poor Laws were gradually sapping the vitals of the country; and whatever miseries I suffered, I had no post to whisk my complaints for a single penny to the remotest corners of the empire . . .

   Attitude: _____

"Condition of Ireland," *The Illustrated London News*
"Progress in Personal Comfort" by Sydney Smith

Literary Analysis: Journalistic Essay

Journalistic essays are short prose pieces that describe current events or trends. Unlike personal essays, which focus on a writer's inner reflections and personal reactions to experiences, journalistic essays examine news, facts, and events and try to make them directly relevant to a wider audience. The writer of a journalistic essay gathers facts and weaves them into a unified story.

DIRECTIONS: Answer the following questions.

1. What purely factual information does the journalistic essay "Condition of Ireland" present about the Famine and Britain's Poor-Laws?

_____

_____

_____

_____

_____

2. What voice is used in *The Illustrated London News* article? What perspective does this voice provide on the facts surrounding the famine? Name specific examples from the selection that demonstrate the writer's perspective.

_____

_____

_____

_____

_____

3. According to "Progress in Personal Comfort," what inventions and services came about during Sydney Smith's life?

_____

_____

_____

_____

_____

4. How might you describe the voice of Sydney Smith in "Progress in Personal Comfort"? What unique story about progress and a changing world does he tell? Give specific examples of Smith's perspective on these events.

_____

_____

_____

_____

_____

"Opening Statement for the Inaugural Session of the Forum for Peace and Reconciliation" by Judge Catherine McGuinness

Build Vocabulary: The Language of Reconciliation

When making the case for peace and reconciliation in an area of conflict, a writer or speaker must choose his or her vocabulary with care. Judge McGuinness applies diplomacy in the words she uses in her speech.

DIRECTIONS: Write the word from the box that best completes each numbered blank in the paragraph. Then use the word in a sentence of your own that relates to the quest for reconciliation in contemporary conflicts around the globe.

stability	respect	rights
validity	traditions	democratic
trust	cooperation	understanding

The diplomats who work for the United Nations have a difficult job. Being assigned by the organization to help bring about (1) _____ in tumultuous situations is a daunting undertaking. Often these diplomats, sometimes known as special envoys, must deal with people whose cultures and (2) _____ are quite different from their own. Such practices must be treated with (3) _____ ; one must not judge the (4) _____ of other people's cultural and political practices. In some situations, the diplomat must be a patient negotiator, attempting to have two sides in a conflict agree to meet in an atmosphere of (5) _____ , even if absolute (6) _____ comes later. At other times, a diplomat must take a sterner tack, lecturing those outside the bounds of international law on the importance of respecting human (7) _____ , even with the (8) _____ that different countries around the globe have differing conceptions of the (9) _____ process.

1. sentence: _____

2. sentence: _____

3. sentence: _____

4. sentence: _____

5. sentence: _____

6. sentence: _____

7. sentence: _____

8. sentence: _____

9. sentence: _____

"Opening Statement for the Inaugural Session of the Forum for Peace and Reconciliation" by Judge Catherine McGuinness

Thematic Connection: Reconciling the Empire

Northern Ireland has been the scene of one of the world's most intractable conflicts. In recent years, hopes for peace have been raised time and again only to be dashed later in a seemingly unbreakable cycle of violence. Judge Catherine McGuinness's opening statement is an eloquent plea for reconciliation. What concrete actions might the Forum agree on to achieve the goal of peace?

DIRECTIONS: Use the questions below to help formulate your own contribution to the quest for peace in Northern Ireland. Answer the questions as if you were preparing a memo to the Forum participants or to the peace negotiators in which you present your findings and suggestions.

What are the roots of the conflict in Northern Ireland?

_____

_____

_____

_____

_____

What specific issues divide the opposing sides in the conflict?

_____

_____

_____

_____

_____

_____

What specific recommendations can you make to help foster reconciliation and bring about peace?

_____

_____

_____

_____

_____

_____

_____

_____

_____

"Remembrance" by Emily Brontë
"The Darkling Thrush" and **"'Ah, Are You Digging on My Grave?'"**
by Thomas Hardy

Build Vocabulary

Spelling Strategy Words ending in silent e drop the e before a suffix beginning with a vowel: *rapture + -ous = rapturous.*

Using the Root *-terr(a)-*

A. DIRECTIONS: Match each word in the left column with its definition in the right column. Write the letter of the definition on the line next to the word it defines.

____ 1. territorial

____ 2. terrace

____ 3. subterranean

____ 4. terra-cotta

____ 5. terrarium

a. beneath the earth

b. fired clay used as building material

c. a glass container containing a garden of small plants and perhaps some small land animals

d. relating to a geographical area

e. a flat roof or paved outdoor space

Using the Word Bank

languish	rapturous	gaunt	terrestrial

B. DIRECTIONS: On the line, write the Word Bank word that best completes the meaning of the sentence as a whole.

1. The thrush in Hardy's poem sings a _____ song.

2. While in mourning, the woman refused to eat and became _____ and pale.

3. The turn of the century causes the speaker to _____ rather than celebrate.

4. Unable to fly, the ostrich is a more _____ creature than other birds.

C. DIRECTIONS: Match each word in the left column with its definition in the right column. Write the letter of the definition on the line next to the word it defines.

____ 1. languish

____ 2. rapturous

____ 3. gaunt

____ 4. terrestrial

a. of the earth

b. weaken

c. thin

d. ecstatic

"Remembrance" by Emily Brontë
"The Darkling Thrush" and **"'Ah, Are You Digging on My Grave?'"**
by Thomas Hardy

Grammar and Style: Pronoun Case Following *Than* or *As*

An incomplete construction is a clause in which key words are not stated, even while their meaning is understood. Sentences are often abbreviated in real speech, as well as in dialogue in poetry and prose, especially after the words *than* or *as*. A common mistake is using an incorrect pronoun to follow these words. To make sure you choose the pronoun after *than* or *as* correctly, mentally complete the sentence.

In the following example, an incomplete construction contains the pronoun *I* following the word *as*. The word in brackets is the unspoken word that is understood and that completes the clause.

And every spirit upon earth / Seemed fervorless *as I* [was].

A. Practice: Circle the pronoun that correctly completes each construction.

1. Few siblings were closer to one another than (*they, them*).

2. Everyone at the New Year's party seemed to have a better time than (*he, him*).

3. No one was as disappointed by the party as (*I, me*).

4. I enjoy poetry more than (*she, her*).

5. No group was more prepared for the presentation than (*we, us*).

6. My partner was as nervous as (*I, me*).

B. Writing Application: Complete each construction with an appropriate pronoun.

1. No one enjoyed the play more than _____.

2. The lead actor was more impressive than _____.

3. Few actors are as talented as _____.

4. Everyone was as pleased with the performance as _____.

"**Remembrance**" by Emily Brontë
"**The Darkling Thrush**" and "'**Ah, Are You Digging on My Grave?**'"
by Thomas Hardy

Reading Strategy: Reading Stanzas as Units of Meaning

Like paragraphs in prose, stanzas in poetry are usually a unit of meaning—they convey a main idea. Sometimes, a stanza will create a unified mood. Taken together, the stanzas of a poem express a larger theme or idea. As you read, analyze the stanzas in a poem for a progression of thoughts, a sequence of events, or a building of an argument or mood within the poem.

A. Directions: On the lines, write your answers to the following questions.

1. In "Remembrance," what progression of thoughts or sequence of events does the speaker describe in stanzas one through five?

_____

2. What change in the speaker's attitude occurs in stanzas six through eight?

_____

3. What pattern is established in the first four stanzas of "Ah, Are You Digging on My Grave"?

_____

4. What is the meaning of stanzas five and six? Do they have more than one meaning? Explain.

_____

B. Directions: On the flow chart, write a summary of each stanza in "The Darkling Thrush." Then write a sentence stating how the stanzas work together to create meaning.

Stanza 1:

↓

Stanza 2:

↓

Stanza 3:

↓

Stanza 4:

↓

Overall Meaning:

Remembrance/Darkling Thrush/Digging on My Grave **203**

"Remembrance" by Emily Brontë
"The Darkling Thrush" and **"Ah, Are You Digging on My Grave?"**
by Thomas Hardy

Literary Analysis: Stanza Structure and Irony

A **stanza** usually contains a certain number of lines arranged to show a recurring pattern, rhythmic structure, and rhyme scheme. **Irony** is a deliberate contradiction between expectation and reality. Poets can establish certain expectations in their readers through a regular stanza structure. When poets then inject surprising events or ideas within the stanza structure, they create irony. The contrast between expectation and reality can make a poem more memorable.

DIRECTIONS: Write your answers to the following questions on the chart.

Questions for Analysis	"Remembrance"	"The Darkling Thrush"	"Ah, Are You Digging on My Grave?"
1. How many stanzas are in the poem?			
2. What is the stanza type (number of lines, meter, rhyme scheme)?			
3. What expectation is established by the stanza structure?			
4. What change or surprise occurs in the poem?			
5. What is the irony in the poem?			

"God's Grandeur" and "Spring and Fall: To a Young Child"
by Gerard Manley Hopkins
"To an Athlete Dying Young" and "When I Was One-and-Twenty"
by A. E. Housman

Build Vocabulary

Spelling Strategy With the exception of the words *trite* and *contrite*, words that contain a long *i* sound followed by a *t* are spelled with the letter combination *ight*, as in the word *blight*.

Using Coined Words

A. DIRECTIONS: In "Spring and Fall," Hopkins uses *unleaving* to describe the falling of the leaves from the branches. This coined word concisely and descriptively expresses the poet's idea. For each of the following phrases, either coin a noun that names the idea or image in a descriptive way, or coin an adjective that would suit the subject.

1. a puddle _____

2. the first leaf buds of spring _____

3. puppies _____

4. a playground full of children _____

Using the Word Bank

grandeur	blight	rue

B. DIRECTIONS: Choose the letter of the word or phrase most nearly *similar* in meaning to each numbered word below. Write the letters on the lines provided.

____ 1. blight
    a. disease
    b. rotten
    c. dim
    d. understandable

____ 3. rue
    a. mourning
    b. rejoice
    c. blush
    d. regret

____ 2. grandeur
    a. more grand
    b. larger
    c. magnificence
    d. haughtiness

C. DIRECTIONS On the line, write the Word Bank word that best completes the sentence.

1. The great cathedral had a _____ that took one's breath away.

2. The tumble-down shack in the middle of the block was a _____ on the neighborhood.

3. My decision to leave before the end of the performance later caused me much _____.

Unit 5: Progress and Decline (1833–1901)

"God's Grandeur" and "Spring and Fall: To a Young Child"
by Gerard Manley Hopkins
"To an Athlete Dying Young" and "When I Was One-and-Twenty"
by A. E. Housman

Grammar and Style: Capitalization: Compass Points

When a compass point—a direction word—is used to refer to a region, the word is capitalized.

I find the **S**outhwest a fascinating place to read about.

I decorated my bedroom in **S**outhwestern style.

I have lived in the **E**ast all my life.

When a compass point is used to indicate direction, the word is not capitalized.

We drove **s**outh about twenty miles to the riding stables.

Once there, we wandered **e**astward along a stream.

Later, we saw the city lights glowing to the **n**orth of us.

A. Practice: Write a *D* in front of each sentence in which the italicized word indicates direction. Write an *R* in front of each sentence in which the italicized word refers to a region, and capitalize the first letter of the word.

_____ 1. Driving *westward* at sunset, we almost wished for a cloud to block the bright sun.

_____ 2. Our morning schedule took us *north* to view a historic site.

_____ 3. The *west* was our destination, and once we reached the Black Hills, we felt as if we had made it.

_____ 4. The next day, our progress was slowed by road construction on the *westbound* lanes of the highway.

_____ 5. Two days later I saw Mt. Rainier looming in the distance and knew that we had reached the *northwest*.

_____ 6. Our homeward journey, though pleasant, had little of the excitement of our *western* travels.

B. Writing Application: Follow the instructions to write sentences that contain compass points, or direction words. Remember to capitalize a word that refers to a region.

1. Make a statement about the states of Georgia and South Carolina. Refer to the region in which those states lie.

_____

2. Write a sentence about traveling from Texas to Montana.

_____

3. Write a sentence about California and the region in which it lies.

_____

4. In what direction would you have to travel to get to Maine? In your answer, name the region in which Maine lies.

_____

"God's Grandeur" and **"Spring and Fall: To a Young Child"**
by Gerard Manley Hopkins
"To an Athlete Dying Young" and **"When I Was One-and-Twenty"**
by A. E. Housman

Reading Strategy: Applying Biography

Knowing something about a poet can help readers understand that person's poetry more fully. Even simple details, such as knowing whether a poet is a man or a woman, can make a poem's meaning more clear. Whenever you read an author's **biography** in a textbook or anthology, be sure to apply what you learn to that person's writings.

Perhaps the most significant and startling fact about Gerard Manley Hopkins, for example, is that he was a Jesuit priest for all of his adult life. As you read his poems, look for signs of his religious beliefs. You may also see signs of the conflict he felt between his vocation and his other interests.

DIRECTIONS: Use the charts on this page to record what you learn about each poet from the biographies on page 856. Then look for evidence of each man's character or personality in his poems. Quote lines or phrases from the poems that reveal the poets' backgrounds. An example entry has been provided.

Characteristic of Hopkins	Where Characteristic Is Seen in Poems
strong religious beliefs	"The world is charged with the grandeur of God." ("God's Grandeur," line 1)

Characteristic of Housman	Where Characteristic Is Seen in Poems

"God's Grandeur" and **"Spring and Fall: To a Young Child"**
by Gerard Manley Hopkins
"To an Athlete Dying Young" and **"When I Was One-and-Twenty"**
by A. E. Housman

Literary Analysis: Rhythm and Meter

Rhythm is the alternation of strong and weak—or stressed and unstressed—syllables, which creates a flow or movement. **Meter** describes or "measures" rhythm when it follows a regular pattern. When poets or readers examine the meter of a poem, they "scan" the poem, marking stressed syllables with a ´ mark and unstressed syllables with a ˘ mark.

The meter of a poem is measured in feet. A foot is a combination of two or more syllables, at least one of which is typically stressed. There are specific kinds of feet. Here are two examples.

Metrical Foot	Pattern of Syllables	Example
iamb trochee	one unstressed, one stressed (˘ ´) one stressed, one unstressed (´ ˘)	The time you won your town the race It will come to such sights colder

Another way to measure and label meter is to count how many feet there are in a line. In the iambic example in the chart, the line contains four iambic feet. Thus the line is said to be in iambic *tetrameter*. The words *trimeter* and *pentameter* refer to lines of poetry with three feet and five feet, respectively.

Hopkins is known for experimenting with rhythm. He uses counterpoint rhythm, which consists of two opposing rhythms in one line of poetry. He also uses what he called "sprung rhythm," which he felt closely imitates the flow of natural speech. In sprung rhythm, each foot begins with a stressed syllable, which may then be followed by any number of unstressed syllables. Scanning a poem written in sprung rhythm reveals its lack of conventional meter.

DIRECTIONS: Follow the instructions given to examine the meter of Hopkins's and Housman's poems. (Scansion is not an exact science, but you should be able to find general patterns.)

1. Scan the second stanza of "To an Athlete Dying Young." Then identify the meter of each line.

   Today, the road all runners come,

   Shoulder-high we bring you home,

   And set you at your threshold down,

   Townsman of a stiller town.

2. Scan these two lines from "God's Grandeur."

   And for all this, nature is never spent:

   There lives the dearest freshness deep down things; . . .

3. Scan these lines from "Spring and Fall: To a Young Child."

   Now no matter, child, the name:

   Sorrow's springs are the same.

   What effect does the meter have on the meaning of these lines?

"Eternity" by Arthur Rimbaud

Build Vocabulary

Poets and writers of prose must have at hand a vocabulary to describe innumerable situations—from the heights of glory to the depths of gloom.

A. DIRECTIONS: Match each word in the left column with its definition in the right column. Write the letter of the definition on the line next to the word it defines.

____	1. recovered	a. pain, extreme unease
____	2. eternity	b. burning coals
____	3. vow	c. won back
____	4. sanctions	d. passion
____	5. ardor	e. penalties
____	6. embers	f. endless period of time
____	7. anguish	g. solemn promise

B. DIRECTIONS: Choose the word from the left column above that best completes each sentence below. Write each word in the correct blank.

1. I hoped that this happy feeling would last an _____.

2. He made a _____ that he would never forget what happened.

3. As I poked at the _____ of the fire, I felt nothing but contentment.

4. What _____ could possibly equal the horrible crime that was committed?

5. I have _____ the joy of my youth.

6. The poet's _____ was evident from the passion of his verses.

7. His face was twisted in _____ at his loss.

"Eternity" by Arthur Rimbaud

Thematic Connection: Gloom and Glory

The poets in this section focus on the contradictory aspects of the human experience: gloom and glory, birth and death, love and loss, civilization and nature. The writers may be said to explore the cycles of life and its passing. Contemporary artists have explored similar themes in a variety of ways. In the song "Glory Days," Bruce Springsteen examines the passing of youth and its heights of accomplishment and emotion. The popular Broadway musical *Sunset Boulevard* offers a searing portrait of an actress, Norma Desmond, who refuses to acknowledge the changes time has brought. The character is caught and cannot move on.

DIRECTIONS: Consider how you might explore in a song or poem of your own the themes focused on by the poets in this section. First, reread the poem "Eternity" by Arthur Rimbaud. Then, use the graphic organizer to list the images Rimbaud uses to explore his theme. Finally, use the remaining lines on the page to list a topic you would like to explore and sketch out images you would include.

"Eternity" by Arthur Rimbaud
Images

_____

_____

_____

_____

_____

_____

_____

_____

Poetry of William Butler Yeats

Build Vocabulary

Spelling Strategy The suffix -*ous* is pronounced *us* and means "having," "full of," or "characterized by." If a word is an adjective ending in the *us* sound, spell it *ous*. Examples include *beauteous*, *righteous*, and *clamorous*.

Using the Root -*ques*-

The root -*ques*- derives from the Latin verb *quaerere*, which means "to ask."

A. DIRECTIONS: The words in the list use the -*ques*- root. Choose the word that best completes each sentence and write in on the line.

request   quest

1. The explorer's _____ for adventure caused him to undertake a voyage around the world.

2. The employee had to _____ another copy of the company's pension plan.

Using the Word Bank

clamorous	conquest	anarchy
conviction	paltry	artifice

B. DIRECTIONS: Each item consists of a word from the Word Bank followed by four lettered words or phrases. Choose the word or phrase most nearly *opposite* in meaning to the Word Bank word. Circle the letter of your choice.

1. clamorous
   a. miserable
   b. joyful
   c. quiet
   d. timid

2. conquest
   a. defeat
   b. plunder
   c. strategy
   d. battle

3. anarchy
   a. faith
   b. order
   c. power
   d. hope

4. conviction
   a. freedom
   b. certainty
   c. weakness
   d. doubt

5. paltry
   a. simple
   b. valuable
   c. clear
   d. kind

6. artifice
   a. destruction
   b. ingenuity
   c. dumbness
   d. incivility

Poetry of William Butler Yeats

Grammar and Style: Noun Clauses

Subordinate clauses of every type can function as single parts of speech. One type of clause, a **noun clause**, can serve any function that a noun can serve in a sentence. Here are examples of noun clauses:

Subject: *What Yeats believed about history* shows in his poems.

Direct Object: Yeats thought *that history runs in cycles.*

Indirect Object: Yeats gives *what he believes* free rein in some poems, but not all.

Object of Preposition: His general theory of *what determines history* produces sometimes complicated imagery.

Predicate Noun or **Subject Complement:** The important thing to remember is *that one need not understand all Yeats's theories to enjoy the poetry.*

Appositive: The essential thing, *what one should go by,* is whether a poem speaks to you.

A. Practice: Underline the noun clauses in the following sentences. Above each, indicate how the noun clause functions.

1. In "When You Are Old," the speaker expresses an idea of what the thoughts of a woman he once loved might one day be.

2. Who you are may determine whether you believe "The Lake Isle of Innisfree" refers to a type of place or a kind of work.

3. Knowledge that the world will go on without you, that stark recognition, glides also across the water in "The Wild Swans at Coole."

4. In "Sailing to Byzantium," an aging man hopes that he can make himself eternal through intellect and artwork.

B. Writing Application: Write a sentence that uses the noun clause in the way indicated in parentheses.

1. That Yeats is the best Irish poet (subject)

_____

_____

2. How Yeats creates memorable images (complement)

_____

_____

3. What Yeats says about aging (direct object)

_____

_____

4. Who the reader is (object of preposition)

_____

_____

Poetry of William Butler Yeats

Reading Strategy: Applying Literary Background

Many readers focus closely on the words of a poem for understanding. After understanding the writer's work as it exists on the page, though, readers may find it helpful and interesting to consider a work in the larger context of the artist's life. What might have led a writer to a specific subject? What was he or she doing when this work was composed? What was the social or historical climate of the period?

It is not necessarily safe or correct, however, to assume that what is in a writer's work gives the exact story of his or her life. Events in writers' lives may not adequately explain their work. For example, one need not know or understand the full details of Yeats's involvement with Irish politics to appreciate his poetry. In some of his poems, however, having knowledge of the issues helps explain references and attitudes.

DIRECTIONS: For each poem, use the third column to write the impact the information in the second column might have had on the poem's composition. Cite specific lines or sections when you can.

Poem	Background Information	Impact on the Poem
1. "When You Are Old"	Actress Maud Gonne, a founder of Sinn Fein, met Yeats three years before the poem was written. She starred in his first play. He proposed, but she married another Irish revolutionary.	
2. "The Wild Swans at Coole"	Yeats summered for years at Coole Park, elegant home of Lady Gregory, founder of the Irish National Theater.	
3. "The Second Coming"	The poem was written in 1920. After the Russian revolution in 1917, counterrevolution, chaos, and famine persisted in the new state into the 1920's.	
4. "Sailing to Byzantium"	In a prose work, *The Vision*, Yeats wrote "I think that if I were given a month of antiquity . . . I would spend it in Byzantium [circa 535 AD] . . ."	

Poetry of William Butler Yeats

Literary Analysis: Symbolism

A **symbol** is a word, character, object, or action that stands for something beyond itself. To determine whether a word has symbolic meaning, consider it within the context of the poem. For example, the city of Byzantium, which symbolically represents the poetic imagination, is central to the meaning of "Sailing to Byzantium." It is in Byzantium that the speaker finds "the singing masters of (his) soul." That Byzantium is part of the title is another clue to its significance.

Following is an anonymous poem. Read the poem and answer the questions that follow.

In the Garden

In the garden there strayed
A beautiful maid
As fair as the flowers of the morn;
The first hour of her life
She was made a man's wife,
And buried before she was born.

1. The "maid" of this poem is an allusion to Eve in the Biblical story of creation. What evidence in the poem indicates that "maid" is symbolic?

_____

_____

_____

_____

_____

_____

_____

2. According the Bible, God created Adam's mate, Eve, by fashioning her from one of Adam's ribs. This means that Eve was never actually "born" in the normal sense of the word. Given this information, how can Eve be interpreted as a symbol for women in general?

_____

_____

_____

_____

_____

_____

_____

"Preludes," "Journey of the Magi" and "The Hollow Men"
by T. S. Eliot

Build Vocabulary

Spelling Strategy For words ending in two consonants, keep both consonants when adding a suffix starting with either a vowel or consonant. For example, the suffix *-ed* added to the word *gall* forms the word *galled*.

Using the Root *-fract-*

In "Journey of the Magi," T. S. Eliot describes camels as "sore-footed and *refractory*." The word *refractory* means "stubborn" or "hard to manage." It contains the root *-fract-*, meaning "to break." A *refractory* camel is one that breaks away from the path which you want to take.

A. Directions: Complete each sentence with a word from the following list.

refract   fractional   fractious

1. He ate only a _____ portion of his meal.

2. Guards were trying to control the loud and _____ crowd.

3. A prism hanging in a window will _____ sunlight into different colors.

Using the Word Bank

galled	refractory	dispensation
supplication	tumid	

B. Directions: Choose a lettered pair that best expresses a relationship *similar* to that expressed in the numbered pair. Circle the letter of your choice.

1. GALLED : FRICTION ::
   a. worked : accomplishment
   b. consume : food
   c. rested : sleep
   d. injury : sore

2. REFRACTORY : STUBBORN ::
   a. generous : unselfish
   b. organize : arrange
   c. ancient : contemporary
   d. quietly : whisper

3. DISPENSATION : BELIEF ::
   a. creation : invent
   b. theory : philosophy
   c. operation : machine
   d. thought : concentrate

4. SUPPLICATION : PRAYER ::
   a. organization : society
   b. belief : knowledge
   c. education : lesson
   d. instruction : learn

5. TUMID : SHRIVELED ::
   a. pester : annoy
   b. heat : scorching
   c. massive : miniature
   d. simple : plain

"Preludes," "Journey of the Magi" and **"The Hollow Men"**
by T. S. Eliot

Grammar and Style: Adjectival Modifiers

An **adjectival modifier** is any word or word group that functions as an adjective. The poems of T. S. Eliot contain many examples of prepositional phrases, participial phrases, and adjective clauses used as adjectival modifiers. For example:

    Prepositional phrase: "In this valley of dying stars"

The prepositional phrase *of dying stars* modifies *valley.*

    Participial phrase: ". . . And the silken girls bringing sherbet."

The participial phrase *bringing sherbet* modifies *girls.*

    Adjective clause: "I am moved by fancies/that are curled around these images . . ."

The adjective clause *that are curled around these images* modifies *fancies.*

A. Practice: For each of the following excerpts from "Preludes," "Journey of the Magi," and "The Hollow Men," underline the adjectival modifier and circle the word it modifies. Then, on the line following the excerpt, identify the modifier as a prepositional phrase, a participial phrase, or an adjective clause.

1. And now a gusty shower wraps / The grimy scraps / Of withered leaves . . . _____

2. The worlds revolve like ancient women / Gathering fuel . . . _____

3. Those who have crossed / With direct eyes . . . _____

4. And newspapers from vacant lots . . . _____

5. With all its muddy feet that press . . . _____

6. Then the camel men cursing and grumbling . . . _____

B. Writing Application: Write a description of the scene in "Preludes," using a variety of adjectival modifiers. Experiment with prepositional phrases, participial phrases, and adjective clauses. Underline each modifier in your paragraph.

_____

_____

_____

_____

_____

_____

_____

_____

_____

_____

"Preludes," "Journey of the Magi" and "The Hollow Men"
by T. S. Eliot

Reading Strategy: Interpreting

In order to understand the themes in T. S. Eliot's poetry, you must **interpret**, or find meaning, in repeated images, words, and phrases. By linking these elements, you can find the meanings they suggest. For example, notice the images Eliot presents of urban life in "Preludes." If you put these images together, what do you learn about Eliot's view of the modern world?

DIRECTIONS: As you read the poems, use the following questions as a guide to search for meaning in the images and patterns of Eliot's poems.

1. What images does Eliot use to describe the city in "Preludes"? What feeling is created by these images? What do these images say about his perception of modern, urban life?

   _____

   _____

   _____

2. What images in "Preludes" relate directly to the actions of humans in the urban setting? What does the pattern of these images suggest about the lives of the people?

   _____

   _____

3. In "Journey of the Magi," what images does Eliot give of the journey? What do these images suggest about the journey?

   _____

   _____

   _____

4. What images and repeated words in "Journey of the Magi" describe the feelings of the Magi after their journey? What do these elements suggest about the importance of the journey?

   _____

   _____

   _____

5. What images in "The Hollow Men" describe specific limitations of the hollow men? What do these details reveal about the men's situation in life?

   _____

   _____

   _____

6. What images describe directly the world in which the hollow men live? What do these images reveal about Eliot's perception of the world?

   _____

   _____

"Preludes," "Journey of the Magi" and "The Hollow Men"
by T. S. Eliot

Literary Analysis: Modernism

Modernism was a literary movement of the early-to-mid twentieth century in which writers attempted to break away from traditional forms and styles of the past. Modernist literature was highly influenced by industrialization and by World War I, which many writers felt left the world chaotic, fragmented, and sad. In poetry, the Modernist movement brought forth a technique known as imagism. Imagist poets, including T. S. Eliot, stood back from their subjects, not commenting outright on feeling or meaning. They used suggestive, musical language and clear images to evoke emotions in readers. Their images are like snapshots, which capture important moments of perception.

DIRECTIONS: Connect the elements of Modernism with the following excerpts from the Modernist poems you have read.

1. The morning comes to consciousness . . . From the sawdust-trampled street / With all its muddy feet that press / To early coffee-stands. / With the other masquerades / That time resumes, / One thinks of all the hands / That are raising dingy shades / In a thousand furnished rooms.

   In what way is the style and theme of this excerpt from "Preludes" uniquely Modernist?

   _____

   _____

   _____

   _____

2. And the night-fires going out, and the lack of shelters, / And the cities hostile and the towns unfriendly / And the villages dirty and charging high prices: / A hard time we had of it. / At the end we preferred to travel all night. / Sleeping in snatches, / With the voices singing in our ears, saying / That this was all folly.

   In what way is the style of this excerpt reflective of the Modernist movement? In what way does the subject matter of "The Journey of the Magi," and the faithful dedication of the Magi revealed in this excerpt, set it apart from the strictly Modernist viewpoints expressed in the other two poems?

   _____

   _____

   _____

   _____

3. The eyes are not here / There are no eyes here / In this valley of dying stars / In this hollow valley / This broken jaw of our lost kingdoms / In this last of meeting places / We grope together / And avoid speech / Gathered on this beach of the tumid river

   What attitude toward people and the modern world is expressed in this excerpt from "The Hollow Men"? In what way is its style and theme similar to that of "Preludes"?

   _____

   _____

   _____

   _____

"In Memory of W. B. Yeats" and **"Musée des Beaux Arts"**
by W. H. Auden
"Carrick Revisited" by Louis MacNeice
"Not Palaces" by Stephen Spender

Build Vocabulary

Spelling Strategy Many words ending in *y* form their plurals by adding *-es* or *-ies* to the base word as in *affinity* + *ies* = *affinities*.

Using the Root *-top-*

A. DIRECTIONS: Knowing that the word root *-top-* means "place" and drawing upon your knowledge of other word roots, circle the letter of the best answer for each question.

1. What does a *topographer* do?
   (a) designs buildings
   (b) plans cities
   (c) records geographical features
   (d) studies the use of electricity

2. Where would you find a *utopia*?
   (a) nowhere
   (b) in the ocean
   (c) on a plain
   (d) in a distant galaxy

Using the Word Bank

sequestered	topographical	affinities
prenatal	intrigues	

B. DIRECTIONS: Choose the phrase that is the most appropriate description for each numbered word. Circle the letter of your choice.

1. sequestered
   a. a small fish in a big pond
   b. a knight on a mission
   c. a dancer on a stage
   d. a patient in quarantine

2. topographical
   a. a political map of Britain
   b. a spinning carnival ride
   c. a relief chart of a park
   d. a featureless, grassy plain

3. affinities
   a. a group of total strangers
   b. a network of interpersonal relationships
   c. an endless universe
   d. a structure made of building blocks

4. prenatal
   a. a ship being repaired
   b. a poet's first book
   c. a check-up for a mother-to-be
   d. a cat lapping up a large saucer of cream

5. intrigues
   a. conspirators' plots
   b. pilots' instruments
   c. students' textbooks
   d. priests' vestments

"In Memory of W. B. Yeats" and **"Musée des Beaux Arts"**
by W. H. Auden
"Carrick Revisited" by Louis MacNeice
"Not Palaces" by Stephen Spender

Grammar and Style: Parallel Structure

Parallel structure is the repeated use of the same grammatical form or pattern. Poets may use parallel structure to create a natural rhythm or flow in their writing or to emphasize an idea. In the following lines from "Not Palaces," the parallel prepositional phrases are underlined:

> It is too late for rare accumulation,

> For family pride, for beauty's filtered dusts.

A. Practice: Rewrite the italicized words to make the sentence structures parallel.

1. W. H. Auden wrote poetry and *was a teacher* in numerous universities.

    _____

2. Auden speaks of Yeats as a poet and *he was* a man.

    _____

3. Returning to his childhood home makes MacNeice recall his youth and *he considers* his identity.

    _____

4. For Spender, poetry has a way of changing attitudes and *it can promote* social equality.

    _____

B. Writing Application: Rewrite each of the following sentences, incorporating parallel sentence structure.

1. Yeats died on a day that was dark, and it was cold.

    _____

    _____

2. The "Old Masters" refers to artists from Belgium and Holland and others from Italy.

    _____

    _____

3. Bruegel enjoyed painting scenes of laborers, including harvesters and hunting scenes.

    _____

    _____

4. The speaker in "Carrick Revisited" admires the landscape and is remembering his childhood.

    _____

    _____

"In Memory of W. B. Yeats" and **"Musée des Beaux Arts"**
by W. H. Auden
"Carrick Revisited" by Louis MacNeice
"Not Palaces" by Stephen Spender

Reading Strategy: Paraphrasing

When you **paraphrase** a poet's words, or restate them in your own words, you can check your understanding of the poem's basic idea. Then you can interpret the poet's original work and appreciate how its language, imagery, and tone add depth to its meaning.

A. DIRECTIONS: Write a paraphrase for each set of lines.

"Musée des Beaux Arts"

1. . . . even the dreadful martyrdom must run its course
   Anyhow in a corner, some untidy spot
   Where the dogs go on with their doggy life . . .

   _____

   _____

"Carrick Revisited"

2. Time and place—our bridgeheads into reality
   But also its concealment! Out of the sea
   We land on the Particular and lose
   All other possible bird's-eye views, the Truth
   That is of Itself for Itself—but not for me.

   _____

   _____

"Not Palaces"

3. It is too late for rare accumulation,
   For family pride, for beauty's filtered dusts;
   I say, stamping the words with emphasis,
   Drink from here energy and only energy
   To will this time's change.

   _____

   _____

B. DIRECTIONS: Write an explanation of how each paraphrase in Part A helps you understand the poet's original words.

1. _____

2. _____

3. _____

"In Memory of W. B. Yeats" and **"Musée des Beaux Arts"**
by W. H. Auden
"Carrick Revisited" by Louis MacNeice
"Not Palaces" by Stephen Spender

Literary Analysis: Theme

A poem's **theme**, which is its central idea, concern, or purpose, may be directly stated. In some cases, theme may be implied by the poet's choice of words, images, tone, or mood.

DIRECTIONS: State what each set of lines indicates about the poem's theme. Determine whether the lines express theme directly or indirectly.

"In Memory of W. B. Yeats"

1. Now he is scattered among a hundred cities
   And wholly given over to unfamiliar affections;
   To find his happiness in another kind of wood
   And be punished by another code of conscience.
   The words of a dead man
   Are modified in the guts of the living.

   _____

   _____

"Musée des Beaux Arts"

2. . . . the expensive delicate ship that must have seen
   Something amazing, a boy falling out of the sky,
   Had somewhere to get to and sailed calmly on.

   _____

   _____

"Carrick Revisited"

3. Torn before birth from where my fathers dwelt,
   Schooled from the age of ten to a foreign voice,
   Yet neither western Ireland nor southern England
   Cancels this interlude; what chance misspelt
   May never now be righted by my choice.

   _____

   _____

"Not Palaces"

4. No spirit seek here rest. But this: No one
   Shall hunger: Man shall spend equally;
   Our goal which we compel: Man shall be man.

   _____

   _____

"Shooting an Elephant" by George Orwell

Build Vocabulary

Spelling Strategy Adding the suffix *-ity* changes a word into a noun. For example, the adjective *senile* becomes the noun *senility*. Remember to drop the silent *e* before adding a suffix that begins with a vowel.

Using Related Words About Politics

A. DIRECTIONS: In a few sentences, describe Orwell's experiences as a British police officer in Burma. Use the following words: *imperialism, despotic, dominion.*

_____

_____

_____

_____

_____

_____

_____

_____

_____

_____

_____

_____

_____

_____

Using the Word Bank

prostrate	imperialism	despotic
squalid	dominion	senility

B. DIRECTIONS: Match each word in the left column with its definition in the right column. Write the letter of the definition on the line next to the word it defines.

_____ 1. prostrate   a. miserably poor; wretched

_____ 2. imperialism   b. defenseless; in a prone or lying position

_____ 3. despotic   c. mental or physical decay due to old age

_____ 4. squalid   d. rule or power to rule; a governed territory

_____ 5. dominion   e. tyrannical

_____ 6. senility   f. policy and practice of forming and maintaining an empire in order to control raw materials and world markets by the conquest of other countries and the establishment of colonies

"Shooting an Elephant" by George Orwell

Grammar and Style: Restrictive and Nonrestrictive Participial Phrases

Participial phrases, or groups of words with a participle, modify nouns and pronouns. A **restrictive participial phrase** is essential to the meaning of the word it modifies and is not separated by commas. A **nonrestrictive participial phrase** is not essential to the meaning and can be separated by commas. Note the differences in the following examples:

Restrictive: I . . . saw a man's dead body *sprawling in the mud.*

Nonrestrictive: Some more women followed, *clicking their tongues and exclaiming . . .*

A. Practice: For each sentence, underline the participial phrase. On the line, indicate whether it is restrictive or nonrestrictive, and write the word it modifies.

1. ". . . the insults hooted after me when I was at a safe distance got badly on my nerves."

   _____

2. "It was a very poor quarter, a labyrinth of squalid bamboo huts, . . . winding all over a steep hillside."

   _____

3. "An old woman with a switch in her hand came round the corner of a hut, violently shooing away a crowd of naked children."

   _____

4. "He was lying on his belly with arms crucified and head sharply twisted to one side."

   _____

5. "Here was I, the white man with his gun, standing in front of the unarmed native crowd . . ."

   _____

B. Writing Application: In a few sentences, describe a situation in which you felt uncomfortable in front of an audience or crowd. Use at least one restrictive participial phrase and one nonrestrictive participial phrase in your description.

_____

_____

_____

_____

_____

_____

_____

_____

_____

_____

"**Shooting an Elephant**" by George Orwell

Reading Strategy: Recognizing the Writer's Attitudes

Orwell reveals in his essay that his attitudes toward British rule in Burma are not always clear cut. At times, he expresses conflicting attitudes. When you recognize the writer's attitudes, you uncover clues to the meaning in a literary work.

DIRECTIONS: Complete each cluster diagram by writing words and phrases, including quotations from the essay, that reflect Orwell's conflicting attitudes. Add branches to the diagram as needed. On the lines following each diagram, write your conclusion about Orwell's attitudes.

1.

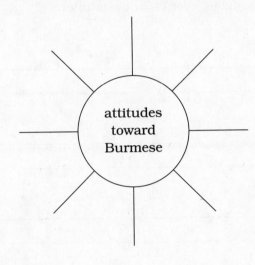

_____

_____

_____

2.

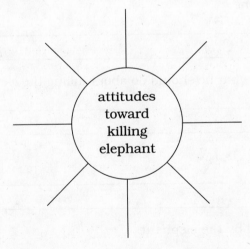

_____

_____

_____

Name _____ Date _____

Literary Analysis: Irony

Irony is a literary device that brings out contradictions between appearance and reality, or between expectation and reality, or between words and reality. In **verbal irony**, the intended meaning of words clashes with their usual meaning, as when Orwell describes the dangerous elephant as "grandmotherly." In **irony of situation**, events contradict what you expect to happen, as when the young Buddhist priests are revealed to be the most insulting toward the British.

DIRECTIONS: Explain what is ironic about the following facts, events, or descriptions.

1. Orwell's attitude toward Buddhist priests

_____

_____

2. Burmese population's lack of weapons

_____

_____

3. "Grinning" mouth of man trampled by elephant

_____

_____

4. Crowd gathering to watch shooting of elephant

_____

_____

5. Value of a living elephant compared to a dead one

_____

_____

6. Orwell's assessment that it was "perfectly clear" what he should do about killing the elephant

_____

_____

7. Comparison of rifle to something "beautiful"

_____

_____

8. Orwell's gladness that the coolie had been killed by the elephant

_____

_____

"The Demon Lover" by Elizabeth Bowen

Build Vocabulary

Spelling Strategy When adding the suffix -*tion* to a word that ends in *te*, such as *dislo-cate*, drop the final two letters; then add the suffix -*tion*, for *dislocation*.

Using the Root -*loc*-

A. DIRECTIONS: Each word in the following list contains the root -*loc*-, meaning "place." Choose the word from the list that correctly completes each sentence, and write it on the line.

allocation   localism   locality

1. Based on her accent, it was apparent that the _____ of her up-bringing was the deep South.

2. The residents' customs gave the town its sense of _____.

3. Each employee received a memo about the _____ of bonuses at the end of the year.

Using the Word Bank

spectral	dislocation	arboreal
circumscribed	aperture	

B. DIRECTIONS: Match each word in the left column with its definition in the right column. Write the letter of the definition on the line next to the word it defines.

____ 1. spectral   a. a condition of being out of place

____ 2. arboreal   b. ghostly

____ 3. circumscribed   c. limited

____ 4. dislocation   d. opening

____ 5. aperture   e. of, near, or among trees

"The Demon Lover" by Elizabeth Bowen

Grammar and Style: Sentence Beginnings—Participial Phrases

A participle is a verb form that functions as an adjective. Most participles end in *-ing* or *-ed*. A **participial phrase** is made up of a participle and its modifiers and complements.

The Londoners, *dreading nightfall*, listened for the drone of the German planes.

In this sentence, the participial phrase "dreading nightfall" modifies *Londoners.*

To create variety in your writing, you can begin sentences with participial phrases. Make sure, though, that the word your participial phrase modifies follows soon after the phrase.

Confusing: Looking about her, the unfamiliarity of her own home perplexed her.

Clear: Looking about her, she was perplexed by the unfamiliarity of her own home.

A. Practice: Circle the number of each sentence that begins with a participial phrase. For each sentence that begins with a participial phrase, underline the phrase and circle the word it modifies.

1. Everything smelled vaguely of ashes from the unused fireplace.

2. Proceeding upstairs, Mrs. Drover had not yet shaken her discomfort.

3. On the table lay a letter addressed to her.

4. Annoyed at the caretaker, she picked up the letter, which bore no stamp.

5. Polishing a clear patch in the mirror, Mrs. Drover peered closely at her face.

B. Writing Application: Revise the following paragraph so that three of the sentences begin with participial phrases. You may either combine or rearrange the existing sentences, or add your own details to create the participial phrases. Rewrite the paragraph in the space provided.

Elizabeth Bowen, described as a writer of "finely wrought prose," is praised highly for her stories. Her characters are mostly from the upper middle class in England and Ireland. Bowen "knew" her characters well, for she was born into that class. Her novel *The Hotel*, published in 1927, contains a typical Bowen heroine. The girl, trying to cope with a life for which she is not prepared, might remind some of a young Elizabeth Bowen.

_____
_____
_____
_____
_____
_____
_____
_____
_____
_____
_____

"The Demon Lover" by Elizabeth Bowen

Reading Strategy: Responding

When you are reading and interpreting fiction, try to find the relationship between the details the author presents and the meaning of the piece. One way to find that meaning is to think about your own **response.** Did the piece grab your attention? Were you frightened? Did it remind you of something in your own life? Identify your own reaction and judge whether your response was intended by the author, and how he or she evoked it.

DIRECTIONS: Use the following questions to record your own response to "The Demon Lover."

1. What was your response to the mood set at the beginning of the story?

_____

_____

_____

2. What was your response to the letter sent to Mrs. Dover?

_____

_____

_____

3. What was your response to the story's ending?

_____

_____

_____

4. Were there parts of the story that reminded you of your own experiences? If so, what were they?

_____

_____

_____

5. What parts of the story grabbed your attention or emotions? Why?

_____

_____

_____

6. Do you think the author intended to get these responses from you? Why would the author want this kind of response?

_____

_____

_____

Name _____ Date _____

"The Demon Lover" by Elizabeth Bowen

Literary Analysis: The Ghost Story

During the nineteenth-century romantic movement, the focus of literature turned to the personal lives of everyday people. Some of these stories were of people with dark or mysterious events in their lives. One of the offshoots of this movement was the development of gothic novels, so named for settings that often included castles or other buildings of gothic architecture. Inevitably such stories began to include tales of folklore and other metaphysical events. Others were written with an emphasis on the supernatural. The **ghost story**, long an oral tradition, became a popular literary form as well.

Part of the appeal of a good ghost story is that it is about normal people who do everyday things. Somehow, though, their normality is disrupted by something that cannot be easily explained or dismissed. Readers relate to the ordinariness of the characters, and are, therefore, intrigued when something unusual happens. Most writers of ghost stories build tension throughout the story by dropping hints or including small details that could be interpreted in more than one way.

DIRECTIONS: Use the following chart to record the "normal" elements in "The Demon Lover" as well as the unusual aspects that creep in almost from the very beginning.

Scene or Detail	What is normal?	What is unusual?
outside Mrs. Drover's house		
inside Mrs. Drover's house		
the letter		
the farewell, 25 years ago		
Mrs. Drover's marriage and family		
catching the taxi		

"The Diameter of the Bomb" by Yehuda Amichai
"Everything Is Plundered" by Anna Akhmatova
"Testament" by Bei Dao

Build Vocabulary: Language of a Grim Reality

In many respects, the twentieth century has been a grim catalogue of barbarity and cruelty, from the horrible carnage of World War I in the early 1900's to the murderous civil strife afflicting such areas as Algeria and the former Yugoslavia today. To provide a clear-eyed description of the unsettling aspects of our century, many writers use a vocabulary of grim reality.

DIRECTIONS: Choose the word from the box that best completes each numbered blank within the paragraph. Then, write a sentence of your own using the words to describe a situation of grim reality.

betrayed	pain
bomb	plundered
graveyard	ruined
mourning	wounded

I could hear the crying of the (1) ____ even before arriving in the town's central marketplace. The marketplace was (2) ____ , devastated by the explosion of a (3) ____ , which had blown up at the stroke of noon. I was struck by the figure of an old man standing over a dead body, (4) ____ the loss of a loved one. What (5) ____ he must have been feeling!

To add to the horror, in the chaos and confusion thieves had (6) ____ some of the shops. "We have been (7) ____!" sobbed a survivor. "All those empty promises of peace . . ." Her voice trailed off as she watched a grim-faced group of people begin to carry victims to the (8) ____ for burial.

1. word: _____ sentence: _____
   _____

2. word: _____ sentence: _____
   _____

3. word: _____ sentence: _____
   _____

4. word: _____ sentence: _____
   _____

5. word: _____ sentence: _____
   _____

6. word: _____ sentence: _____
   _____

7. word: _____ sentence: _____
   _____

8. word: _____ sentence: _____
   _____

"The Diameter of the Bomb" by Yehuda Amichai
"Everything Is Plundered" by Anna Akhmatova
"Testament" by Bei Dao

Cultural Connection: Waking From the Dream

In their poetry, Yehuda Amichai, Anna Akhmatova, and Bei Dao each respond to the grim reality of the dark side of the twentieth century. Without a doubt, problems persist around the globe as the century turns. Do the troubles that each of the poets confronted still fester? Have they been resolved in some way? If so, has the resolution caused problems of its own? What other contemporary problems are deserving of literary exploration?

DIRECTIONS: Use the chart to examine the context of the poems you read in this section. In the first box under each title, describe the conflict or historical circumstance that the poet is exploring or confronting. Then, in the second box, describe the status of the conflict today, explaining if a resolution has occurred that the poet might celebrate or whether the poet would have no cause to change his or her view.

	"The Diameter of the Bomb" by Yehuda Amichai	**"Everything Is Plundered"** by Anna Akhmatova	**"Testament"** by Bei Dao
Conflict in Poem			
Status of the Conflict Today			

"The Soldier" by Rupert Brooke
"Wirers" by Siegfried Sassoon
"Anthem for Doomed Youth" by Wilfred Owen
"Birds on the Western Front" by Saki (H. H. Munro)

Build Vocabulary

Spelling Strategy Words that end in the letter *y* preceded by a consonant form their plurals by dropping the *y* and adding *-ies*. Examples include *fly = flies; rally = rallies; symphony = symphonies; try = tries*; and the Word Bank word *mockeries*, from *mockery*.

Using the Root *-laud-*

The word *laudable*, which means "praiseworthy," originates from the Latin verb *laudere*, which means "to praise." Other related words are *laud, laudatory*, and *laudation*.

A. DIRECTIONS: Complete the following sentences with one of the words in the preceding paragraph that use the *-laud-* root.

1. Wilfred Owen's poem is powerful enough to _____ young soldiers and say that they "die like cattle" at the same time.

2. Is Brooke's _____ of England different in tone from one a homesick German might imagine for his country?

3. Saki's _____ remarks about birds gloss an ironic view of human beings.

Using the Word Bank

| stealthy | desolate | mockeries | pallor |
| laudable | requisitioned | disconcerted | |

B. DIRECTIONS: Each item consists of a word from the Word Bank followed by four lettered words or phrases. Choose the word or phrase most nearly *similar* in meaning to the Word Bank word. Circle the letter of your choice.

1. stealthy
   a. furtive
   b. luxurious
   c. pilfered
   d. invisible

2. desolate
   a. absent
   b. disconnected
   c. selected
   d. deserted

3. mockeries
   a. imitations
   b. farces
   c. symbols
   d. vanities

4. pallor
   a. salon
   b. companionship
   c. gloom
   d. paleness

5. laudable
   a. humorous
   b. flexible
   c. praiseworthy
   d. clamorous

6. requisitioned
   a. relocated
   b. investigated
   c. ordered
   d. recovered

7. disconcerted
   a. silenced
   b. confused
   c. detached
   d. failed

"The Soldier" by Rupert Brooke
"Wirers" by Siegfried Sassoon
"Anthem for Doomed Youth" by Wilfred Owen
"Birds on the Western Front" by Saki (H. H. Munro)

Grammar and Style: Using *Who* and *Whom* in Adjective Clauses

The pronouns *who* and *whom* sometimes cause confusion when they occur in clauses. A clause has both a subject and predicate and serves as a sentence element. In a sentence with an **adjective clause**, the entire clause modifies a noun or pronoun.

Determine which pronoun to use by what the pronoun is doing *within the clause.* If the pronoun serves as a subject, appositive, or complement in the clause, use *who*, the nominative form. If the pronoun serves as an object, indirect object, or object of a preposition in a clause, use *whom*, the objective form, regardless of how the entire clause functions. For example:

Sassoon, *whom* Owen met, published Owen's poetry after the war.

The pronoun *whom* serves as the object of *met*, the verb within the adjective clause. Because it is the object of a verb, *whom* is the correct pronoun, even though the clause is part of the subject.

A. Practice: Write either *who* or *whom* on the line to complete each of the following sentences.

1. In World War I, the killing efficiency of modern machine guns shocked

   those _____ had romantic notions of the glory of war.

2. Brave soldiers, _____ unprepared generals thought would attack as

   they always had, were mown like grass.

3. Tanks and airplanes were dismissed as interesting novelties by strategists

   _____ four years of slaughter taught little.

4. Warfare became stalemate mixed with suicidal attacks by those

   _____ had no choice and little chance.

B. Writing Application: Write sentences with adjective clauses using *who* or *whom*. Follow the prompts provided.

1. Write a sentence using *who* about Rupert Brooke and talented writers dying in World War I.

   _____

   _____

2. Write a sentence using *whom* about Siegfried Sassoon. The world discovered him in war and he wrote about peace in later life.

   _____

   _____

3. Write a sentence using *whom* about families that soldiers left behind—a subject on Wilfred Owen's mind as he writes his poem.

   _____

   _____

"The Soldier" by Rupert Brooke
"Wirers" by Siegfried Sassoon
"Anthem for Doomed Youth" by Wilfred Owen
"Birds on the Western Front" by Saki (H. H. Munro)

Reading Strategy: Making Inferences

An **inference** is a conclusion drawn by reasoning. We make inferences all the time in daily life. Someone stands in the hall with wet hair and a dripping umbrella, and we conclude that it has been raining outside. If the sprinkler system had gone off in the building ten minutes ago, however, we might make a different inference. In short, we infer based on all available evidence. In daily life, we do this quickly, almost automatically.

In literature, we may have to make inferences more consciously. Writers engage readers by portraying a world of details or evidence and understand that readers will draw conclusions from clues they read.

Much in literature is implied, especially in poetry, so picking up quickly on setting, images, language, tone, and theme is a valuable skill for a reader. What do you know about the setting and speaker? How do you know it? What's going on? How soon do you find out? What clues do you use? What is the tone and message of the work? What language lets you make the inference?

Use the following chart to practice making inferences.

DIRECTIONS: Write down the inference you make about each element of "Birds on the Western Front." In the Clues column, identify specifically the evidence that you used to make the inference.

Element	Inference	Clues
Setting (Where?)		
Speaker (Who?)		
Action/Topic (What?)		
Tone (Attitude)		
Theme (Message)		

"The Soldier" by Rupert Brooke
"Wirers" by Siegfried Sassoon
"Anthem for Doomed Youth" by Wilfred Owen
"Birds on the Western Front" by Saki (H. H. Munro)

Literary Analysis: Tone

The **tone** of language conveys an attitude toward the audience or the subject. We recognize tone in spoken language quickly. The way in which words are spoken, as well as the speaker's volume and facial expressions help us sort out his or her attitude. Some of these advantages aren't available to the writer, who must create tone with language alone. In literature, tone is transmitted primarily through choice of words and details.

Details selected may imply an attitude about the subject. In "The Soldier," Rupert Brooke represents England with "her flowers to love" and "the suns of home." Apart from descriptive language, these choices tell us part of what Brooke feels for his country.

The particular words selected matter greatly. When Wilfred Owen writes of "shrill, demented choirs of wailing shells," we get a clear sense of his attitude toward war. A writer's manner of speaking, or voice, conveys tone, too. Is it formal or informal? Serious or light? Lofty or low? How does the language help you make these decisions?

DIRECTIONS: Analyze the tone of each of the following passages. For each one, explain what impression details, word choices, and voice make. Then describe the overall tone of the passage.

"Wirers"		
. . . I heard him carried away, / Moaning at every lurch; no doubt he'll die today. / But we can say the front-line wire's been safely mended.		
Details:	Word Choice:	Voice:
Tone:		

"Birds on the Western Front"		
. . . once, having occasion to throw myself down with some abruptness on my face, I found myself nearly on the top of a brood of young larks. Two of them had already been hit by something and were in rather a battered condition, but the survivors seemed as tranquil and comfortable as the average nestling.		
Details:	Word Choice:	Voice:
Tone:		

"Wartime Speech" by Winston Churchill
"Defending Nonviolent Resistance" by Mohandas K. Gandhi

Build Vocabulary

Spelling Strategy A prefix attached to a word *never* affects the spelling of the original word. Examples include Word Bank words *dis-* + *affection* = *disaffection*, and *en-* + *durance* = *endurance* (although *durance* is an uncommon word). Other examples are *intolerable*, *reeducate*, *ennoble*, *mistake* and *unexceptional*.

Using the Root *-dur-*

The Latin word *durus* is an adjective meaning "hard." It is an ancestor of the Word Bank word *endurance*, which means "stamina" or "resistance to wear." Most words with a *-dur-* root carry this connotation of toughness.

A. DIRECTIONS: For each of the sentences, write the word from among the following that can replace the underlined words:

duration   durability   obdurate

1. For the time the war wore on, Churchill never let show his fear. _____

2. Gandhi was hard and unyielding in not compromising his position. _____

3. Though they differed on the role of the British Empire, the resistance to corruption of their reputations has outlived both the men and the issues that divided them. _____

Using the Word Bank

intimidated	endurance	formidable
invincible	retaliate	disaffection
diabolical	extenuating	excrescence

B. DIRECTIONS: Complete each sentence with the best choice from the Word Bank.

After the Germans tore through France early in World War II, there appeared no way to defeat them. The Nazi war machine looked (1) _____. Hitler, however, feared crossing water for military action, and the British Navy was still (2) _____. German planes began to bomb England in an effort to terrorize Britons. The British, however, were unafraid and not (3) _____. Churchill chose to bomb Berlin. Hitler was shocked that the English had the means to (4) _____. Bombing raids struck at civilians, an evil development in the (5) _____ history of war. This horrible tactic, an (6) _____ of previous military strategy, became common. With unbelievable stamina, civilians went about daily life with incredible (7) _____. In spite of their suffering, British citizens showed little (8) _____ with the war effort. The recognition that this was total war for both sides may be an (9) _____ factor in the decision to bomb civilians, but it doesn't make less terrible the death of innocent millions.

"Wartime Speech" by Winston Churchill
"Defending Nonviolent Resistance" by Mohandas K. Gandhi

Grammar and Style: Parallel Structure

Parallel structure is the use of matching grammatical forms or patterns to express related ideas. Parallel structure adds rhetorical power through rhythm, repetition, and balance. Writers may repeat single words, phrases, or clauses in parallel structure. In a parallel structure, each part of the coordinating structure must be of the same grammatical form.

A. Practice: Underline parallel structures in the following passages and identify the grammatical element of each.

"Wartime Speech"

1. And if the French Army, and our own Army, are well handled, as I believe they will be; if the French retain that genius for recovery and counter-attack for which they have so long been famous; and if the British Army shows the dogged endurance . . . of which there have been so many examples in the past—then a sudden transformation might spring into being.

2. Only a very small part of that splendid army has yet been heavily engaged; and only a very small part of France has yet been invaded.

3. After this battle in France abates its force, there will come the battle for our island—for all that Britain is, and all that Britain means.

"Defending Nonviolent Resistance"

4. Nonviolence is the first article of my faith. It is also the last article of my creed.

5. No sophistry, no jugglery in figures can explain away the evidence that the skeletons in many villages present to the naked eye.

B. Writing Application: Rewrite each of the following items to use parallel structure.

1. Churchill wanted to explain the situation so he could encourage the Army and reassure the people. He also wanted to prepare both Army and people and inspire them for the long struggle he foresaw.

_____

_____

_____

_____

2. Gandhi did not dispute the British charges. He disputed the British right of administration. He objected to their application of the law and imposition of justice. He opposed British rule of India.

_____

_____

_____

_____

"Wartime Speech" by Winston Churchill

"Defending Nonviolent Resistance" by Mohandas K. Gandhi

Reading Strategy: Identifying Main Points and Support

One of the most important reading skills is the ability to recognize main points and supporting details. Readers and listeners look for main ideas and supporting details almost intuitively. You can see the principle operating in even a single sentence:

Churchill was a great wartime leader who refused to quit and inspired his people.

The main idea is that Churchill was a great wartime leader. The rest of the sentence gives evidence for the idea. Here is a graphic representation of the idea and support:

Main Idea	Churchill was a great wartime leader
Support 1	He refused to quit.
Support 2	He inspired his people.

The same principles of analysis work in paragraphs. In most paragraphs, a topic sentence near the beginning identifies the main idea. Other sentences provide support.

You can extend this type of analysis even to whole documents. The main idea of the Declaration of Independence, for example, is that the bonds of government between the King and the colonies must be broken. Thomas Jefferson gives about twenty-five reasons.

DIRECTIONS: Use the grid below to list the main idea and supporting features for the following paragraph. Label the supporting features S1, S2, and so on.

We must not allow ourselves to be intimidated by the presence of these armored vehicles behind our lines. If they are behind our Front, the French are also at many points fighting actively behind theirs. Both sides are therefore in an extremely dangerous position. If the French Army, and our own Army are well handled, as I believe they will be; if the French retain that genius for recovery and counter-attack for which they have so long been famous; and if the British Army shows the dogged endurance and solid fighting power of which there have been so many examples in the past—then a sudden transformation of the scene might spring into being.

Main Idea	
S1	

"Wartime Speech" by Winston Churchill
"Defending Nonviolent Resistance" by Mohandas K. Gandhi

Literary Analysis: Speech

Although different in rhetorical style, Churchill and Gandhi were excellent persuasive speakers. Both understood that the audience for a speech has needs different from the audience for a written work, and developed speaking styles to meet those needs.

The purpose of a speech may be to entertain, inform, or persuade, but to do any of these, it must capture and hold the attention of its audience. Features of an effective speech include:

An engaging introduction Depending on its purpose, a speech may begin with an announcement, brief statement of purpose, entertaining anecdote, or surprising declaration. The introduction serves as a "hook" to capture the interest of the audience. Churchill knows his audience is worried about war news, and begins there. Gandhi begins a "defense" by admitting guilt.

Clear organization The audience for a speech cannot stop and reread for information, so clarity and organization are especially important in a speech. Churchill uses simple statements followed by explanations and Gandhi addresses his points chronologically, but neither is hard to follow.

Concrete language and vivid images Although Churchill uses more formal rhetoric, his terms are familiar, and when he speaks of "gashed" Holland, or when Gandhi refers to "skeletons in many villages", the words have impact.

Examples Churchill gives specific examples of British heroism in the air and service at home, and Gandhi traces precisely the causes of his disaffection with British rule.

A strong conclusion In many speeches, the conclusion summarizes main points in an appealing way. In a persuasive speech, appeals to high ideals may be made. Gandhi and Churchill do both.

DIRECTIONS: Cite specific examples or passages from each selection that correspond to features of an effective speech.

1. Engaging Introduction:_____
   _____
   _____

2. Clear Organization: _____
   _____
   _____

3. Concrete Language/Vivid Images: _____
   _____
   _____

4. Examples: _____
   _____
   _____

5. Strong Conclusion: _____
   _____
   _____

"The Fiddle" by Alan Sillitoe

Build Vocabulary

Spelling Strategy When adding an ending that begins with a vowel to a word that ends in *y*, you almost always change the *y* to an *i* and add the ending. For example, *harry + -ed = harried.*

Using Forms of *Sublime*

A. DIRECTIONS: The following words are forms of *sublime*, which means "lofty, exalted, supreme." Choose the word that correctly completes each sentence, and write it on the line.

sublimate   subliminal

1. The politician succeeded in part because of his ability to _____ his personal desires into the fulfilling of his official duties.

2. It was only October, but the subtle, _____ message from the jingling tunes on the store's sound system was "shop for the Holidays."

Using the Word Bank

persistent	obliterate	sublimity	harried

B. DIRECTIONS: Each question below consists of a related pair of words in CAPITAL LETTERS, followed by four lettered pairs of words. Choose the pair that best expresses a relationship *similar* to that expressed in the pair in capital letters. Circle the letter of your choice.

1. HARRIED : BESET ::
   a. stressed : tired
   b. thrilled : successful
   c. angry : conflict
   d. anticipated : expected

2. OBLITERATE : CREATE ::
   a. express : utter
   b. contribute : complete
   c. emerge : disappear
   d. level : flat

3. PERSISTENT : STEADY ::
   a. margin : footnote
   b. eager : fervent
   c. doctor : medicine
   d. hopeful : desire

4. SUBLIMITY : MAGNIFICENCE ::
   a. investment : wealth
   b. subtlety : clarity
   c. talent : aptitude
   d. observation : prediction

"The Fiddle" by Alan Sillitoe

Grammar and Style: Vary Sentence Beginnings

When you write, you begin each sentence with different words because you have different things to say. Good writers make sure that not only their beginning words, but their beginning *structures*, are different. **Varying sentence beginnings** keeps your writing from becoming repetitious and dull. Generally, sentences can begin in four different ways.

> **Subject:** *Harrison's Row* had a character all of its own.
>
> **Introductory adverb:** *Occasionally*, the stream flowed over its banks.
>
> **Introductory phrase:** *In summer*, an old tin hip bath would come from one of the houses.
>
> **Introductory clause:** *When they did get Ted Griffin*, he was pulled out of bed one morning . . .

Remember that a phrase, such as the adverb phrase "in summer," does not contain a subject or a verb. A clause is a group of words that contains a subject and a verb.

A. Practice: Identify the type of beginning of each of the following sentences from "The Fiddle." Write *subject, adverb, phrase,* or *clause* next to each sentence to identify its beginning.

1. "On a fine evening late in August one of the unemployed husbands might be seen looking across at the noise."

2. "Instead I saw myself wading or swimming the Leen from Harrison's Row."

3. "When they did get Ted Griffin he was pulled out of bed one morning even before he'd had time to open his eyes."

4. "To a child it seemed as if the songs lived in the hard collier's muscle at the top of his energetic arm."

5. "Anyone with a wireless would turn it down or off."

6. "Two years later the Second World War began, and not long afterwards meat as well as nearly everything else was put on the ration."

B. Writing Application: Write sentences according to the following instructions.

1. Tell about Harrison's Row. Begin with a subject.

_____

_____

2. Write a sentence about Jeff Bignal. Begin with an introductory phrase.

_____

_____

3. Tell about Jeff's fiddle playing. Begin with an introductory clause.

_____

_____

4. Beginning with an adverb, tell what Jeff did with his fiddle.

_____

_____

"The Fiddle" by Alan Sillitoe

Reading Strategy: Predicting Effect of Setting

The **setting** of a story can influence, to some extent, the outcome of the story. It was probably not possible for Jeff Bignal, for example, to make a living as a fiddle player, given the setting and circumstances of his life.

Readers may be able to predict some events or story elements based on the setting as well as on the prior knowledge that they bring to the story. Harrison's Row is described as a set of closely built cottages, and the residents seem to mix across their back gardens and the stream. It probably comes as no surprise, then, that news of Jeff selling his fiddle spreads quickly from one cottage to the next.

DIRECTIONS: As you read, record observations in the following chart about the setting of "The Fiddle." Then indicate what effect the setting has on the characters. Finally, predict plot events or what will happen to the characters, based on the setting. Some details have been filled in for you.

Details of Setting	Effect on Characters	Predictions
the cottages were in a "ruinous condition"		
the story takes place in England in the 1930's		

"**The Fiddle**" by Alan Sillitoe

Literary Analysis: Setting and Atmosphere

The **setting** of a story provides the background, just as if the story were a play being acted out on a stage with scenery in the background. Is the setting dark or well lit? Does the action take place in a neat, tidy room or in a crude, dingy one?

The author of a short story answers these questions—and more—by describing the sights, sounds, and smells of a place, as well as by establishing a time setting. All of the details of the setting combine to create the **atmosphere**, or the overall feeling or mood of a story. Following is a passage in which Sillitoe creates an atmosphere of hopelessness. Note how the author accomplishes this in just two sentences.

> A rent man walked down cobblestoned Leen Place every week to collect what money he could. This wasn't much, even at the best of times which, in the "thirties," were not too good—though no one in their conversation was able to hark back to times when they had been any better.

DIRECTIONS: Following is a list of different atmospheres that Sillitoe creates in "The Fiddle." Identify one point in the story where each atmosphere occurs, citing details that create the mood.

1. bleakness _____
   _____
   _____

2. tranquillity _____
   _____
   _____

3. relaxation _____
   _____
   _____

4. determination _____
   _____
   _____

5. oppression _____
   _____
   _____

6. resignation _____
   _____
   _____

"The Distant Past" by William Trevor

Build Vocabulary

Spelling Strategy Adding the suffix -*ment* to a word usually does not change the spelling of the root word. The word *internment* illustrates this point.

Using the Suffix -*ity* (-*ty*)

A. DIRECTIONS: Complete each sentence with the appropriate word from the list. Note how the -*ity* (-*ty*) suffix, meaning "the quality of" or "the state of," contributes to each word.

| conductivity | eternity | maternity | productivity | sterility |

1. A supervisor is concerned with the _____ of her employees.

2. Someone who is looking for the Fountain of Youth is interested in _____.

3. Operating room personnel demand _____ in their surroundings.

4. An electrician tests a circuit for _____.

5. Expectant mothers and fathers are now eligible for _____ leave.

Using the Word Bank

| countenance | adversity | sovereignty |
| anachronism | internment | |

B. DIRECTIONS: Match each word with its definition. Write the letter of the definition on the line next to the word it defines.

____ 1. countenance   a. misfortune, trouble

____ 2. adversity   b. supreme political authority

____ 3. sovereignty   c. something out of its proper time in history

____ 4. anachronism   d. confinement during war

____ 5. internment   e. face, facial features

"The Distant Past" by William Trevor

Grammar and Style: Restrictive and Nonrestrictive Adjective Clauses

An **adjective clause** modifies a noun or pronoun. Adjective clauses are always subordinate clauses. This means they contain a subject and a verb, but do not express complete thoughts. Adjective clauses usually begin with a relative pronoun—*that, which, who, whom,* or *whose*—or a relative adverb—*when* or *where.*

A **restrictive adjective clause** is *not* set off by commas and *is* necessary to the meaning of a sentence.

> **Restrictive:** Catholics *who remained in Northern Ireland after 1922* experienced political and economic discrimination.

Note that removing the adjective clause would alter the meaning of this sentence.

A **nonrestrictive adjective clause** *is* set off by commas and is *not* necessary to the meaning of the sentence.

> **Nonrestrictive:** Trevor, *who has received much recognition as a writer,* was originally a sculptor.

This adjective clause adds information to the sentence, but could be removed without affecting the sentence's message.

A. Practice: Underline the adjective clause in each sentence. Label each sentence with an *R* if it contains a restrictive clause or an *N* if it contains a nonrestrictive clause

____ 1. The Middletons inherited the estate where they had lived all their lives.

____ 2. The Catholic Dublin woman, whom they blamed for their decreased fortunes, was never quite forgotten.

____ 3. The red setters, which always accompanied them to town, had become a symbol for Carraveagh.

____ 4. Miss Middleton chatted with the shopkeepers who took care of her requests.

____ 5. Mr. Middleton's remark that it was a great day for the Commonwealth amused Fat Driscoll.

B. Writing Application: Write sentences about the story "The Distant Past" according to the following specific guidelines.

1. Use *that* in a restrictive clause.

_____

_____

2. Use *when* in a restrictive clause.

_____

_____

3. Use *who* in a nonrestrictive clause.

_____

_____

"The Distant Past" by William Trevor

Reading Strategy: Cause and Effect

Every event has a **cause**, even though it may not always be apparent. In addition, almost every event has an **effect**, or a consequence. Keeping track of causes and effects in a short story can help you understand both the characters and why the plot develops as it does.

As you read, ask yourself why events happen. Then continue by asking what consequences each event has. Here's an example.

Event the Middletons inherit only 12 acres

What caused the event? their father's lifestyle

What effect did the event have? They live simply on the remains of the estate.

Keep in mind as you question events that there may be more than one cause and more than one effect for any one event or occurrence.

DIRECTIONS: As you read, look for the causes and effects of the events or occurrences listed in the table.

Event or Occurrence	What caused the event?	What effect did the event have?
1. The Middletons go to town twice a week.		
2. Rev. Bradshaw replaces Rev. Packham.		
3. The Middletons display a union jack.		
4. Post offices in Belfast are blown up.		
5. British soldiers arrive in the North.		
6. The Middletons are snubbed in the town.		

"The Distant Past" by William Trevor

Literary Analysis: Social Conflict

Throughout most of "The Distant Past," the conflict, or struggle, between characters is not a personal one but a social one. A **social conflict** is a struggle between people who hold opposing views about the society in which they live.

The long-standing social conflict between Irish and British citizens provides the fabric for Trevor's story. Without the characters' differing social views, there would be no plot—no story. Trevor introduces some difference immediately in the first paragraph—the Middletons are "peculiar" and "odd." Then, more specifically in the third paragraph, Trevor reveals their resistance to the "new national regime." He indicates that the Middletons believed times were better in "the days of the union jack," meaning when British rule of Ireland was unchallenged.

DIRECTIONS: As you consider the questions that follow, refer to the story as well as to the Background for Understanding on page 992.

1. When the Middletons were children, Britain ruled all of Ireland. Why was there an armed conflict in the Middletons' home at this time?

   _____

   _____

   _____

2. Almost all of the action in the story takes place *after* 1922. What is the significance of that date? How would it have affected the Middletons?

   _____

   _____

   _____

3. What lies at the bottom of the social conflict Trevor portrays in this story?

   _____

   _____

4. Aside from the social conflict that still exists in Ireland, what current social conflicts can you think of? Name two.

   _____

   _____

   _____

5. Now consider one of those current social conflicts. What lies at the bottom of this conflict? See if you can trace the conflict down to the very essence of the opposing views.

   _____

   _____

   _____

"Follower" and **"Two Lorries"** by Seamus Heaney
"Outside History" by Eavan Boland

Build Vocabulary

Spelling Strategy When forming the plurals of nouns, add *-es* if the noun ends in *h, s,* or *x*. Add only *-s* if the noun ends with any other letter. The word *inklings* is an example.

Using the Root *-mort-*

A. DIRECTIONS: Each of the following words contains the root *-mort-*, meaning "dead" or "death." Match each word with its definition. Write the letter of the definition on the line next to the word it defines.

____ 1. mortify

____ 2. mortally

____ 3. postmortem

a. in a deadly or fatal manner

b. to subject to severe embarrassment

c. after death

Using the Word Bank

| furrow | nuisance | inklings |
| mortal | ordeal | |

B. DIRECTIONS: Choose the lettered word or phrase that is most *similar* in meaning to the numbered word. Circle the letter of your choice.

1. furrow
   a. groove
   b. mold
   c. measurement
   d. ditch

2. inklings
   a. notes
   b. blotches
   c. suggestions
   d. ideas

3. mortal
   a. impermanent
   b. prone to error
   c. inexact
   d. everlasting

4. nuisance
   a. boredom
   b. excitement
   c. distress
   d. annoyance

5. ordeal
   a. comedy club
   b. severe test
   c. new freeway
   d. light supper

"Follower" and **"Two Lorries"** by Seamus Heaney
"Outside History" by Eavan Boland

Grammar and Style: Concrete and Abstract Nouns

You already know that a noun names a person, place, thing, or idea. More specifically, a **concrete** noun names something that can be perceived by the senses. An **abstract** noun names an idea, a quality, or a characteristic. Following are some examples:

Concrete: salt, fire, field, clang, sunset

Abstract: ability, ego, wit, cleverness, certainty

The kinds of nouns you use in your writing affect the impact your writing has on your readers. Concrete nouns tend to create vivid pictures because readers can perceive with their senses the objects being named. The use of abstract nouns tends to create impressions rather than images, and readers have to grasp the meaning with something other than their senses.

A. Practice: Following are lines from the poems in this section. Above each italicized noun, write *C* if the noun is concrete or *A* if the noun is abstract.

1. An *expert*. He would set the *wing*
   And fit the bright steel-pointed sock.
   The *sod* rolled over without breaking.
   At the *headrig*, with a single pluck

   Of *reins*, the sweating *team* turned round
   And back into the *land*.
               ("Follower," ll. 5–10)

2. And *films* no less! The *conceit* of a coalman . . .
   She goes back in and gets out the black lead
   And emery paper, this nineteen-forties *mother*,
   All *business* round her stove, half-wiping *ashes*
   With a backhand from her *cheek* as the bolted *lorry*
   Gets revved and turned and heads for *Magherafelt*
               ("Two Lorries," ll. 13–18)

B. Writing Application: Write sentences using concrete and abstract nouns according to the instructions that follow.

1. Describe the farmer in "Follower" using only concrete nouns.

_____

2. Now describe the farmer using at least two abstract nouns.

_____

3. Write a sentence about what the boy in "Follower" does, using only concrete nouns.

_____

4. Tell about the boy's relationship with his father, now that he is grown. Use abstract nouns.

_____

"Follower" and **"Two Lorries"** by Seamus Heaney
"Outside History" by Eavan Boland

Reading Strategy: Summarizing

A summary is a restatement of main ideas in a condensed, or shortened, form. Creating a summary is a useful study tool because it makes you think critically about material you've read, identifying main ideas and pushing aside unnecessary details or examples. When you **summarize** a poem you will do the same thing—identify and restate the main ideas aside from the poem's images.

For poetry, it may be helpful to note the main points of each stanza and then build a complete summary from there. Here is a portion of "Outside History" (lines 7-12), accompanied by notes about the main ideas of these two stanzas.

They keep their distance. Under them remains
a place where you found
you were human, and

discovery of humanness—being alive

a landscape in which you know you are mortal.
And a time to choose between them.
I have chosen:

discovery of mortality; must choose

DIRECTIONS: Use the space on this page to note the main idea of each stanza of "Two Lorries" as you read. Then use your notes to summarize the essence of the whole poem.

"Two Lorries"

Stanza 1: _____

Stanza 2: _____

Stanza 3: _____

Stanza 4: _____

Stanza 5: _____

Stanza 6: _____

Stanza 7: _____

Summary of "Two Lorries":

_____

_____

_____

_____

_____

_____

_____

_____

"Follower" and **"Two Lorries"** by Seamus Heaney
"Outside History" by Eavan Boland

Literary Analysis: Diction and Style

Style refers to these poetic elements: **diction,** or word choice; imagery; rhythms; poetic form; and theme. How each poet *uses* these elements is that poet's style. The style of a poem adds meaning to the poem and affects how a reader responds to that poem. Though generalizations can be made, a poet's style varies from poem to poem.

Following is the first stanza of "Follower." Read it and then refer to the table for an explanation of Heaney's style.

My father worked with a horse plow,
His shoulders globed like a full sail strung
Between the shafts and the furrow.
The horses strained at his clicking tongue.

Elements of Style	Examples
Diction—Is the poet's word choice formal or informal, conversational or stilted, concrete or abstract?	Diction is informal and easy to read, just as if a boy were talking to the reader. Poet uses many concrete words.
Imagery—Is the imagery easily perceived by the senses? Or does it create unusual or abstract pictures? Do the images tell a story, or do they just stand next to each other?	The imagery appeals to the senses of sight and hearing. Poet creates a vivid image of the father's strong shoulders.
Rhythm—Does the poet use rhyme? Does the poet use rhythm? How much? Are they conventional or irregular?	Poet uses a traditional *abab* rhyme scheme.
Form—Are there stanzas? Are they regular or irregular? Does the poet write in free verse?	Poet uses regular, four-line stanzas.

DIRECTIONS: Using the table on this page as a model, examine the first stanza of "Two Lorries" for style. Write your evaluation of each element of style in the space provided.

Diction: _____

_____

Imagery: _____

_____

Rhythm: _____

_____

Form: _____

_____

"No Witchcraft for Sale" by Doris Lessing

Build Vocabulary

Spelling Strategy When adding an *-ly* suffix to a word that ends in a consonant, do not double the final consonant, as in the words *reverently* and *incredulously*.

Using Forms of *Skeptical*

A. DIRECTIONS: The word *skeptical* means "doubting" or "not easily persuaded." Use one of the following words related to *skeptical* to complete each sentence correctly.

skeptically   skeptic   skepticism

1. The pleasure of the circus may be somewhat deflated for an audience member who is a

   _____.

2. The child looked at the circus performer _____ after the clown had apparently pulled an egg out of the child's ear.

3. There was even more _____ on the part of the child's parents, whose eyes told them one thing, but whose minds told them another.

Using the Word Bank

reverently	defiantly	efficacy
incredulously	skeptical	

B. DIRECTIONS: Choose the lettered word or phrase that is most nearly *opposite* in meaning to the numbered word. Circle the letter of your choice.

1. defiantly
   a. uncertainly
   b. aggressively
   c. blindly
   d. obediently

2. efficacy
   a. affectation
   b. lack of effectiveness
   c. aftereffect
   d. self-sufficiency

3. incredulously
   a. trustingly
   b. curiously
   c. childishly
   d. massively

4. reverently
   a. religiously
   b. disrespectfully
   c. earnestly
   d. truthfully

5. skeptical
   a. abstract
   b. hesitating
   c. believing
   d. artificial

"No Witchcraft for Sale" by Doris Lessing

Grammar and Style: Correct Use of *Like* and *As*

The words *like* and *as* have become almost interchangeable in casual conversation. This informal usage can lead to errors in formal speaking or writing. Sometimes *like* is a verb meaning "to prefer." When used for comparisons, however, *like* is always a preposition. Remember that a prepositional phrase consists of a preposition followed by a noun or pronoun and any related words.

> Gideon, *like the Farquars,* dotes on Teddy.

In casual speech, we often use *like* as a conjunction to introduce a subordinate clause. (Remember that a subordinate clause contains a subject and a verb, but does not express a complete thought and cannot stand alone.) In formal speaking or writing, use *as* in such situations.

> *As the scientist suspects,* Gideon will not reveal the source of his medicine.

In general, use *like* to compare people or things. Use *as* to compare or demonstrate actions or states. If you are unsure about which word to use, look for a verb form. If the phrase in question contains a verb, use *as* to complete your subordinate clause.

A. Practice: Each of the following sentences uses *like* or *as*. Write *C* if a sentence is correct. Write *I* if a sentence is incorrect.

_____ 1. As the other servants, Gideon calls Teddy "Little Yellow Head."

_____ 2. The Farquars, as many colonials, kept a number of servants to run their household.

_____ 3. Gideon, like many other Africans, had been educated in a mission school.

_____ 4. Mrs. Farquar believed, like her husband did, that Gideon's help was half knowledge and half miracle.

_____ 5. Later, Gideon was unable to be as comfortable with Teddy as he once had been.

_____ 6. As Teddy, Gideon's youngest son was fascinated with the scooter.

B. Writing Application: Write comparative constructions using *like* and *as* according to the instructions that follow.

1. Use *like* to compare Teddy with other young children.

_____

_____

2. Use *as* to compare Mrs. Farquar with other mothers.

_____

_____

3. Describe Teddy's treatment of Gideon's son, using a subordinate clause that begins with *as*.

_____

_____

4. Compare Mrs. Farquar's and Gideon's reactions to Teddy's accident, using the preposition *like*.

_____

_____

"No Witchcraft for Sale" by Doris Lessing

Reading Strategy: Analyzing Cultural Differences

All short stories contain a conflict of some sort. Often the conflict is between two individuals or between an individual and nature. Sometimes, as is the case in "No Witchcraft for Sale," the conflict is between the characters' cultures. For the most part, the characters themselves are not in conflict. Differences in their cultures, however, lead to misunderstandings or actions that cause conflict.

Analyzing the cultural differences among characters can increase your understanding of the characters themselves as well as of the story as a whole. When comparing the similarities and differences of two things, it is helpful to do so in chart form.

A. DIRECTIONS: In the Venn diagram, note details about the Farquars that are unique to them and their way of thinking in the circle labeled "Farquars." In the circle labeled "Gideon," note details that are unique to Gideon's culture and way of thinking. In the center, where the circles intersect, write ideas or attitudes that the Farquars and Gideon share.

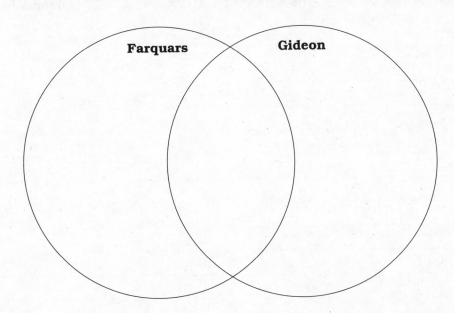

B. DIRECTIONS: Now that you have analyzed the cultural differences in the story, answer this question.

1. If the characters' cultural differences—that is, the cultural conflict—did not exist, what would be left of the plot? Describe what this story would be without the cultural differences. Would it still be an engaging story? Why or why not?

_____

_____

_____

_____

_____

_____

_____

"No Witchcraft for Sale" by Doris Lessing

Literary Analysis: Cultural Conflict

Doris Lessing's story is based on the premise that Gideon's culture and the Farquars' culture are in conflict. In spite of the fact that the characters seem accepting of their roles and live relatively compatibly, they possess different customs, ideas, and values.

Perhaps, in the workings of everyday life, the cultural differences between the Farquars and Gideon were invisible. In the aftermath of Teddy's accident, however, differing ideas revealed themselves. In fact, Lessing even introduces a third culture in the form of the scientist who comes to learn about the cure Gideon used for Teddy's eyes. His added ideas from the scientific and commercial world serve to emphasize the conflict between the Farquars and Gideon, who otherwise live harmoniously.

DIRECTIONS: List below the viewpoints represented by members of each of the three cultures over the issue of the medicine. Then answer the questions that follow.

The Farquars' Attitudes	The Scientist's Attitudes	Gideon's Attitudes

1. How do the attitudes of the Farquars bring them into conflict with the scientist?

_____

_____

2. How do the Farquars' attitudes bring them into conflict with Gideon?

_____

_____

_____

3. How do the scientist's attitudes cause him to conflict with Gideon?

_____

_____

_____

"The Rights We Enjoy, the Duties We Owe" by Tony Blair

Build Vocabulary: The Language of Building a New Society

Much nonfiction writing today addresses contemporary political and social issues, many of which are related to ways in which nations around the world are building new societies. In these pieces—which will include news articles, speeches, and political analyses—you will come across certain vocabulary words again and again.

A. DIRECTIONS: Match each word in the left column with its definition in the right column. Write the letter of the definition on the line next to the word it defines.

____ 1. prosper   a. endured or borne together

____ 2. strong   b. accountable

____ 3. cohesive   c. mutually reliant

____ 4. interdependent   d. obligation

____ 5. shared   e. sticking together

____ 6. responsible   f. group of people

____ 7. duty   g. powerful, healthy

____ 8. community   h. working together

____ 9. cooperative   i. flourish

____ 10. competitive   j. involving rivalry

B. DIRECTIONS: Choose the word from the left column above that best completes each sentence below.

1. Every citizen has a _____ to be involved in the political process.

2. Creating a real _____ among people with diverse backgrounds and interests can be quite difficult.

3. The _____ nature of the country's society was the envy of more fractious nations.

4. The economic health of an individual country is increasingly _____ on that of other nations in this age of globalization.

5. If we work together in a _____ manner we could accomplish much more.

6. Working together harmoniously does not mean that peoples' _____ instincts must be discouraged.

7. A country cannot be said to _____ unless the benefits reach all members of its society.

8. The effects of a truly _____ economy will be felt worldwide.

9. All members of the community _____ in the task of rebuilding the city.

10. Political leaders must be _____ for the welfare of their nation and its allies.

Name _____ Date _____

"The Rights We Enjoy, the Duties We Owe" by Tony Blair

Thematic Connection: Conflicts at Home and Abroad

In his speech, British Prime Minister Tony Blair reaffirms the importance of rights and responsibilities, arguing for "practical policies" guided by "values" that stress "the good of all." Many commentators have stressed the similarities between Blair's notion of a new social order and the aims of President Bill Clinton of the United States. Others have contended that any similarities are only on the surface, having more to do with style and packaging than with substantive issues. What relevance do the ideas presented by Blair have for the United States, both in terms of domestic policy and foreign affairs?

DIRECTIONS: Review each of the quotations below, all taken from Tony Blair's speech on rights and duties. Assess what relevance each may have for the United States, both in terms of its domestic affairs and how the United States conducts its affairs overseas. In your response, consider how Blair's ideas may have different shades of meaning in Britain than they have in America.

. . . a strong society should not be confused with a strong state, or with powerful collectivist institutions.
. . . the Right started to define personal responsibility as responsibility not just for yourself but to yourself.
People need rules which we all stand by, fixed points of agreement which impose order on chaos. That does not mean a return to the old hierarchy of deference.

"The Lagoon" by Joseph Conrad
"Araby" by James Joyce

Build Vocabulary

Spelling Strategy Words ending in *y* preceded by a consonant form their plurals by changing the *y* to *i* and adding *es* to the base word as in *litany* + *-ies* = *litanies*.

Using the Root *-vinc-*

A. DIRECTIONS: In each sentence, cross out the italicized word or phrase and replace it with one of the following words: *convince, evince, invincibility*.

1. I have doubts about this alarm system's *unconquerable quality*.

2. What can you do to *conquer the doubt in* me?

3. If you *show* clear, overwhelming evidence of the system's performance, perhaps I'll buy it.

Using the Word Bank

portals	invincible	propitiate	conflagration	august
imperturbable	litanies	garrulous	derided	

B. DIRECTIONS: For each related pair of words in CAPITAL LETTERS, choose the lettered pair that best expresses a *similar* relationship. Circle the letter of your choice.

1. PORTALS : ENTRANCES ::
   a. gates : iron
   b. locks : keys
   c. tunnels : bridges
   d. roads : pathways

2. INVINCIBLE : VICTORY ::
   a. strong : muscular
   b. confident : success
   c. fear : doubt
   d. clouds : sunshine

3. PROPITIATE : OFFEND ::
   a. welcome : greet
   b. freeze : thaw
   c. develop : innovate
   d. hasten : hurry

4. CONFLAGRATION : SPARK ::
   a. flood : droplet
   b. burn : destroy
   c. thunder : lightning
   d. boots : mud

5. AUGUST : REVERE ::
   a. November : spring
   b. authoritative : obey

c. powerful : weak
d. monarch : queen

6. IMPERTURBABLE : DISRUPT ::
   a. anger : hatred
   b. wealthy : inherit
   c. contented : dismay
   d. acceptance : agreement

7. LITANIES : PRAYER ::
   a. clergy : congregation
   b. songs : music
   c. snow : sleet
   d. games : children

8. GARRULOUS : TALKATIVE ::
   a. sickly : healthy
   b. yawning : tired
   c. brilliance : sunlight
   d. energetic : lively

9. DERIDED : TEASE ::
   a. ran : sprint
   b. stretched : squeeze
   c. grasped : release
   d. scripted : plagiarize

"The Lagoon" by Joseph Conrad
"Araby" by James Joyce

Grammar and Style: Adverb Clauses

Adverb clauses are subordinate clauses that modify verbs, adjectives, and adverbs. As modifiers, adverb clauses add specificity and vivid detail to writing. In the following sentence from "The Lagoon," the adverb clause shown in italics modifies the adverb *paler*:

The stars shone paler *as if they had retreated into the frozen depths of immense space.*

A. Practice: Underline the adverb clauses in the following sentences. Circle the word each adverb clause modifies.

1. ". . . his voice and demeanor were composed as he asked, without any words of greeting— 'Have you medicine, Tuan?'"

2. "She lay still, as if dead; but her big eyes, wide open, glittered in the gloom. . . ."

3. "But since the sun of today rose she hears nothing—she hears not me."

4. "He had known Arsat years ago, in a far country in times of trouble and danger, when no friendship is to be despised."

5. "When we returned to the street, light from the kitchen windows had filled the areas."

6. "She could not go, she said, because there would be a retreat that week in her convent.'

7. "When he was midway through his dinner I asked him to give me the money to go to the bazaar."

8. "I lingered before her stall, though I knew my stay was useless, to make my interest in her wares seem the more real."

B. Writing Application: For each of the following, write a sentence containing an adverb clause that answers the question.

1. Why does the white man stay with Arsat in "The Lagoon"?

_____

_____

2. In "The Lagoon" when do Arsat and his brother kidnap the young woman?

_____

_____

3. How does the boy in "Araby" feel about Mangan's sister?

_____

_____

4. In "Araby," what circumstance prevents the boy from going to the bazaar when he wants?

_____

_____

"The Lagoon" by Joseph Conrad
"Araby" by James Joyce

Reading Strategy: Picturing Action and Situation

Conrad and Joyce place great importance on the psychological states of their characters. As you read modernist fiction, pause to picture the action and situation. Pay particular attention to the characters' internal responses to what is happening. For example, in "The Lagoon," as the narrator details the crew's thoughts about Arsat, try to picture the physical scene and imagine what the white man might be thinking at the same moment.

DIRECTIONS: Read the following passages from the stories. For each, write a few sentences describing what the characters do and see as well as what they might think or feel.

1. The white man . . . murmured sadly without lifting his head—
   "We all love our brothers."
   Arsat burst out with an intense whispering violence—
   "What did I care who died? I wanted peace in my own heart."

   _____

   _____

   _____

   _____

   _____

   _____

2. At nine o'clock I heard my uncle's latchkey in the hall door. I heard him talking to himself and heard the hallstand rocking when it had received the weight of his overcoat. I could interpret these signs. When he was midway through his dinner I asked him to give me the money to go to the bazaar. He had forgotten.

   _____

   _____

   _____

   _____

   _____

3. Nearly all the stalls were closed and the greater part of the hall was in darkness. I recognized a silence like that which pervades a church after a service. I walked into the center of the bazaar timidly.

   _____

   _____

   _____

   _____

   _____

   _____

"The Lagoon" by Joseph Conrad
"Araby" by James Joyce

Literary Analysis: Plot Devices

In "The Lagoon," Conrad uses a **story within a story**, a plot device in which a character in a fictional narrative tells a story. Conrad's plot device focuses attention on Arsat's story by framing it with another narrative. In "Araby," Joyce uses an **epiphany**, a plot device in which a character has a sudden and profound revelation in an ordinary moment, to heighten the story's climax.

DIRECTIONS: Write your answers to the following questions.

1. As you read "The Lagoon," what clues signal the beginning and the end of the story within the story?

   _____

   _____

   _____

   _____

2. In "The Lagoon," is Arsat's story ever interrupted by the outside narrative? If so, what is the effect?

   _____

   _____

   _____

   _____

3. Would Arsat's story in "The Lagoon" have the same effect if it had been told on its own? Explain.

   _____

   _____

   _____

   _____

4. What is the epiphany in "Araby"?

   _____

   _____

   _____

5. In "Araby," what is the boy doing or looking at when he has an epiphany?

   _____

   _____

   _____

6. Why do you suppose the epiphany in "Araby" occurs at this moment? In other words, why does this moment trigger an epiphany for the boy?

   _____

   _____

   _____

"The Lady in the Looking Glass: A Reflection" by Virginia Woolf
"The First Year of My Life" by Muriel Spark

Build Vocabulary

Spelling Strategy In most words, the vowels *ie* following *c* are spelled *ei*. However, when *ie* follows an *sh* or *ch* sound, *i* comes before *e* as in *omniscient*.

Using the Prefix *trans-*

A. DIRECTIONS: Knowing that *trans-* means "through" or "across," use the following words to complete the sentences.

transatlantic   translucent   transom   transmutation

1. The glass panel is _____, allowing light to shine through it.

2. Opening the _____ above the door allowed the breeze to pass through.

3. The scientific experiment caused a _____ of the chemical substance.

4. During World War I, how many days did a _____ crossing require?

Using the Word Bank

suffused	transient	upbraidings	evanescence
reticent	omniscient	authenticity	discerned

B. DIRECTIONS: Match each word in the left column with its definition in the right column. Write the letter of the definition on the line next to the word it defines.

____ 1. suffused

____ 2. transient

____ 3. upbraidings

____ 4. evanescence

____ 5. reticent

____ 6. omniscient

____ 7. authenticity

____ 8. discerned

a. temporary; passing through quickly

b. gradual disappearance, especially from sight

c. silent; reserved

d. recognized as separate or different

e. filled

f. quality or state of being genuine

g. stern words of disapproval for an action

h. having infinite knowledge; knowing all things

"The Lady in the Looking Glass: A Reflection" by Virginia Woolf
"The First Year of My Life" by Muriel Spark

Grammar and Style: Subject–Verb Agreement in Inverted Sentences

In inverted sentences, which often begin with *there* or *here*, the verb precedes the subject. However, the verb must still agree in number with its subject. Look at the following sentence from "The First Year of My Life":

> There *were* those black-dressed people, females of the species to which I appeared to belong. . . .

The verb *were* agrees with the plural subject *people*, not with *There*.

A. Practice: Underline the subject or subjects of each sentence, and circle the verb that agrees with your choice.

1. Here (*is, are*) a letter and an invitation delivered by the postman.

2. There (*was, were*) a suggestion of depth and intelligence in the occupant's room.

3. In the end, there (*is, are*) no interesting thoughts in Isabella's brain.

4. There (*was, were*) many soldiers scarred and killed by poisonous gas during the war.

5. In this anthology (*is, are*) poems by Wilfred Owen and Alan Seegar.

6. Here (*is, are*) an interesting theory on infant development.

B. Writing Application: Write a paragraph describing the first birthday party you can recall, either your own or someone else's. Use at least two inverted sentences. Make sure to use the correct subject-verb agreement in your inverted sentences.

_____

_____

_____

_____

_____

_____

_____

_____

_____

_____

_____

_____

_____

_____

"The Lady in the Looking Glass: A Reflection" by Virginia Woolf

"The First Year of My Life" by Muriel Spark

Reading Strategy: Questioning

When reading experimental works, like those of Virginia Woolf and Muriel Spark, you must continually ask questions to find your way through each story and determine its meaning. Two areas of focus are *who* is narrating and *why* the narrator emphasizes an incident. For example, as you begin "The Lady in the Looking Glass," you must ask who is the narrator. Questioning and suggesting possible answers can help you determine the story's meaning.

DIRECTIONS: Write a question and answer for each of the following passages.

"The Lady in the Looking Glass: A Reflection"

1. As for facts, it was a fact that she was a spinster; that she was rich; that she had bought this house and collected with her own hands . . . the rugs, the chairs, the cabinets, which now lived their nocturnal life before one's eyes. Sometimes it seemed as if they knew more about her than we, who sat on them, wrote at them, and trod on them so carefully, were allowed to know.

   Question: _____

   Answer: _____

2. At last there she was, in the hall. She stopped dead. She stood by the table. She stood perfectly still. At once the looking glass began to pour over her a light that seemed to fix her; that seemed like some acid to bite off the unessential and superficial and to leave only the truth. It was an enthralling spectacle.

   Question: _____

   Answer: _____

"The First Year of My Life"

3. I wailed for my feed. . . . They rocked the cradle. I never heard a sillier song. Over in Berlin and Vienna the people were starving, freezing, striking, rioting and yelling in the streets. In London everyone was bustling to work and muttering that it was time the whole . . . business was over.

   Question: _____

   Answer: _____

4. . . . occasionally I beamed over to the House of Commons which made me drop off gently to sleep. Generally, I preferred the Western Front where one got the true state of affairs. It was essential to know the worst, blood and explosions and all, for one had to be prepared, as the boy scouts said.

   Question: _____

   Answer: _____

"The Lady in the Looking Glass: A Reflection" by Virginia Woolf
"The First Year of My Life" by Muriel Spark

Literary Analysis: Point of View: Modern Experiments

Point of view is the perspective from which a writer tells a story. Many writers, including Woolf and Spark, have experimented with point of view to reflect the state of modern life. Woolf uses **stream-of-consciousness narration**, which attempts to convey the random flow of thoughts in a character's mind. Spark experiments with the **omniscient narrator**, who knows every character's thoughts. Spark's narrator displays omniscience in an extreme sense—she knows everything that is going on everywhere in the world.

DIRECTIONS: Write your answers to the following questions.

1. Identify a stream-of-consciousness passage in Woolf's story. Explain what elements of stream of consciousness it demonstrates.

   _____

   _____

   _____

2. Does the narrator in "The Lady in the Looking Glass" convey reliable information about Isabella? Why or why not?

   _____

   _____

   _____

3. Why might Woolf have chosen this type of narrator?

   _____

   _____

   _____

4. How is the narrator of "The First Year of My Life" unusual?

   _____

   _____

   _____

5. How does Spark's omniscient narrator affect her story's tone?

   _____

   _____

   _____

6. Why might Spark have chosen this type of narrator?

   _____

   _____

   _____

"The Rocking-Horse Winner" by D. H. Lawrence
"A Shocking Accident" by Graham Greene

Build Vocabulary

Spelling Strategy Words of two or more syllables ending in *c* add *-ally* to form an adverb as in *intrinsic* + *-ally* = *intrinsically*.

Using the Prefix *ob-*

A. DIRECTIONS: Replace the italicized word or words with the word *object, obscures,* or *obstacles.*

1. During a solar eclipse, a celestial body *blocks* our view of the sun.

2. I *firmly am opposed* to your interpretation of the scientific findings.

3. We must remove any *items that block the way* before we can proceed.

Using the Word Bank

discreet	brazening	careered	obstinately	uncanny
remonstrated	apprehension	embarked	intrinsically	

B. DIRECTIONS: For each numbered word, choose the word or phrase that is the most *similar* in meaning. Circle the letter of your choice.

1. discreet
   a. showing good judgment
   b. behaving wildly
   c. showing favor
   d. acting mysteriously

2. brazening
   a. acting courageously
   b. thinking innovatively
   c. daring shamelessly
   d. accepting willingly

3. careered
   a. skidded
   b. dashed
   c. jumped
   d. glided

4. obstinately
   a. regretfully
   b. admittedly
   c. stubbornly
   d. happily

5. uncanny
   a. unique
   b. feverish
   c. unfamiliar
   d. eerie

6. remonstrated
   a. reverted
   b. exemplified
   c. protested
   d. approved

7. apprehension
   a. reluctance
   b. misgiving
   c. refusal
   d. avoidance

8. embarked
   a. made a start
   b. planned a party
   c. left the scene
   d. greeted a host

9. intrinsically
   a. thoroughly
   b. quickly
   c. superficially
   d. innately

"The Rocking-Horse Winner" by D. H. Lawrence
"A Shocking Accident" by Graham Greene

Grammar and Style: Subjunctive Mood

The **subjunctive mood** of a verb is used to state a wish or condition contrary to fact. It is usually expressed with the verb *were*. Notice the use of the subjunctive mood in the following sentence from "The Rocking-Horse Winner":

> "I needn't worry, mother, if I *were* you."

The subjunctive is also used in *that* clauses of recommendation, command, or demand. Used with third-person singular subjects, the subjunctive form is the present form of the verb without *s*. For the verb *to be*, the present subjunctive form is *be* and the past is *were*.

Recommendation: It is suggested that Paul *go* to the seaside.

Demand: His mother insisted that the money *be* advanced all at once.

A. Practice: Circle the correct verb in parentheses for each of the following sentences.

1. When he was on his rocking horse, Paul looked as if he (*was, were*) possessed.

2. Initially, Oscar recommended that Paul (*is, be*) cautious with his betting.

3. Paul wished that the house (*was, were*) satisfied.

4. The housemaster's shoulders shook as if he (*was, were*) laughing.

5. Jerome wishes that his father (*were, be*) remembered for his writing, not his bizarre death.

6. It is important to Jerome that Sally (*respond, responds*) appropriately to the story.

B. Writing Application: Write a brief paragraph describing a dream, wish, or goal you have. Use the subjunctive mood at least twice in your description.

_____

_____

_____

_____

_____

_____

_____

_____

_____

_____

_____

_____

Unit 6: A Time of Rapid Change (1901–Present)

"The Rocking-Horse Winner" by D. H. Lawrence
"A Shocking Accident" by Graham Greene

Reading Strategy: Identifying With a Character

When you **identify with a character**, or put yourself in that character's place, you can better understand his or her thoughts, feelings, problems, or motivations. Identifying with a character can lead you to understand a writer's purpose and a literary work's overall theme. For example, identifying with Paul when he first discusses his winners with Uncle Oscar means putting yourself in the boy's situation. You imagine that Paul is proud of his luck, careful not to reveal too much, and concerned that an adult might disapprove of his actions. Empathizing with Paul makes it easier to understand his actions.

DIRECTIONS: For each situation described, identify the character's thoughts, feelings, problems, or motivations. Then state how you would respond.

"The Rocking-Horse Winner"

1. Paul proclaims to his mother that he is lucky, but she doesn't believe him.

   _____

   _____

   _____

   _____

2. After Paul's mother receives the five thousand pounds, Paul hears the house screaming for even more money.

   _____

   _____

   _____

   _____

"A Shocking Accident"

3. After his classmates learn the details of his father's death, Jerome is called Pig.

   _____

   _____

   _____

   _____

4. Jerome delays telling Sally the story of his father's death.

   _____

   _____

   _____

   _____

"The Rocking-Horse Winner" by D. H. Lawrence
"A Shocking Accident" by Graham Greene

Literary Analysis: Theme and Symbol

In most short stories, a **theme** conveys a main idea or message about life to the reader. Writers often use symbols to enhance their themes. A symbol is a person or object that represents an idea or a connection point for several ideas. Lawrence uses the rocking horse as a symbol with multiple meanings. Greene, in "A Shocking Accident," strengthens his theme by using the pig as a symbol for what is out of place.

DIRECTIONS: Write your answers to the following questions.

1. What is the literal meaning of the rocking horse in "The Rocking-Horse Winner"?

_____

_____

_____

_____

_____

2. What other meanings might the rocking horse have in Lawrence's story? In other words, what does the rocking horse symbolize?

_____

_____

_____

_____

_____

3. How does the symbol of the rocking horse help you define the theme of "The Rocking-Horse Winner"?

_____

_____

_____

_____

_____

4. How does the pig serve as a symbol in "A Shocking Accident"?

_____

_____

_____

_____

_____

"**The Book of Sand**" by Jorge Luis Borges

Build Vocabulary: The Language of Philosophical Ideas

Jorge Luis Borges's tale "The Book of Sand" is a story of fantasy inspired by philosophical ideas. The words in the box range from the technical, such as *hypervolume*, to the common, such as *end*. The meaning or connotation of a word used to represent a philosophical idea can be determined from its context.

DIRECTIONS: Write a word from the box to complete each sentence.

infinite	hypervolume	random	beginning	end
arbitrary	space	point	time	

1. A series of seemingly _____ acts may sometimes end up being related in some way.

2. In its unconcern for human emotions, the dealings of fate are completely _____.

3. A universal idea may be considered _____, with no beginning and no end.

4. The energy of a young child can only be measured in terms of _____.

5. When one is at the _____ of a journey, the first few steps can be the most difficult to take.

6. Does _____ pass more or less quickly when you are enjoying yourself?

7. One could open the book at any _____ and be sure to find some new and puzzling bit of information.

8. Humankind's hopes and fears, dreams and terrors, are enough to fill all the reaches of _____.

9. In the _____, all a person can hope for is to have lived a life of both reflection *and* action.

"The Book of Sand" by Jorge Luis Borges

Literary Connection: The Short Story

"The Book of Sand" is a short story told as if it recounted actual autobiographical events. It plays with the questions of what is reality and what is fiction. This short story, like the others in this section, resembles the novel, but with some important differences:

- A short story is much briefer.
- A short story has a simpler plot and setting.
- In a short story, characters are revealed at a crucial moment, rather than developed through many incidents.

The writers in this section helped make the short story an important literary form in the twentieth century. As your reading indicates, short-story writers have made use of a wide variety of fictional techniques, ranging from Joseph Conrad's story-within-a-story narrative to Virginia Woolf's stream of consciousness.

DIRECTIONS: Complete the entries below to help plan a short story of your own.

Who are my characters? _____

_____

_____

What is the setting? _____

_____

_____

What are the basic events in the plot? _____

_____

_____

_____

_____

_____

Around what crucial incident will the story revolve? _____

_____

_____

_____

_____

What fictional techniques will be used? _____

_____

_____

_____

_____

"Do Not Go Gentle into That Good Night" and **"Fern Hill"**
by Dylan Thomas
"The Horses" and **"The Rain Horse"** by Ted Hughes

Build Vocabulary

Spelling Strategy When forming the past tense of a verb that ends in a silent *e*, drop the *e*. Then add *-ed*. With few exceptions, this is true whenever you add a suffix that begins with a vowel to a word that ends in a silent *e*. The verbs *grieved* and *exasperated* demonstrate this rule.

Using the Root *-vol-*

A. DIRECTIONS: The following words contain the root *-vol-*, meaning "to will" or "to wish." Complete each sentence by writing the appropriate word in the blank.

volition   voluntarily   voluntarism

1. The not-for-profit organization relied almost completely on _____ for its work among the community of homeless people.

2. Though her parents expressed their opinions, Sheila chose the field of social work of her own _____.

3. After seeing the news report, dozens of residents _____ turned out to show their support for preserving the historical building.

Using the Word Bank

grieved	transfiguring	exasperated
nondescript	malevolent	

B. DIRECTIONS: Each numbered word is followed by four lettered words or phrases. Choose the word or phrase that is most *similar* in meaning to the numbered word, and circle the letter of your choice.

1. exasperated
   a. out of breath
   b. without hope
   c. very irritated
   d. filled with longing

2. grieved
   a. sighed
   b. mourned
   c. hailed
   d. resented

3. nondescript
   a. lacking authority
   b. having no destination
   c. lacking form or shape
   d. without character

4. malevolent
   a. wishing harm
   b. hard or brittle
   c. against one's will
   d. clearly disinterested

5. transfiguring
   a. moving from place to place
   b. changing form
   c. performing experiments
   d. calculating values

"Do Not Go Gentle into That Good Night" and **"Fern Hill"**
by Dylan Thomas
"The Horses" and **"The Rain Horse"** by Ted Hughes

Grammar and Style: Sentence Beginnings: Adverb Clauses

An adverb modifies a verb, an adjective, or another adverb. Similarly, an **adverb clause** is a subordinate clause that modifies a verb, an adjective, or an adverb, telling *how, when, where, why, to what extent*, or *under what condition*. In the sentence below, the italicized adverb clause modifies the verb *defend* and tells *under what condition*.

There were deep hollows in the river-bank, shoaled with pebbles, . . . perfect places to defend himself from *if the horse followed him out there*.

Adverb clauses are always introduced by subordinating conjunctions. Here are some common subordinating conjunctions.

after	as though	since	when
although	because	so that	whenever
as	before	than	where
as if	if	through	wherever
as long as	in order that	unless	while
as soon as	provided that	until	

To create variety—and, therefore, interest—in your writing, you can begin sentences with adverb clauses, as Ted Hughes does.

Since the horse seemed to have gone on down the wood, his way to the farm over the hill was clear.

A. Practice: Circle the number of each sentence that begins with an adverb clause. For each sentence that does begin with an adverb clause, underline the clause and circle the word it modifies.

1. "At the woodside he paused, close against a tree."

2. "As he went, he broke a yard length of wrist-thick dead branch from one of the oaks."

3. "Through the bluish veil of bare twigs he saw the familiar shape out in the field below the wood."

4. "Whenever it seemed to be drawing off he listened anxiously until it closed in again."

5. "In the middle of the last field he stopped and looked around."

B. Writing Application: Write three sentences about "The Rain Horse." Begin each sentence with an adverb clause, and use three different subordinating conjunctions.

1. _____

2. _____

3. _____

Name _____ Date _____

"Do Not Go Gentle into That Good Night" and "Fern Hill"
by Dylan Thomas
"The Horses" and "The Rain Horse" by Ted Hughes

Reading Strategy: Judging the Message

Whenever you read a poem, a story, or an editorial, it is only natural to weigh the writer's ideas or events against your own experience. Does the writer's expression of an idea or an event match with your own experience, or have you had a different experience?

Readers should **judge the message** of what they read. Some ideas you come across simply won't make sense to you; other ideas will contradict what you may already believe or know to be true. Test a writer's message against your own experience and accept or reject ideas accordingly.

DIRECTIONS: As you read each poem in this section, note its message in the appropriate area in the table. Then judge each message, deciding whether you agree or disagree, accept or reject the message.

Poem	Message	Reader's Judgment and Explanation
"Do Not Go Gentle into That Good Night"		
"Fern Hill"		
"The Horses"		

"Do Not Go Gentle into That Good Night" and **"Fern Hill"**
by Dylan Thomas
"The Horses" and **"The Rain Horse"** by Ted Hughes

Literary Analysis: Voice

What did you "hear" when you read these poems by Dylan Thomas and Ted Hughes? Did you hear Thomas raging against death? Did you hear Hughes relishing his memory? What is it, exactly, that causes you to "hear" anything in a poem? What produces a poem's voice?

Voice in literature is usually produced by variations in word choice, rhythm, and diction. Writers use these elements carefully to produce the "sound" they want. Many writers, like Dylan Thomas, have a characteristic voice, although most can vary their sound considerably.

Word choice, or vocabulary, affects the voice. A word like *hush* is an obvious example of a word that readers can "hear." In a similar way, Hughes's use of the word *frost* seems almost hushed, and adds to the image he is creating.

Rhythm also makes a difference. Hughes sets up his sentences in stanzas so that they cannot be read quickly, and in "Fern Hill," Thomas's lilting rhythm invites the poem to be read aloud to play with its voice.

Diction affects voice. Diction is the way words are put together, and includes language level, narrative form, and grammatical structure. Are sentences complex or simple? Is the language casual or formal? Choices about word order also make the rhythm, of course, but so do repetitions. When Thomas repeats *rage* in "Rage, rage against the dying of the light," you can almost hear the rolling Welsh *r*'s. This line is a good example of word choice, rhythm, and diction combining to make a distinctive voice.

DIRECTIONS: Review "Fern Hill" and record lines or phrases in the following table that seem particularly indicative of the voice of the poem. Then indicate whether the effect is produced by word choice, rhythm, or diction. Then, in the third column, describe the voice of the passage and what effect it has on the poem as a whole.

Line or Passage	How Voice Is Produced	Description of Voice

"An Arundel Tomb" and **"The Explosion"** by Philip Larkin
"On the Patio" by Peter Redgrove
"Not Waving but Drowning" by Stevie Smith

Build Vocabulary

Spelling Strategy Whenever you hear the sound *j*, or soft *g*, in the middle of an English word, you can be sure that the letter that makes the sound is a *g*, as in *effigy*.

Using the Root *-fid-*

A. DIRECTIONS: The root *-fid-*, meaning "faith," is included in each of the numbered words. Match each numbered word with its definition. Write the letter of the definition next to the word it defines.

____ 1. confidant   a. one to whom secrets are entrusted

____ 2. confidential   b. faithless

____ 3. perfidious   c. private, secret

Using the Word Bank

effigy	supine	fidelity	larking

B. DIRECTIONS: Complete each sentence by writing the appropriate Word Bank word in the blank.

1. Without knowing anything about the earl and countess, it is hard to tell whether their _____ was the sculptor's imagination or not.

2. Many tombs of royalty traditionally include a(n) _____ of the noble person, in commemoration of his or her rank and importance.

3. The children were only _____; they hadn't meant to tramp through old Mrs. Wilson's flower garden.

4. When performing CPR, the victim should be lying _____ unless other injuries prevent him or her from being so positioned.

C. DIRECTIONS: Choose a lettered pair that best expresses a relationship *similar* to that expressed in the numbered pair. Circle the letter of your choice.

1. EFFIGY : LIKENESS ::
   a. canvas : easel
   b. water : wet
   c. portrait : painting
   d. horse : animal

2. FIDELITY : TRUST ::
   a. greed : money
   b. hope : future
   c. anger : calm
   d. betrayal : disloyalty

3. LARKING : PLAYFUL ::
   a. working : easy
   b. aiming: target
   c. troubling : avoidance
   d. studying : scholarly

4. SUPINE : ERECT ::
   a. recline : stand
   b. careful : mistake
   c. favorable: false
   d. run : jog

"An Arundel Tomb" and **"The Explosion"** by Philip Larkin
"On the Patio" by Peter Redgrove
"Not Waving but Drowning" by Stevie Smith

Grammar and Style: Sequence of Tenses

The tense of a verb indicates the time of the action or state of being expressed by the verb. Each verb has six tenses. The following summary focuses on just four tenses.

Tense	The tense expresses . . .	Examples
Present	an action that is occurring now	I *write* a story.
Past	an action that occurred in the past and did not continue into the present	I *wrote* a story.
Present Perfect	an action that occurred at some indefinite time in the past, or that began in the past and continues into the present	I *have written* a story. (Requires *has* or *have* + past participle.)
Past Perfect	an action that was completed in the past before some other past occurrence	I *had written* a story. (Requires *had* + past participle.)

When you write, it is important to make sure that your verbs express actions in the order in which they occurred. Writers must pay attention to this **sequence of tenses** to make sure their writing is clear and accurate. Using the sequence of tenses carefully can also add expressiveness to your writing, as it does to Philip Larkin's in "An Arundel Tomb."

A. Practice: Identify the tense of the italicized verb in each of the following sentences.

1. Time *has transfigured* them into untruth. _____

2. The earl and countess *lie* in stone. _____

3. Rigidly they *persisted*, linked, through lengths of time. _____

4. The sculptor *had taken* a liberty, thinks the speaker. _____

B. Writing Application: Write sentences according to the instructions.

1. Use a past perfect verb in a sentence about a book you've read. Show that one action happened before another. _____

2. Use a present tense verb in a sentence about your morning routine. _____
_____

3. Use a past tense verb in a sentence about something you did yesterday. _____
_____

4. Use a present perfect tense verb about something you started last week that you haven't completed. _____

"An Arundel Tomb" and **"The Explosion"** by Philip Larkin
"On the Patio" by Peter Redgrove
"Not Waving but Drowning" by Stevie Smith

Reading Strategy: Reading in Sentences

The key to reading and understanding poetry is to read the punctuation rather than the line endings. The rhythm or rhyme of a poem may seem to require a reader to pause at the end of each line, but one must think beyond the physical line endings to the sense of the words. If you **read in sentences**, ignoring the line endings, you will find that sense.

In Philip Larkin's "An Arundel Tomb," each of the first three stanzas is one sentence. Though some lines end with a comma, a dash, or a colon, the unit of thought does not end until the end of the stanza.

A. DIRECTIONS: Write each sentence in stanzas 4–7 of "An Arundel Tomb." Do not pay attention to line endings; write the sentences in the space provided as if they are in narrative form.

Sentence 1: _____

_____

Sentence 2 _____

_____

Sentence 3: _____

_____

Sentence 4: _____

_____

Sentence 5: _____

_____

Sentence 6: _____

_____

Sentence 7: _____

_____

Sentence 8: _____

B. DIRECTIONS: Now review the entire poem. Remember that each of the first three stanzas is one sentence. Practice reading them in sentences. Then continue to stanzas 4–7, which you have written on this page. Mark places to pause and breathe that fit with the meaning of the sentences. Practice several times, and then read the poem aloud to an audience.

"An Arundel Tomb" and **"The Explosion"** by Philip Larkin
"On the Patio" by Peter Redgrove
"Not Waving but Drowning" by Stevie Smith

Literary Analysis: Free Verse and Meter

Whether a poet uses free verse or a conventional form of poetry, the lines of poetry likely have some kind of rhythm, or alternation of strong and weak—or stressed and unstressed—syllables. That rhythm may or may not create a regular pattern, or meter. Whether it does or not, though, the poet probably uses the rhythm to add to the meaning of the poem.

The meter of a poem is measured in feet. One foot is made up of one stressed syllable and any number of unstressed syllables. Following is a summary of the kinds of meter Larkin uses in "An Arundel Tomb" and "The Explosion."

Meter	Pattern of Syllables	Example
iambic tetrameter	four sets of iambs per line (˘ ´)	The earl and countess lie in stone
trochaic tetrameter	four sets of trochees per line (´ ˘)	Shadows pointed towards the pithead:

When poets vary the rhythm of a conventional meter, they add emphasis to a line or give special significance to the meaning of the line. Free-verse poets vary their rhythms frequently to add to or create meaning in their poems.

DIRECTIONS: Examine the rhythm and meter in the poems in this section, as directed by the following questions.

1. Following is the first line of "An Arundel Tomb." Notice how the stressed and unstressed syllables fall.

   Side by side, their faces blurred,

   How is this line different from the other lines in the poem? Why do you think Larkin made this line different?

   _____

   _____

2. Scan line 15 of "The Explosion." How many feet does it have? What effect does its rhythm have?

   Scarfed as in a heat-haze, dimmed.

   _____

   _____

3. In "On the Patio," lines 5–8 are shorter than those in the rest of the poem. What connection is there between these shorter lines and the image the poet creates with them?

   _____

   _____

"B. Wordsworth" by V. S. Naipaul

Build Vocabulary

Spelling Strategy When adding *-ly* to a word that ends in a consonant, the spelling of the base word does not change. For example, in the base word *keen*, adding *-ly* creates the word *keenly*.

Using Related Forms of *patron*

The Word Bank word *patronize* is a form of the word *patron*, which means "customer, supporter, or benefactor."

A. DIRECTIONS: Write the form of the word *patron* that best completes each of the following sentences. Use context clues and your knowledge of the word *patron* to choose the correct word.

patronize	patronizing	patronage	patroness

1. The wealthy _____ entered the gallery dressed in jewels and a lavish gown.

2. Unfortunately, the shopkeeper's _____ manner turned away many customers.

3. The wisest shopkeepers appreciate the _____ of each and every customer.

4. We decided to _____ the new Italian restaurant in our neighborhood.

Using the Word Bank

rogue	patronize	distill	keenly

B. DIRECTIONS: Match each word in the left column with its definition in the right column. Write the letter of the definition on the line next to the word it defines.

____ 1. keenly   a. to be a customer of a store

____ 2. rogue   b. to obtain the essential part

____ 3. patronize   c. sharply or intensely

____ 4. distill   d. scoundrel

C. Complete each of the sentences with the most appropriate word from the Word Bank.

1. The poet sought to _____ life in a single line of poetry.

2. "What a _____ am I!" exclaimed Don Juan.

3. Writers seek to express thoughts and feelings _____.

4. Great minds _____ the resources of great literature.

Name _____ Date _____

Grammar and Style: Pronoun Case in Compound Construction

Pronoun case refers to the different forms a pronoun takes to indicate its function in a sentence. The subjective case is used when the pronoun performs the action—acts as the subject of the sentence—or when it renames the subject. The objective case is used when the pronoun receives the action of the verb—as a direct or an indirect object—or is the object of a preposition.

Subjective case pronouns: *I, we, you, he, she, it, they*

Objective case pronouns: *me, us, you, him, he, it, them*

The following sentences show the use of subjective and objective pronoun cases:

Subjective case: The narrator eats a fresh mango.

> *He* is delighted with the flavor.

Objective case: B. Wordsworth tells the narrator a secret.

> The poet asks *him* to keep a secret.

When **personal pronouns** are used in **compound structures**, that is, when they are linked by conjunctions such as *and* or *or*, they use the case that would be correct if the pronoun were used alone.

Subjective case: *He and B. Wordsworth* become friends.

> B. *Wordsworth and I* talked about poetry.

Objective case: Orion shined brightly in the sky for the *poet and him.*

> The yard on Miguel Street is a secret between *B. Wordsworth and me.*

A. Practice: Circle the correct pronouns for each sentence.

1. The poet and (*I, me*) live on Miguel Street.

2. The narrator's mother and (*he, him*) do not have a close relationship.

3. They became friends, B. Wordsworth and (*he, him*).

4. Suddenly, the world was an exciting place for (*he, him*) and (*I, me*).

B. Writing Application: Each of the following sentences contains a compound pronoun construction. Rewrite each of these sentences, replacing the italicized word or words with a pronoun in the correct case.

1. Mr. Wordsworth and *the narrator* take long walks together.

_____

2. *Mr. Wordsworth and the narrator* live on the same street.

_____

3. The relationship between the narrator and *his mother* is not loving.

_____

"B. Wordsworth" by V. S. Naipaul

Reading Strategy: Responding to Character

You can become a more active reader by envisioning the world a writer creates. One way to do this is to **respond to character** as you read. Each character reveals himself or herself through words, actions, personal qualities, and responses to other characters. For example, when B. Wordsworth asks the narrator if he may watch the bees, you are alerted to the character's unusual behavior. Then, when B. Wordsworth says, "I can watch a small flower like the morning glory and cry," you experience a glimpse of the man's sensitivity to the world around him.

DIRECTIONS: As you read "B. Wordsworth," record in the following chart your responses to the behavior, words, and qualities expressed by B. Wordsworth and the narrator as they encounter specific events.

Character: B. Wordsworth

Behavior/Words/Qualities	My Responses
Event:	
Event:	
Event:	

Character: the narrator

Behavior/Words/Qualities	My Responses
Event:	
Event:	
Event:	

Name _____   Date _____

"B. Wordsworth" by V. S. Naipaul

Literary Analysis: First-Person Narrator

Point of view determines what the author can or cannot tell readers about a character's thoughts and actions. For instance, when we read a story written in **first-person narration,** we see, hear, and learn everything through the narrator. As a result, we can only guess why B. Wordsworth takes a liking to the narrator, what his motive might be, and whether or not he is what and who he says he is. We know only what the narrator tells us, and he can share information only from his own senses: what he sees, hears, thinks, imagines, assumes.

The following sentences are written from a variety of points of view. Identify with the word "yes" those sentences that could have been included in "B. Wordsworth" because they are written in the first person. Write "no" next to those sentences that are *not* in first person. Beneath each sentence marked "no," rewrite the sentence in first-person narration, as if it were part of the story.

_____ 1. I was glad to see B. Wordsworth again and happy to be invited to eat his mangoes.

_____

_____

_____

_____ 2. B. Wordsworth was glad to see the boy.

_____

_____

_____ 3. His mother was angry with the boy for coming home late from school and wondered where he'd been.

_____

_____

_____

_____ 4. B. Wordsworth told me, "I think you have the poet's eye."

_____

_____

_____

_____ 5. B. Wordsworth told him a story about a girl poet and a boy poet.

_____

_____

_____

_____ 6. B. Wordsworth and the boy took long walks through parks and along the waterfront.

_____

_____

_____

"The Train from Rhodesia" by Nadine Gordimer

Build Vocabulary

Spelling Strategy If a word ends in *y* and an ending is added that begins with *-ist*, *-ing*, or *-ish*, the base word keeps the final *y*. For example, the word *splay* keeps the final *y* when adding *-ing* to form the word *splaying*.

Using the Prefix *a-*

One of the meanings of the prefix *a-* is "without or not." When using this meaning of the prefix *a-*, the meaning of the base word is negated. For example, the Word Bank word *atrophy* means "without nourishment."

A. DIRECTIONS: Complete each of the following sentences. Form the missing word by using the italicized context clue and your knowledge of the prefix *a-*.

1. The _____ character in the story displayed a *lack of moral judgment.*

2. *Without a tonal center or key*, the _____ composition sounded like a chorus of squabbling birds.

3. Our _____ meal of popcorn was *not typical* of our dinner eating habits.

Using the Word Bank

impressionistic	elongated	segmented
splaying	atrophy	

B. DIRECTIONS: Match each word in the left column with its definition in the right column. Write the letter of the definition on the line next to the word it defines.

____ 1. atrophy   a. conveying a quick, overall picture

____ 2. impressionistic   b. separated into parts

____ 3. elongated   c. waste away

____ 4. segmented   d. spreading

____ 5. splaying   e. lengthened; stretched

C. DIRECTIONS: Rewrite each sentence using an appropriate word from the Word Bank.

1. Her memories of the incident were sketchy.

_____

2. After long hours on the train, he felt his muscles begin to lose strength.

_____

3. The suitcase fell, spreading its contents across the corridor.

_____

4. The journey was more restful because it was broken into manageable parts.

_____

5. Her face sagged, stretched by fatigue.

_____

"The Train from Rhodesia" by Nadine Gordimer

Grammar and Style: Absolute Phrases

An **absolute phrase** is a group of words containing a noun or pronoun modified by a participle or participial phrase. In the following sentence from "The Train from Rhodesia," the absolute phrase is italicized.

The stationmaster was leaning against the end of the train, *green flag rolled in readiness.*

As you can see in the preceding example, an absolute phrase modifies the rest of the sentence in which it appears, instead of modifying a particular word. An absolute phrase is always set off by a comma. The details included in an absolute phrase can heighten suspense and bring a scene to life.

A. Practice: Underline the absolute phrase in each of the following sentences from Gordimer's story.

1. "A man passed beneath the arch of reaching arms meeting gray-black and white in the exchange of money for the staring wooden eyes, the stiff wooden legs sticking up in the air."

2. "Joints not yet coordinated, the segmented body of the train heaved and bumped back against itself."

3. "She was holding it away from her, . . . the wonderful ruff of fur facing her."

4. "He stood astonished, his hands hanging at his sides."

5. "She sat down again in the corner and, her face slumped in her hand, stared out of the window."

B. Writing Application: Revise each of the following sentences by adding an absolute phrase.

1. The train pulled into the station.

_____

_____

_____

_____

2. The young woman stood on the platform.

_____

_____

_____

3. The stationmaster rang the bell.

_____

_____

_____

_____

"The Train from Rhodesia" by Nadine Gordimer

Reading Strategy: Reading Between the Lines

Writers do not always explain the meaning or significance of an event in a story. Just as a character needs to reflect and consider the significance of events that occur, the reader needs to **read between the lines** of the story to discover clues to meaning. Consider the following passage from the story:

> All up and down the length of the train in the dust the artists sprang, walking bent, like performing animals, the better to exhibit the fantasy held toward the faces on the train. Buck, startled and stiff, staring with round black and white eyes. More lions, standing erect, grappling with strange, thin, elongated warriors who clutched spears and showed no fear in their slits of eyes.

What is significant in the passage's contrasting description of the artists "walking bent" and the fearless "elongated warriors"?

DIRECTIONS: As you read "The Train from Rhodesia," record in the first column events that you or a character do not fully understand. After you read between the lines, explain in the second column the full meaning or significance of the event.

Event	Meaning of Event

"The Train from Rhodesia" by Nadine Gordimer

Literary Analysis: Conflict and Theme

A **conflict** in a literary work is a struggle between two characters, or between a character and some outside force, such as society or nature. A **theme** is a literary work's central idea. To bring alive a theme for readers, writers often dramatize it by showing a character struggling with a conflict. The writer's theme is developed through the way in which a character resolves, or fails to resolve, the conflict. In simple stories with simple themes, the resolution may be straightforward. In more complex stories, the conflict may remain unresolved.

In Gordimer's story, there are many conflicts. The main character, a young woman, is not able to resolve the major conflict, but she finally does, through her own inner struggle and that with her husband, reach an understanding of what the true conflict is.

DIRECTIONS: For each of the following passages from "The Train from Rhodesia," explain how conflict helps dramatize the theme.

1. . . . she thought of the lion and smiled. That bit of fur round the neck. But the wooden buck, the hippos, the elephants, the baskets that already bulked out of their brown paper under the seat and on the luggage rack! How will they look at home? Where will you put them? What will they mean away from the places you found them? Away from the unreality of the last few weeks? The man outside. But he is not part of the unreality; he is for good now. Odd . . . somewhere there was an idea that he, that living with him, was part of the holiday, the strange places.

   _____

   _____

   _____

   _____

   _____

2. She was holding it [the lion] away from her, the head with the open jaws, the pointed teeth, the black tongue, the wonderful ruff of fur facing her. She was looking at it with an expression of not seeing, of seeing something different.

   _____

   _____

   _____

   _____

   _____

3. If you wanted the thing, she said, her voice rising and breaking with the shrill impotence of anger, why didn't you buy it in the first place? If you wanted it, why didn't you pay for it? Why didn't you take it decently, when he offered it? Why did you have to wait for him to run after the train with it, and give him one-and-six? One-and-six!

   _____

   _____

   _____

   _____

Name _____ Date _____

from *Midsummer*, XXIII and **from *Omeros* from Chapter XXVIII**
by Derek Walcott
"From Lucy: Englan' Lady" by James Berry

Build Vocabulary

Spelling Strategy Most adjectives ending in a hard *c* sound form that sound by means of the letter *c* alone, as in the word *antic*. Other examples include *cardiac*, *domestic*, and *poetic*.

Using the Root *-duc-*

The Word Bank word *inducted* contains the Latin root *-duc-*, which means "to lead." Many other words, such as *education* or *ductwork*, that connote "leading" or "bringing something toward" also share this origin.

A. Directions: Match each word with the *-duc-* word root in the left column with its meaning in the right column. Write the letter of the definition on the line next to the word it defines.

_____ 1. ductile   a. to lead or take away

_____ 2. ducat   b. to trace a course of thought

_____ 3. deduce   c. a cutting back in number or amount

_____ 4. abduct   d. easily drawn or shaped, as metal

_____ 5. reduction   e. a coin bearing the image of a duke

Using the Word Bank

antic	rancor	eclipse	inducted

B. Directions: Each item consists of a related pair of words in CAPITAL LETTERS, followed by four lettered pairs of words. Choose the pair that best expresses a relationship *similar* to that expressed in the pair in capital letters. Circle the letter of your choice.

1. ANTIC : DIGNIFIED ::
   a. comic : funny
   b. rushed : sedate
   c. crazy : oddity
   d. frantic : nervous

2. RANCOR : ANIMOSITY ::
   a. malice : generosity
   b. spite : jealousy
   c. kindness : courtesy
   d. revenge : charity

3. INDUCTED : MEMBER ::
   a. honored : hero
   b. called : answer
   c. gave : donor
   d. rejected : quality

4. ECLIPSE : LIGHT ::
   a. darken : darkness
   b. dim : bright
   c. orbit : planet
   d. shade : sun

from *Midsummer*, XXIII and from *Omeros* from Chapter XXVIII
by Derek Walcott
"From Lucy: Englan' Lady" by James Berry

Grammar and Style: Commonly Confused Words: *Affect* and *Effect*

Two words commonly confused are **affect** and **effect**. The words sound similar, and although *affect* is a verb, *effect* may be a noun or a verb, adding to the confusion.

Affect is nearly always a verb. The usual meaning of *affect is* "to influence." For example, "Caribbean backgrounds strongly *affect* the poetry of Walcott and Berry." You could substitute *influence* without changing the meaning.

Effect is usually a noun meaning "result." For example, "The *effect* of Walcott's poem is a new perspective of England." You can substitute *result* without changing the meaning.

When *effect* is a verb, it means "to bring about," or "achieve." The sense of *effect* when used as a verb is one of completion, as in "Walcott hopes to effect political change in England."

A. Practice: Indicate whether each sentence uses *affect* or *effect* correctly. Write *C* in the blank if the sentence is correct or *I* in the blank if the sentence is incorrect.

____ 1. One *effect* of England's economic problems of the 1980's was increased competition for scarce jobs.

____ 2. This competition could not fail to *effect* an already tense racial climate.

____ 3. In order to *affect* reform, the country needed to improve its entire economy.

____ 4. The tension had its *effect* on every aspect of a long-overlooked issue.

B. Writing Application: Write sentences using *affect* or *effect* according to the instructions given for each item.

1. Write a sentence about the result of reading the selection from *Omeros* and your imagination of the slave trade.

_____

_____

_____

2. Write a sentence about the way the selection "From Lucy: Englan' Lady" influences your thinking about the personal life of royalty.

_____

_____

_____

3. Write a sentence about what change Walcott had hoped to bring about in British theater.

_____

_____

_____

from *Midsummer*, XXIII and **from *Omeros* from Chapter XXVIII**
by Derek Walcott
"From Lucy: Englan' Lady" by James Berry

Reading Strategy: Applying Background Information

Sometimes it is helpful to **apply background information** to extend your understanding of a literary work. The fact that Derek Walcott was in England, for example, probably explains Brixton rather than Miami or Los Angeles, as a setting for a poem. First, focus closely on the words the writer has chosen to use in the work. After considering what exists on the page, you might seek more information from the larger context of the artist's life.

It is not always safe to assume that a writer's work gives the exact story of his or her life, or that events in a writer's life adequately explain his or her work. Having knowledge of a writer's life may help explain references and attitudes, though, such as Walcott's disappointment in English theater, or where James Berry may have gotten an idea. Applying background information can enlarge your understanding and expand your comprehension of the artist's world and yours.

DIRECTIONS: Use the background information from the biographical material and footnotes in your text to consider the following passages. For each, write what background information may apply, and how you think it affects the particular passage or how it may have influenced the ideas represented.

Passage	Background Information	Effect or Influence on on the Passage
1. "I was there to add some color to the British theater." *Midsummer*		
2. "Now he heard the griot muttering his prophetic song/of sorrow that would be the past." *Omeros*		
3. "Yet/sometimes, deep, deep, I sorry for her./Everybody expec' a show/from her." "From Lucy: Englan' Lady"		

Name _____ Date _____

from *Midsummer*, XXIII and from *Omeros* from Chapter XXVIII
by Derek Walcott
"From Lucy: Englan' Lady" by James Berry

Literary Analysis: Theme and Context

The **theme** is the main idea or basic meaning that a writer communicates in a literary work. Theme expresses a clear point of view about some aspect of life and human experience. The theme is understood through exploring the **context**—the local conditions from which it comes. Very often poets and other writers choose to reveal their themes indirectly—thorough characters' behavior, figurative language, details of setting or atmosphere, dialogue, and other elements—rather than to state their message directly.

DIRECTIONS: Answer each of the following questions.

1. One of Walcott's themes in both *Midsummer* and *Omeros* concerns the brutality and injustice that result from racial prejudice. Put the theme in context by listing the images and phrases from these poems in which Walcott touches on this idea.

   from *Midsummer*, XXIII: _____

   _____

   _____

   _____

   _____

   from *Omeros*, from Chapter XXVIII: _____

   _____

   _____

   _____

   _____

2. Reread the second stanza of "From Lucy: Englan' Lady." In a sentence or two, state the theme Berry explores by juxtaposing images of the Queen's background with images of the toils of English workers.

   _____

   _____

   _____

   _____

   _____

   _____

   _____

Name _____ Date _____

"A Devoted Son" by Anita Desai

Build Vocabulary

Spelling Strategy Some adjectives end in *ant*, such as the word *complaisant*. Other examples are *pleasant*, *compliant*, and *valiant*. Some adjectives that may sound similar end in *ent*, such as *recent* or *complacent*. The only way to be absolutely certain whether to use *ant* or *ent* is to check a dictionary, but it is a good idea to memorize the spellings of words that may cause confusion.

Using the Root -fil-

The Latin word *filius* means "son," and *filia*, "daughter." The Word Bank word *filial* comes from these roots, literally meaning "of or befitting a son or daughter." Words formed from the root *-fil-* imply obligation and association.

A. Directions: Match each word derived from the *-fil-* word root in the left column with its definition in the right column. Write the letter of the definition on the line by the word it defines.

____ 1. affiliate (verb)   a. relationship between parent and child

____ 2. filiation   b. voluntary connection

____ 3. affiliate (noun)   c. to join or associate

____ 4. affiliation   d. a member or colleague

Using the Word Bank

exemplary	filial	encomiums	complaisant	fathom

B. Directions: Each item consists of a word from the Word Bank followed by four lettered words or phrases. Choose the word or phrase most nearly *similar* in meaning to the Word Bank word. Circle the letter of your choice.

1. exemplary
   a. model
   b. necessary
   c. released
   d. principal

2. filial
   a. equine
   b. teeming
   c. belated
   d. respectful

3. encomiums
   a. campgrounds
   b. tributes
   c. environments
   d. savings

4. complaisant
   a. protesting
   b. supplement
   c. agreeable
   d. courtesy

5. fathom
   a. assist
   b. comprehend
   c. deny
   d. create

"A Devoted Son" by Anita Desai

Grammar and Style: Sentence Variety

Just as effective speakers change voice inflection to hold audiences, effective writers vary sentences to keep language moving.

Sentences vary by length. Some paragraphs begin with a short crisp sentence to make a point, followed by longer ones to provide details. Others may begin with long sentences to set the scene, and drive home a point with a single, blunt insight.

Sentences vary by type. Beginning a paragraph with a question or exclamation grabs readers' attention. Sentences are declarative, interrogative, imperative, or exclamatory.

Sentences vary by structure. Simple sentences, compound sentences (two or more independent clauses, but no subordinate clauses), or complex sentences (at least one independent and one subordinate clause) mix to vary the cadence of a paragraph.

Sentences vary in placement of elements. Within these types of variation exist options for more variety. Clauses, phrases, subjects, and predicates may shift for sentence diversity.

A. Practice: Identify the length, type, and structure of each sentence in the following passage. Then describe how all of the sentences work together to dramatize events in the paragraph.

> The old man who had been lying stretched out on his bed, weak and feeble after a day's illness, gave a start at the very sound, the tone of these words. He opened his eyes—rather, they fell open with shock—and he stared at his son with a disbelief that darkened quickly to reproach. A son who actually refused his father the food he craved? No, it was unheard of, it was incredible. But Rakesh had turned his back to him and was cleaning up the litter of bottles and packets on the medicine shelf and did not notice while Veena slipped silently out of the room with a little smirk that only the old man saw, and hated.

1. Sentence 1: _____

2. Sentence 2: _____

3. Sentence 3: _____

4. Sentence 4: _____

5. Sentence 5: _____

6. Paragraph Description: _____

_____

B. Writing Application: Experiment with sentence variety by rewriting the third-to-last paragraph of "A Devoted Son." Reorder or recast sentences in the paragraph that begins "Varma's mouth. . . ."

_____

_____

_____

_____

_____

_____

"**A Devoted Son**" by Anita Desai

Reading Strategy: Evaluating Characters' Decisions

In good writing, characters and the situations they face often seem real. One test of a good story is whether you wonder about the characters outside the context of the story. Is Rakesh's father still alive? What is Rakesh like now? Has he learned what his father really needs?

As you read, you compare the things that characters do to what you think they ought to do, and develop attitudes about them. In much fiction, just as in life, actions have consequences, some of them not foreseen by the characters (or the reader). When Rakesh first did well on his exams, could his father have anticipated how success might affect his relationship with his son? Could you? As you read, try to **evaluate characters' decisions** in terms of the world of the story. What is being decided? What are the choices and consequences? How is each decision made? What are the values on which the decision is based?

DIRECTIONS: Use the following chart to help you consider decisions the characters make in the story. The first column lists a decision that has been made. In the second column, write what you think the reason for that decision is, and how the decision is made. In the third column, write the consequences of the decision. What does it lead to in terms of events, and what effect does it have on this or other characters? In the fourth column, note your assessment or thoughts about the decision and the character.

Decision	Motivation	Consequences	Evaluation
1. Rakesh pursues a career in medicine			
2. Rakesh seeks advanced education in America.			
3. Rakesh returns to India and sets up a clinic.			
4. Varma becomes increasingly irritable.			
5. Varma decides he wants to die.			

"A Devoted Son" by Anita Desai

Literary Analysis: Static and Dynamic Characters

Anita Desai's "A Devoted Son" presents an unusual example of **static** and **dynamic** characters. A static character is one who does not change during the course of a work, and a dynamic character is one who undergoes change as a result of what happens in the work. Readers might expect that the young man would be the one to change, but Desai reverses our expectations.

To understand static and dynamic characters, we need to consider what we mean by change. Varma never leaves the village. Yet he is not the same person at the end of the story as he was when Rakesh first showed him his test results. His feelings about the world and his son have altered dramatically. By contrast, Rakesh has many experiences, for he begins the story as a student, studies in America, returns, marries, raises a family, and founds a successful clinic. Yet Desai presents him as the same dutiful son at the end of the story as at the beginning, apparently unaffected internally by the things he has done.

How does Desai show the changes in Varma and the lack of change in Rakesh? Because the change occurs emotionally, we can look at descriptions of characters' feelings or responses to situations to follow each character's progress.

DIRECTIONS: Answer the following questions by analyzing indications of change in Rakesh and Varma in "A Devoted Son."

1. Describe Varma's emotional state at the beginning, middle, and at the end of the story.

   _____

   _____

   _____

   _____

2. Identify three paragraphs from the beginning, the middle, and the end of the story that indicate this change. Write phrases or sentences from the paragraphs that evidence change.

   _____

   _____

   _____

   _____

3. Describe Rakesh at the beginning and at the end of the story.

   _____

   _____

   _____

   _____

4. Identify three paragraphs from the beginning, the middle, and the end of the story that support your description of Rakesh. Write phrases or sentences from the paragraphs that support your interpretation.

   _____

   _____

   _____

   _____

from "We'll Never Conquer Space" by Arthur C. Clarke

Build Vocabulary

Spelling Strategy When adding the prefix *in-* or *im-*, meaning "not," to a word that begins with an *r*, the prefix changes to *ir-*, as in *irrevocable*.

Using the Suffixes *-ible* and *-able*

A. DIRECTIONS: Many words in the English language contain the suffixes *-ible* or *-able*, meaning "able to," "having qualities of," or "worthy of." Match the following words with their definitions. Write the letter of the definition next to the word it defines.

____ 1. applicable   a. capable of being traversed or dealt with

____ 2. commendable   b. able to be disregarded

____ 3. negligible   c. capable of being brought into action

____ 4. negotiable   d. worthy of praise

Using the Word Bank

ludicrous	irrevocable	instantaneous
enigma	inevitable	zenith

B. DIRECTIONS: Each item consists of a Word Bank word followed by four lettered words or phrases. Choose the lettered word or phrase that is most nearly *opposite* in meaning to the Word Bank word, and circle the letter of your choice.

1. enigma
   a. query
   b. widely known
   c. negative image
   d. solution

2. inevitable
   a. sure
   b. unlikely
   c. satisfied
   d. unsafe

3. instantaneous
   a. delayed
   b. lacking attention
   c. rough-skinned
   d. precise

4. irrevocable
   a. without words
   b. changeable
   c. finely tuned
   d. permanent

5. ludicrous
   a. boring
   b. serious
   c. miserable
   d. not playful

6. zenith
   a. lowest point
   b. farthest point
   c. nearest point
   d. distant point

Name _____ Date _____

Grammar and Style: Linking Verbs and Subject Complements

A **linking verb** connects its subject with a word that identifies or describes that subject.

Arthur C. Clarke *is* a *writer*. (The word *writer* identifies the subject, *Clarke*.)

Following are the most commonly used linking verbs.

all of the forms of *be* (*am, is, are, was, were, will be, has been, could have been, and so on*)	*appear*	*seem*
	become	*smell*
	feel	*sound*
	grow	*stay*
	look	*taste*
	remain	*turn*

The word or words that identify or describe the subject, such as *writer* in the previous example, are called the **subject complement**. There are two kinds of subject complements, the predicate nominative and the predicate adjective. A predicate nominative refers to the person or thing that is the subject of the verb. The previous example has a predicate nominative. Here is another example.

Arthur C. Clarke *was* once a radar *instructor*.

A predicate adjective is an adjective that follows a linking verb and modifies, or describes, the subject of the verb.

Clarke's essay *is interesting*. (The adjective *interesting* modifies the subject, *essay*.)

A. Practice: In each sentence, circle the linking verb and underline the subject complement. Indicate whether the subject complement is a predicate nominative or a predicate adjective by writing *PN* or *PA* above the complement.

1. "The facts are far otherwise."

2. "In all earlier ages than ours, the world was wide indeed."

3. "Once again we are face to face with immensity."

4. "The velocity of light is the ultimate speed limit."

5. "Again they are wrong."

6. "It is a sphere which will grow at almost the speed of light."

B. Writing Application: Use two different forms of the verb *be* and two other linking verbs to write sentences about Arthur Clarke or his essay. Underline the subject complement in each sentence.

1. _____

2. _____

3. _____

4. _____

from "We'll Never Conquer Space" by Arthur C. Clarke

Reading Strategy: Challenging the Text

Do you believe, and accept, everything you read? Books, magazine articles, newspapers, office memoranda, and corporate newsletters all convey information. Is the newspaper's reporting unbiased? Does the memo address the heart of the issue, or just someone's side of it? Is the company revealing what employees have a right to know?

When you read an essay, even one by a famous, well-respected writer, you should **challenge the text,** just as you should challenge materials you read at school and home. Clarke's essay, in particular, addresses a controversial subject and should raise questions as you read. Some of Clarke's statements are straight facts. Others are opinions, assumptions, or speculations about what might—or might not—come to be. Test his ideas by raising those questions.

DIRECTIONS: Following are some statements from Clarke's essay that are worthy of being challenged. For each statement, write a question with which to challenge the statement. (You need not know the answer to the question.) An example has been done for you.

> Because we have annihilated distance on this planet, we imagine that we can do it once again.

Have we really "annihilated distance" on earth? Do people assume we can do it again, as Clarke claims?

1. ". . . when the satellite communication network is established, we will be able to see friends on the far side of the earth as easily as we talk to them on the other side of the town."

   _____

   _____

   _____

2. "We have abolished space here on the little earth; we can never abolish the space that yawns between the stars."

   _____

   _____

3. "This achievement [using nuclear energy for spaceflight], which will be witnessed within a century, might appear to make even the solar system a comfortable, homely place . . ."

   _____

   _____

4. "It will never be possible to converse with anyone on another planet."

   _____

   _____

   _____

from "We'll Never Conquer Space" by Arthur C. Clarke

Literary Analysis: Prophetic Essay

It is not hard for readers to guess what Clarke's viewpoint is as they begin to read *We'll Never Conquer Space*. Clarke's title makes it no secret. As in any essay, though, Clarke needs to back up his viewpoint with facts and evidence. Also, because Clarke's is a **prophetic essay**, readers may also expect predictions and speculations.

A modern prophetic essay is, in some ways, no different from ancient prophecies. The person who writes or speaks the prophecy wants to convince his or her audience of the accuracy and truth of the prophecy. Modern writers do this by using persuasive literary techniques such as presenting facts or evidence, making logical and/or emotional appeals, creating images, and using quotable language. Here are some examples from Clarke's essay.

Fact: Radio and light waves travel at the same speed of 186,000 miles a second.

Logical appeal: Our age is in many ways unique, full of events and phenomena which never occurred before and can never happen again.

Image: The remotest of the planets will be perhaps no more than a week's travel from the earth.

Quotable language: Man will never conquer space.

Keep in mind that these are persuasive techniques. Your job as a reader is to determine whether they *really* support Clarke's argument or not.

DIRECTIONS: State the main point, or thesis, of Clarke's essay in your own words. Then identify four major points that Clarke uses to support his thesis. For each point, identify whether it is a fact, logical/emotional appeal, an image, a speculation, or whether it is stated in quotable language. Some points may be a combination of techniques.

Clarke's thesis: _____

Support 1: _____

_____

Support 2: _____

_____

Support 3: _____

_____

Support 4: _____

_____

ANSWERS
Unit 1: From Legend to History (449–1485)

"The Seafarer,"
translated by Burton Raffel
"The Wanderer,"
translated by Charles Kennedy
"The Wife's Lament,"
translated by Ann Standford

Build Vocabulary (p. 1)

A. 1. sweetness; sample answer: The sweetness of the cake upset her stomach.
2. brightness; sample answer: The brightness of the light gave me a headache.
3. eagerness; sample answer: Ryan's eagerness was easy to see.
4. helpfulness; sample answer: The teacher was impressed with Alan's helpfulness.

B. 1. f 2. g 3. d 4. b 5. h 6. a 7. i 8. e 9. c 10. j

C. 1. d 2. b 3. b

Grammar and Style: Compound Predicates (p. 2)

A. 1. Compound predicate: called me eagerly out, sent me over / The horizon; subject: soul
2. Compound predicate: ages and shrinks; subject: honor
3. Compound predicate: grieved each dawn / wondered where my lord my first on earth might be; subject: I
4. Compound predicate: took me, swept me back / and forth in sorrow and fear and pain, / showed me suffering; subject: sea
5. Compound predicate: ages and droops into death; subject: earth

B. Sample responses:
1. Hardship groaned and wrenched around my heart.
2. The weakest survives and eventually thrives.
3. Lonely and wretched I wailed and moaned my woe.
4. Ever I know and bemoan the dark of my exile.
5. I must far and near bear and lament the anger of my beloved.

Reading Strategy: Connecting to Historical Context

Suggested responses:
1. The life of a seafarer was always at risk. They were frequently far from home, or in exile. All of these conditions can bring sorrow, fear, and pain.
2. Warriors were dependent upon their lords for proteciton and provisions. The loss of a master could bring great despair and financial insecurity.
3. Women had few rights and were subjected to whatever their fathers, masters, husbands, or lovers demanded.
4. Answers will vary.

Literary Analysis: Anglo-Saxon Lyric Poetry (p. 4)

1. But there isn't a mán on eárth so próud,
So bórn to greátness, so bóld with his yóuth,
Grówn so bráve, or so gráced by Gód
That he féels no féar as the sáils unfúrl.
2. two: greatness, brave
3. Those pówers have vánished, those pleásures are deád.
The weákest súrvives and the wórld contínues.
Kept spínning by tóil. All glóry is tárnished.
4. wave-tumult

from *Tristia* by Ovid
"Far Corners of Earth" by Tu Fu

Build Vocabulary: Words of Exile (p. 5)

A. 1. besieged; sample sentence: We were *besieged* by doubts as to whether we could endure the loneliness and fear.
2. impassable; sample sentence: I came up against an *impassable* wall of despair.
3. dread; sample sentence: I was filled with *dread* at having to face the unknown.
4. menace; sample sentence: This new world appeared to be filled with *menace*.
5. barbarous; sample sentence: The people around me seemed *barbarous* and strange.

from *Tristia* by Ovid
"Far Corners of Earth" by Tu Fu
(continued)

B. misery; I can't convey my *misery* at having to leave my home.

Thematic Connection: Exile (p. 6)
Suggested responses:

Students will not be able to make entries for each part of the chart. For example, the reader is unaware of the reason the person in "Far Corners of the Earth" was exiled. For "Other Exiles," students may list a character from literature, such as the exile in "Man Without a Country," or an exile or group of exiles from real life, such as refugees from conflict in the Balkans.

from *Beowulf,*
translated by Burton Raffel

Build Vocabulary (p. 7)
A. 1. *Disconsolate* means depressed and dejected, because there was no comfort they could find for the loss of their companions to Grendel.
  2. *Consoled* means relieved or lessened the grief from loss.
  3. *Inconsolably* means unable to be comforted.
  4. A *consolation* tournament is meant to "comfort" players who have lost in the main contest.

B. 1. large and imposing; 2. disgusting; 3. cleanse; purify; 4. twisting and turning; 5. comfort; relief; 6. amends; making up for wrongs

Grammar and Style: Appositives and Appositive Phrases (p. 8)
A. 1. Circle *monsters*; murderous creatures banished/By God
  2. Circle *years*; Twelve winters of grief for Hrothgar
  3. Circle *Beowulf*; Higlac's /Follower and the strongest of the Geats
  4. Circle *Geats*; bold and warlike; circle: Beowulf; Their lord and leader
  5. Circle *home*; in a place/You've not seen

B. 1. Fourteen men went with Beowulf, their fearless leader.

2. They sailed in a mighty vessel, the master of the sea.
3. Hrothgar welcomed Beowulf and his men to Herot, the strongest hall ever built.

Reading Strategy: Paraphrasing (p. 9)
Student passages will differ, but all columns should be filled in order to paraphrase the passage.

Literary Analysis: The Epic (p. 10)
Sample responses: (All of these passages are serious in tone.)
1. Descriptions of Grendel as "mankind's enemy" and Hrothgar's "glorious throne protected by God" make these characters larger than life. Grendel is portrayed as a force of evil in a Christian context in that he can't know the love of God.
2. Beowulf uses elevated, formal language to present himself and his heroic deeds. Herot and Hrothgar, too, come across as grander and larger than life. The recognition of a duty to help others reflects Christian values.
3. Beowulf addresses Hrothgar in elevated language. His desire to conquer on his own reflects a cultural value of self-reliance. He recognizes that Grendel represents evil, and so implies that he is on the side of good.

"The Prologue" from *Gilgamesh,*
translated by David Ferry
from the *Iliad* by Homer

Build Vocabulary: Words of Heroic Values and Beliefs (p. 11)
Sample responses:

The general rode forward to join the *vanguard* of his army.

The soldier was awarded a medal for her *valor*.

Prince Ivan, his castle in flames, took on the role of *avenger*.

The metal of the hero's *helm* glinted in the bright sunlight.

The army began the *rite* of burial for the fallen warriors.

His *destiny* was to spend his years in battle.

Thematic Connection: The Epic (p. 12)
Suggested responses:

The details included in the chart should

reflect the content of the two excerpts. For themes and values, students should cite bravery, courage, duty, faithfulness, and valor. For epics of today, students might point to such cinematic epics as the *Star Wars* trilogy or to a western movie or miniseries they have seen, such as *Lonesome Dove*.

Students' paragraphs of comparison and contrast should provide specific similarities and differences, each of which is supported by specific examples from the epics.

from *A History of the English Church and People* by Bede
from *The Anglo-Saxon Chronicle*, translated by Anne Savage

Build Vocabulary (p. 13)

A. Sample responses:

1. barricade—Barricade the gate or the draft animals will get out!

2. masquerade—The dancers were wearing elaborate costumes at the masquerade ball.

3. ambuscade—The king had not suspected an ambuscade and was consequently astonished to find himself surrounded.

4. promenade—The riders had their horses promenade through the town square.

B. 1. Innumerable; 2. stranded; 3. promontories; 4. barricaded; 5. ravaged

C. 1. c 2. d 3. a 4. b 5. d

Grammar and Style: Compound Sentences (p. 14)

A. 1. (not a compound sentence)

2. They were nearly twice as long as the others; some had sixty oars, some more.

3. The Danes went out with three ships against them, and three stood higher up the river's mouth, beached on dry land; the men from them had gone inland.

4. (not a compound sentence)

5. Alfred died, who was town reeve at Bath; and in the same year the peace was fastened at Tiddingford, just as king Edward advised, both with the East Anglians and the Northumbrians.

B. Sample responses:

1. Ireland is broader than Britain, and its climate is superior.

2. There are no reptiles; no snake can exist there.

3. The island abounds with milk and honey, and there is no lack of vines, fish, and birds; deer and goats are widely hunted.

4. In these latitudes the sun does not remain long below the horizon; consequently, both summer days and winter nights are long.

5. Britain is rich in grain and timber; it has good pasturage, and vines are cultivated.

Reading Strategy: Breaking Down Sentences (p. 15)

A. 1. these Picts asked wives of the Scots—The Picts asked the Scots for women who could be wives to them.

2. because the Picts had no women with them

3. The Scots consented, or gave the Picts permission to take Scots women for their wives.

4. The Scots consented on the condition that when any dispute arose, they [the Picts] should choose a king from the female royal line rather than the male. In other words, if the Picts found themselves in need of a new ruler they would have to select one from female [Scots] royal line rather than the male [Picts], which would give the Scots an element of control over the Picts.

B. Student responses will differ depending upon which sentences they choose to break down.

Literary Analysis: Historical Writing (p. 16)

Possible responses:

1. The wording suggests that this story has been handed down orally. Because of its importance to the British, care was probably taken to transmit the story accurately from generation to generation.

2. Again, the wording suggests an oral tradition. The accuracy of the details is not strictly ascertainable.

3. Because this information relates to royal history, it is probable that it was recorded in court records. Its accuracy is most likely trustworthy, as the lineage should be traceable.

4. This wording suggests an oral interpretation of the events. The speaker determines

from **A History of the English Church and People** by Bede
from **The Anglo-Saxon Chronicle,**
translated by Anne Savage (continued)

that the English got away because their enemies ran aground.

5. This passage suggests that the records of the deaths came from an official source such as church or court records. This information could be verified.

The Prologue from *The Canterbury Tales* by Geoffrey Chaucer

Build Vocabulary (p. 17)

A. Nouns: contribution, congregation, recreation, navigation, decoration

1. decoration; 2. recreation; 3. contribution; 4. navigation

B. 1. sanguine; 2. absolution; 3. avouches; 4. garnished; 5. solicitous; 6. prevarication; 7. commission

Grammar and Style: Past and Past Perfect Tenses (p. 18)

A. 1. had followed (past perfect), had achieved (past perfect)

2. had burnished (past perfect), dangled (past)

3. had learned (past perfect), dipped (past)

4. had found (past perfect), lived (past)

5. had stocked (past perfect), arrayed (past)

B. 1. Chaucer had intended to write 124 tales, but had completed only 24 by the time he died.

2. The narrator had decided to go to Canterbury before he met the other pilgrims but agreed to travel with them once he made their acquaintance.

3. The narrator wanted to write down what he had observed of each pilgrim while he still had the time and space to do so.

Reading Strategy: Analyzing Difficult Sentences (p. 19)

1. He knew the taverns well and every innkeeper and barmaid.

2. He didn't know the lepers, beggars, and slum-and-gutter dwellers as well because they weren't his class of people

and nothing good could come to him from knowing them.

3. If the enemy vessel sank, leaving him prisoners, he "sent them home."

4. He did this by making them walk the plank.

5. The Cook stood alone.

6. He stood alone for cooking flavorful chicken.

7. This is about the Doctor.

8. He can talk about medicine and surgery better than anyone else alive.

9. He watches his patient's favorable star and, using his knowledge of astronomy and his own Natural Magic, knows which hours and planetary degrees would be the luckiest for making charms and magic effigies.

10. He sings an Offertory.

11. He knows he'll have to preach and use his speaking skills to win silver from the crowd.

12. He wants to do the best job he can to win the most silver he can.

Literary Analysis: Characterization (p. 20)

1. Circled item(s) (direct characterization) should include the following: "she was known as Madam Eglantyne"

(indirect characterization:) Her way of smiling very simple and coy. / Her greatest oath was only "By St. Loy!"; well she sang a service, with a fine / Intoning through her nose, as was most seemly; she spoke daintily in French, extremely, / After the school of Stratford-atte-Bowe; French in the Paris style she did not know; At meat her manners were well taught withal/No morsel from her lips did she let fall,/Nor dipped her fingers in the sauce too deep;/But she could carry a morsel up and keep/The smallest drop from falling on her breast.

Sample response: The Nun is the kind of person who tries to act like a well-mannered and delicate lady but is actually rather vain, affected, and lower-class.

2. Circled item(s) (direct characterization) should include the following: "Wary and wise"; "Discreet he was"; "of noted excellence"

(indirect characterization:) who paid his calls; for clients at St. Paul's ; a man to reverence, / Or so he seemed, his sayings were so wise.

Sample response: The Sergeant at the Law seems to be a man who boasts of his own discretion and accomplishments and feels himself wise enough to make remarks for the benefit of others—all of which suggests that he may be more "wary, wise, and discreet" in his own opinion than he actually is.

3. Circled item(s) (direct characterization) should include the following: "worthy woman"; "somewhat deaf"; "Her hose were of the finest scarlet red/And gartered tight; her shoes were soft and new."

(indirect characterization:) In making cloth she showed so great a bent / She bettered those of Ypres and of Ghent. / In all the parish not a dame dared stir / Towards the altar steps in front of her. / And if indeed they did, so wrath was she / As to be quite put out of charity. / Her kerchiefs were of finely woven ground; / I dared have sworn they weighed a good ten pound, / The ones she wore on Sunday on her head.

Sample response: This woman appears to be a vain, materialistic, competitive, show-off type of person.

4. Circled item(s) (direct characterization) should include the following: "a chap of sixteen stone./A great stout fellow big in brawn and bone"; "Broad, knotty and short-shouldered"

(indirect characterization:) he could go / And win the ram at any wrestling show: he would boast / He could heave any door off hinge and post, / Or take a run and break it with his head.

Sample response: The Miller is the kind of person who relies on his brute strength, is proud of his physique and abilities, and isn't very smart.

"The Nun's Priest's Tale" and "The Pardoner's Tale" from *The Canterbury Tales*
by Geoffrey Chaucer

Build Vocabulary (p. 21)
A. 1. captain; the chief officer of a ship or airplane
2. capsize; to turn over or sink headfirst
3. capacity; maximum amount or highest limit
4. apologize; to acknowledge wrong-doing or offense

5. apothegm; a saying or maxim
B. 1. timorous; 2. stringent; 3. capital; 4. maxim; 5. apothecary; 6. derision; 7. prating; 8. pallor; 9. hoary

Grammar and Style: Pronouns (p. 22)
A. 1. she, S; 2. him, O; 3. he, S
B. 1. O, him; 2. S, she; 3. S, he; 4. S, She
C. 1. <u>Who long before the morning service bell</u>; modifies *rioters*
2. <u>Who kills us all round here</u>; modifies *thief*
3. <u>who singles out/And kills the fine young fellows hereabout</u>; modifies *traitor*
4. <u>who draws the longest</u>; modifies *one.*
5. <u>Who lent him three large bottles</u>; modifies *man*

Reading Strategy: Context Clues (p. 23)
A. 1. roar and scream; start
lurch: to start or move suddenly
2. timorous; what cowardice
poltroon: coward
3. Down in a yard with oxen and a plow. . . lodging
refuge: shelter, lodging, a safe place to stay
B. Sample Responses:
1. The boy's warning is clearer during the second reading. Not only does it become clearer that he is talking about Death, it is also clear that Death really is everywhere since all three men die in the end.
2. The vow of the men to destroy Death is clearer during a second reading. They are going to destroy what has destroyed their friends, and they vow before God to do so.
3. The old man's directions become clearer after rereading because the death that meets them under the tree is in the form of the gold florins, and the men bring about their own death through their greed.

Literary Analysis: Parody and *Exemplum* (p. 24)
A. 1. Yes; 2. No
B. Sample Responses:
1. No longer was it Death those fellows sought.

"The Nun's Priest's Tale" and "The Pardoner's Tale" from *The Canterbury Tales*
by Geoffrey Chaucer

2. "Then draw your dagger and do the same. / Then all this money will be ours to spend . . ."

3. "Lord, to think I might / Have all that treasure to myself alone! / Could there be anyone beneath the throne / Of God so happy as I then should be?"

4. Trust me, no ghastlier section to transcend / What these two wretches suffered at their end. / Thus these two murderers received their due, / So did the treacherous young poisoner too.

"Elizabeth II: A New Queen," *The London Times*

Build Vocabulary: Words of Royalty (p. 25)

Sample responses:

"The queen gave a lengthy address on her *accession* to the throne.

The news of the king's marriage was confirmed in a royal *proclamation*.

The queen presides at two *sittings* of her council of advisers every week.

All members of the realm gave an oath of *allegiance* to the new sovereign.

There are very detailed rules that govern the *succession* of a new monarch.

The *abdication* of a king or queen is very rare.

The new queen did not enjoy the *ceremonial* aspects of her position.

The Royal Navy made plans for the *commissioning* of a new ship in honor of the queen.

A modern king travels his *dominions* by plane, not by carriage.

A royal appearance is full of pomp and *pageantry*.

Thematic Connection: A National Spirit (p. 26)

Students will have to use research sources such as an encyclopedia or biography to complete the chart. Through their entries they should make the point that the British monarch has no political role beyond a ceremonial function. Students may point to obvious political figures such as the president or important congressional leaders as their candidates for symbols of the national spirit of the United States. You may wish to encourage students to consider exploring other areas of public life as they develop their proposals, such as athletics, philanthropy, medicine, environmental advocacy, and so on.

from *Sir Gawain and the Green Knight,* translated by Marie Borroff
from *Morte d'Arthur*
by Sir Thomas Malory

Build Vocabulary (p. 27)

A. Sample responses:

1. Because of his *adroitness* with a football, Charley was able to make the football team. *or* Because of his *maladroitness* with a football, Charley was unable to make the football team.

2. Amber was very *adroit* at gymnastics, so she knew she might go to the Olympics. *or* Amber was very *maladroit* at gymnastics, so she knew she would never go to the Olympics.

3. correct

4. Tad prides himself on his *adroitness*, having never broken a leg in all his years as a skier.

B. 1. assay; 2. feigned; 3. righteous; 4. adjure; 5. peril; 6. adroitly; 7. entreated; 8. largesse; 9. interred

Grammar and Style: Comparative and Superlative Forms (p. 28)

A. 1. larger: comparative
2. finer: comparative
3. largest: superlative
4. more beautiful: comparative
5. coldest: superlative

B. 1. Marcie is the most compassionate person I know.

2. Katrusha will be happier working outdoors than in an office this summer.

3. Fresh fruit and a bagel makes a more nutritious breakfast than coffee and a donut.

4. Angelo explained to his grandfather that writing a letter is easier with a computer than with a pen and paper.

5. Up in the hills, it's always chilliest in the morning before the sun comes up.

Reading Strategy: Summarizing (p. 29)

Sample responses: Sir Lucan left because he was hurt very badly. He saw pillagers and robbers who killed people after they robbed them. He told the king what he saw.

Sir Lucan was badly hurt, so he left. As he walked he saw pillagers and robbers stealing from the nobles. As soon as he could, he told the king about it.

Literary Analysis: Medieval Romance (p. 30)

Possible responses from *Sir Gawain and the Green Knight*:

1. The Green Knight himself—given his size, color, and ability to disguise himself—is an example. Another is the green girdle; although in fact it was part of the Green Knight's scheme and probably not magical after all, the girdle still conveyed a sense of the supernatural earlier in the story.

2. At Arthur's court, the knights are dressed in armor, sitting on a high dais. The New Year's Eve feast was very elaborate, "With all dainties double, dishes rare, / With all manner of meat and minstrelsy both . . ."

3. Gawain courageously offers to take Arthur's place. He also courageously presents himself at Green Chapel even though he fears the place is inhabited by Satan.

4. Traveling in search of Green Chapel and finding a wondrous castle where Gawain stays with "strangers" can be viewed as examples of a hero engaged in adventure.

Possible responses from *Morte d' Arthur*:

1. King Arthur dreams a wonderful dream full of rich detail and supernatural elements such as hideous black water, serpents, and worms. Sir Lucan reminds Arthur of his dream and what the spirit of Sir Gawain has taught him.

2. Courtly life is seen in the number of lords, ladies, and knights that appear.

3. Sir Gawain refers to all of the ladies he has fought for and the fact that God has given them grace.

4. A sense of adventure permeates the story as Mordred controls England when Arthur returns and a battle ensues. Just before Gawain dies, he manages to send word to Lancelot that Arthur needs help.

Letters of Margaret Paston
"Lord Randall," "The Twa Corbies," "Get Up and Bar the Door," and "Barbara Allan," Anonymous

Build Vocabulary (p. 31)

A. 1. *Certain* means "sure beyond a doubt."
   2. *Certificate* means a "document verifying the truth of something."
   3. *Certitude* means "sureness."

B. 1. ransacked; 2. alderman; 3. remnant; 4. enquiry; 5. assault; 6. succor; 7. asunder; 8. certify

Grammar and Style: Direct Address (p. 32)

A. Line 1: Lord Randall, my son
   Line 2: my handsome young man
   Line 3: mother

B. Are you hungry, Lord Randall, for there's plenty to eat,

Eat hearty, my love, of the bread and the broth.

Now surely, my darling, there's room in you still.

'Twas a pleasure, dear man, to cook you this food.

Be off, stupid hounds, there's no scraps for you!

Now go home, gentle knight, you've eaten quite well,

Reading Strategy: Understanding Dialect (p. 33)

first stanza: alane, twa corbies, mane, tane, tither, Whar sal, gang, dine the day

second stanza: behint yon auld fail dyke, wot, naebody kens

Rewritten stanzas:

As I was walking all alone,
I heard two ravens making a moan.
The one unto the other did say,
"Where shall we go to dine today?"

In behind yonder old bank of earth
I know there lies a new-slain knight;
And nobody knows that he lies there
But his hawk, his hound, and his lady fair.

Letters of Margaret Paston
"Lord Randall," "The Twa Corbies," "Get Up and Bar the Door," and "Barbara Allan,"
Anonymous *(continued)*

Literary Analysis: Letter and Folk Ballad (p. 34)

A. Sample responses:

Title: "Barbara Allan";

Details: "'Young man, I think you're dying.'"; "'O it's I'm sick . . .'";

Challenge: In the Middle Ages, people often died from disease because the medicines they needed had not yet been discovered.

Title: "The Letters of Margaret Paston";

Details: "They made your tenants of Hellesdon and Drayton, with others, break down the walls of both the place and the lodge—God knows full much against their wills . . .";

Challenge: Corrupt politicians could force tenants to help them destroy a landowner's property even if the tenants supported and worked for the landowner.

"How Siegfried Was Slain" from *The Nibelungenlied,* translated by A. T. Hatto

Build Vocabulary: Language of Perils and Adventures (p. 35)

Sample responses:

1. daring; In an act of daring, he leapt from the castle tower into the ocean.
2. ill-omened; The uprooted tree was an ill-omened sight as they began their journey.
3. thwarted; The bandits were thwarted in their attempt to rob the caravan.
4. dispatched; She dispatched her assailant with his very own sword.
5. quarry; Our quarry was the monster who inhabited the dark forest.
6. noble; To release the prisoners was a noble gesture.
7. sinister; He was known to be sinister, but an act this evil was inconceivable.
8. treacherous; Many boats had been lost on the treacherous rapids they were about to navigate.

Thematic Connection: Perils and Adventures (p. 36)

In the first column, students should list entries such as poor sanitation, a social structure divided between peasants and nobles, superstitious beliefs, and crude technologies. In the second column, students may list attributes of contemporary life such as modern technology (the computer and the telephone), a flatter social stratum, stresses associated with modern life, better transportation, and so on.

Unit 2: Celebrating Humanity (1485–1625)

Sonnets 1, 35 and 75 by Edmund Spenser
Sonnets 31 and 39 by Sir Philip Sidney

Build Vocabulary (p. 37)

A. 1. languor
   2. languid
   3. languid
   4. languish
   5. languor

B. 1. e   2. b   3. a   4. c   5. f   6. d

C. Suggested response: The paragraph should contain the vocabulary words in sentences that reflect the following meanings: *deign*—to condescend; *assay*—to try; *devise*—to work out or plan; *wan*—sickly, pale; *languished*—grew weak; *balm*—something that heals.

Grammar and Style: Capitalization of Proper Nouns (p. 38)

A. 1. Kate
   2. Dawn
   3. Tom; Southridge High School

B. Sample responses:
   2. O Wind, the winter comes. The wind blows.
   3. My brother Bill is thirteen. The bill for repairs came yesterday.
   4. My homeroom teacher is Ms. Carpenter. A carpenter will build the new deck.

5. My sister attends Cook School. My dad is a professional cook.

6. The school is on Grove Street. That is a one-way street.

Reading Strategy: Paraphrasing (p. 39)

Sample responses:

Students should paraphrase each by breaking it into parts and summarizing/paraphrasing each section, focusing on the main ideas rather than all the images.

Literary Analysis: The Sonnet and Sonnet Sequence (p. 40)

A. "Lyke as a ship that through the ocean wyde . . ."—lines 1-4: *ABAB*

"So I whose star, that wont with her bright ray . . ."—lines 5-8: *BCBC*

"Yet hope I well, that when this storme is past . . ."—lines 9-12: *CDCD*

"Till then I wander carefull comfortlesse . . ."—lines 13-14: *CC*

B. Sample responses:
1. a. moon;   b. sleep
2. a. sympathy or understanding;
   b. peaceful sleep
3. a. bitter, or unhappy;   b. longing or need

Sonnets 29, 106, 116, and 130
by William Shakespeare

Build Vocabulary (p. 41)

A. chronic, chronologer, chronology, synchronicity, synchronize, chronicle

B. 1. prefiguring;   2. impediments;   3. scope;   4. chronicle;   5. alters;   6. sullen

Grammar and Style: Participles as Adjectives (p. 42)

A. blesséd wood [circle *wood*]

dancing chips [circle *chips*]

living lips [circle *lips*]

B. Sample responses:
1. an outstanding or accomplished playwright
2. renowned or lauded Globe Theater
3. devastating or ravaging plague
4. daunting or amazing variety
5. betrayed or discontented speaker

Reading Strategy: Paraphrasing (p. 43)

Sample responses:

Students shoul paraphrase each by breaking it into parts and summarizing/paraphrasing each section, focusing on the main ideas rather than all the images.

Literary Analysis: Shakespearean Sonnet (p. 44)

A. a, b, a, b, c, d, c, d, e, f, e, f, g, g

B. 1. Shakespearean

2. The premise is that the world is in a constant state of change. To support this idea, the speaker lists historical events that have occurred since his love first began.

3. The conclusion is that although events are uncertain, the speaker will remain constant to his beloved.

4. Both poets express concern about the uncertain course of events over which they have no control, and both express faith in the ability of love and poetry to give meaning to life.

Sonnets 18 and 28 by Petrarch
Sonnets 69 and 89 by Pablo Neruda

Build Vocabulary (p. 45)

1. prospects; sample sentence: The smile in my love's eyes show my prospects as promising.

2. muse; sample sentence: With you as my muse I can write poetry for the ages.

3. light; sample sentence: Meet me by the light of the moon and I'll sing you a song of love.

4. destiny; sample sentence: From the minute I met you, I knew you were my destiny.

5. woe; sample sentence: My woe at being parted from you cannot be measured.

6. vanquished; sample sentence: My anguish is vanquished by your presence.

7. beauties; sample sentence: Your inner beauties are even lovelier than your graceful form.

8. sublime; sample sentence: Each fond memory of you is sublime.

Cultural Connection: Love Poetry (p. 46)

Students' chart entries are likely to include contemporary references that are less romantic or idyllic than the images found in the sonnets of Neruda and Petrarch.

from *Utopia* by Sir Thomas More
Elizabeth's Speech Before Her Troops by Queen Elizabeth I

Build Vocabulary (p. 47)

A. 1. consequence; 2. inconsequential;
   3. sequentially; 4. sequel;
   5. non sequitur

B. Sample responses:
   1. confiscation; 2. sloth; 3. stead;
   4. fraudulent; 5. abrogated; 6. treachery;
   7. forfeited; 8. subsequently

Grammar and Style: Complex Sentences (p. 48)

A. Sample responses:
   1. The royals loved their jester *because* he never failed to make them laugh.
   2. *Although* the general worshiped his queen, he was still forced to fight against her.
   3. *When* the king called for an end to taxes, his subjects cried for joy.

B. Sample response:

The queen enjoyed her morning ritual. *While* she drank her tea, she read the paper. Then, she watered the plants in her room, *because* she didn't trust her staff with such delicate specimens. *After* Her Majesty ate a delicious royal breakfast, she strolled the grounds of the main house. *When* the groundskeeper spoke with her about landscaping matters, the resident rabbit was scared off by their loud voices. *If* the queen extended her stroll, it was a sure sign that her mood had soured. She continued on a long walk *until* the dignitaries from France arrived. *Although* it seemed she might be cross, the queen still looked cheerful.

Reading Strategy: Summarizing (p. 49)

Sample response:

Passage: Let him curb crime, and by his wise conduct prevent it rather than allow it to increase, only to punish it subsequently.

Main Idea: Let him curb crime. . . .

Supporting Ideas: The crime rate can be lowered by prevention rather than punishment.

Summary: The wise ruler prevents crime rather than punishing criminals.

Literary Analysis: The Monarch as Hero (p. 50)

Sample responses:

1. strength, safeguard, honor, heart of a king, general, judge, rewarder, care, efforts, authority, majesty of kingship, noble, exalted spirit, wise conduct

Students' paragraphs should reflect the universal lessons about heroic leadership conveyed by Sir Thomas More and/or the heroic courage and strength that Elizabeth implies.

2. Students might argue it was necessary for a monarch to have exceptional intelligence—and from More's perspective, tremendous generosity, nobility, and exaltedness of spirit—and extreme courage (to the point of laying down his or her life for the people) to tackle the problems of the day, which often included threats to the very stability of the kingdom.

3. Some students might say that given the enormous task of overseeing an entire kingdom, monarchs would seem to require almost superhuman capabilities, especially given the hardships of the time such as pestilence, famine, and war. However, others might point out that intelligence, generosity, and courage make for an excellent leader, then as well as now.

from The King James Bible

Build Vocabulary (p. 51)

A. 1. Static: sentence should indicate the idea that something stands motionless.
   2. Thermostat: sentence should indicate that a thermostat marks where temperature stands.
   3. Station: sentence should include the idea that a station is the place or position a person occupies.
   4. Status: sentence should include the idea that status is a person's relative standing within a group.

B. 1. a 2. c 3. a 4. d 5. c

Grammar and Style: Infinitive Phrases (p. 52

A. 1. to raise his hand in class, ADV (modifies *afraid*)
   2. to answer the question, N (direct object of *refused*)

3. to work evenings, ADJ (modifies *someone*)

B. 1. To save lives, N

2. to begin the race, ADJ

3. to watch the argument, ADV

4. to save money for college, ADV

5. to discriminate against others, ADJ

6. to talk on the phone, N

Reading Strategy: Inferring Meaning (p. 53)

Suggested responses: Students should clearly state what they know about the passage; clues listed should give insights into the meaning of the passage; entries under the column "meaning" should be appropriate and should relate to the entries under the other columns.

Literary Analysis: Psalm, Sermon, and Parable (p. 54)

1. narrative structure; dialogue

2. a. that God takes care of birds, and he will take care of people; b. sermon

3. a. Metaphors for guidance and support are green pastures, still waters, paths of righteousness; b. God; c. It is a lyric poem in praise of God.

from *A Man for All Seasons*
by Robert Bolt

Build Vocabulary: Language of Power (p. 55)

Sample responses:

1. The licentious conduct of the ruling monarch led to his downfall.

2. It is important for a leader to have his or her people's trust.

3. The wise king took no pride in the fact that the people feared him.

4. The ministers were shocked at the decision Her Majesty issued.

5. Even though you are my king, I must be honest in giving you my opinion.

6. He gained the crown for no reason other than being the eldest son.

7. The people had no respect for the wicked, unjust prince.

8. The queen insisted on hearing the truth, not fearing its consequences.

9. The opposition quickly became united in face of the abuse of civil rights under the current regime.

10. He believed that a citizen has a duty to resist an unjust law.

Thematic Connection: Power of Contemporary Rulers (p. 56)

In their contemporary references, students may include leaders from the United States and other democratic countries, noting that they derive their power from the franchise exercised by the people. They may, however, point to democratic leaders who abused their power, such as Richard Nixon or Joseph McCarthy. They may also cite leaders as diverse as Pope John Paul II, Nelson Mandela, Joseph Stalin, Mother Teresa, Queen Elizabeth II, and so on.

The Tragedy of Macbeth, Act I,
by William Shakespeare

Build Vocabulary (p. 57)

A. senator, senate, president, vice president, representative, mayor, governor, Republican, Democrat

B. 1. valor; 2. treason; 3. liege; 4. imperial; 5. sovereign

C. 1. c 2. b 3. a 4. a 5. d

Grammar and Style: Action Verbs and Linking Verbs (p. 58)

A. 1. underline (will) sail, (will) do

2. underline hover

3. circle *are*; underline live, may question

4. underline speak, can; circle are

5. underline bade, call, hail; circle is

6. circle was, art, is; underline overtake

7. underline comes

B. Sample responses:

1. Lady Macbeth is eager for her husband to become king.

2. The witches conjure up an evil plot.

3. King Duncan is far too trusting.

4. Duncan's sons act like guilty men when they run away.

5. Macbeth is desirous of the crown.

Reading Strategy: Using Text Aids (p. 59)

Suggested responses: Students should find stage directions and margin notes in the text of the play and use the graphic organizer to show what they tell about the action and characters in the play.

The Tragedy of Macbeth, Act I,
by William Shakespeare *(continued)*

Literary Analysis: Elizabethan Drama (p. 60)

Sample responses:

1. Audiences might assume the witches represent evil, temptation, or danger. They may say that the witches also represent the devil or some force against God.

2. Confession, request for forgiveness, and repentance are all concepts common to Christian faiths.

3. Lady Macbeth feels that her husband is too soft to seize what he wants; she thinks he is too kind to make his ambition a priority, and therefore he may never get what he wants. Audiences may easily sympathize with a person who is too good-hearted to put his own desires foremost.

The Tragedy of Macbeth, Act II,
by William Shakespeare

Build Vocabulary (p. 61)

A. 1. vociferously; 2. provocative; 3. evocative; 4. vocation; 5. vocalize

B. 1. a 2. d 3. b 4. a 5. d 6. b

Build Grammar Skills: Commonly Confused Words: *Lie* and *Lay* (p. 62)

A. 1. OK; 2. OK; 3. OK; 4. lie; 5. lay

B. Sample responses:

1. Uncle Martin tries to lie down for a nap every afternoon.

2. I had laid my good jacket on the chair, so I decided to hang it up.

3. A layer of thick black dust had lain over the old rocker for at least a decade.

4. Yesterday the cat lay on the rug for eight hours.

5. Tamika is lying down for a little while; she's not feeling well.

6. The farmer told me that the hens had not been laying many eggs.

Reading Strategy: Reading Verse for Meaning (p. 63)

1. three

2. The danger that threatened us has not overtaken us and our most prudent act is to get away before it does.

3. So let's leave on horseback and be quick about it. There's justification for leaving quickly when our lives are in grave danger.

4. We must get away before we are murdered.

Literary Analysis: Blank Verse (p. 64)

1. rhyme; 2. rhyme; 3. blank verse; 4. prose

"The Kíng háth háppilý recéivéd, Mácbéth,
The néws óf thý succéss. Ánd whén hé réads
Thý pérsónal véntúre ín the rébéls' fíght,
His wóndérs ánd his práisés dó conténd
Which should bé thíne or hís.

The Tragedy of Macbeth, Act III,
by William Shakespeare

Build Vocabulary (p. 65)

A. Sample responses:

1. The airplane engine continued to malfunction during a routine inspection.

2. Sheri was maladjusted to her new school environment.

3. The doctor said my problem with digesting proteins came from malabsorption.

4. Every time Tomas comes for a visit, I remember that he is a malcontent.

5. The company was cited for malfeasance.

B. 1. d 2. a 3. a 4. d 5. c

Grammar and Style: Subject-Verb Agreement (p. 66)

A. 1. Are; 2. shine; 3. attempt; 4. is; 5. Have

B. 1. The three murderers who were hired by Macbeth are upset when Fleance escapes.

2. Macbeth is shocked that no one else sees the ghost of Banquo.

3. OK

4. Lady Macbeth becomes alarmed when she sees that Macbeth is out of control.

5. She tells the dinner guests that Macbeth is prone to this kind of fit.

Reading Strategy: Reading Between the Lines (p. 67)

Sample responses:

1. He is telling the murderers that he has a grievance with Banquo that runs as deep as their own.

2. Macbeth wants to get the murderers on his side so that they will carry out his orders and murder Banquo. He feels he must justify his deed by saying there is a terrible rift between himself and Banquo.

3. Macbeth is flattering the murderer by telling him that he is the best at his trade.

4. He is flattering the murderer because he wants the deaths of both Banquo and Fleance.

Literary Analysis: Conflict (p. 68)

Sample responses:

1. Macbeth has told the murderers that Banquo has been the cause of their misfortune in the past. This makes them want to get even with Banquo and to curry favor with Macbeth.

   Quotation: **MACBETH.** Both of you / Know Banquo was your enemy.

   BOTH MURDERERS. True, my lord.

2. Banquo suspects that Macbeth has killed the king.

   Quotation: **BANQUO.** Thou hast it now: King, Cawdor, Glamis, all, / As the weird women promised, and I fear / Thou play'dst most foully for 't.

3. His guilty conscience makes him see the image of dead Banquo seated in his chair.

   Quotation: **MACBETH.** Avaunt! and quit my sight! Let the earth hide thee!

4. She fears he will give away the secret that he was Duncan's murderer, which will prove the undoing of both of them.

   Quotation: **LADY MACBETH.** What, quite unmanned in folly?

The Tragedy of Macbeth, Act IV,
by William Shakespeare

Build Vocabulary (p.69)

A. 1. credentials; 2. credibility; 3. credence

B. 1. f 2. d 3. e 4. a 5. b 6. c

C. 1. judicious; 2. avarice; 3. credulous; 4. pernicious; 5. sundry; 6. intemperance

Grammar and Style: Possessive Forms (p. 70)

A. 1. witches; 2. glass's; 3. sisters'; 4. Scotland's; 5. ladies'; 6. Macbeths'; 7. Ross's

B. Sample responses:

2. The eight kings' heirs filled the hall.

3. Fleance's escape was a matter of pure luck.

4. The three apparitions' prophesies satisfy Macbeth.

5. The messenger's words frighten Lady Macduff.

6. The murderers' gruesome deeds cannot go unpunished.

Reading Strategy: Using Your Senses (p. 71)

Sample responses:

Quotation: "This tyrant, whose sole name blisters our tongues / Was once thought honest . . ."

Appeals to Sense of: touch

Quotation: ". . . To offer up a weak, poor, innocent lamb / T' appease an angry god."

Appeals to Sense of: sight

Quotation: "Each new morn / New widows howl, new orphans cry . . ."

Appeals to Sense of: hearing

Quotation: "Double, double, toil and trouble; / Fire burn and caldron bubble."

Appeals to Senses of: sight and touch

Quotation: "Thy crown does sear mine eyelids."

Appeals to Senses of: sight and touch

Literary Analysis: Imagery (p. 72)

1. Imagery: thunder, lightning, rain

   Connection: darkness, rough weather, stormy seas

2. Imagery: the fires or brightness of stars; black and deep desires

   Connection: the contrast of the light of goodness and the dark evil of Macbeth's desire for power

3. Imagery: spurring a horse, which leaps and falls upon another horse and rider

   Connection: An out-of-control animal has the same qualities as Macbeth's ambitions for power.

4. Imagery: feeling constricted, tied up

   Connection: Macbeth is trapped.

The Tragedy of Macbeth, Act V,
by William Shakespeare

Build Vocabulary (p. 73)

Sample responses:

A. 1. My aunt was extremely perturbed about her tax increase.
   2. The roar of the turbine was almost deafening.
   3. Suri had never seen a turbojet take off from the airport before.
   4. The turbid river water flowed from the hydroelectric plant upstream.

B. 1. d   2. c   3. a   4. b

C. 1. pristine;   2. harbingers;
   3. perturbation;   4. clamorous

Grammar and Style: Pronouns and Antecedents (p. 74)

A. 1. he;   2. his;   3. her;   4. his, him;
   5. her;   6. him

B. Sample responses:

1. When Macduff hears of the death of his children, he determines to seek justice against Macbeth.

2. The three witches give Macbeth information that makes him feel he can't lose in battle against his enemies.

3. Lady Macbeth spends several nights sleepwalking and washing her hands over and over again.

Reading Strategy: Inferring Beliefs of the Period (p. 75)

Suggested response: Students should look through the play, find excerpts that might reveal information about the time in which Shakespeare lived, and fill in the table with the excerpts and their own interpretations. For example:

Quotation: LENNOX. Where we lay, / our chimneys were blown down, and, as they say, / Lamentings heard i' th' air, strange screams of death, / And prophesying with accents terrible / Of dire combustion and confused events / New hatched to th' woeful time: the obscure birds / Clamored the live long night. Some say, the earth / Was feverish and did shake.

Meaning: Throughout the play there are references to omens and harbingers of good or ill fortune, as illustrated by this quotation from Lennox about the night on which King Duncan was murdered. This seems to indicate that people were fairly superstitious in Shakespeare's time.

Literary Analysis: Shakespearean Tragedy (p. 76)

Sample responses:

1. Students will probably say that the events would have turned out the same way even if Macbeth had never encountered the witches. In a tragedy, the tragic figure brings about his or her own downfall. The witches allow Macbeth to see an opportunity to gain the throne, but it is his own ambition, and not the prophesies of the witches, that brings about his inevitable undoing.

2. There are several places where it is clear that Macbeth is aware of his own deep character flaw. Students may cite Macbeth's quote: "The Prince of Cumberland! That is a step / On which I must fall down, or else o'erleap, / For in my way it lies . . ." or "I have no spur / To prick the sides of my intent, but only / Vaulting ambition, which o'erleaps itself / And falls on th' other . . ."

3. Students should know that Lady Macbeth doubts her husband's ambition at the beginning of the play. She fears his kind nature and feels that he is ambitious without being wicked enough to attain his ambitions. Representative quotes: ". . . Yet do I fear thy nature; / It is too full o' th' milk of human kindness / To catch the nearest way. Thou wouldst be great / Art not without ambition, but without / The illness should attend it . . ."; "Art thou afeard / To be the same in thine own act and valor / As thou art in desire? . . ."

from *Oedipus, the King*
by Sophocles

Build Vocabulary: Language of Tragedy (p. 77)

1. pestilence;   2. wreck;   3. prophesied;
4. burden;   5. guilt;   6. destroying;
7. sorrows;   8. oracles

Literary Connection: Dramatic Tragedy
(p. 78)

Students should make the basic point that while Oedipus's tragedy stemmed from a fate seemingly beyond his control or beyond his awareness, Macbeth was an active participant in or designer of his tragedy. Both men, however, were tragic figures who did make choices and perform acts that led to their own destruction. The contemporary characters students create should have experiences grounded in contemporary life. Their tragic hero may be a bureaucrat who compromises his integrity for personal gain or a high school athlete who fails at life outside the sports arena.

Unit 3: A Turbulent Time (1625–1798)

Works of John Donne

Build Vocabulary (p. 79)
A. Sample responses:
1. among nations
2. meet each other
3. going between them
4. between the events
5. with each other

B. 1. breach, laity
2. contention, intermit
3. trepidation, piety
4. profanation
5. covetousness

Grammar and Style: Active and Passive Voice (p. 80)
A. 2. active
3. Fate, chance, kings, and desperate men enslave death.
4. The image of a drawing compass with two legs represents the two lovers.
5. active

B. Sample responses:
1. The horse was trained by the boy.
2. The artist draws a circle with the compass.
3. Death will separate the lovers.
4. The earth is eroded by the sea.
5. Donne was dismissed by his employer.
6. The poet weeps and sighs for his lover.

Reading Strategy: Recognizing the Speakers Voice and Motivation (p. 81)
Sample responses:
From "Meditation 17"

Speaker's Words: ". . . but this bell that tells me of his affliction digs out and applies that gold to me, if by this consideration of another's danger, I take mine own into contemplation.

Why: He is contemplating the death of someone he knows, and focuses on his own mortality.
From "Song"

Speaker's Words: "When though sigh'st, thou sigh'st not wind/But sigh'st my soul away; . . ."

Why: He is grieved at leaving her, but her grief over his leaving makes him even more sorrowful.
From "A Valediction: Forbidding Mourning"

Speaker's Words: "Our two souls therefore, which are one,/Though I must go, endure no yet/A breach, but an expansion/Like gold to airy thinness beat."

Why: He is putting a positive light on their farewell by saying that their love will be expanded rather than divided by the separation.
From "Holy Sonnet 10"

Speaker's Words: "One short sleep past, we wake eternally,/And death shall be no more; Death, thou shalt die."

Why: He is viewing death through his religious faith that overcomes death in the end.

Literary Analysis: Metaphysical Poetry (p. 82)
Possible responses:
1. Death is being compared to a person who looks strong and indomitable, but is in fact powerless.
2. Like the two legs of a compass, the poet and his lover will always be connected and look to each other for support, no matter how far apart they are. Their love is being compared to the compass.

"On My First Son," "Song: To Celia," and "Still to Be Neat" by Ben Jonson

Build Vocabulary (p. 83)

A. dost, do; thou, you; thy, your; wert, were

B. Across: 2. hast; 3. wert; 5. thou
Down: 1. dost; 2. hath; 3. wast; 4. dost

Grammar and Style: The Placement of *Only* (p. 84)

A. 1. a   2. b   3. b

B. Sample responses:

1. The word *only* may be placed before
   a. "the dark forest" (The dark forest is all we saw.)
   b. "window" (There is just one window.)
   c. "cabin" (There is just one cabin.)
2. The word *only* may be placed before
   a. "for advice" (My purpose was just to get advice.)
   b. "to borrow" (My purpose was to get advice as well as borrow your radio.)
   c. "radio" (My purpose was not to borrow the one radio you own.)
3. The word *only* may be placed before
   a. "day" (We spent just one day together.)
   b. "listening" (We only listened to music.)
   c. "music" (There is just one kind of music we both love.)

Reading Strategy: Hypothesizing (p. 85)

Sample responses:

2. "Or leave a kiss but in the cup/And I'll not look for wine." ("Song: To Celia," lines 2–3) Hypothesis: The speaker probably has an idealistic vision of his lady. Supporting Lines: Line 13: "It could not withered be." Lines 15–16: "it grows and smells . . . / Not of itself, but thee." Final Hypothesis: The speaker claims that his lady only breathed on the wreath and it continued to grow and smell of her. These lines confirm his idealistic vision of her.

3. "Still to be neat, still to be dressed," "Still to be powdered, still perfumed." ("Still to Be Neat," lines 1 and 3) Hypothesis: "Still" means always; repetition of this word sounds like a negative comment—the speaker probably doesn't like to see a woman always neat. Supporting Lines: Lines 7–8: "Give me a look, give me a face / That makes simplicity a grace." Final Hypothesis: These lines further confirm that the speaker prefers simplicity to artificial neatness.

4. "Though art's hid causes are not found/All is not sweet, all is not sound." ("Still to Be Neat," lines 5–6) Hypothesis: The speaker seems to imply that the artificial neatness conceals something unsavory. Supporting Lines: "Than all th'adulteries of art." Final Hypothesis: The use of the word *adulteries*, meaning "corruptions," further confirms the idea of something unwholesome.

Literary Analysis: Epigrams (p. 86)

A. Students should circle the numbers 2, 3, 4, 5.

B. Guidelines for student responses:
Epigrams should be at least two lines. They may rhyme and may be either humorous or serious.

"To His Coy Mistress" by Andrew Marvell
"To the Virgins, to Make Much of Time" by Robert Herrick
"Song" by Sir John Suckling

Build Vocabulary (p. 87)

A. Sample responses:

1. Our primary goal for the afternoon is to complete the composition.
2. The gallery was established primarily to promote young artists.
3. In our school, the class president has primacy.
4. If the primary were held now, the incumbent would win.
5. Babe Ruth was in his prime when he hit 61 home runs.

B. 1. prime;   2. coyness;   3. amorous;
4. wan;   5. languish

Grammar and Style: Irregular Forms of Adjectives (p. 88)

A. 1. best; superlative
2. better; comparative
3. more; comparative
4. worst; superlative
5. less; comparative

B. 1. It is better to read the poem now while you are not so tired rather than after you have studied hard all day.

2. Although they also studied Shakespeare and Milton, most students preferred the metaphysical poets.

3. The judges decided that the best poem of all those they had read was written by a high-school student.

Reading Strategy: Inferring Speakers' Attitudes (p. 89)

Possible responses:

1. A flower that is beautiful today will be dead tomorrow. The speaker feels sadness that time and beauty are fleeting.

2. The speaker feels that time is right behind him, overtaking him. The poem implies a sense of urgency and helplessness in facing the passage of time.

3. In the first stanza, the speaker seems solicitous. In the second, he seems less tolerant; the person he is addressing is now a "young sinner" rather than a "fond lover." In the third stanza, the speaker seems exasperated as he urges the person to "quit, for shame."

Literary Analysis: *Carpe Diem* Theme (p. 90)

Sample responses:

1. The sun is used as a symbol in the second stanza.

2. The lines claim that not only is life short, but the best years of life—those of youth—are even briefer. After they are gone, life gets worse and worse.

3. He says there's nothing wrong with coyness except that it takes time and life is too short for that.

4. "But at my back I always hear/Time's winged chariot hurrying near:/And yonder all before us lie/Deserts of vast eternity."

5. The speaker wants his mistress to be his lover. Sample lines from the poem:

That long-preserved virginity,
And your quaint honor turn to dust,
And into ashes all my lust:
The grave's a fine and private place,
But none I think do there embrace.

"Freeze Tag" by Suzanne Vega
"New Beginning" by Tracy Chapman

Build Vocabulary: Language of Time (p. 91)

1. beginning; 2. fading; 3. wake up;
4. past; 5. fragments; 6. change;
7. indecision; 8. cycle

Cultural Connection: Theme of Time (p. 92)

Sample responses:

Marvell—the Flood, sensitivity, time's winged chariot, the marble vault, the grave

Herrick— rosebuds, old time still flying, lamp of heaven, warm blood of youth

Vega—sun fading fast, wintertime, fading to black, slides into the past, swings of indecision

Chapman—new beginning, waking up and looking around, endings, coming together, breaking the chain, breaking the cycle

Poetry of John Milton

Build Vocabulary (p. 93)

A. Sample responses:

1. turn on the light; 2. brightness;
3. bright

B. 1. guile; 2. obdurate; 3. semblance;
4. ignominy; 5. tempestuous;
6. illumine; 7. transgress; 8. supplicant;
9. transcendent

Grammar and Style: Correct Use of *Who* and *Whom* (p. 94)

A. 1. Circle *whom*; 2. Circle *who*; 3. Circle *whom*; 4. Circle second *who*; 5. Circle *whom*; 6. Circle *who*

B. 1. *Who*; 2. *who, whom*; 3. *who*; 4. *who, who*; 5. *whom*

Reading Strategy: Breaking Down Sentences (p. 95)

Sample responses:

2. Passage: "Th' infernal Serpent; he it was, whose guile / Stirred up with envy and revenge, deceived / The mother of mankind, what time his pride / Had cast him out from Heav'n, with all his host / Of rebel angels, by whose aid aspiring / To set himself in glory above his peers . . . ." (lines 34–39)

Main Clause: He it was.

Poetry of John Milton (continued)

Supporting Ideas: He is the infernal Serpent. Out of envy and revenge he deceived the mother of mankind. Because of his pride he had been cast out of heaven along with his host of rebel angels with whom he was aspiring to set himself in glory above his peers.

3. Passage: "Yet not for those, / Nor what the potent Victor in his rage / Can else inflict, do I repent or change. . . ." (lines 94–96)

   Main Clause: I do not repent or change.

   Supporting Ideas: Satan maintains this view despite "those" (his punishments and God's power) and whatever else God can do.

4. Passage: "To bow and sue for grace / With suppliant knee, and deify his power / Who from the terror of this arm so late / Doubted his empire, that were low indeed. . . ." (lines 111–114)

   Main Clause: That were low indeed.

   Supporting Ideas: Satan considers it beneath him to bow and sue for grace on suppliant knee and deify God's power. Satan thinks that his power caused God to question the strength of His kingdom.

Literary Analysis: Epic Poetry (p. 96)

Of man's first disobedience, and the fruit
Of that forbidden tree, whose mortal taste
Brought death into the world, and all our woe,
With loss of Eden, till one greater Man
Restore us, and regain the blissful seat,
Sing Heav'nly Muse, that on the secret top
Of Oreb or of Sinai, didst inspire
That shepherd, who first taught the chosen
seed . . .

from "Eve's Apology in Defense of Women" by Amelia Lanier
"To Lucasta, on Going to the Wars" and "To Althea, from Prison"
by Richard Lovelace

Build Vocabulary (p. 97)

A. Sample responses:

1. Richard said, "The owner of that car should be cited for a breach of the peace."

2. The subcontractor who failed to build the foundation on time was cited for breach of contract.

3. The knights finally made a breach in the town's defenses.

B. 1. c   2. d   3. a

Grammar and Style: Correlative Conjunctions (p. 98)

A. 1. Lanier's poetry is both sincere and insightful.

2. The reader is forced to wonder whether Eve was justly punished or if Adam should have shared the blame.

3. Richard Lovelace was neither a Catholic nor a Puritan.

4. Lovelace was both arrested and imprisoned by anti-Royalists.

5. The poetry that Lovelace wrote while in prison was not only beautiful but also some of his finest.

B. Sample responses:

1. In "Eve's Apology in Defense of Women" Lanier says that *both* Adam *and* Eve are guilty of sin.

2. Lovelace's tone is *both* coy *and* serious in his poem about going to the wars.

3. The poem addressed to Lucasta is *not so* playful in its imagery *as* the poem addressed to Althea.

4. "To Althea, from Prison" is *not only* a poem about love *but also* a profound statement on the nature of freedom.

Reading Strategy: Using Historical Context (p. 99)

Suggested response:

"Eve's Apology in Defense of Women"

Students should point out that women in seventeenth-century England were considered second-class citizens in all walks of life. Lanier claims that the root reason for this discrimination is an injustice. She argues that Adam in the biblical story of Adam and Eve should share equal blame for the guilt of humanity. The poem is ultimately an argument that if men and women share equal guilt in the biblical story, they should share equal privileges in society.

"To Lucasta, on Going to the Wars"

Students should point out that English society in the mid-seventeenth century underwent a massive upheaval. Both the authority of the king and of wealthy landowners were being questioned, and Lovelace was a wealthy landowner. In the poem he is saying that his love of duty, king, and honor are greater than his love of Lucasta. He is revealing his conservative beliefs in a time of radical social upheaval.

"To Althea, from Prison"

Student responses should include the observation that after the English Civil War, many Royalists and conservatives, including Lovelace, were persecuted and imprisoned by the anti-Royalists. In the poem he is stating his undying devotion to the king in such phrases as "loyal flames" and "glories of my King."

Literary Analysis: Tradition and Reform (p. 100)

Possible responses:

1. Lanier is referring to the eating of the apple in the Garden of Eden. After Adam and Eve ate the apple, they were cast out of paradise. Although both Adam and Eve were punished for their actions, Eve generally is assigned a greater blame because she tempted Adam with the apple. Lanier states that Adam deserves a greater share of the blame than he received.

2. According to Lanier, Adam's guilt is greater because his motives were less noble than Eve's. Eve bit the apple because she wanted the knowledge that would come from it. Adam bit the apple because it looked good.

3. Men claim a greater knowledge of worldly matters and a privilege over women in society. They claim this because of the traditional story of Adam and Eve. Lanier is saying that if you reinterpret the story you will see that men and women were both equally to blame from the start, and that men and women should therefore be equal in society.

from *The Diary* by Samuel Pepys
from *A Journal of the Plague Year* by Daniel Defoe

Build Vocabulary (p. 101)

A. 1. disheveling; 2. distribute; 3. disinfect; 4. disgust; 5. disgrace; 6. dispel

B. 1. g 2. i 3. c 4. d 5. h 6. f 7. e 8. b 9. a

Build Grammar Skills: Gerunds (p. 102)

A. 1. Not a gerund; 2. Gerund; 3. Gerund; 4. Not a gerund; 5. Not a gerund

B. Sample responses:

1. Summarizing is an important strategy for understanding difficult poetry.
2. Bicycling wastes less energy than driving.
3. The economy of this town is based on farming.
4. Chewing food with your mouth open is impolite.
5. Performing before audiences is part of an actor's job.

Reading Strategy: Drawing Conclusions (p. 103)

Sample responses:

1. At first, Pepys was not very worried about the fire.
2. A person who walked around London freely during the plague risked becoming infected with it.
3. People infected with the plague became despondent and wanted to die quickly.

Literary Analysis: Diary or Journal (p. 104)

A. Sample responses:

1. The fire followed a long drought; 2. High wind drove the fire into the city; 3. Few people fought the fire, because most were distracted and trying to save their possessions; 4. Houses were built very close together; 5. Combustible materials in the houses and warehouses fed the fire.

B. Sample responses:

1. A future historian might discover what high-school students learned at school, the types of extracurricular activities they participated in, what types of relationships they had, and how they felt about historical events of the time.

2. The reader might feel less involved with the narrator and the characters of the story. The journal form makes the events in the story seem more compelling and immediate, as though one is hearing a first-hand account.

from *Gulliver's Travels*
by Jonathan Swift

Build Vocabulary (p. 105)

A. Sample responses:

1. downcast; 2. a flu shot; 3. throw in

B. 1. c 2. d 3. b 4. b

Grammar and Style: Correct Use of *Between* and *Among* (p. 106)

A. 1. between; 2. among; 3. between;
4. Among; 5. between

B. Sample responses:

1. Among the members of the jury there was no argument.

2. An argument broke out between the linebacker and the quarterback.

3. Gossip was among the things that my grandmother couldn't tolerate.

4. Gossip flowed steadily between Mrs. McReady and her neighbor.

5. The zoning dispute among the townspeople caused tempers to flare.

6. The land dispute between the two property owners dragged on for years.

7. Communication among the members of the committee proved difficult.

8. Communication between the friends continued via email.

Reading Strategy: Interpreting (p. 107)

Sample responses:

2. "I observe among you some lines of an institution, which in its original might have been tolerable, but these half erased, and the rest wholly blurred and blotted by corruptions."—The king observes that the doctrines that countries are founded upon can sometimes be interpreted in such a way as to distort the original meaning.—This phenomenon can be seen today in the way people seek to redefine the meaning of the Constitution and other documents.

3. "He was perfectly astonished with the historical account I gave him of our affairs during the last century, protesting it was only a heap of conspiracies, rebellions, murders, massacres, revolutions, banishment . . ."—The king sees England's history through the eyes of an outside observer and can therefore describe the country's deeds as murderously violent and corrupt.—Many countries have over the course of history used their political and military might to gain advantage over other, weaker countries.

4. "I would hide the frailties and deformities of my political mother and place her virtues and beauties in the most advantageous light."—Gulliver is describing a form of nationalism in which a person defends his or her country right or wrong.—Many people feel that love of country justifies almost any political or military deed.

Literary Analysis: Satire (p. 108)

Sample responses:

1. A big city hospital

2. Disorganization and lack of compassionate concern prevents the hospital from offering truly good care to patients.

3. A prototypical Metropolitan General Hospital, with its peeling paint and dilapidated conditions, can be the setting for the satire.

4. Patient X and Patient Y, (students should come up with an amusing name), along with their respective injuries or ailments

5. Red tape and bureaucratic procedures tie up treatment for Patients X and Y.

6. Metropolitan General Hospital does everything in its power to encourage patients to get well; the proof is that they all want to leave as soon as possible. A hospital administrator says that he is sure their hospital is the best around because no patient ever returns.

from *An Essay on Man* and from *The Rape of the Lock*
by Alexander Pope

Build Vocabulary (p. 109)

A. Sample responses:

1. The court was associated with the royal family and its entourage. Therefore, the upper classes vied to stay in the court's favor.

2. A ball was a huge formal dance. It served as an important social occasion for the members of the upper class.

3. Reputation, or a person's estimated social worth, was very important in Pope's time, which is one of the reasons his poetry often takes aim at supposedly

reputable members of the upper class who behave badly.

4. Snuff was a preparation made of pulverized tobacco. When men "took snuff" they inhaled this preparation through their nostrils. It was considered the mark of a gentleman to indulge in this practice. Fans were a part of women's fashion and played a significant role in the social mores of the day. Women used their fans to flirt as well as to maintain their modesty or hide their emotions. Fans also served as screens behind which women could gossip.

5. Barons were noblemen of various ranks.

B. 1. disabused; 2. destitute; 3. assignations; 4. obliquely; 5. plebeian; 6. stoic

Grammar and Style: Inverted Word Order (p. 110)

A. 1. His giant limbs spread in unwieldy state . . .

2. Clubs, diamonds, hearts seen in wild disorder . . .

3. The exulting nymph fills the sky with shouts . . .

4. "Let wreaths of triumph now twine my temples. . . ."

5. While nymphs take treats, or give assignations . . .

B. Sample responses:

2. When winter weather goes from bad to worse / Think I sometimes that I might need a nurse.

3. In springtime when the heart may turn to love / 'Tis then takes wing the happy turtle dove.

4. How happy are the children in the park, / But yet how frightened be they of the dark.

Reading Strategy: Recognizing Author's Purpose (p. 111)

Sample responses:

2. The author makes a point about the shallowness of judges who, with little thought, sentence criminals to hang; he implies that the judges' motivation is not a wish to parcel out justice but rather an eagerness to get to their dinners.

3. The author is poking fun at Belinda for taking the card game so seriously. He likens her calling up spades as trump to the orders of a powerful general.

4. The author likens the cutting of a small lock of hair to a death or an evil deed that can never be undone. The fact that everyone knows that hair grows back serves to point up the absurdity.

5. The author is ridiculing the fuss that Belinda and the others have made over the stolen lock of hair. His point is that after Belinda has died, all that will be known of the battle will be the poem that Pope has written about it.

Literary Analysis: Mock Epic (p. 112)

Sample responses:

1. The subject is the theft by the baron of a lock of Belinda's hair.

2. They link the grand and the trivial.

3. The war is a card game between Belinda and the baron.

4. "While through the press enraged Thalestris flies, / And catters death around from both her eyes."

5. "This lock, the Muse shall consecrate to fame, / And midst the stars inscribe Belinda's name."

from *The Preface to A Dictionary of the English Language* and *A Dictionary of the English Language* by Samuel Johnson
from *The Life of Samuel Johnson* by James Boswell

Build Vocabulary (p. 113)

A. 1. dictator; 2. predict; 3. dictate; 4. diction

B. 1. j 2. f 3. e 4. i 5. a 6. g 7. c 8. b 9. d 10. h

Grammar and Style: Commas with Parenthetical Expressions (p. 114)

A. 1. The character of Samuel Johnson has, I trust, been so developed in the course of this work. . . .

2. Man is, in general, made up of contradictory qualities. . . .

**from *The Preface to A Dictionary of the English Language* and *A Dictionary of the English Language* by Samuel Johnson
from *The Life of Samuel Johnson***
by James Boswell (*continued*)

3. Ridicule has gone down before him, and, I doubt, Derrick is his enemy.

4. . . . so that the unavoidable consciousness of his superiority was, in that respect, a cause of disquiet.

5. his poetical pieces, in general, have not much of that splendor. . . .

B. Sample responses:

1. The property owner said that the tree was diseased and had to be cut down; but, on the contrary, the tree was healthy.

2. Did you, incidentally, have a chance to look at my essay?

3. I was going to say that her car was blue, but, to tell the truth, it was purple.

4. In some respects I agree with you, but, on the other hand, I mainly disagree.

5. I finally had a chance to meet your mother, and she, indeed, is very tall.

Reading Strategy: Establishing a Purpose (p. 115)

Sample responses:

from *The Preface to A Dictionary of the English Language*

What I Know: A preface often explains why an author wrote a particular work.

What I Want to Find Out: Why did Johnson write his famous dictionary?

What I Learned: Johnson wrote the *Dictionary* in order to set standards of usage in a changing language.

from *A Dictionary of the English Language*

What I Know: Johnson wrote a dictionary of the English language.

What I Want to Find Out: What are the differences between Johnson's dictionary and modern dictionaries?

What I Learned: Unlike modern dictionaries, Johnson indicated that an entry was a verb by placing the word *to* in front of it.

from *The Life of Samuel Johnson*

What I Know: Boswell wrote a biography of Samuel Johnson.

What I Want to Find Out: What was the relationship between Johnson and Boswell?

What I Learned: Boswell was in awe of Johnson when they first met.

Literary Analysis: Dictionary (p. 116)

A. Sample responses:

Johnson's Dictionary: (This circle should be blank because there are no features that are unique to the entry for *gang* in Johnson's dictionary.)

Overlapping area: Number of syllables, definition, usage, synonyms

Modern Dictionary: Phonetic information, etymology, word definition in different parts of speech, multiple meanings, word in context

"Elegy Written in a Country Churchyard" by Thomas Gray
"A Nocturnal Reverie"
by Ann Finch, Countess of Winchilsea

Build Vocabulary (p. 117)

A. Sample responses:

1. winds or circles around

2. moves around

3. a ring or arena

4. walking around in a circle

B. 1. temperate; 2. forage; 3. nocturnal;
4. venerable; penury 5. ignoble; ingenuous;
6. circumscribed

Grammar and Style: Pronoun-Antecedent Agreement (p. 118)

A. 1. their; 2. his; 3. their; 4. its; 5. his

B. Sample responses:

1. My sister or I will take my books to school.

2. The mothers and the children had their picnic behind the school.

3. The cemetery is locked up at night and its gate is bolted.

4. Thomas Gray is remembered as a fine poet even though his literary output was rather small.

5. Ann Finch, Countess of Winchilsea, wrote her poems despite public mockery.

Possible responses:

2. "Let not Ambition mock their useful toil, / Their homely joys, and destiny obscure; / Nor Grandeur hear with a disdainful smile / The short and simple annals of the poor." ("Elegy," lines 29–32); Don't think that the hard work, simple pleasures, and obscurity of the poor lack importance.

3. "Perhaps in this neglected spot is laid / Some heart once pregnant with celestial fire; / Hands, that the rod of empire might have swayed, / Or waked to ecstasy the living lyre." ("Elegy," lines 45–48); Perhaps the person buried here could have been a great ruler or a wonderful musician.

4. "There at the foot of yonder nodding beech, / That wreathes its old fantastic roots so high, / His listless length at noontide would he stretch, / And pore upon the brook that babbles by." ("Elegy," lines 101–104); At the foot of that great tree where the roots are exposed and tangled, the poet used to lie lazily and look steadily into the bubbling stream.

5. "No farther seek his merits to disclose, / Or draw his frailties from their dread abode / (There they alike in trembling hope repose), / The bosom of his Father and his God." ("Elegy," lines 125–128); Don't talk any more of his good qualities or his past errors; they have died with him and now belong to God.

Literary Analysis: Preromantic Poetry (p. 120)

Sample responses:

1. Gray is saying that every person who dies is important, whether a nobleman, a poet, or a farmer.

2. According to Gray, even the rudest monument to the most lowly person is important as a symbol of continuance, a reminder of the past, and a guide for those who will die in the future.

3. Being at one with nature and away from the aggravations of daily life gives the speaker a feeling of peace, of spiritual understanding, and of freedom from confusion. This feeling exemplifies preromantic poetry in that it is derived from enjoying the mystery and serenity of nature with the heart, not from examining the world with reason and the mind.

from *The Analects* by Confucius
from The Declaration of Independence by Thomas Jefferson

Build Vocabulary: Language of Governing (p. 121)

Across	Down
1 political	1 powers
6 principles	2 trusts
8 right	3 consent
9 equal	4 moral
11 homage	5 superior
12 order	7 authority
13 respect	10 rules
14 separate	

Cultural Connection: Governors and the Governed (p. 122)

Confucius:

- The ideal citizen is a person who is respectful of others and of those in authority, as long as they act in a way deserving of respect.

- The ideal ruler rules not through force or by law alone, but by the example of moral force; he or she inspires the trust of the ruled.

Jefferson:

- The ideal citizen should act on his or her beliefs after careful consideration. Citizens have the responsibility to be ever vigilant so that their rights are not jeopardized or taken away.

- The ideal ruler does not seek to establish tyranny or despotism over the ruled.

"On Spring" by Samuel Johnson
from "The Aims of the Spectator"
by Joseph Addison

Build Vocabulary (p. 123)

Sample responses:

A. 1. looked at all its parts
2. examined it from every angle
3. watch something unusual or entertaining

B. 1. procured; 2. embellishment; 3. trifles; 4. affluence; 5. divert; 6. speculation; 7. transient; 8. contentious

"On Spring" by Samuel Johnson
from "The Aims of the Spectator"
by Joseph Addison *(continued)*

Grammar and Style: Adjective Clauses (p. 124)

A. 1. Samuel Johnson's *Dictionary of the English Language*, which was wildly popular in its day, greatly influenced the format of later dictionaries. (*which*)

2. Irony and satire were popular tools of writers who hoped to make their mark in eighteenth-century literature. (*who*)

3. The art of essay writing, which many writers hold to be among the most difficult, dates to the sixteenth century. (*which*)

B. Sample responses:

1. the poet whose biography was published
2. a barking dog that ran in circles
3. the president whom I admire the most
4. ironic essays that teach lessons about human behavior
5. the dancer who leapt from the stage

Reading Strategy: Drawing Inferences (p. 125)

Sample responses:

2. "But we solace ourselves with some new prospect, and press forward again with equal eagerness." ("On Spring," 2nd paragraph) Johnson considers this trait with amusement. People have expectations which they believe time alone will bring to reality. Johnson is saying that people never seem to learn.

3. "The vernal flowers, however beautiful and gay, are only intended by nature as preparatives to autumnal fruits." ("On Spring," 2nd paragraph) Johnson is saying that the observations and lessons made in youth will prepare a person for the experiences of adulthood.

4. "So that if I allow twenty readers to every paper, which I look upon as a modest computation." ("The Aims of the Spectator," 1st paragraph) Twenty readers for every paper sounds like an exaggeration. Addison is humorously inflating the number of people who read *The Spectator*.

5. "[Readers] who I hope will take care to distinguish themselves from the thoughtless herd of their ignorant and inattentive brethren." ("The Aims of the Spectator," 1st paragraph) Addison is being humorous about the possible advantages of reading *The Spectator*.

Literary Analysis: Essay (p. 126)

Possible responses:

1. From this and other passages in the essay it is clear that Addison wants *The Spectator* to spread learning and wisdom beyond schools and libraries, making it available to everyone. He especially recommends the periodical to those who usually give their attentions to trivial matters and to women who, because of the limitations of society, don't have many opportunities to obtain an education.

2. The type of person Addison is describing here is concerned mainly with trivia, weather, and gossip. This might be because they are unused to being exposed to more important or beneficial matters. *The Spectator* will provide these types of people with weightier and more important information and wisdom.

3. Earlier in the essay Johnson wrote about people who don't know how or are afraid to be alone. The paradox relates to the essay because being able to take a walk is a way of enjoying solitude and appreciating springtime and the wonders of nature.

"Homeless" by Anna Quindlen

Build Vocabulary: Language of Social Awareness (p. 127)

1. certainty; 2. wrong; 3. problems;
4. survival; 5. predictability; 6. stability;
7. world; 8. participation; 9. pain;
10. discussion; 11. privacy

Genre Connection: The Essay (p. 128)

Students' responses should reveal that they have grasped the basic attributes of the informal essay.

Unit 4: Rebels and Dreamers (1798–1832)

"To a Mouse" and "To a Louse"
by Robert Burns
"Woo'd and Married and A'"
by Joanna Baillie

Build Vocabulary (p. 129)

A. Sample responses:

1. Making tired or bored
2. Arousing disgust or loathing
3. Bothering or irritating

B. 1. discretion; 2. impudence;
   3. inconstantly; 4. dominion; 5. winsome

Grammar and Style: Interjections (p. 130)

A. 1. My gosh! 2. Hey! 3. Good grief!
   4. Aha! 5. Yikes! 6. Whew!

B. Sample responses:

1. Well! Now the dentist wants to fill three of my teeth.
2. Hurrah! The team will compete in the playoffs!
3. Hey! I don't see why I should wash the dishes when it is your turn.
4. Alas! Many died during the famine.
5. Whoa! Where are you going with my car keys?
6. Oh! I forgot Margo's birthday.
7. My goodness! I didn't study for the test!

Reading Strategy: Translating Dialect (p. 131)

1. run—context ("an' chase")
2. at times—reading the footnote
3. house—look for similarities with a standard English word
4. leave—noting that the apostrophe stands for the omitted *v*
5. cannot—listening for similarities with a standard English word

Literary Analysis: Dialect (p. 132)

Possible responses:

1. "Little, sleek, cowering, timorous beast"; by using dialect to address the mouse, the speaker achieves a friendly and affectionate tone.
2. "An occasional ear of grain in a bundle/

Is a small request"; the use of expressions familiar to a Scottish farmer stresses the strong bond that exists between the land and all creatures.
3. "And nothing, now, to build a new one"; dialect effectively expresses the speaker's tenderness toward the mouse's plight.
4. "To withstand the winter's sleety drizzle/ And cold frost"; using the harsh sounding words *cranreuch cauld* emphasizes the speaker's strong empathy for the mouse.
5. "But, Mousie, you are not alone"; the use of dialect reinforces the bond of shared experience.

"The Lamb," "The Tyger," "Infant Sorrow," and "The Chimney Sweeper" by William Blake

Build Vocabulary (p. 133)

A. Sample answers:

1. is full of life
2. felt a loss of spirit or energy
3. waited to see what would come to be, or arise
4. came to an end
5. has an impact on the reader's life

B. 1. b 2. a 3. c

C. 1. vales; 2. symmetry; 3. aspire

Grammar and Style: *Rise* and *Raise* (p. 134)

A. 2. risen (*rise*: past participle)
   3. raised (*raise*: past tense)
   4. raised (*raise*: past participle)
   5. rise (*rise*: present infinitive)

B. 1. The sun rises over the far horizon.
   2. We rose and gathered up our camp equipment.
   3. Abigail and John had raised the kayak onto the roof of the car.
   4. I watched as morning mist rose from the nearby river.
   5. I raised the tent yesterday and now I have to take it down.

**"The Lamb," "The Tyger,"
"Infant Sorrow,"and "The Chimney
Sweeper"** by William Blake
(continued)

Reading Strategy: Using Visuals as a Key to Meaning (p. 135)

Sample answers:

2. "The Tyger"—The tiger appears solitary and fearsome, and it lives in a dark wood. This image supports the poem's description of the "fearful symmetry" of the tyger.

3. "The Chimney Sweeper"—The children in the illustration look miserable. The setting is dark and the mood is tragic. The chimney sweeps in the poem live miserable lives.

4. "Infant Sorrow"—The scene depicted in the illustration would be a perfect example of the "dangerous world" described in the poem.

Literary Analysis: Symbols (p. 136)

1. *Meaning:* Jesus Christ
   Source: Bible
2. *Meaning:* Jesus Christ
   Source: Bible
3. *Meaning:* the Baby Jesus
   Source: Bible
4. *Meaning:* innocent
   Source: Bible
5. *Meaning:* place where human fates are created
   Source: Norse mythology
6. *Meaning:* messenger
   Source: Bible

Introduction to *Frankenstein*
by Mary Wollstonecraft Shelley

Build Vocabulary (p. 137)

A. Sample responses:

1. imaginary; 2. ghost; 3. daydream; 4. place that exists only in the imagination; 5. bizarre and unbelievable

B. 1. acceded; 2. platitude; 3. phantasm; 4. ungenial; 5. incitement; 6. appendage

Grammar and Style: Past Participial Phrases (p. 138)

A. 1. annoyed by the platitude of prose; circle *poets*

2. cradled in healthy sleep; circle *youths*
3. snapped from the stalk; circle *flowers*
4. left to itself; circle *spark*

B. Sample responses:

1. On Friday, all her best students, exhausted as they were by the test they had taken Thursday, were late to class.
2. The plants on Sara's windowsill, parched from neglect, withered and died.
3. Built in the eighteenth century, the house was more dilapidated than haunted.
4. Several of the stuffed animals, crowded onto the shelf above Magda's bed, were in danger of falling to the floor.
5. Samuel, angered by the loss of his ticket, did not listen to the train conductor's announcements and consequently missed his stop.

Reading Strategy: Predicting (p. 139)

Suggested responses:

1. The story will be a hideous tale, perhaps shocking even to the author.
2. Her story *will* rival those stories they had been discussing. Additionally, the story will invoke some fear all humans have, possibly fears about death, life, personal identity, love, and so on.
3. Her story will dwell on the discovery and communication of life to a non-human.
4. Her nightmare that night will become the essence of *Frankenstein*.

Literary Analysis: The Gothic Tradition (p. 140)

Possible responses:

1. The mountains and lake are beautiful, romantic, and mysterious. The constant rain adds an atmosphere of gloom and forces the poets indoors, where their thoughts turn to ghost stories.
2. The ghost stories are filled with horrifying, gloomy details and deal with untimely deaths forced on the young with sorrowful irony.
3. It is the product of her fevered imagination, which creates vivid images of a horrifying animated corpse. The images appear mysteriously, seeming to come out of thin air from "beyond the usual bounds of reverie."

The descriptive language is varied and rich and terrifying: "pale student of unhallowed arts"; "hideous phantasm"; "uneasy, half vital motion"; "odious handiwork"; "horror-stricken"; "hideous corpse"; "horrid thing"; "yellow, watery . . . eyes."

"The Oval Portrait" by Edgar Allan Poe

Build Vocabulary: Language of the Supernatural (p. 141)

Sample responses:

1. spirited: The paintings were so spirited they seemed to be alive.

2. delirium: In my delirium, I was visited by people from the past.

3. dreamy: My dreamy condition lasted well into the day, long after I had awakened.

4. secret: What dark secret was hidden in the dusty safe?

5. spell: The old man had cast a spell on the unsuspecting villagers.

6. fancy: Ignoring the warning signs, the young man took a fancy to the visitor from the mountains.

Cultural Connection: Supernatural Horror (p. 142)

Chart entries for "The Oval Portrait" should include: the slow revealing of the secret of the portrait (suspense), the effect the room and the paintings have on the narrator as well as the psychological ordeal suffered by the young wife (psychological terror), the way the narrator seems to float in and out of consciousness (dreamlike states), the finely detailed descriptions of the room and lifelike description of the production of the painting (semblance of reality).

Poetry of William Wordsworth

Build Vocabulary (p. 143)

A. Sample responses:

1. to dissect or separate body parts for study

2. a scalpel or other type of knife

3. their internal organs

4. It analyzes the details of the crime.

B. 1. a   2. a   3. b   4. c   5. d   6. b   7. d

Grammar and Style: Present Participial Phrases (p. 144)

A. 1. yes

2. No, because it is one word, not a phrase.

3. No, because *beatings* is used as a noun rather than an adjective, so it is not a participle.

4. yes

5. No, because it is one word, not a phrase.

B. Sample responses:

1. Walking to school, I lost my key.

2. That dog sitting over there looks like my dog.

3. The car rolling down the hill is out of control.

4. The man sitting next to me seems familiar.

5. The movie playing downtown is great!

Reading Strategy: Using Literary Context (p. 145)

Possible responses:

2. "that serene and blessed mood, / In which the affections gently lead us on" ("Tintern Abbey," lines 41–42)—These lines deal with emotions rather than with intellect and reason.

3. "O sylvan Wye! . . . / How often has my spirit turned to thee!" ("Tintern Abbey," lines 56–57)—The Wye valley is a special place to the narrator because of his personal connection to it.

4. "While here I stand, not only with the sense / Of present pleasure, but with pleasing thoughts / That in this moment there is life and food / For future years." ("Tintern Abbey," lines 62–65)—These lines describe an emotional rather than a rational response.

5. "Oh! yet a little while / May I behold in thee what I was once, / My dear, dear Sister!" ("Tintern Abbey," lines 119–121)—These lines describe a personal rather than a universal experience.

Literary Analysis: Romanticism (p. 146)

Suggested responses:

1. He describes his younger self as being like a roe. By comparing himself to an animal, he may be implying that before he grew up, he—and perhaps all young people—were more a part of nature.

2. No; Wordsworth felt that people had become too far removed from nature and he was saying—undoubtedly rhetorically—that it would be better to err in the other direction, to believe in pagan nature gods, than to ignore nature completely.

3. By comparing him to a star, the sea, and the heavens; they are all aspects of nature. To Wordsworth, nature was an ideal; he was trying to show how good Milton was by comparing him to the best there is—the natural world.

"The Rime of the Ancient Mariner" and "Kubla Khan"
by Samuel Taylor Coleridge

Build Vocabulary (p. 147)

A. 1. journey;   2. journalism;   3. journal;   4. adjourn;   5. du jour

B. 1. a   2. d   3. b   4. d   5. a   6. b

Grammar and Style: Inverted Word Order (p. 148)

A. 1. The subject (*an Albatross*) and verb (*did cross*) have been inverted.

   At length an Albatross did cross.

2. The prepositional phrase (*about my neck*) precedes what it modifies (*hung*) instead of following it.

   Instead of the cross, the Albatross was hung about my neck.

3. The subject (*mingled measure*) and verb (*was heard*) are inverted.

   Where the mingled measure was heard from the fountain and the caves.

4. The verb (*saw*) and its direct object (*damsel with a dulcimer*) are inverted.

   Once I saw in a vision a damsel with a dulcimer. . . .

B. Sample responses:

1. In that light saw I a sprite.

2. Around the pole his fingers wrapped; that it would snap I knew.

3. To the port came we, the boats to see.

4. Up the walk ran the man and his dog, the injured bird to fetch.

5. Into my ears slipped music soft and sent me right to sleep.

Reading Strategy: Analyzing Poetic Effects (p. 149)

Sample responses:

2. "About, about, in reel and rout / The death fires danced at night. . . ." ("Rime," lines 127–128) Internal rhyme and alliteration. Internal rhyme in the words *about* and *rout* emphasizes the rhythmic, omnipresent nature of the death fires. Alliteration of *reel* and *rout* and of *death* and *danced* draws attention to the key words in this passage.

3. "'A speck, a mist, a shape, I wist! / And still it neared and neared. . . .'" ("Rime," lines 153–154) Alliteration, internal rhyme, and repetition. Alternation of the alliteration of *speck* and *shape* with the internal rhyme of *mist* and *wist* produces the sense that the ship is coming closer, as does the repetition of *neared* and *neared*.

4. "'Alone, alone, all, all alone, / Alone on a wide wide sea!" ("Rime," lines 232–233) Repetition and alliteration. Repetition of the words *alone, all,* and *wide* emphasizes the Mariner's horror at being the only one left alive, and alliteration of the *w* sound creates a hissing noise like a howling wind.

5. "'Farewell, farewell! but this I tell / To thee, thou Wedding Guest!'" ("Rime," lines 610–611) Repetition, internal rhyme, and alliteration. Repetition of the word *farewell* alerts the reader that the Mariner is about to give his final comments, while internal rhyme of *farewell* and *tell* and alliteration of *this, thee,* and *thou* create a rhythm that draws the reader to pay particular attention.

Literary Analysis: Poetic Sound Devices (p. 150)

1. consonance;   2. assonance;   3. alliteration;   4. internal rhyme;   5. consonance;   6. alliteration;   7. assonance;   8. internal

rhyme;   9. assonance;   10. alliteration;   11. alliteration;   12. alliteration;   13. alliteration;   14. assonance;   15. internal rhyme

"She Walks in Beauty," from *Childe Harold's Pilgrimage* and **from *Don Juan*** by George Gordon, Lord Byron

Build Vocabulary (p. 151)

A. 1. delicious;   2. adventurous, ominous;   3. famous, humorous;   4. miraculous;   5. rebellious

B. 1. f   2. a   3. c   4. d   5. b   6. g   7. i   8. e   9. h

Grammar and Style: Subject-Verb Agreement (p. 152)

A. 1. agree;   2. tell;   3. is;   4. are, melt;   5. Has dried;   6. agree

B. Sample responses:

1. A raindrop falls on the mountain and begins its rush to the sea.
2. A professional dancer usually attends classes every day.
3. Coffee and tea are best served hot.
4. Olives can be put on top of pizza, pressed into oil, or even baked in bread.
5. The two strangers did not know where to buy tokens for the subway.
6. Grammar is studied by many and understood by few.

Reading Strategy: Questioning (p. 153)

Sample responses:

1. Who is the speaker of the poem?
   A thirty-year-old man
2. What is the subject of this excerpt?
   The subject is the speaker's reflections on the meaning of his life and what will remain of him after he has died.
3. What does the speaker think of fame?
   He considers it to be overrated.
4. Why does the speaker think that he has wasted his youth?
   He apparently spent it partly on love affairs and drinking, and partly writing poetry.
5. Why does the speaker quote Southey at the end of this excerpt?

He's making fun of Southey, and thinks that if Southey can be remembered, certainly he (the speaker) could be, too.

Literary Analysis: Figurative Language (p. 154)

A. 1. personification;   2. metaphor;   3. simile;   4. personification;   5. simile

B. Sample responses:

1. The storm clouds glowered over the trembling town.
2. Courage blanketed his anxious fears.
3. A feeling of peacefulness washed over her like a spring rain.
4. An eagle cradled the sky in its tender wings.
5. His thoughts roared to her doorstep on the wheels of his dreams.

"Ozymandias," "Ode to the West Wind," and "To a Skylark" by Percy Bysshe Shelley

Build Vocabulary (p. 155)

A. 1. pulsar;   2. compulsive;   3. impulsiveness;   4. repulse

B. 1. sepulcher;   2. profuse;   3. vernal;   4. visage;   5. satiety, verge;   6. blithe;   7. impulse

Grammar and Style: Subjunctive Mood (p. 156)

A. The following verbs should be underlined:

If I *were* a dead leaf . . .;

If I *were* a swift cloud . . .;

I *were* as in my boyhood, and *could be* . . .

I *would* ne'er have striven . . . .

B. Sample responses:

1. That apple should not fall far from the tree.
2. Samantha could hurt herself if she loses her balance on those slippery steps.
3. I wish you were happier about this decision.
4. Marty would not resign from the company.
5. Bruno could not talk, even if he wanted to—he's only a dog.

"Ozymandias," "Ode to the West Wind, "
and "To a Skylark" by Percy Bysshe Shelley
(continued)

Reading Strategy: Responding to Imagery
(p. 157)

Sample responses:

2. "Angels of rain and lightning: there are spread / On the blue surface of thine aery surge, / Like the bright hair uplifted from the head / Of some fierce Maenad. . . ." ("West Wind," lines 18–21) Description: The sky is blue but it is possible to see the storm approaching in the distance, where it is already raining. One can hear and smell the approaching rain and feel the damp wind. Senses: sight, smell, touch

3. "Scatter, as from an extinguished hearth / Ashes and sparks, my words among mankind!" ("West Wind," lines 66–67) Description: The image is of a fireplace in which a fire has recently gone out, and the wind kicks up still hot ashes and sparks. Senses: sight, smell, hearing

4. "Like a highborn maiden / In a palace tower, / Soothing her love-laden / Soul in secret hour / With music sweet as love, which overflows her bower . . ." ("Skylark," lines 41–45) Description: The image is a castle tower from which one can hear a young woman's sweet song. Senses: sight, hearing

5. "Like a rose embowered / In its own green leaves, / By warm winds deflowered, / Till the scent it gives / makes faint . . ." ("Skylark," lines 51–55) Description: A rose bud stays contained with the greenery of a bush until winds cause the flower to open and lose its odor. Senses: sight, smell, hearing (the sound of wind)

Literary Analysis: Imagery (p. 158)

Sample responses:

1. sight, touch (one might imagine touching the sand or the sculpture)

2. curiosity, possibly fear or resentment of the "sneer of cold command"

3. This passage illustrates that grandeur in life cannot be maintained after death.

4. sight, touch, hearing (The wreck is probably surrounded by noticeable silence, because

there is nothing else there except a vast expanse of desert.)

5. awe that nothing remains of the civilization except the wreck, or satisfaction that this dictatorial ruler is no longer remembered or recognized

6. This passage illustrates that even a totalitarian ruler cannot command time, and eventually his dictatorial rule will pass into oblivion.

Poetry of John Keats

Build Vocabulary (p. 159)

A. 1. quality of draining or being drained; 2. state of being married or wed; 3. state of being bound or tied up; 4. state of being in short supply; 5. state of being wrecked or broken

B. 1. surmise; 2. gleaned; 3. requiem; 4. vintage; 5. teeming; 6. ken

Grammar and Style: Direct Address (p. 160)

A. 1. Thou still unravished bride of quietness Thou foster child of silence and slow time, Sylvan historian

2. Fair youth

3. happy, happy boughs!

4. O Attic shape! Fair attitude!

5. Thou, silent form . . . Cold Pastoral!

B. Sample responses:

1. O thoughtless man, I wish I could forget you and your wicked birds.

2. Some day, misguided folk, you will all see that I'm no child, that I knew the truth.

3. If only you would look my way, old friend, you'd know my mind.

4. Great, towering castle, I wonder what secrets hide behind those bricks of yours.

5. Sweet, gentle form, did you know that the sight of you knocks me speechless?

Reading Strategy: Paraphrasing (p. 161)

Sample responses:

1. When I fear that I might die before I've written down the ideas that fill my brain . . .

2. Fade away, dissolve, and forget the weariness, sickness, and worry that you have never known while living in the leaves.

3. Maybe the same song that Ruth heard, weeping and homesick in the cornfields of a strange land . . .

Literary Analysis: Ode (p. 162)

"Ode to a Nightingale"

8 stanzas; 10 lines in each stanza; rhyme scheme is *abab cdecde*; meter is iambic pentameter, with iambic trimeter in eighth line of each stanza; it is a Horatian ode.

"Ode on a Grecian Urn"

5 stanzas; 10 lines in each stanza; rhyme scheme is *abab cdecde*, except for the first stanza: *abab cdedce*, and the second stanza: *abab cdeced*; meter is iambic pentameter; it is a Horatian ode.

"The Lorelei" by Heinrich Heine
Haikus by Bashō, Yosa Buson, and Kobayashi Issa

Build Vocabulary: Emotional Language of Romantic Lyric Poetry (p. 163)

1. sadness; 2. clouds; 3. reflected; 4. veiled; 5. anguish; 6. vision; 7. devoured; 8. cry; 9. beautiful; 10. cold

Literary Connection: Contemporary Lyrical Works (p. 164)

In their charts, students should cite such attributes of romantic lyric poetry as the emotional emphasis of "The Lorelei," the precision, simplicity, and suggestiveness of the haiku, and, for both sets of poems, the achieving of a single, unified effect.

"Speech to Parliament: In Defense of the Lower Classes"
by George Gordon, Lord Byron
"A Song: 'Men of England'"
by Percy Bysshe Shelley
"On the Passing of the Reform Bill"
by Thomas Babington Macaulay

Build Vocabulary (p. 165)

A. 1. c 2. d 3. b 4. e 5. a
B. 1. c 2. b 3. b 4. d 5. a 6. b

Grammar and Style: Correlative Conjunctions (p. 166)

A. 1. . . . both Shelley and Byron

2. . . . whether Lord Byron is considered a Romantic or a Victorian
3. Neither Byron nor Shelley
4. Just as repetition can underscore a poem's musicality, so too can it intensify
5. . . . contains not only examples of Shelley's verses, but also a selection

B. Sample responses:

1. You may write your research report on the life and literary works of either Percy Bysshe Shelley or Mary Shelley.
2. Poets must consider carefully not only the connotations but also the sounds of the words they choose to express their ideas.
3. Whether you are writing a speech or a persuasive essay, you must pay close attention to your audience.
4. Neither Samuel Taylor Coleridge nor John Keats was as politically active as Shelley.

Reading Strategy: Setting a Purpose for Reading (p. 167)

Sample responses:

Purpose: to learn about the lives of nineteenth-century working-class people in England; Passages: (1) "Men of England, wherefore plough / For the lords who lay ye low?" (lines 1–2)—Farmers toiled for upper-class lords; (2) "Wherefore feed and clothe . . . / Those ungrateful drones who would / Drain your sweat—nay, drink your blood?" (lines 5–8)—The upper class treated the working class poorly; (3) "Have ye leisure, comfort, calm, / . . . Or what is it ye buy so dear / With your pain and with your fear?" (lines 13–16)—The working class probably did not live comfortable lives with sufficient leisure time; (4) "Forge arms—in your defense to bear." (line 24)—The working class may have been kept unarmed to prevent a revolution.

Literary Analysis: Political Commentary (p. 168)

Possible responses:

1. Shelley encourages "the Men of England" to recognize that they are exploited and controlled by their employers. He indicates that they should consider the possibility of armed revolt against their masters.

"Speech to Parliament: In Defense of the Lower Classes"
by George Gordon, Lord Byron

"A Song: 'Men of England'"
by Percy Bysshe Shelley

"On the Passing of the Reform Bill"
by Thomas Babington Macaulay
(continued)

2. The poet hopes to raise the consciousness—if not the weapon-bearing arm—of the "common men" of England.

3. Not only is poetry Shelley's preferred form, but a "song" can also be easily read, understood, memorized, and recited. Rhyming verses such as these could be useful to workers trying to unite and protest as a group.

4. Shelley's intended audience includes the vast multitudes of manual laborers all across England.

5. Shelley uses simple vocabulary—such as *plough, weave, feed, clothe, cradle, food, seed, cellars*—to describe the tasks and objects of working-class British life in the early years of the Industrial Revolution.

"On Making an Agreeable Marriage"
by Jane Austen

from *A Vindication of the Rights of Woman* by Mary Wollstonecraft

Build Vocabulary (p. 169)

A. Sample responses:

1. in a loud, strong way; 2. strongly barricaded; 3. strengthen; 4. strong attempt

B. 1. solicitude; 2. specious; 3. gravity; 4. vindication; 5. fastidious; 6. fortitude; 7. preponderates; 8. scruple; 9. amiable

Grammar and Style: Commas in a Series (p. 170)

A. 1. Fanny and her friends and family addressed the problem of her impending marriage.

2. Fanny might have spoken to Ellen, Jane(,) or any of Jane's sisters.

3. correct

4. Mary Wollstonecraft felt that young women were taught to behave in a deceptive, conniving(,) and ridiculous way.

B. Sample responses:

1. Women were expected to be pleasant, cunning, and pretty.

2. Large families produced male heirs, strong workers, and women who seemed to have no real place in the world.

3. Jane Austen, though unmarried herself, expected others to marry based on love, honor, and trust.

Reading Strategy: Determining the Writer's Purpose (p. 171)

Sample responses:

Paragraph 2: Although her tone is still sad, Wollstonecraft addresses her subject matter-of-factly.—The author's purpose is to heap more facts on top of her argument.—Wollstonecraft is embittered by the fact that a woman of her day can't rise through any means except marriage. This is less of a factor today, depending upon where women live.

Paragraph 3: The author appeals to the rational side of men by suggesting rather sarcastically that women should become more like men so that they can in turn command the respect of men.—The author's purpose is to point up the absurdity of the current situation.—The author is making a strong point.

Paragraph 4: The author's tone is incredulous. She uses strong words like *bugbear, fortitude,* and *prejudices.*—The author seeks to appeal to men's sense of fair play.—Since the whole piece is about fair play, this is an excellent path to take.

Paragraph 5: The author's tone is firm.—Her message is clear: Give women a chance and let them prove whether or not they deserved that chance.—Although things have improved for some women today, there are still times when women are held back from success. Everyone should be treated equally.

Literary Analysis: Social Commentary (p. 172)

Sample responses:

1. Austen points out that many people are made happier by the chase than they are by the conquest. She points out that her niece is hopelessly in love until she wins the devotion of the object of her desire. Then she promptly loses interest in him.

2. Wollstonecraft asserts that society breeds women for nothing more than childish pursuits, when actually the raising of children and the running of a household are pursuits that require educated, mature processing skills.

from the Screenplay of *Sense and Sensibility* and Diaries
by Emma Thompson

Build Vocabulary: Language of Social Awareness (p. 173)

1. circumstances; 2. idle; 3. politician;
4. private; 5. orator; 6. church; 7. useless;
8. army; 9. inherited; 10. fortune

Thematic Connection: Contemporary Social Reformers (p. 174)

Sample responses:

In works such as *Sense and Sensibility*, Austen seeks to expose the unfairness of eighteenth-century standards of gender and class. In his "A Song: 'Men of England,'" Shelley hopes to inspire workers to fight for their rights. In his speech to Parliament, "In Defense of the Lower Classes," Byron defends the common worker from the tyranny of aristocrats. In *A Vindication of the Rights of Woman*, Wollstonecraft argues for the equality of women.

Cesar Chavez worked to secure rights and better working conditions for migrant workers. Princess Diana worked to ban landmines and to alleviate the sufferings of people with AIDS. Martin Luther King, Jr., worked to achieve equality for African Americans. Willie Nelson devotes much of his career to helping the ordinary family farmer.

Unit 5: Progress and Decline (1833–1901)

from "In Memoriam, A.H.H.," "The Lady of Shalott," "Ulysses," and from *The Princess*: "Tears, Idle Tears" by Alfred, Lord Tennyson

Build Vocabulary (p.175)

A. 1. tithe: a tax of one-tenth of one's income in support of the local church

2. buckler: a small shield

3. wimple: a scarf-like piece of clothing that covers the head, neck, and chin

B. 1. c 2. b 3. d 4. a

Grammar and Style: Parallel Structure (p. 176)

A. 1. There she sees the highway near
Winding down to Camelot:
There the river eddy whirls.
And there the surly village churls
And the red cloaks of market girls
Pass onward from Shallot. (adverbs)

2. Let Love clasp Grief lest both be drowned
Let darkness keep her raven gloss
Ah, sweeter to be drunk with loss,
To dance with death, to beat the ground.
(imperative verbs; infinitive phrases)

B. Sample responses:
1. The damsels, the abbot, the shepherd, the page, and the knight may see Camelot, but not the Lady of Shalott.

2. In order to bear the fate of the curse, the Lady should not look at, wonder about, dream of, or go to Camelot.

3. To share, to strive, to question, and to discover is to live, whatever one's age, says Tennyson in "Ulysses."

4. What is faith? What is friendship? What is memory? What is life itself? "In Memoriam, A.H.H." asks these essential questions about relationships in the face of death.

Reading Strategy: Judging the Poet's Message (p. 177)

Sample responses:

Students will have different judgments depending on their evaluation of the poet's message and their own lives. Be sure that students rely on a clear understanding of the poet's message, as well as specific experiences and observations from their own life.

from "In Memoriam, A.H.H.,"
"The Lady of Shalott," "Ulysses," and
from *The Princess:* "Tears, Idle Tears"
by Alfred, Lord Tennyson
(continuFed)

Literary Analysis: The Speaker in Poetry
(p. 178)

Possible responses:

1. Ulysses reveals his impatience with the domestic duties of kingship and his need for action in order to stay "honed like a sword's cutting edge."

2. Ulysses's affectionate, confident tone is intended to inspire confidence and good feelings both in his son and among his subjects. Words like *well-loved, discerning,* and *fulfill* have connotations that can help create a positive atmosphere for transfer of power.

3. Ulysses speaks to his loyal followers, reminding them of the good and bad times they have shared on their adventures. Calling them "my mariners," he appeals strongly to their feelings of loyalty and to their spirits rather than to their physical natures. This is wise on Ulysses's part because his followers are old men now and have naturally declined in physical prowess.

4. Ulysses here speaks both to himself and to his mariners, offering them a chance to regain the difficult but satisfying life of forward motion and excitement they once knew. Having convinced them of the futility of remaining on the island, he holds out the appealing image of the "newer world" and the environment of the "sounding furrows" in which the men could once more take a vital, active role.

"My Last Duchess," "Life in a Love" and "Love Among the Ruins"
by Robert Browning
Sonnet 43 by Elizabeth Barrett Browning

Build Vocabulary (p. 179)

A. 1. absence; 2. presence; 3. diligence; 4. innocence

B. 1. e 2. a 3. b 4. f 5. h 6. d 7. g 8. c

Grammar and Style: The Use of *Like* and *As*
(p. 180)

A. 1. like; 2. like; 3. as; 4. as; 5. like; 6. like

B. Paragraphs must include at least one instance each of *like* and *as* used correctly.

Reading Strategy: Making Inferences About the Speaker (p. 181)

Sample responses:

1. The Duke seems not to have cared for his wife. He believes she was too easily pleased by any little thing; perhaps he feels she was too generous to others.

2. The Duke appears jealous. By characterizing the giver as an "officious fool," he reveals his own pettiness.

3. The speaker is attracted to the girl and loves her. He eagerly awaits the moment of first seeing her and wants to linger, just looking at her, before they kiss.

4. The speaker is a romantic. He imagines every detail of meeting his beloved; he does not want to "rush" the pleasure and joy he feels when first seeing her.

Literary Analysis: Dramatic Monologue
(p. 182)

A. Possible responses:

"My Last Duchess"

Setting: sixteenth-century Italian castle; Speaker: Duke; Listener: agent for Count; Conflict: Duke hopes to marry the Count's daughter and, while negotiating with the agent, discusses his former wife.

"Life in a Love"

Setting: present day; Speaker: a spurned lover; Listener: object of speaker's affections; Conflict: The speaker pursues a woman who does not return his affections.

"Love Among the Ruins"

Setting: countryside near ruins of ancient civilization; Speaker: shepherd; Listener: unspecified, perhaps a fellow shepherd; Conflict: The speaker's admiration of the past and its glories conflicts with his stronger desire to meet his beloved.

B. Sample responses:

1. The reader imagines how the Count's agent must be reacting to the Duke's words. One would suspect that the agent does not view the Duke favorably and that the tension over the question of marriage becomes greater as the Duke reveals himself to be arrogant, jealous, and petty.

2. Most likely, the conflict will not be resolved. The speaker states his position at the beginning—"Escape me? / Never—" and does not back down. He seems not to mind, either; he concedes that "the chase takes up one's life, that's all."

3. "Love Among the Ruins" mirrors the poem's conflict between the drama of past glories and the thrill of present desire.

"You Know the Place: Then"
by Sappho
"Invitation to the Voyage"
by Charles Baudelaire

Build Vocabulary: The Language of Relationships (p. 183)

Sample responses:

1. treacherous; His treacherous eyes spoke of an untrustworthiness I couldn't ignore.

2. richness; The richness of the sauce made it fit for a monarch's table.

3. pleasure; It was with pleasure that we welcomed them into our lives.

4. leave; When you leave, I will feel a void in my life.

5. love; Might love be richer the second time it is experienced?

6. deep; The low gurgling of the brook lulled me into a deep sleep.

7. sacred; The building is a sacred site of pilgrimage for many believers.

8. waiting; I grew tired of waiting for him to arrive.

Cultural Connection: Relationships (p. 184)

Students should identify the relationship explored by Sappho as that between human beings and the divine, listing such images as sacred precincts, pleasant groves, leaves pouring down deep sleep, and the filling of gold cups

with love. Students should identify the relationship explored by Baudelaire as an ideal love relationship, listing the various images of the poet's alternate world. Relationships that students identify to fill the chart might include those between a citizen and the government (political), a human being and the world of nature (environmental), and a person and his or her past or dreams of the future (psychological).

from *Hard Times* by Charles Dickens
from *Jane Eyre* by Charlotte Brontë

Build Vocabulary (p. 185)

A. 1. monolithic
   2. monogram
   3. monophony
   4. monosyllabic

B. 1. d   2. c   3. a   4. b   5. c   6. a   7. d   8. d

Grammar and Style: Punctuation of Dialogue (p. 186)

A. 1. After a pause, one half of the children cried in chorus, "Yes, Sir!"
   2. "You must paper it," said Thomas Gradgrind, "whether you like it or not."
   3. "Fact, fact, fact!" said the gentleman.
   4. "Why," thought I, "does she not explain that she could neither clean her nails nor wash her face, as the water was froze?"

B. I thought I heard Mr. Gradgrind shout, "Just give me facts!" Did he really say, "Facts alone are needed in life"?

In response to his statements, the fearful children in the room said, "Yes, sir!"

"I don't understand," Sissy Jupe said.

"What is so difficult to understand?" Mr. Gradgrind asked. "Just stick to facts. Root out everything else."

Reading Strategy: Recognizing the Writer's Purpose (p. 187)

Possible responses:

1. The schoolroom is described as being a "plain, bare, monotonous vault." The speaker is described as having a "wide, thin, hard set" mouth; an "inflexible, dry, and dictatorial" voice; bristling hair; and a square, boxy figure. The author sees the schoolroom as a boring, rigid, unwelcoming place.

from *Hard Times* by Charles Dickens
from *Jane Eyre* by Charlotte Brontë
(continued)

2. Sissy is shy and unable to fit into the rigid classroom. Bitzer is responsive and precise; he is able to give the teachers exactly what they want. In the sunlight, Sissy appears natural and glowing, while Bitzer appears drained of all color. Sissy's clash with her teachers reinforces the author's negative view of the classroom and its teachers. The author does not approve of the teachers' rigid teaching styles, and the way they ban imagination and individuality from their classroom.

3. Brontë describes how Miss Scatcherd repeatedly criticizes Helen, who is a quiet, studious young woman. Scratcherd even attacks Helen for not having clean fingernails, thrashing her with a bundle of twigs. This scene shows the unhappy circumstances under which the girls in the school live. Brontë is criticizing the school and its abusive treatment of its students.

4. Jane does not understand how Helen can keep silent and never become angry when she is abused. Helen says that the teachers are only trying to correct her faults, and that students should be grateful for such instruction. She says she can tolerate unhappiness in this life, because she is always looking to its end, when she will be rewarded. This conversation reveals the problems the girls experience at Lowood, and contrasts the anger Jane feels at injustice with Helen's "saintly" forbearance.

Literary Analysis: The Novel and Social Criticism (p. 188)

1. He does not like Gradgrind's aggressive teaching style, which destroys all imagination and wonder and fills students' heads with only facts. He is criticizing the way in which the school is run.

2. He refers to her in this way because he thinks of students as parts of a system, not as individuals. Dickens is critical of this approach to education.

3. Helen's faults are not really faults; she is guilty only of occasionally having trouble adjusting to the rigid rules of the school.

Brontë is criticizing the cold, rigid world of Lowood.

4. Helen places little value on her own life. Her humility is worlds away from the routine, petty abusiveness of Scatcherd. Brontë suggests that only a saint could survive at Lowood.

from *War and Peace* by Leo Tolstoy

Build Vocabulary: The Language of Human Experience (p. 189)

1. blunders; 2. pitiful; 3 inspired; 4. abandon; 5. greatness; 6. dignity; 7. ashamed; 8. panic; 9. intuition; 10. guilty

Literary Connection: The Novel (p. 190)

Suggested response:

Students' plot outlines should present a coherent narrative ambitious enough to warrant novelistic treatment. The incidents they list should have sufficient depth to have universal significance. Possibilities include family relationships, school friendships, academic difficulties, youthful romances, and other human experiences that students are likely to have encountered.

"Dover Beach" by Matthew Arnold
"Recessional" and "The Widow at Windsor" by Rudyard Kipling

Build Vocabulary (p. 191)

A. Possible responses:

1. To *dominate* is to rule, control, or exert influence over someone or something. To *domineer* is to exercise arbitrary or overbearing control.

2. The *Dom* signifies a position of importance or influence, and implies that the person is a "master."

3. An *indomitable* enemy is one that cannot be overpowered or overcome, one that cannot be mastered.

B. 1. d 2. a 3. e 4. c 5. b

Grammar and Style: Present Tense (p. 192)

A. The following sentences contain present tense verbs: 1, 3, 4, 6, 7, 8, 10.

B. Suggested response: Students should use present tense verbs throughout this activity. If any students have difficulty, suggest that they imagine they are seeing the ocean or mountain, for example, right now.

Reading Strategy: Drawing Conclusions
(p. 193)

Sample responses:

"Dover Beach"

Detail: the world only "seems / To lie before us like a land of dreams"; the world has "neither joy, nor love, nor light, / Nor certitude, nor peace, nor help for pain. . . ." Conclusion: The speaker is pessimistic about the ability of people to struggle successfully in a world without God.

"Recessional"

Detail: The speaker addresses "God of our fathers, known of old—" to "be with us yet"; Conclusion: The speaker feels that God is no longer as close as He once was, but he still wishes for God's guidance.

Detail: Four of the five stanzas end with "Lest we forget—lest we forget!" Conclusion: The speaker recognizes that the dominion the nation has won did not come easily and could easily be abused.

"The Widow at Windsor"

Detail: "us poor beggars in red"; the fair wind takes "us to various wars"; "we" have bought her the half of creation she owns. Conclusion: The speaker is a soldier in Queen Victoria's forces.

Detail: Kings and emperors stop when the "widow" says stop; "From the pole to the Tropics"; "round the earth." Conclusion: The speaker sees the queen as powerful and believes her influence reaches throughout the world.

Literary Analysis: Mood as a Key to Theme
(p. 194)

Possible responses:

1. The rhythm of the passage's image—"Begin, and cease, and then again begin,"—is calming. The poet seems to want to establish an everyday image into which sadness enters so readers understand that the sadness is "here."

2. Navies "melt away" is a sobering euphemism for soldiers being killed in battle. The allu-

sions to Nineveh and Tyre are bold and alarming. The poet almost threatens that *this* nation could pass into obscurity as did these cities of old.

3. The image of "flopping" around the earth till you're dead seems to imply that the soldiers go unwillingly. Nonetheless, wherever they go, the British flag always flies overhead, signifying, ironically, their victory.

"Condition of Ireland,"
The Illustrated London News
"Progress in Personal Comfort"
by Sydney Smith

Build Vocabulary (p. 195)

A. 1. sluggish or slow
2. warm or cheerful

B. 1. indolence; 2. exonerate; 3. requisites;
4. depredation; 5. sanction; 6. melancholy

Grammar and Style: Coordinating Conjunctions (p. 196)

A. 1. I can walk, by the assistance of the police, from one end of London to the other, without molestation: *or*, if tired, get into a cheap *and* active cab . . .

2. Calmly *and* quietly, *but* very ignorantly . . . did the decree go forth which has made the temporary *but* terrible visitation of a potato rot the means of exterminating, through the slow process of disease *and* houseless starvation, nearly the half of the Irish.

B. Sample responses:

1. Most people believe progress is always good, but "Condition of Ireland" reveals something different.

2. In the name of economic progress, many people suffered and died.

3. The Poor-Laws were supposed to provide relief for the people in Ireland, but the laws instead caused their destruction.

4. People lost their land, so they lost their livelihoods.

5. "Condition of Ireland" calls for compassion and change.

"Condition of Ireland,"
The Illustrated London News
"Progress in Personal Comfort"
by Sydney Smith *(continued)*

Reading Strategy: Distinguishing Emotive and Informative Language (p. 197)

Sample responses:

1. emotive: "instrument of their destruction," "terrible distress," and "temporary calamity." informative: "The Poor-Law, said to be for the relief of the people" and "they were to have no relief unless they gave up their holdings." Attitude: critical of Poor-Law; sympathetic to people.

2. emotive: "Calmly and quietly, but very ignorantly," "a terrible blunder." informative: "did the decree go forth." Attitude: critical of the decree from Westminster.

3. emotive: "I suffered between 10,000 and 12,000 severe contusions" informative: "It took me nine hours to go from Taunton to Bath, before the invention of the railroads, and I now go in six hours from Taunton to London!" Attitude: approving of railroads; bemoans pain of earlier transportation.

4. emotive: "sapping the vitals of the country," "whatever miseries," "remotest corners of the empire." informative: "There were no banks to receive the savings of the poor." Attitude: powerless to voice protest against Poor-Laws.

Literary Analysis: Journalistic Essay (p. 198)

Possible responses:

1. The Irish potato crop failed due to disease. The Poor-Laws, which were supposed to help people by reducing unemployment, forced farmers with small holdings to give up their land, rendering them homeless. Because they could not grow food for themselves or find employment, many people emigrated or starved.

2. The voice's perspective is standing apart from the events, as a witness or a judge. The writer criticizes the actions of the government, calling them "ignorant and vicious." Students might also list details that reveal the writer's view of the suffering of the Irish.

3. Inventions include the gaslight, steam engine, paved roads, the umbrella, medicines, and the post office.

4. Smith is amazed and thrilled by the changes. He celebrates the inventions that help him to feel more comfortable. Students might list his descriptions of inventions and the comparisons he makes between his life before and after the changes.

"Opening Statement for the Inaugural Session of the Forum for Peace and Reconciliation"
by Judge Catherine McGuinness

Build Vocabulary: The Language of Reconciliation (p. 199)

Sample responses:

1. stability; A number of areas around the globe are lacking in stability.

2. traditions; Sometimes people with different traditions come into conflict.

3. respect; A first step in resolving a conflict is to respect others' points of view.

4. validity; There may be validity to the claims made by both sides in a conflict.

5. cooperation; Cooperation is the opposite of conflict.

6. trust; If the negotiators do not win the trust of the warring sides, there will be no hope for peace.

7. rights; The peace treaty laid out in detail the rights of minorities.

8. understanding; The two sides came to an understanding.

9. democratic; A democratic structure was put into place to give the people a voice in settling the conflict.

Thematic Connection: Reconciling the Empire (p. 200)

Students should be able to trace the roots of the conflict in Northern Ireland to Great Britain's original colonial presence in Ireland. When the Irish Republic gained its independence, Great Britain retained control of certain northern provinces in which the majority was Protestant and loyal to Great Britain. The conflict involves differences between the Protestant and Catholic populations that are religious in some degree, but also involve issues of class, education, and political representation. Students may offer a variety of peace proposals, including the holding of an increased number of forums where ordinary citizens can meet to discuss their differences or the convening of an international peace conference where nations such as the United States help to mediate the conflict.

"Remembrance" by Emily Brontë
"The Darkling Thrush" and
"'Ah, Are You Digging on My Grave?'"
by Thomas Hardy

Build Vocabulary (p. 201)

A. 1. d 2. e 3. a 4. b 5. c

B. 1. rapturous; 2. gaunt; 3. languish; 4. terrestrial

C. 1. b 2. d 3. c 4. a

Grammar and Style: Pronoun Case Following *Than* or *As* (p. 202)

A. 1. they; 2. he; 3. I; 4. she; 5. we; 6. I

B. 1. No one enjoyed the play more than we.

2. The lead actor was more impressive than he.

3. Few actors are as talented as she.

4. Everyone was as pleased with the performance as I.

Reading Strategy: Reading Stanzas as Units of Meaning (p. 203)

A. Sample responses:

1. The speaker describes how she has grieved for her love, who has been dead for fifteen years.

2. In stanzas six through eight, the speaker realizes that she cannot spend her life grieving and that she has learned to live without her love.

3. In each stanza, the speaker guesses who is digging on her grave, and the digger answers. Each answer conveys the idea that a person is forgotten after death.

4. The final two stanzas create two effects: they are humorous, but they also reinforce the idea that death means the disappearance of a person from the world, and even from memory.

B. Possible responses:

Stanza 1: Images create a desolate mood.

Stanza 2: Death seems to surround the speaker.

Stanza 3: A frail bird sings a joyful song.

Stanza 4: The bird knows a reason for hope of which the speaker is unaware.

Overall Meaning: Even in the bleakest of situations, one can find hope.

Literary Analysis: Stanza Structure and Irony (p. 204)

Possible responses:

"Remembrance"

1. eight

2. four lines, with five feet in each, often starting with a trochee; *abab* rhyme scheme

3. The consistency of stanza structure makes reader expect each stanza will focus on the same theme.

4. In stanza six, speaker explains that she has learned to live without her love.

5. The regular stanza structure leads reader to expect that speaker will follow her love to the grave, when in fact, she decides to live.

"The Darkling Thrush"

1. four

2. eight alternating lines of four and three iambic feet, *abab cdcd* rhyme scheme

3. The consistent stanza structure creates expectation that all stanzas will have the same gloomy mood and subject matter.

4. In stanza three a bird sings a joyful song, which leads speaker to concede in stanza four that there might be hope.

5. The reader is lulled into complacency by the singsong quality of the stanzas, only to be surprised, as the speaker is, by the thrush's hopeful song.

"Ah, Are You Digging on My Grave?"

1. six

2. six lines of four feet each, except the second and the last, which have three; *abcccb* rhyme scheme

3. Reader expects a question and answer in each stanza; the repeated question also builds suspense.

"Remembrance" by Emily Brontë
"The Darkling Thrush" and
"'Ah, Are You Digging on My Grave?'"
by Thomas Hardy *(continued)*

4. In stanza four, reader learns the digger is not, like the others asked, a human being, but is the speaker's dog. In stanza six, the dog states that he has also forgotten his mistress.

5. The speaker and reader both expect the digger will care for the speaker. Also, the serious subject matter now becomes darkly humorous.

"God's Grandeur" and **"Spring and Fall: To a Young Child"**
by Gerard Manley Hopkins
"To an Athlete Dying Young" and **"When I Was One-and-Twenty"**
by A. E. Housman

Build Vocabulary (p. 205)

A. Possible responses:

1. duckdelight, splashbeggar, socksoaker
2. leafpromises, summerhopes, the first sun-eager leaf buds of spring
3. the puppies tumbletripped to the food dish, their rasptongues scraped my cheek
4. sunsprawling metal-antheap; childbursts

B. 1. a   2. c   3. d

C. 1. grandeur;   2. blight;   3. rue

Grammar and Style: Capitalization: Compass Points (p. 206)

A. 1. D;   2. D;   3. R—West;   4. D;
   5. R—Northwest;   6. R—Western

B. Possible responses:

1. The Southern states, such as Georgia and South Carolina, are full of Civil War history.
2. We drove north for what seemed like an eternity.
3. California is the epitome of what the West is all about—it has mountains, deserts, and ocean beaches.
4. Student responses will depend on where they live. Students should use the capitalized word *Northeast* to name the region.

Reading Strategy: Applying Biography (p. 207)

Sample responses:
Hopkins

Trait: belief in uniqueness of all things; "There lives the dearest freshness deep down things;" ("God's Grandeur," line 10)

Trait: love of nature; the image of "worlds of wanwood leafmeal" ("Spring and Fall," lines 2, 8)

Housman

Trait: studied Greek and Latin; reference to laurel wreath, a classical Greek symbol for an athlete's victory ("To an Athlete Dying Young," line 25)

Trait: bitterness; There is bitterness as well as humor in the lines "And I am two-and-twenty, / And oh, 'tis true, 'tis true." ("When I Was One-and-Twenty," lines 15–16)

Literary Analysis: Rhythm and Meter (p. 208)

Suggested responses:

1. Today, the road all runners come,
   iambic tetrameter
   Shoulder-high we bring you home,
   trochaic tetrameter
   And set you at your threshold down,
   iambic tetrameter
   Townsman of a stiller town.
   trochaic tetrameter

2. And for all this, nature is never spent:
   There lives the dearest freshness deep down things:
   1st line: *counterpoint rhythm*
   2nd line: *iambic pentameter*

3. Now no matter, child, the name:
   Sorrow's springs are the same.
   sprung rhythm

Students may observe that the meter gives the words dramatic expressiveness and contributes to the mood of a poem.

"Eternity" by Arthur Rimbaud

Build Vocabulary (p. 209)

A. 1. c   2. f   3. g   4. e   5. d   6. b   7. a

B. 1. eternity;   2. vow;   3. embers;
   4. sanctions; 5. recovered;   6. ardor;
   7. anguish

Thematic Connection: Gloom and Glory (p. 210)

Students should include some or all of the following images from the Rimbaud poem: the sea and sun representing eternity, a "night so void," a "fiery day," "human sanctions" and "common transports," "satin embers," "duty exhaling." Students may list any number of topics for their own songs or poems. They may take a cue from the Bruce Springsteen example and explore the theme of what happens after youth and its accomplishments have passed.

Unit 6: A Time of Rapid Change (1901–Present)

Poetry of William Butler Yeats

Build Vocabulary (p. 211)

A. 1. quest; 2. request
B. 1. c 2. a 3. b 4. d 5. b 6. c

Grammar and Style: Noun Clauses (p. 212)

A. 1. In "When You Are Old," the speaker expresses an idea of what the thoughts of a woman he once loved might one day be. (object of preposition)

2. Who you are may determine whether you believe "The Lake Isle of Innisfree" refers to a type of place or a kind of work. (subject)

3. Knowledge that the world will go on without you, that stark recognition, glides also across the water in "The Wild Swans at Coole." (appositive)

4. In "Sailing to Byzantium," an aging man hopes that he can make himself eternal through intellect and artwork. (direct object)

B. Sample responses:

1. Subject: That Yeats is the best Irish poet of the twentieth century seems beyond question.

2. Complement: The use of graceful, carefully chosen language is how Yeats creates memorable images.

3. Direct object: Some may find what Yeats says about aging cruel, but he was feeling himself aging as he wrote "Sailing to Byzantium."

4. Object of preposition: A reader's response to some of Yeats' philosophy may depend upon his or her personal experiences.

Reading Strategy: Applying Literary Background (p. 213)

Possible responses:

1. It's easy to assume this is Yeats's prediction for Gonne; language like "glad grace" and "loved your beauty with love false or true" and "pilgrim soul" fit squarely with Gonne's appearance and career.

2. Yeats's many summers gave him much opportunity to watch, reflect on, and feel the coming autumn at Coole.

3. Lines 3–8, with their reference to things falling apart seem to refer to the fall of the Tsars who had ruled Russia for centuries. Wave after wave of bloodthirsty vengeance by those fighting for control foreshadowed for Yeats an ugly modern world with much violence, a redefined authority, and an absence of belief—exactly the state Russia was becoming.

4. Yeats's dreamy fascination with an ancient city provides him a place of imaginative escape that turns up in his poem as a place safe from physical decay.

Literary Analysis: Symbolism (p. 214)

Sample responses:

1. The fact that Eve is referred to as "a beautiful maid" indicates that the poet is speaking symbolically of all women.

2. Traditionally, women were predestined to become wives, even before they were born. Because their entire lives were devoted to their husbands and families, the poet maintains that they were never actually "born" in the sense of having fully separate identities.

"Preludes," "Journey of the Magi" and "The Hollow Men" by T. S. Eliot

Build Vocabulary (p. 215)

A. 1. fractional; 2. fractious; 3. refract

B. 1. c   2. a   3. b   4. c   5. c

Grammar and Style: Adjectival Modifiers (p. 216)

A. 1. "of withered leaves" modifies *scraps*; prepositional phrase

2. "gathering fuel" modifies *ancient women*; participial phrase

3. "who have crossed" modifies *those*; adjective clause

4. "from vacant lots" modifies *newspapers*; prepositional phrase

5. "that press" modifies *feet*; adjective clause

6. "cursing and grumbling" modifies *men*; participial phrase

B. Sample response:

The poem "Preludes," features a city of despair. The poet writes of showers beating on blinds, a lonely horse stamping and steaming, and the smell of steaks. Morning brings hands that raise dingy shades and the sad masquerades of humans.

Reading Strategy: Interpreting (p. 217)

Suggested responses:

1. Students might list some of the following images: "The grimy scraps of withered leaves about your feet"; "The showers beat on broken blinds and chimney pots"; "Newspapers from vacant lots"; "A lonely cab horse steams and stamps." Students should notice that these images reveal a feeling of quiet, loneliness, and sadness. Eliot seems to be saying that modern, urban life is lonely and depressing.

2. Students might list some of the following images: "With all its muddy feet that press"; "One thinks of all the hands / That are raising dingy shades."; "You curled the papers from your hair, / Or clasped the yellow soles of feet / In the palms of both soiled hands"; "And short, square fingers stuffing pipes." These images show only parts of people, as they focus on simple tasks. The people are fragmented, and words such as

"muddy," "dingy," "soiled," and "yellow" give the impression that their lives are tarnished and unhappy.

3. Students might list some of the following details: "The ways deep and the weather sharp"; "the camels galled, sore-footed, and refractory"; ". . . the night-fires going out, and the lack of shelters"; ". . . the cities hostile and the towns unfriendly / And the villages dirty and charging high prices . . ." These images suggest that the journey is difficult, and that the Magi would not endure it if not for an important reason.

4. The Magi are left thinking about birth and death, and they have a sense of unease when they return home to old traditions. The journey changed their lives, and the images imply that the birth they were honoring will have an important effect on the world.

5. The hollow men have a "headpiece filled with straw," "dried voices" that are "quiet and meaningless," and they are "sightless." They are also described as a "paralyzed force, gesture without motion." These images emphasize the misery of the hollow men, who have no self-knowledge and no ability to reach out to find meaning in their lives.

6. Students might list the following images: "This is the dead land / This is cactus land" and "In this valley of dying stars / In this hollow valley / This broken jaw of our lost kingdoms." With these images, Eliot creates a scene of hopelessness and despair.

Literary Analysis: Modernism (p. 218)

Suggested responses:

1. Students should understand that the clear images, presented without the commentary of the author, are characteristic of Modernism. Students should also understand that the bleak outlook on urban life and the lives of people is a common Modernist theme.

2. The clear images reflect the Modernist style, but unlike the other poems, the people in this work find meaning in their lives. They are guided by a religious belief that helps them through the chaotic world.

3. The world is described as "hollow," "broken," and "lost." People seem unable to communicate or understand themselves and their surroundings. Like "Preludes," the poem uses clear images intended to create emotion in readers and it presents a sad view of modern life.

"In Memory of W. B. Yeats" and "Musée des Beaux Arts" by W. H. Auden
"Carrick Revisited" by Louis MacNeice
"Not Palaces" by Stephen Spender

Build Vocabulary (p. 219)

A. 1. c 2. a
B. 1. d 2. c 3. b 4. c 5. a

Grammar and Style: Parallel Structure (p. 220)

A. 1. taught; 2. as; 3. consider; 4. promoting
B. Sample responses:
1. Yeats died on a day that was dark and cold.
2. The "Old Masters" refers to artists from Belgium, Holland, and Italy.
3. Bruegel enjoyed painting scenes of laborers, including harvesters and hunters.
4. The speaker in "Carrick Revisited" admires the landscape and remembers his childhood.

Reading Strategy: Paraphrasing (p. 221)

A. Possible responses:
1. Nature is indifferent to human suffering.
2. Returning to a place we know mostly from memory limits our perception of the place.
3. Art cannot be kept and collected. It must be created, with energy, if there is any hope that art can change the world.

B. Suggested responses:
1. The phrase "dogs go on with their doggy life" emphasizes nature's indifference to human suffering.
2. The imagery of sea and land underscore the speaker's feelings of ambivalence about the truth of memory.
3. The juxtaposition of "filtered dusts" with "stamping," "emphasis," and "Drink from here energy" sharply contrasts the old and new ideas about art.

Literary Analysis: Theme (p. 222)

Sample responses:
1. A central idea in the poem is that Yeats's death blurs the line between Yeats himself and his poetry. Auden's word choice implies the theme: "wholly given over to unfamiliar affections" and "words of a dead man / Are modified in the guts of the living."
2. The poem's theme—tragedy matters only to those who are affected by it—is indirectly expressed. Auden's word choice and tone—"expensive delicate ship" and "sailed calmly on"—imply the theme.
3. These lines express the theme directly. The speaker grapples with his identity, and the lines describe these different identities. The poet's tone, which is both angry and melancholy, implies the theme.
4. The idea that art can bring about social justice is directly stated. The poet's forceful tone implies the theme.

"Shooting an Elephant" by George Orwell

Build Vocabulary (p. 223)

A. Sample response:
   While serving as a police officer in Burma, Orwell came to despise imperialism. He viewed it as a despotic form of government. He noted the irony in the supposed dominion the colonizers had over the colonized.

B. 1. b 2. f 3. e 4. a 5. d 6. c

Grammar and Style: Participial Phrases: Restrictive and Nonrestrictive (p. 224)

A. 1. hooted after me when I was at a safe distance; restrictive; insults
2. winding all over a steep hillside; nonrestrictive; labyrinth
3. violently shooing away a crowd of naked children; nonrestrictive; woman
4. sharply twisted to one side; restrictive; head
5. standing in front of the unarmed native crowd; nonrestrictive; I

"Shooting an Elephant"
by George Orwell (continued)

B. Sample response:

At my first violin recital I was very nervous and uncomfortable. My fingers, drenched in sweat, slipped on my violin strings. I rarely looked up from the pages clipped to my music stand.

Reading Strategy: Recognizing the Writer's Attitudes (p. 225)

Sample responses:

1. attitudes toward Burmese: perplexed, upset by hatred; knows they're oppressed; "wretched prisoners"; "rage against the evil-spirited little beasts"; "prostrate peoples"; wants to drive bayonet into Buddhist priest; Conclusion: Orwell believes the Burmese are oppressed by the British and, logically, can understand their hatred. However, part of him wants to react to their hatred with rage and revenge.

2. attitudes toward killing elephant: "vaguely uneasy"; no intention of shooting it; feels pressure of crowd's expectations; "absurd puppet"; wears a mask and is not himself; later rationalizes his action; Conclusion: If the decision were left to him, Orwell would not have shot the elephant. However, he felt pressured by the expectation of the crowd and his own perception of what he should do, as a representative of the ruling group.

Literary Analysis: Irony (p. 226)

Sample responses:

1. One would expect a certain respect to be shown toward priests. Orwell believes they are oppressed, but he also thinks of them as "evil spirited" and has fantasies of killing them.

2. The British seem heavily armed—Orwell has several types of rifles—against a population that has no weapons, but the Burmese control the behavior of the British.

3. "Grinning" connotes happiness in a situation that is morbid.

4. The crowd showed little interest in the elephant while it was ravaging the bazaar.

5. Orwell feels compelled to kill the elephant, even though he knows its worth is far greater living than dead.

6. The situation is anything but "perfectly clear." Orwell's original resolve not to kill the animal becomes clouded by many concerns, such as embarrassment and pressure from the crowd.

7. A dangerous weapon, which Orwell uses to perform an unseemly task, contrasts sharply with traditional ideas of beauty.

8. The death of the coolie, who was not valued, gave Orwell an excuse for doing something he did not really want to do—shooting the valuable elephant.

"The Demon Lover"
by Elizabeth Bowen

Build Vocabulary (p. 227)

A. 1. locality

2. localism

3. allocation

B. 1. b 2. e 3. c 4. a 5. d

Grammar and Style: Sentence Beginnings: Participial Phrases (p. 228)

A. Sentences 2, 4, and 5 begin with participial phrases.

2. "Proceeding upstairs" modifies *Mrs. Drover.*

4. "Annoyed at the caretaker" modifies *she.*

5. "Polishing a clear patch in the mirror" modifies *Mrs. Drover.*

B. Sample response:

Described as a writer of "finely wrought prose," Elizabeth Bowen is highly praised for her stories. Her characters are mostly from the upper middle class in England and Ireland. Born into that class, Bowen "knew" her characters well. Her novel *The Hotel*, published in 1927, contains a typical Bowen heroine. Trying to cope with a life for which she is not prepared, the girl might remind some of a young Elizabeth Bowen.

Reading Strategy: Responding (p. 229)

Sample Responses:

Student reactions to the story will depend on their own life experiences. Be sure that students go beyond their own responses to evaluate whether the author intended that response, and why.

Literary Analysis: The Ghost Story (p. 230)

Sample responses:

outside Mrs. Drover's house: *normal*: deserted because of war, autumn so humid and rainy; *unusual*: "unfamiliar queerness" due to street's lack of activity

inside Mrs. Drover's house: *normal*: dark because windows boarded up, usual things are visible (smoke stain, ring on desk, bruise in wallpaper); *unusual*: she is "perplexed," one door is ajar

the letter: *normal*: letters were not uncommon; *unusual*: how it came to be delivered and laid on hall table, vaguely sinister message from former lover who is presumed dead

the farewell, 25 years ago: *normal*: saying good-bye to a soldier would have been a common scene during a war; *unusual*: his face not visible, pressure of buttons on hand, she eager to have the farewell done with, "sinister troth" made

Mrs. Drover's marriage and family: *normal*: courtship, marriage, home, and children, she busy being utterly dependable for her family; *unusual*: [no "unusual" details are given]

catching the taxi: *normal*: the street is busy as usual, the taxi is right where it should be; *unusual*: taxi seems to be waiting for her, starts up without instructions, Mrs. Drover screams when she sees the driver's face, taxi speeds off into the deserted streets

"The Diameter of the Bomb"
by Yehuda Amichai
"Everything Is Plundered"
by Anna Akhmatova
"Testament" by Bei Dao

Build Vocabulary: Language of a Grim Reality (p. 231)

1. wounded; sample sentence: The number of wounded in the bombing numbered in the hundreds.
2. ruined; sample sentence: A number of historical landmarks were ruined during the war in Yugoslavia.
3. bomb; sample sentence: Special precautions must be taken to make sure a bomb cannot be brought onto the airplane.
4. mourning; sample sentence: Citizens of the city were in mourning for the loss of so many inhabitants.
5. pain; sample sentence: The dictator ignored the pain felt by the citizens.
6. plundered; sample sentence: The rebels attacked and plundered the city.
7. betrayed; sample sentence: The informer betrayed the location of the army's supply storehouses.
8. graveyard; sample sentence: A memorial to unknown soldiers was built in the graveyard.

Cultural Connection: Waking From the Dream (p. 232)

Students should identify the three conflicts explored in the poems as the atmosphere of terror in the Middle East, the harshness and misery of Stalinist Russia, and the repressive nature of the Chinese government. Students should point out that conflict still plagues the Middle East, with the threat of terrorism a daily reality. Students should note that in China, the government still rules with an iron hand, although at least some observers point to the adoption of free market economic practices as pointing toward an eventual lessening in political repression. Students should also point out that the Soviet regime passed into history in the late 1980's. Of the three poets, then, only Akhmatova might be able to write from a different point of view. Students may point out, however, that life in Russia continues to be a difficult experience.

"The Soldier" by Rupert Brooke
"Wirers" by Siegfried Sassoon
"Anthem for Doomed Youth"
by Wilfred Owen
"Birds on the Western Front"
by Saki (H. H. Munro)

Build Vocabulary (p. 233)

A. 1. laud; 2. laudation; 3. laudatory
B. 1. a 2. d 3. b 4. d 5. c 6. c 7. b

Grammar and Style: Use of *Who* and *Whom* in Adjective Clauses (p. 234)

A. 1. who; 2. whom; 3. whom; 4. who

"The Soldier" by Rupert Brooke
"Wirers" by Siegfried Sassoon
"Anthem for Doomed Youth"
by Wilfred Owen
"Birds on the Western Front"
by Saki (H. H. Munro) *(continued)*

B. Sample responses:

1. Rupert Brooke was one of many talented writers who died in World War I.

2. Siegfried Sassoon, whom the world first noticed in war, wrote of peace in later life.

3. The families whom the soldiers left behind are on the mind of Wilfred Owen in "Anthem for Doomed Youth."

Reading Strategy: Making Inferences (p. 235)

Possible responses:

Setting: War zone; "seems to be very little corresponding disturbance," eyewitness account

Speaker: Observer of some sort, then clearly a soldier; eyewitness observations, then, "I once saw a pair of crows," "throw myself down with abruptness" indicating he is a soldier.

Action/Topic: Bird behavior in wartime; any of various bird behaviors in scarred landscape.

Tone: Ironic and detached; studied language and formal expression, as if in a club or over dinner rather than on a battlefield.

Theme: Absurdity of war, a life and death struggle, as contrasted against bird behavior, also a life and death struggle. Gentle satire of English reserve and mannerisms.

Literary Analysis: Tone (p. 236)

Sample responses:

"Wirers" *Details:* Doomed soldier carried off in great pain; Cost of life to repair barb-wire fence. Impact of image is horror. *Word Choice:* "Moaning" "lurch" are direct and graphic. "No doubt he'll die today" is matter-of-fact. *Voice:* Voice is direct plain speech, a credible soldier, and an understated account of death. Bitter in last line. *Tone:* Overall tone is stark in reporting the casual details of death, turning bitter as the lost life is measured against the minor gain of fence repair

"Birds on the Western Front" *Details:* Narrator falls on nestlings. Two were dead, the others uninjured. Underscores random nature of death in wartime, and the absurdity

of war as nature tries to go on. *Word Choice:* "with some abruptness" rather than a terrified dive; "rather a battered condition" means dead; "tranquil and comfortable," even for a bird, seems incredible in the circumstances. *Voice:* Formal diction of an upper class, as if writing a letter back to a local birdwatching club. The voice is gently absurd in these conditions. *Tone:* Overall tone is ironic, focusing closely on birds while in mortal peril.

"Wartime Speech" by Winston Churchill
"Defending Nonviolent Resistance"
by Mohandas K. Gandhi

Build Vocabulary (p. 237)

A. 1. duration; 2. obdurate; 3. durability

B. 1. invincible; 2. formidable;
3. intimidated; 4. retaliate; 5. diabolical;
6. excrescence; 7. endurance;
8. disaffection; 9. extenuating

Grammar and Style: Parallel Structure (p. 238)

A. 1. And if the French Army, and our own Army, are well handled, as I believe they will be; if the French retain that genius for recovery and counter-attack for which they have so long been famous, and if the British Army shows the dogged endurance of which there have been so many examples in the past—then a sudden transformation might spring into being. *Adverbial clause*

2. Only a very small part of that splendid army has yet been heavily engaged; and only a very small part of France has yet been invaded. *Adjective phrase*

3. After this battle in France abates its force, there will come the battle for our island—for all that Britain is, and all that Britain means. *Noun clause*

4. Nonviolence is the first article of my creed. It is also the last article of my faith. *Complement*

5. No sophistry, no jugglery in figures can explain away the evidence that the skeletons in many villages present to the naked eye. *Subject*

B. 1. Churchill wanted to explain the situation, to encourage the Army, to reassure the people, to prepare and to inspire them for the long struggle he foresaw.

2. Gandhi did not dispute the charges against him, but he disputed British right of administration, British application of law, British imposition of justice, and British rule of India.

Reading Strategy: Identifying Main Points and Support (p. 239)

Sample responses:

Main Idea	We must not be intimidated by these developments.
S1	If they're behind our front, we're behind theirs.
S2	All armies are in danger, so the battle may be even.
S3	French and British armies will be well handled.
S4	The French have a genius for counter-attack.
S5	The British Army has always shown dogged endurance.
S6	The situation could therefore improve suddenly.

Literary Analysis: Speech (p. 240)

Possible responses:

1. *Churchill:* ". . . solemn hour for the life of our country, of our Empire, of our Allies, and above all, of the cause of Freedom. A tremendous battle is raging in France and Flanders."

   Gandhi: ". . . I entirely endorse the learned advocate-general's remarks in connection with my humble self. I think he was entirely fair to me . . ."

2. *Churchill:* Status, followed by cause for hope, followed by praise for forces, followed by expectation of battle in Britain, followed by call for commitment, concluded by invocation of history.

   Gandhi: Admission of guilt by law; history of his own loyalty, disaffection through chronology of abuse, details, reiteration of guilt by immoral law, appeal to higher morality.

3. *Churchill:* "clawing down three to four to one of our enemies," "foulest and most soul-destroying."

Gandhi: "mad fury of my people," "to invite and cheerfully submit."

4. *Churchill:* Specifics of battles; request for munitions; call for labor.

   Gandhi: Any examples from history of Gandhi's service to the Empire.

5. *Churchill:* Roll call of conquered nations; appeal to British history on Trinity Sunday.

   Gandhi: Reiteration of guilt; acceptance of penalties; appeal to judge to step down and not participate in injustice.

"The Fiddle" by Alan Sillitoe

Build Vocabulary (p. 241)

A. 1. sublimate; 2. subliminal

B. 1. d 2. c 3. b 4. c

Grammar and Style: Vary Sentence Beginnings (p. 242)

A. 1. phrase; 2. adverb; 3. clause;
4. phrase; 5. subject; 6. clause

B. Sample responses:

1. The buildings had been built a century ago.

2. During the winter, Jeff hated not seeing daylight for weeks at a time.

3. While his neighbors worked and played, Jeff sat in his back garden and played for all to hear.

4. Finally, Jeff sold his fiddle for four quid.

Reading Strategy: Predicting Effect of Setting (p. 243)

Possible responses:

Detail: the cottages were in a ruinous condition; Effects: low morale of residents; Predictions: cottages not likely to be fixed up, since they were a century old already

Detail: story takes place in England in the 1930's; Effects: worldwide depression hit especially hard in England; Predictions: national economic difficulties will make it especially hard for people to change their lives

Detail: Harrison's Row was right on the edge of Nottingham; Effects: feeling of separation or isolation from city; Predictions: future expansion may jump over—or over run—Harrison's Row

"The Fiddle" by Alan Sillitoe *(continued)*

Detail: Jeff Bignal could play the fiddle; Effects: held a special position in the neighborhood, different from neighbors; Predictions: his differentness may give him an outlet that other residents don't have

Detail: coal mining was brutal, draining work; Effects: miners didn't see daylight in winter, wasn't very satisfying work; Predictions: miners might try to change their circumstances

Detail: Jeff Bignal is twenty-four years old; Effects: he is young and energetic and still has ambition, he is eligible for the draft; Predictions: his youth might help him change his circumstances, but circumstances may also turn him into a soldier

Literary Analysis: Setting and Atmosphere (p. 244)

Possible responses (multiple options given for each mood):

1. bleakness: cottages in "ruinous condition," a "cut-off place," the "persistent rain of one autumn. . . ."

2. tranquillity: "the back doors and windows looked across the stream into green fields,"; "Across the Leen, horses were sometimes to be seen in the fields. . . ."; "After tea in summer . . . he would sit in his back garden playing the fiddle. . . ."

3. relaxation: "But his face was almost down and lost to the world as he sat on his chair and brought forth his first sweet notes of a summer's evening."; "Jeff played for himself, for the breeze against his arm. . . ."

4. determination: "I'd do anything,"; "But I'll do summat, you can be sure of that."

5. oppression: "In the middle of the winter Jeff's fiddling was forgotten."; ". . . he complained to Blonk that it was hard on a man not to see daylight for weeks at a time."

6. resignation: "I sold it."; "He never had much chance to make a proper start in life, though people said that he came out all right in the end."

"The Distant Past" by William Trevor

Build Vocabulary (p. 245)

A. 1. productivity; 2. eternity; 3. sterility; 4. conductivity; 5. maternity

B. 1. e 2. a 3. b 4. c 5. d

Grammar and Style: Restrictive and Nonrestrictive Adjective Clauses (p. 246)

A. 1. R; where they had lived all their lives
2. N; whom they blamed for their decreased fortunes
3. N; which always accompanied them to town
4. R; who took care of her requests
5. R; that it was a great day for the Commonwealth

B. Sample responses:
1. It was the general opinion that the Middletons were peculiar.
2. It was something of an occasion when they went to town.
3. Fat Driscoll, who was Catholic, even joked with the Middletons.

Reading Strategy: Cause and Effect (p. 247)

Sample responses:

Event 1: Cause—They have eggs to sell, things to buy, and want to attend church; Effect—They develop "convivial relationships" with the townspeople.

Event 2: Cause—Rev. Packham died; Effect—The prayers for the Royal Family are no longer said; Middletons are disappointed.

Event 3: Cause—Queen Elizabeth II is crowned; Effect—Townspeople are amused by the Middleton's continuing support of British royalty.

Event 4: Cause—Catholic-Protestant hostilities; Effect—The differences between the Middletons and the townspeople become more apparent.

Event 5: Cause—"Incidents" occurred in Belfast, Derry, Fermanagh, and Armagh; Effect—The town's tourist trade decreases; hostilities spread to the South.

Event 6: Cause—Old suspicions and bad feelings arise in the town; Effect—The Middletons lose their friends, conclude that nothing will ever change, and see that they will "die friendless."

Literary Analysis: Social Conflict (p. 248)

Possible responses:

1. Some Irish citizens, particularly Protestants, were absolutely in favor of British rule. Other

Irish citizens, particularly Catholics, resisted British rule and were fighting for Irish independence. The Middletons were locked up to prevent them from aiding the British soldiers against the Irish "revolutionaries."

2. Most of Ireland won home rule in 1922. The six counties of Northern Ireland remained part of Britain. The Middletons, who lived in southern Ireland, had supported British rule and would have been disappointed by the onset of home rule in 1922.

3. It goes back to the 1600's when Scottish Protestants were allowed, even encouraged, to confiscate Irish Catholic lands in northern Ireland. The Protestants became the dominant force, in spite of two hundred years of Catholic resentment and resistance. In general terms, social change brought about the conflict.

4. Guidelines for student response: Students are likely to think of local conflicts between members of different ethnic groups, neighborhoods, or schools. Larger social conflicts include the Serbo-Croatian conflict, the English-only argument for American education, and views on the effects of violence on television and in the media.

5. Guidelines for student response: Students need to go beyond the first incident, or who did what to whom, to the basic ideas that are in opposition and why or how those ideas came to be. If traced far enough, many social conflicts go back to social change, which causes some behaviors or actions to become inappropriate. Differences occur when people change their behaviors or recognize the inappropriateness of their behaviors at different points in time.

"Follower" and "Two Lorries"
by Seamus Heaney
"Outside History" by Eavan Boland

Build Vocabulary (p. 249)

A. 1. b 2. a 3. c

B. 1. a 2. c 3. a 4. d 5. b

Grammar and Style: Concrete and Abstract Nouns (p. 250)

A. 1. *expert*—A; *wing*—C; *sod*—C; *headrig*—C; *reins*—C; *team*—C; *land*—C

2. *films*—C; *conceit*—A; *mother*—C; *business*—A; *ashes*—C; *cheek*—C; *lorry*—C; *Magherafelt*—C

B. Possible responses:

1. The farmer works with a horse plow and plows a straight furrow.

2. The boy knows his father is strong and an expert at what he is doing.

3. The boy stumbles over the furrows and sod, following in his father's wake.

4. The boy hints that his father is a nuisance, whether he is actually following the boy around or whether it is just his memory that follows the boy.

Reading Strategy: Summarizing (p. 251)

Sample responses:

Stanza 1: coalman sweet-talking my mother

Stanza 2: mother "moved" by coalman

Stanza 3: mother goes back to work, cleaning stove

Stanza 4: a lorry blows up a bus station

Stanza 5: I imagine my mother dead after the explosion in Magherafelt

Stanza 6: Which lorry is it?

Stanza 7: the coalman now represents death or violence

Summary: The speaker has two memories or visions of a lorry. In one lorry is a coalman who flirts with his mother. Another lorry at another time blows up a bus station. The speaker imagines his mother dead in the aftermath. The coalman, representing death, returns.

Literary Analysis: Diction and Style (p. 252)

Sample responses:

Diction: The contractions lend an informal feeling to this scene-setting, story-telling first stanza. The question in line 5, in which the speaker adopts the coalman's voice, adds to the conversational feeling.

Imagery: Vivid, concrete images of the scene: rain, black coal, warm wet ashes, tire-marks, old lorry, Belfast accent

Rhythm: The stanza does not have rhyme. The rhythm is irregular.

Form: The poem is in six-line stanzas.

"No Witchcraft for Sale"
by Doris Lessing

Build Vocabulary (p. 253)
A. 1. skeptic; 2. skeptically; 3. skepticism

B. 1. d 2. b 3. a 4. b 5. c

Grammar and Style: Correct Use of *Like* and *As* (p. 254)
A. 1. I; 2. I; 3. C; 4. I; 5. C; 6. I

B. Possible responses:
1. Like other young children, Teddy was thrilled with the speed of his scooter.
2. Mrs. Farquar was horrified, as most other mothers would be, by Teddy's accident with the snake.
3. Teddy treated Gideon's son disrespectfully, as he had probably seen other colonists do.
4. Gideon, like Mrs. Farquar, reacted strongly to Teddy's injury.

Reading Strategy: Analyzing Cultural Differences (p. 255)
A. Sample responses:

Farquars: believe white people to be superior to African natives; believe it would be best for Gideon to reveal source of his medicine; are "at home" on their homestead

Farquars and Gideon (in circle intersection): belief in Christian God; devoted to Teddy; shared understanding that the destiny of a white child is different from that of a black child; share some belief in the efficacy of herbal medicines

Gideon: trained by his medicine-man father; conscious of his "place" despite family's affection for him; refuses to reveal source of medicine; is comfortable in bush

B. Possible response:

Without the cultural differences, the story would be about a child's run-in with a poisonous snake. The parents' and the cook's attitudes about the accident and about the cure would be the same. The disagreement over revealing the source of the medicine would not occur. The story could still be engaging, but it would carry much less impact.

Literary Analysis: Cultural Conflict (p. 256)
Possible responses:

The Farquars' Attitudes

Others could benefit from this medicine.

It would be nice if something good came about because of them.

There is no reason not to share this "miracle" with others.

The Scientist's Attitudes

Perhaps a handful of these native cures are any good; most of them are pure imagination.

There is money to be made if there is any truth in one of these cures or medicines.

Gideon's Attitudes

Knowledge of the medicine belongs to him and his culture.

The British have their own medicine and don't really believe in the efficacy of African medicines.

1. Their feelings about the medicine and the "miracle" were deep and religious. They were uncomfortable when the scientist talked about money.
2. When they ask a servant a question, they expect a prompt and truthful answer. They don't understand Gideon's resistance, especially after explaining what good the medicine could do. They view Gideon as stubborn and selfish.
3. He is skeptical about the usefulness of any of the native African medicines or cures about which amazing stories were told. He *assumes* that Gideon will not reveal the source of the medicine, which just proves his point about the lack of usefulness of African medicines.

"The Rights We Enjoy, the Duties We Owe" by Tony Blair

Build Vocabulary: The Language of Building a New Society (p. 257)
A. 1. i 2. g 3. e 4. c 5. a 6. b 7. d 8. f 9. h 10. j

B. 1. duty; 2. community; 3. cohesive; 4. interdependent; 5. cooperative; 6. competitive; 7. prosper; 8. strong; 9. shared; 10. responsible

Students will probably point out the relevance of the three quotations for the United States. First, currently there is a mistrust of the government as the source of solutions to our society's problems. Second, as the emphasis on personal responsibility grows, many social observers, among them President Clinton, have also contended that citizens have a responsibility to help others. Third, modern societies throughout the world are seeking fixed points of reference in order to navigate on an increasingly interdependent planet. Students may note how certain emphases in the quotations apply to British society in a different way than they do to America. For example, the "old hierarchy of deference" is a reference to a rigid British class structure that did not exist to the same degree in the United States.

"The Lagoon" by Joseph Conrad
"Araby" by James Joyce

Build Vocabulary (p. 259)

A. 1. invincibility; 2 .convince; 3. evince

B. 1. d 2. b 3. d 4. a 5. b 6. c 7. b 8. d 9. a

Grammar and Style: Adverb Clauses (p. 260)

A. 1. as he asked, without any words of greeting— "Have you medicine, Tuan?"; composed

2. as if dead; still

3. since the sun of today rose; hears

4. when no friendship is to be despised; had known

5. When we returned to the street; had filled

6. because there would be a retreat that week in her convent; could not go

7. When he was midway through his dinner; asked

8. though I knew my stay was useless; lingered

B. Sample responses:

1. The white man stays with Arsat because he once fought with him in the war.

2. When the others are distracted by the fish hunt, Arsat and his brother kidnap the young woman.

3. The boy feels as if Mangan's sister is a force moving him beyond his control.

4. The boy cannot go to the bazaar until his uncle returns home.

Reading Strategy: Picturing Action and Situation (p. 261)

Possible responses:

1. The white man contemplates the people in his life he has left behind, losses for which he cannot accept responsibility and for which he has not allowed himself to grieve.

2. When he hears his uncle at the door, the boy instantly feels excited because he can now go to the bazaar. When he hears the signs of his uncle's drunkenness, however, his heart sinks. He knows that he will have to wait longer and negotiate for something his uncle had promised earlier.

3. The boy's small frame looks even smaller in the midst of the hall's immense darkness and barrenness. He is overcome by feelings of uncertainty, disappointment, and sadness.

Literary Analysis: Plot Devices (p. 262)

Sample responses:

1. Quotation marks around Arsat's narrative signal the beginning and the end of the story within the story.

2. Arsat's story is occasionally interrupted by observations from the omniscient narrator. The effect is to remind the reader of the present situation—that the two men sit surrounded by darkness and groping with their own inner darkness as well.

3. Arsat's story told on its own would not have the same effect. It conveys deeper meaning within the context of the outside story in which the white man has a history with Arsat and the reader learns what has become of Arsat since his choice.

4. The boy realizes that his desires will never be satisfied.

5. The boy is standing in the empty hall and looking up into the darkness.

6. The emptiness and darkness of the hall mirror the boy's dissatisfaction and echo his feelings of emptiness and self-loathing.

"The Lady in the Looking Glass: A Reflection" by Virginia Woolf
"The First Year of My Life" by Muriel Spark

Build Vocabulary (p. 263)

A. 1. translucent; 2. transom;
3. transmutation; 4. transatlantic

B. 1. e 2. a 3. g 4. b 5. c 6. h 7. f 8. d

Grammar and Style: Subject-Verb Agreement in Inverted Sentences (p. 264)

A. 1. Here are a letter and an invitation delivered by the postman.

2. There was a suggestion of depth and intelligence in the occupant's room.

3. In the end, there are no interesting thoughts in Isabella's brain.

4. There were many soldiers scarred and killed by poisonous gas during the war.

5. In this anthology are poems by Wilfred Owen and Alan Seegar.

6. Here is an interesting theory on infant development.

B. Sample response:

The first birthday party I recall is my fourth. There were red balloons, red and white streamers, and brightly colored party hats. There was a clown performing magic tricks. In this picture are my mother and father, lighting the four candles on my cake.

Reading Strategy: Questioning (p. 265)

Possible responses:

1. Question: Why would these inanimate objects know more about Isabella?; Answer: Because they observe her when she doesn't think she's being observed.

2. Question: Why does Woolf use the word *acid*?; Answer: Because it implies stripping to the bone, or the truth, of a person.

3. Question: Why does the narrator think the song is silly?; Answer: Because on her other "frequencies," she is tuning in to the war's mass destruction.

4. Question: Why is it "essential to know the worst"?; Answer: Because the atrocities on the Western Front have the most impact on the human consciousness to which the narrator is attuned.

Literary Analysis: Point of View— Modern Experiments (p. 266)

Sample responses:

1. One stream-of-consciousness passage begins with "One must put oneself in her shoes" and ends with "But one was tired of the things that she talked about at dinner." The narrator begins with a figurative saying, addresses its literal meaning, and from there speculates about Isabella's actions and thoughts.

2. Although the narrator bases her information about Isabella on the items in Isabella's room, her impressions have no real basis in reality. They are all imagination and speculation until Isabella appears before the looking glass.

3. Woolf might have chosen this type of narrator to comment on the unreliability of appearance when searching for meaning.

4. The narrator is super-omniscient, claiming not only to remember everything from the moment of her birth but also to have known everything that was going on in the world, including the thoughts of any given person.

5. The narrator's observations create a brisk, amused tone that contrasts with the grim reality of World War I.

6. This narrator allows Spark to comment on the atrocities of war without sounding didactic. This point of view invites the reader to consider the issue from an ironic perspective.

"The Rocking-Horse Winner" by D. H. Lawrence
"A Shocking Accident" by Graham Greene

Build Vocabulary (p. 267)

A. 1. obscures; 2. object; 3. obstacles
B. 1. a 2. c 3. b 4. c 5. d 6. c 7. b 8. a
9. d

Grammar and Style: Subjunctive Mood (p. 268)

A. 1. were; 2. be; 3. were; 4. were; 5. be;
6. respond

B. Sample response:

In my family, it is important that everyone be focused on a goal. My goal is to become a pilot. If I were older, I could take flying lessons.

Reading Strategy: Identifying With a Character (p. 269)

Sample responses:

1. Paul wants to relieve his mother's anxiety about being lucky and is hurt that she doesn't believe him or appreciate his actions on her behalf. Like Paul, a reader might resolve to prove himself right.

2. Paul's anxiety increases. He had hoped that his earnings would alleviate problems, and now he worries that there will never be enough money. In this situation, a reader might wish to escape the house that is the source of such anxiety.

3. Jerome feels embarrassed and isolated from his classmates. Due to circumstances he could not control, he is now an object of ridicule. In this situation, a reader might resolve not to let his feelings show to others.

4. Jerome feels conflicting emotions: he wants to be closer to Sally yet he fears a negative reaction from her. By delaying the story, he increases his own anxiety. A reader might have similar feelings or perhaps would decide to confront the problem directly.

Literary Analysis: Theme (p. 270)

Possible responses:

1. The rocking horse is an expensive toy. Although it looks like a real horse, it cannot go anywhere; it simply rocks back and forth.

2. The rocking horse symbolizes the futility of materialism. The horse may look good, but it is false and it gets the rider nowhere. The faster Paul rocks, the more frenzied he becomes; his actions harm him rather than help him.

3. This symbol underscores the notion that the pursuit of money is useless and self-destructive.

4. The falling pig that kills Jerome's father symbolizes the absurdity of life. Many events in life cannot be predicted or pre-pared for, and death is one of them.

"The Book of Sand"
by Jorge Luis Borges

Build Vocabulary: The Language of Philosophical Ideas (p. 271)

1. random; 2. arbitrary; 3. infinite;
4. hypervolume; 5. beginning; 6. time;
7. point; 8. space; 9. end

Literary Connection: The Short Story (p. 272)

Students' responses to the questions should indicate an understanding of the short story format: the number of characters should be limited, the setting should be fairly simple, and the plot should center on one crucial event. They may choose to utilize a simple narrative technique or one of the fictional techniques exemplified in the unit.

"Do Not Go Gentle into That Good Night" and "Fern Hill"
by Dylan Thomas
"The Horses" and "The Rain Horse"
by Ted Hughes

Build Vocabulary (p. 273)

A. 1. voluntarism; 2. volition; 3. voluntarily
B. 1. c 2. b 3. d 4. a 5. b

Grammar and Style: Sentence Beginnings: Adverb Clauses (p. 274)

A. Sentences 2 and 4 contain adverb clauses.

2. As he went—modifies *broke*
4. Whenever it seemed to be drawing off—modifies *listened*

B. Sample responses:

1. After he reached the top of the hill, he paused.
2. As if the horse had been waiting, it bore down on him.
3. Unless he were able to make the horse veer off, the man could be trampled.

Reading Strategy: Judging the Message (p. 275)

Possible responses:

"Do Not Go Gentle into That Good Night"

Message: One should fight against dying rather than accepting its inevitability. Judg-ment: Students may agree, or they may say that accepting death makes it easier, both for the dying and for the survivors.

"Do Not Go Gentle into That Good Night" and **"Fern Hill"**
by Dylan Thomas
"The Horses" and **"The Rain Horse"**
by Ted Hughes *(continued)*

"Fern Hill"

Message: Childhood is lovely and brief, and we don't realize it until we are past it. Judgment: Some students may disagree with the poet's very agreeable image of childhood. Students may state that children do sometimes, at least, recognize the loveliness of childhood, if not its brevity.

"The Horses"

Message: The poet expresses appreciation of and gratitude for a vivid memory in the midst of a life that is now less "vivid" or satisfying. Judgment: Students may be able to relate to this message through a vivid memory of their own, from an earlier time in their lives when they were less responsible, less burdened with school or work or concerns about the future.

Literary Analysis: Voice (p. 276)

Sample responses:

Line: "And honored among wagons . . . / And once below a time . . ."; diction; Thomas "piles" images with lots of *and*'s.

Line: "the spellbound horses walking warm / Out of the whinnying green stable"; word choice / diction; the repeated *w* sounds pull the image together and help create a warm, gentle feeling, suitable for the reflection in the poem.

Line: "My wishes raced through the house-high hay"; diction; the repeated *h*'s give a "stacked-up" feeling, like the hay.

Line: "green and golden" (lines 15 and 44); word choice; both of the colors bring up images of youth, freshness, vitality.

"An Arundel Tomb" and
"The Explosion" by Philip Larkin
"On the Patio" by Peter Redgrove
"Not Waving but Drowning"
by Stevie Smith

Build Vocabulary (p. 277)

A. 1. a 2. c 3. b

B. 1. fidelity; 2. effigy; 3. larking; 4. supine

C. 1. c 2. d 3. d 4. a

Grammar and Style: Sequence of Tenses (p. 278)

A. 1. present perfect; 2. present; 3. past; 4. past perfect

B. Sample responses:

1. I had read the novel before the movie version came out.

2. In the morning I dress before I eat my breakfast.

3. Yesterday, however, I altered my routine and ate breakfast first.

4. I have wanted to see that movie for some time now.

Reading Strategy: Reading in Sentences (p. 279)

A. Stanzas 4–7 of "An Arundel Tomb"

Sentence 1: They would not guess how early in their supine stationary voyage the air would change to soundless damage, turn the old tenantry away; how soon succeeding eyes begin to look, not read.

Sentence 2: Rigidly they persisted, linked, through lengths and breadths of time.

Sentence 3: Snow fell, undated.

Sentence 4: Light each summer thronged the glass.

Sentence 5: A bright litter of birdcalls strewed the same bone-riddled ground.

Sentence 6: And up the paths the endless altered people came, washing at their identity.

Sentence 7: Now, helpless in the hollow of an unarmorial age, a trough of smoke in slow suspended skeins above their scrap of history, only an attitude remains: Time has transfigured them into untruth.

Sentence 8: The stone fidelity they hardly meant has come to be their final blazon, and to prove our almost-instinct almost true: What will survive of us is love.

B. Suggested responses:

With the stanzas written out in narrative form, students may need to be cautioned about reading too quickly. Emphasize the need to find meaning in the lines, not to get to the end of the sentence.

Literary Analysis: Free Verse and Meter (p. 280)

Possible responses:

1. The first line of the poem starts out in trochees instead of iambs, and is half a foot short. The meter of the first phrase emphasizes the words "side by side."

2. Scarfed as in a heat-haze, dimmed. Line 15 is in trochees, but is half a foot short. It emphasizes the fact that something unnatural has happened; something has thrown things out of kilter, even if just "for a second," as stated in line 14.

3. In lines 5–8, the poet focuses on the pellets that come to dwell in the glass, and on the rusty tabletop. These images are smaller, more concentrated than those of the rest of the poem, which involve cloud, thunder, and so on.

"B. Wordsworth" by V. S. Naipaul

Build Vocabulary (p. 281)

A. 1. patroness; 2. patronizing; 3. patronage; 4. patronize

B. 1. c 2. d 3. a 4. b

C. 1. distill; 2. rogue; 3. keenly; 4. patronize

Grammar and Style: Pronoun Case in Compound Construction (p. 282)

A. 1. I; 2. he; 3. he; 4. him, me

B. 1. Mr. Wordsworth and *he* take long walks together.

2. *They* live on the same street.

3. The relationship between the narrator and *her* is not loving.

Reading Strategy: Responding to Character (p. 283)

Possible responses:

For each character—B. Wordsworth and the narrator—students must note three events and each character's behavior, words, and qualities expressed as they experience this event. Students must explain their response to each character/event. For example, students may note B. Wordsworth's request to "watch bees," and note their response to him as an odd, yet interesting character.

Literary Analysis: First-Person Narrator (p. 284)

1. yes

2. no; I could tell B. Wordsworth was glad to see me.

3. no; My mother was angry with me for coming home late from school and asked me where I'd been.

4. yes

5. no; B. Wordsworth told me a story about a girl poet and a boy poet.

6. no; B. Wordsworth and I took long walks through the parks and along the waterfront.

"The Train from Rhodesia"
by Nadine Gordimer

Build Vocabulary (p. 285)

A. 1. amoral; 2. atonal; 3. atypical

B. 1. c 2. a 3. e 4. b 5. d

C. Sample responses:

1. Her memories of the incident were impressionistic.

2. After long hours on the train, he felt his muscles begin to atrophy.

3. The suitcase fell, splaying its contents across the corridor.

4. The journey was more restful because it was segmented.

5. Her face sagged, elongated by fatigue.

Grammar and Style: Absolute Phrases (p. 286)

A. 1. the stiff wooden legs sticking up in the air

2. Joints not yet coordinated

3. the wonderful ruff of fur facing her

4. his hands hanging at his sides.

5. her face slumped in her hand

B. Possible responses:

1. The train, a sleek black machine humming with life, pulled into the station.

2. The piccanins and dogs circling her, the young woman stood on the platform.

3. The stationmaster rang the bell, an urgent call heeded by the waiting passengers.

"The Train from Rhodesia"
by Nadine Gordimer *(continued)*

Reading Strategy: Reading Between the Lines (p. 287)

Suggested response:

For each event students identify in the first column, they must explain the meaning or significance of in the second column. For example, students may record the incident of the lion's mouth "opened in an endless roar too terrible to be heard." By reading between the lines, students may determine that the lion's roar is the cry of native Africans, grieving their loss of independence and dignity.

Literary Analysis: Conflict and Theme (p. 288)

Sample responses:

1. The character's inner struggle with reality and unreality, symbolized by her husband and carved animals and baskets, dramatizes the conflict between the realities of two cultures—non-African and African—and how each is out of place when put in the other.

2. The character's dawning awareness of the conflict is dramatized in her "seeing something different" when looking at the lion.

3. The husband's success at buying the lion for a cheap amount and degrading the artist by not taking it decently, dramatizes the colonization of Africa and Africans by exploitive Europeans.

from *Midsummer*, XXIII and from *Omeros* from Chapter XXVIII
by Derek Walcott
"From Lucy: Englan' Lady"
by James Berry

Build Vocabulary (p. 289)

A. 1. d 2. e 3. b 4. a 5. c
B. 1. b 2. c 3. a 4. d

Grammar and Style: Commonly Confused Words: *Affect* and *Effect* (p. 290)

A. 1. C 2. I 3. I 4. C
B. Possible responses:

　1. The effect of *Omeros* is to make the reader feel as if he or she were on a slave ship.

2. The *Lucy* poem affects one's opinion about how easy the life of a king or queen really is.

3. Walcott had hoped to effect an increased diversity in Shakespearean theater in England.

Reading Strategy: Applying Background Information (p. 291)

Possible responses:

1. Walcott is a playwright as well as a poet, and a person of color who was in England in 1981; The word "color" here likely means racial integration or diversity, as well as character or tone.

2. A *griot* is a West-African shaman; Walcott's heritage as well as his interest in it probably lead him to employ the authentic term for a speaker of this section of the poem.

3. James Berry, who spent his childhood in Jamaica, now lives in England; Berry's creates a character speaking with the sounds he knew in childhood to make a sensitive observation of day-to-day English life—where the personal life of royalty never leaves the papers.

Literary Analysis: Theme and Context (p. 292)

Sample responses:

1. *Midsummer*: roar of a Brixton riot tunneled by water hoses; die for the sun; leaf stems tug at their chains . . . nearer to apartheid; "But the blacks can't do Shakespeare"; Their thick skulls bled with rancor . . . the Moor's eclipse; Calibans howled; barred streets burning.

　Omeros: leg irons; chains; ashen ancestors; scorching decks; tubers withered; dried fronds; curved spines; dead palms were heaved overside, the ribbed corpses floated; burnt branches; crooked fingers; waiter; lances; ruin; suntraction; the hold's iron door rolled over their eyes; bolt rammed home its echo; there went Ashanti . . . brother. The context reflects the colonial history of the Caribbean region.

2. In English society, the privileged are unnaturally separated from (yet, perhaps ironically, respected by) working-class people.

"A Devoted Son" by Anita Desai

Build Vocabulary (p. 293)
A. 1. c 2. a 3. d 4. b
B. 1. a 2. d 3. b 4. c 5. b

Grammar and Style: Sentence Variety (p. 294)

A. 1. long, complex, declarative

2. long, compound, declarative

3. short, complex, interrogative, fragment (indirect discourse)

4. short, compound, declarative (indirect discourse)

5. long, complex, declarative

6. The paragraph sandwiches two blunt expressions of Varma's shock between long narrative sentences. The first two describe Varma's condition and the realization that shocks him. The final one describes his stunned aftermath and details of his defeat.

B. Sample response:

Varma's mouth worked hard. As if he had a gob of betel in it, though his supply had been cut off years ago, he spat, sharp and bitter as poison, "Keep your tonic—I want none—I won't take any more of your medicines. None. Never." With a wave of his hand, he swept the bottle out of his son's hand. He was suddenly effective. He was grand.

Reading Strategy: Evaluating Characters' Decisions (p. 295)

Possible responses:

1. Family's desire to see son succeed and Rakesh's ambition; Acclaim from the community, some jealousy; At this point, pride is the dominant emotion.

2. Rakesh seeks unheard of success; Still pride and acclaim, but father's simpleness is hinted; One now begins to wonder at the ultimate effect.

3. Rakesh's surprising decision seems unclear, but family still proud; Varma begins to be eclipsed, and fame dies down; It seems clear there will be an ultimate consequence.

4. Varma's wife has died and his modern son thinks him a fool; Rakesh completely takes over and Varma is treated like a child; Rakesh's observation of duty seems self-centered, for he isn't really helping Varma.

5. Varma has completely lost his identity and any reason to live; Rakesh treats him all the more as senile and childish; All that Varma lived for, including his pride in his devoted son, is gone.

Literary Analysis: Static and Dynamic Characters (p. 296)
Sample responses:

1. At the beginning of the story Varma is proud, happy and competent. As he ages, retires, loses his wife, and watches his son take over his household, he becomes resentful and irritated. At the end he is angry and bitter and wants to die.

2. Fifth paragraph (begins "To everyone who came to him . . ."): "He came and touched my feet"; Eleventh paragraph (begins "It was a strange fact . . ."): "He developed so many complaints and fell ill so frequently . . ."; The first complete paragraph on the next to last page (begins "'Let me be,' Varma begged, turning his face away from the pills on the outstretched hand."): "Let me die. It would be better. I do not want to live only to eat your medicines."

3. Rakesh is bland, dutiful, and devoted throughout. He is clearly ambitious, though no overt aggressiveness appears, and he is intent only on his success and repeating the patterns that brought it, throughout the story. No other personality traits appear.

4. First paragraph: ". . . and bowed down to touch his feet." Eighth paragraph (begins "For some years Rakesh worked . . ."): ". . . for he became known not only as the best but the richest doctor in town"; Next to last page (begins "At last the sky-blue Ambassador arrived..."): "Ever a devoted son, he went first to the corner where the father sat gazing . . ."

from "We'll Never Conquer Space"
by Arthur C. Clarke

Build Vocabulary (p. 297)
A. 1. c 2. d 3. b 4. a
B. 1. d 2. b 3. a 4. b 5. b 6. a

from "We'll Never Conquer Space"
by Arthur C. Clarke *(continued)*

Grammar and Style: Linking Verbs and Subject Complements (p. 298)

A. 1. are—otherwise; PA
   2. was—wide; PA
   3. are—face to face; PA
   4. is—limit; PN
   5. are—wrong; PA
   6. is—sphere; PN

B. Possible responses:
   1. Arthur Clarke is a British citizen.
   2. Clarke has been a resident of Sri Lanka for forty years.
   3. Clarke seems comfortable with his subject matter.
   4. He remains technically accurate while writing for nontechnical audiences.

Reading Strategy: Challenging the Text (p. 299)

Possible responses:

1. Will video communication become that accessible?

2. *Have* we "abolished space" on earth? Perhaps abolishing the space between the stars means simply traversing it, not necessarily traversing it quickly.

3. Is technology moving toward using nuclear energy for spaceflight? How "homely" could the solar system be?

4. What does Clarke mean by "converse"?

Literary Analysis: Prophetic Essay (p. 300)

Sample responses:

Thesis: Space travel will never be easy for humans.

Support 1: The vastness of solar space prohibits human travel.—fact/speculation

Support 2: Even interplanetary communication will be problematic, if not intolerable.—emotional appeal

Support 3: Nothing can ever travel faster than light.—fact/speculation

Support 4: The size of the universe is simply beyond human comprehension, which contributes to the likelihood that humans will not "conquer" space.—emotional appeal